IN SEARCH OF STABILITY

In Search of Stability

Economics of Money, History of the Rupee

SASHI SIVRAMKRISHNA

Routledge
Taylor & Francis Group

LONDON AND NEW YORK

First published in paperback 2024

First published 2017
by Routledge
4 Park Square, Milton Park, Abingdon, Oxon OX14 4RN

and by Routledge
605 Third Avenue, New York, NY 10017

Routledge is an imprint of the Taylor & Francis Group, an informa business

Publisher's Note
The publisher has gone to great lengths to ensure the quality of this
reprint but points out that some imperfections in the original copies
may be apparent.

Print edition not for sale in South Asia (India, Sri Lanka, Nepal,
Bangladesh, Afghanistan, Pakistan or Bhutan)

British Library Cataloguing in Publication Data
A catalogue record for this book is available from the British Library

Library of Congress Cataloging in Publication Data
Catalog record for this book has been requested

ISBN: 978-1-138-23481-9 (hbk)
ISBN: 978-1-03-291934-8 (pbk)
ISBN: 978-1-315-27681-6 (ebk)

DOI: 10.4324/9781315276816

Typeset in Garamond
by Kohli Print, Delhi 110 051

MANOHAR

For
Preeta and Kartikeya

Contents

List of Boxes, Figures and Tables

FIGURES

Preface

In July 2010, the new symbol of the Indian Rupee, was introduced to the world. With this, as the country's then Finance Minister Pranab Mukherjee put it, the 'Indian rupee will join the select club of currencies such as the U.S. dollar, British pound sterling, euro and the Japanese yen that have a clear distinguishing identity'. The symbolic identity is no doubt relevant but it is also necessary to question the underlying basis of the rupee's growing significance. The answer is actually quite simple. In spite of being categorized as an economically poor or a lower middle income country on a per capita income basis, India's macronumbers tell a different story. An almost two trillion dollar economy that, in spite of the global recession continues to grow at a rate of around 6 per cent is a clear sign of its dynamism. With every country in the world wanting to be a part of the action, trade with and investment in India could be poised for a structural shift in trajectory. The rising stature of India in the world economy will mean a greater demand to participate in its markets and therefore make the rupee more sought after. Embodying this vision in the symbol ₹ 'reflects the confidence in the future of the Indian economy and of India.

In a matter of just a few years, the new rupee symbol has become common, familiar and almost universally used. In a world where the future is assimilated even before we get there, few of us may know the tumultuous history of the rupee, its journey from a silver coin to a symbol of a country's ambition to become an economic superpower. Behind the rupee lies an entire history of India's monetary system and financial institutions, its evolution through cataclysmic phases and epochs. This book attempts to present the fascinating but intricate history of the rupee so that we don't only think about where we are going but also reflect on where we came from.

It was while watching Niall Ferguson's television series, *The Ascent of Money* that I felt, rather impulsively, that the story of the rupee needs to be told. Perhaps this feeling arose because Ferguson said so little about India or the Indian rupee. While the sweeping narrative of his book may have compelled him to overlook India's part in world monetary history, its place in the evolution of money cannot be ignored. Consider a couple of facts to illustrate the point. The decline of the Roman Empire AD *c.*200 is said to have begun when India stopped accepting the debased Roman denarius. Another interesting fact relates to the concern of the West over India as a sink of precious metals, taking the world's money out of circulation throughout the medieval and early modern period. John Maynard Keynes (1913) once contemplated what could happen if this obsession were to change; 'If a time comes when Indians learn to leave off their unfertile habits and to divert their hoards into the channels of productive industry and to the enrichment of their fields, they will have the money markets of the world at their mercy (p. 100).

But before you presume my objective is to establish the rupee's place in the financial history of the world, I must correct course. This book actually narrates the *history of the rupee* to specifically understand *the underlying economics of money*. I am an economist by training, not a historian and howsoever much my interest in history grows I compulsively articulate events in terms of economic principles. Let me, however, not downplay the importance of history; history helps immensely in grasping economics, in particular, monetary economics. On the other hand, mainstream monetary economics does tell us a lot about money, from how banks create it to its role in business cycles. The danger though with abstraction and conceptually strong arguments is the possibility to miss the *essence* of money. In a highly mystified and dense financial landscape, history helps us see the forest from the trees. The tumultuous journey of the rupee reveals that it is the relentless *search for stability* in value, both internally (in terms of domestic price level) and externally (in terms of exchange rate), that has been its greatest challenge throughout history. Unfortunately, this search continues even today, and in an even more complex environment.

We live in the age of financialization; an emerging reality wherein the real economy or the actual production and distribution of goods and services is increasingly controlled by finance capital through institutional intermediaries like private equity and venture capital funds, insurance companies, pension and hedge funds, large mortgage companies and investment banks. The volumes of global financial markets are not easy to grasp for the human mind. Consider, for example, this report from the Bank for International Settlements: 'Trading on the international derivatives exchanges slowed in the fourth quarter of 2006. Combined turnover of interest rate, currency and stock index derivatives fell by 7 per cent to $431 trillion between October and December 2006'.

In annual terms, derivatives trading in primarily futures contracts on interest rates, foreign currencies, treasury bonds, etc., had reached a level of $1.2 quadrillion! Yes, a quadrillion is 1 with 15 zeroes attached to it. By comparison, U.S. GDP in 2006 was just around $12 trillion. Given these enormous flows of money in pursuit of maximum returns, often through speculative gains, many political economists now argue that the Great Recession of 2008–9 was in effect the outcome of this phenomenon of financialization.

An exploration of financialization is beyond the scope of this book. Nevertheless, it is important to highlight the necessity for each one of us to recognize the power and influence of money and finance over our daily lives, livelihoods and business. Money may have become a part, if not the very meaning of life . . . we live and some even die for it . . . but the world of money remains mysterious and confusing. Many of us still presume that paper money is convertible to gold, bemused as to why the Japanese yen is considered a strong currency when 80 yen make a dollar or puzzled whether credit cards are money or not. So where does one begin?

To me, the answer is history. History cuts through the fog and reveals the *nature* of money, which has, fundamentally speaking, changed little. Monetary history can help us understand with simple factual illustrations the working and implications of the monetary system. It is a bottom-up approach to demystifying the world of money rather than a method based on abstraction, which to the non-economist at least, can sometimes be far more obscure than the issues themselves. More than perhaps any other subject in economics, it is in the study of money that a historical perspective can play an obligatory role.

I began working on this book almost five years ago, alternating between research on this subject and in economic and environmental history. There have been some other attractions and distractions too: documentary filmmaking, teaching and of course, most importantly, family. If there is anyone I must acknowledge for patiently bearing the ordeal of my sermons on money, it is my wife Preeta. My son Kartikeya too deserves a share of the credit for enduring my explanations on some rather abstract notions of money. Every time he dropped a coin into his piggy bank I would tell him how India did pretty much the same thing throughout the medieval period right up to the twentieth century by taking money out of circulation. Kartikeya, however, assured me that he would put it back into circulation soon and even more of it if I wished. I also wish to record my gratitude to Dr. N.C.B. Nath, my father-in-law, who has always encouraged my academic pursuits. Sreedhar, who has managed my business interests over more than a decade, has also endured many a long lectures on money. I also thank Amalendu Jyotishi, my friend and colleague, who gave me several opportunities to speak on the history of the rupee to his students. The fascinating discussions with Mahadev during our road trips around south India retracing Francis Buchanan's *Journey*, fuelled my interest in history. I must also make special mention of the Foundation to Aid Industrial Recovery (FAIR) where I began this project and carried out a substantial portion of the research for this book. In 2011, I joined the Narsee Monjee Institute of Management Studies in Bangalore where I completed this book.

Ever since my days at the University of Bombay (now Mumbai) and then at Cornell, I had been interested in the economics of money. Somewhere along the way I guess I lost my way, perhaps inundated by macroeconomic theory that was so mathematically dense that I could never see the essence of money. After completing my Ph.D., I took a long sabbatical from economics and returned to it after more than a decade. I was then free from institutional pressures and could freely delve into what I wanted to. And it is when I started reading more about the history of money and of the rupee that I was able to get a complete perspective of where we have come from and where we are today. It is this understanding that I share with my readers through this book.

Introduction

Not a single line of these investigations is meant to be a statement about economics.

GEORG SIMMEL

Unlike Simmel's profound discourse on the philosophy of money, the objective of this book is rather mundane: to *understand the economics of money* through a *narrative on the history of the rupee.* Having stated the modest objective of this effort let me explicitly mention some important points on the style adopted in writing this book and who might want to read it. *First,* what it is not; this work is not a critical history of the English East India Company or of British colonial rule over India. I have consciously avoided drifting into a discussion of other important and interesting historical events. *Second,* the underlying thread that runs through our narrative is the positive economics of money and history of the rupee. This is a book that explains what happened rather than raising normative questions on what ought to have happened or what could have been a more appropriate monetary system for India. *Third,* the time period I have delineated for study is from the time of introduction of the rupee is 1542 up to 1971, the latter being the year which marked the beginning of the end of the Bretton Woods era and a fixed exchange rate regime. To highlight the continuity in the rupee's history as the search for stability, I have added an epilogue that brings us right into present times. *Fourth,* the economics of money draws us into understanding the evolution of monetary instruments through history and their impact on the economy. These instruments cannot be separated from the institutions that develop and are developed by them. I, therefore, digress into a study of the origins, nature and development of some of the most important monetary institutions in India. *Fifth,* unlike a historian, I have restricted extensive use of endnotes that often proves to

be a nagging distraction to readers. A complete bibliography including references and sources is given at the end of the book.
Finally, the book is written for students and researchers of monetary
economics and could serve as a textbook for a one- semester course
on the history of the rupee and a complementary text to a more
general course on the history of money. Students of business management who want to understand the evolution of the financial landscape could also find this book particularly relevant. Outside
academia, bank and financial institution managers, policymakers
and the general follower of contemporary social, political and economic issues will find the book useful as it is becoming increasingly evident that many recent financial upheavals that encompass
the economic landscape of the twenty-first century bear an uncanny
resemblance to events of the past. This makes it pertinent to look
back at history to learn important lessons for the future. But I must
confess that the style of the book remains academic and I have not
economized on rigour even if that is at the cost of being a little
demanding. From my own experience in deciphering and grappling with contemporary sources, I thought this clarity ultimately
helps. I have liberally used graphs to make the explanations crisper,
simpler and more convincing. Moreover, and quite honestly, it is
difficult for an economist to give up thinking in terms of demand
and supply. For those who are uncomfortable with such an approach, I have added an Appendix on how equilibrium exchange
rates are determined and fluctuate in foreign exchange markets,
which can of course be found in most elementary international
economics textbooks.

Simple as my objective seemed, the difficulty I faced while going about the task on hand was to ensure that while studying the
economics of money, I did not lose sight of the history of the
rupee. To an extent, the chapter plan of the book reflects my predicament. Each part covers a specific time period but within these
I do not follow a strictly chronological order; an element of non-
linearity in the chapter flow therefore exists. A further complexity
arose; the history of the rupee in the early colonial period was one
where many new forms of money were introduced. Although the
stability of the rupee was critical during this phase, the challenge

of introducing new monetary instruments was replaced by issues pertaining almost exclusively to stability of the rupee, in particular its external value in terms of the exchange rate. This slight realignment in the narrative becomes evident as we draw closer to the end of the nineteenth century.

Part I, which is bounded between the mid-sixteenth and the mid-nineteenth centuries, deals with the several monetary instruments that developed in late medieval and early modern India; each chapter in this part then goes on to introduce certain economic aspects or forms of money and/or critical contexts in which money performed its functions. For instance, in Chapter 1, I discuss the basic economics of metallic currency and then explore the evolution of the rupee coin from its inception in 1542 until the year 1853, the year in which Dalhousie declared a monometallic silver standard with the rupee as legal tender. Chapter 2 introduces remittance money but once again goes back in history and brings in episodes related to remittances from India from the late eighteenth and early nineteenth centuries. I follow this pattern until Chapter 5, which contains a description of the difficulties faced in introducing paper currency in India in the 1860s. This is preceded by two chapters which delve into a study of commercial credit and bank money respectively.

In Part II of the book I cover the entire period between *c*.1860 and 1971. In the early decades of this period, India remained on a monometallic silver standard with the rupee as coin of the realm. Under British colonial rule, India was increasingly subsumed by economic forces of the market system, and with this the role and impact of money (and the rupee) on the real economy became stronger and more pervasive. The international economy was also undergoing a transition in this period with integration of production across the world through trade and commerce. This also shifted the emphasis in international monetary economics from the search for instruments of money transfer to stability in exchange rates and price levels. Major concerns arose after the steep decline in the price of silver and with it depreciation of the rupee, a situation akin to floating exchange rates. The exchange rate depreciation itself was a classic instance of an external shock and not caused by a balance of payments issue. Nonetheless, its repercussions on the domestic price level, on the real economy and government budgets could not be ignored. In the end the government decided to abandon the monometallic silver standard that India had adhered to since 1835. There are, however, some important lessons in monetary history that emerge from this period especially the decline of international bimetallism and the priority extended to stable foreign exchange rates as against domestic inflation. From the year 1893 the rupee was delinked from silver and put on a gold exchange standard. Several hurdles had to be overcome in stabilizing the exchange rate of the rupee and putting India back on a fixed exchange rate regime. What did this entail for the Indian economy? This forms the topic of discussion of Chapter 6.

Chapter 7 explores a phase of relative stability in the Indian monetary system under the gold-exchange standard, as it came to be known. An aberration did occur in 1907 but was surmounted after a few anxious moments. India it seemed was finally getting ready to abandon the rupee once and for all and move on to a gold currency when the world drifted into a major crisis in 1914, the First World War.

How did the rupee behave during the First World War after its anchor, the sterling, suspended its fixed relation with gold? Chapter 8 looks at the rupee-sterling rate and the jagged path traversed in maintaining fixed exchange rates. From an economic slump soon after the commencement of the war, the war years ended with an economic boom. The rupee external value being fixed, its internal value had to bear the brunt of both these extreme economic situations. Surprisingly, it was the boom that created bigger problems for the rupee with the appreciation of silver. As silver prices surged the fear of the rupee being melted for its metallic content meant that the fixed rate of the rupee could not be maintained. The rupee had to be revalued but not without a fierce debate over its repercussions on the Indian economy.

The postwar years put India on a roller-coaster ride, testing the endurance of the fixed exchange regime under different economic conditions. All through this period, except for a couple of years, the government accorded priority to the exchange rate letting the domestic economy absorb the impacts of the international shocks. England meanwhile returned to the gold standard but that was for a relatively short period. In 1931 it once again abandoned gold and with it the rupee too was delinked from gold and pegged to the sterling. The Great Depression of 1929 and the fixed exchange rate with, what was claimed as an overvalued rupee eroded India's balance of merchandise trade. Gold exports came to India's rescue in maintaining exchange rates but this was not without strong reactions from economists and contemporary commentators. The period also saw major changes in India's banking sector with a reorganization of the Presidency Banks into the Imperial Bank in 1921 and later the formation of India's central bank, the Reserve Bank of India in 1935. Along with a discussion of these issues, Chapter 9 outlines the state of the world monetary system at the eve of the Second World War.

The war years are the subject of Chapter 10 of the book. Interestingly several calls for a floating exchange rate were articulated even then but the non-availability of hedging instruments, India's dependence on capital imports as well as remittance of home charges were cited as reasons why a fixed exchange rate regime was more appropriate. The coming of the war also introduced India to the possibility of controlling foreign exchange flows as a way of managing external stability; a legacy that would endure for many decades to come. But the sterling surpluses were drained off to finance the war in return for a massive dose of inflation in India. As a consequence of these events, Bengal suffered a famine in 1943, which took the lives of millions of people.

The disruption of international trade and commerce commencing with the currency wars that ensued during the Great Depression and then the Second World War was increasingly seen as a lose-lose game for all nations of the world. In Chapter 11 of the book we see the return to a fixed exchange rate. While this was considered desirable, without adequate gold reserves a new system had literally to be created. In 1944 at Bretton Woods in the United States of America it was decided that the world would move on to a dollar exchange standard. The rupee's struggle to maintain value only intensified during this period. With post-Independence demands for development increasing, government expenditure expanded rapidly, leading to pressure on domestic price level to rise. In 1966 a devaluation of the rupee became imperative when foreign exchange reserves were depleted to dangerously low levels. This was India's first major economic crisis after securing Independence in 1947.

The Bretton Woods era came to an end in 1971 and soon after the world moved on to a floating exchange rate regime. But India continued to peg the rupee to sterling and later to a basket of international currencies. It was only in 1993 that India too moved on to a market-determined exchange rate regime but with regular interventions by the Reserve Bank of India. The challenges in maintaining stability in the internal and external value of the rupee did not disappear with the new liberalized regime; as I briefly explore in Part III, the Epilogue, in many ways achieving this objective has become even more complex in an era of financialization.

This book highlights the trials and tribulations of the rupee in its historical journey; it, at the same time, explores the tumultuous journey of money searching to find stability in value, domestically and internationally. Money has made exchange smooth so that the division of labour within and across countries is ensured to the maximum. While standards of living have risen enormously, money has struggled to maintain its value across place and time, without definitive success. This has brought with it crises and severe hardships to entire societies; a lesson which the history of the rupee unequivocally reveals.

PART I

DEVELOPMENT OF MONETARY INSTRUMENTS AND THEIR STABILITY
1542–c.1860

CHAPTER 1

Currency Money

The study of money, above all other fields in economics, is one in which complexity is used to disguise truth or to evade truth, not to reveal it.

JOHN KENNETH GALBRAITH

Money plays the largest part in determining the course of history

KARL MARX

Metallic coins, shells or cowries are *currency*, i.e. media of exchange that are generally and readily accepted in the immediate settlement or discharge of debt. Currency is the most commonly used form of money in day-to-day transactions. Convertible or inconvertible paper money is also currency, but I defer its independent study to later. After outlining the economics of currency money, I present the evolution of India's currency money, the silver rupee coin, from its introduction in 1542 until 1853, the year in which Lord Dalhousie declared it to be the sole legal tender (apart from copper coins for fractional transactions) in territories under the rule of the English East India Company.

1.1: THE ECONOMICS OF CURRENCY MONEY

So you think that money is the root of all evil. Have you ever asked what is the root of all money?

AYN RAND

What is money? While you try answering the question let me mention the importance of this chapter; it is the backbone of the book, providing readers a conceptual framework to approach monetary history. Throughout the book I will return to concepts outlined here. Coming back to our question; while most of us have an intuitive idea of what money is, only a few may be able to articulate a precise definition. Money can broadly be defined as a medium or an instrument that is used in settlement of claims or debts that arise from purchase of goods and services. The notion of money is, however, better captured by its functions as a unit of account, a medium of exchange and a store of value. *Simple as these may seem, the difficulty of monetary instruments to fulfil all three functions simultaneously, effectively and efficiently, across space (domestically and internationally) and time (intertemporally), has been and continues to be the root cause of many contemporary national and global financial crises.* Take, for instance, the cries of a currency war that echoed over the economic landscape soon after the Great Recession of 2008, threatening to disrupt foreign trade and investment, or the need for a new international currency in the context of an emerging multi-polar global economic world; these and many other issues, as we will see, are ultimately linked to the search for a stable money that accomplishes its three functions fully and satisfactorily. This search for stability not only connects several cataclysmic episodes through monetary history but is also the thread that strings our narrative on the Indian rupee together.

The functions of money are best understood when we go back into the distant past to a world before money when exchange took place through barter or the direct exchange of one commodity for another. But barters inconvenient in more ways than one. Imagine a village where five sheep trade for twelve blankets, seventeen blankets trade for one cow, seven cows for one ton of iron nails and one kilogram of iron nails for a kilogram of peanuts. How many kilograms of peanuts are required to buy a blanket? Without recourse to conversion calculators, a solution to the above problem would have kept the ablest arithmeticians of those days busy and may well have been a lucrative profession with one hour of his services fetching 50 kg of peanuts.[1] To make life simpler the price of all goods and services could be expressed in terms of any one of the goods ora unit of account, say, sheep. Trading ratios in this village are shown in Table 1.1.

TABLE 1.1: EXCHANGE RATIOS WITH SHEEP AS
THE STANDARD OF VALUE

1 sheep	2.4 blankets
1 sheep	0.14 cow
1 sheep	20 kg nails
1 sheep	20 kg peanuts
1 sheep	2½ hours of arithmetician's time

From this, cross price ratios between goods other than sheep become easier to compute; if 2.4 blankets exchange for 20 kg of peanuts then a blanket would command 8.33 kg of peanuts. Life becomes a little simpler with this common unit of account. In a barter economy, the convenience, if not the necessity of a common unit of account would most probably have sown the seeds for the emergence of money.

Sheep as a unit of account is not yet money for there are other functions that have to be satisfied. Our village, therefore, continues to operate in a barter economy and with it, constraints on exchange. For one, the problem of double coincidence of wants remains. The peanut farmer if he were looking for a blanket would have to find a weaver looking for peanuts, at that very point of time and for quantities he wants to trade. Now this may have been a feasible proposition in a simple economy which included a few small villages with a limited set of occupations and where consumption patterns were well established and predictable. In such communities, exchange was organized on the basis of social, tradition and cultural norms rather than purely economic terms. However, as the number of commodities produced grew and trade became geographically more widespread and impersonal, the double coincidence of wants would have had a debilitating effect on trade and commerce. To overcome the constraint imposed by barter on exchange, it is possible that the unit of account would have evolved into a common medium of exchange. Things, however, may actually have happened the other way around; the evolution of a medium of exchange may have overcome the constraints of barter.

The villagers call a meeting. The chief announces, 'We have been using sheep as the unit of account for all our transactions. Henceforth, let us make it a common medium of exchange for all transactions'. What would owning a sheep now mean in this village? The owner of sheep has a claim over goods and services produced by the other villagers, quantities being in accordance with Table 1.1 Sheep, as a medium of exchange, is nothing but a receipt, a certificate or a bookkeeping entry, which establishes claims over goods and services produced by all others in this society who agreed to the village chief's announcement. In other words, owning a sheep establishes the fact that a person has given society (*a* member of it) something equal in value to one sheep and, therefore, society (*any* member of it) must give her back at anytime goods and services, the value of which must be equal to that of one sheep. If sheep indeed were to become readily and generally acceptable money by one and all in this village, it can be called *currency*.[2] A Rs. 100 currency note serves exactly the same purpose. It is a receipt that you have given someone in India, goods or services worth this amount and therefore have a claim over anyone else, in India at least, for goods and services amounting to Rs. 100 in return. This decree or fiat, and the agreement or compulsion of members in a society to honour it, does away with the problem of double coincidence of wants. Going back to our village economy, the ironsmith can accept a sheep in exchange for nails which the cowherd bought, and then look for a farmer to buy peanuts with sheep in exchange. The cowherd, therefore, need not waste time and resources looking for an ironsmith who wants a cow.

Unfortunately, with sheep as their unit of account and medium of exchange this village will soon face serious problems. What if I wanted just one blanket? At the risk of sounding offensive, I would have to 'divide' my sheep into several parts. Not only would each part be of different value (for that matter even two sheep may not be of equal value) but the sum of all parts would not add up to the whole. Even if I were to divide the sheep into equal parts successfully, it would not retain value for even a few hours as it begins to decompose. I would therefore be forced to settle claims immediately before my money (sheep) turns worthless. This brings us to the third important property that money must possess if it must be useful; it should be a good store of value. Unlike sheep, shells or metals are a better store of value over an extended period of time. But it is not just the perishable nature of sheep which makes it unsuitable as a store of value; a change in the price of sheep could also affect its purchasing power over time.

There is yet another problem with sheep (and other commodities) as money. To rear sheep requires the diversion of the community's resources for this purpose, including cultivable land, shepherds, veterinarians, medicine, and so on. Currency as it changes hands is also subject to wear and tear. Replacing currency which is not resilient to such damage imposes a cost on society. As the economy develops and more currency is required to support trade, the monetary system will become expensive, diverting scarce resources of a society towards physical production of the monetary instrument. Given these disadvantages of sheep, the villagers would rethink their choice of money and look for cheaper and more convenient alternatives.

With all these problems in using sheep as money, the village may soon decide to switch over to iron nails. Not only is it more homogeneous, more easily divisible and of smaller units but it can also retain value over a longer period of time. Unfortunately, nails have their own limitations. Carrying a handful of nails in your pocket would not be comfortable; nails are neither convenient nor a handy medium of exchange. Given the possibility to produce them easily, nails may also be too cheap to be a suitable medium of exchange so that common transactions would entail large amounts of nails to be exchanged. A farmer wanting to sell a ton of peanuts would have to carry back a ton of nails. Moreover, nails can be easily produced. To prevent a fall in its price, the village would have to control its supply. As nails represent a claim over other commodities a serious crisis would develop if people began making nails instead of engaging themselves in other pursuits. If iron ore and charcoal were easily available in this village, the weaver and farmer may decide to produce nails rather than make blankets or cultivate peanuts. Soon all the villagers will do the same. With nothing else but nails produced its price falls relative to all other goods, rendering it worthless.

Assume that access to iron ore is restricted and the village decides that instead of nails, small iron flats are to be considered as currency. Everyone agrees not to make such iron flats illegally so that only a certain fixed quantity will circulate. But can you trust the iron flats that the shepherd gives you in exchange for your blankets? Is it not possible that he cheated by adding some slag and re-melted the iron flat into two pieces? Will the cowherd or the baker accept this iron flat? This concern will only grow as trade and exchange expands beyond the domain of a small village, becoming increasingly impersonal. Certification of authenticity of the iron money becomes necessary if it must perform its task of making exchange smooth and simple. Minting of coins arose from this concern and evolved over centuries from crude symbols stamped on a single side of a flat piece of metal to intricate designs that we see on coins today. Stamping of coins, however, came at a cost and the mint entrusted with this job levied a fee to issue currency called *brassage*.

From our discussion so far, we can summarize the properties a commodity must possess if it is to pass as money. It must be homogeneous and divisible, it must be available in sufficient quantity to enable exchange but at the same time not too easily available, it must not degenerate physically, it must not be easily duplicated, it must be easily identifiable as the commodity it is supposed to be, it must be universally accepted by members of society that it is a receipt or certificate of a member's contribution to society and therefore a legitimate claim over goods and services produced by others in that society and finally the most difficult, it must retain its purchasing power (or value) over a period of time. From beads to fur to cowrie shells to metals to precious metals to paper, societies continuously struggled to find commodities that could serve as money, in particular, as currency. And to a great extent they ultimately did in two precious metals: gold and silver.

What made gold and silver so ideally, though not perfectly suited as currency? Let's begin with gold. Given its imperishable nature and the care people take of it, existing stocks of gold above the earth's surface do not diminish by attrition, loss in manufacture, or accident. Its durability allows the same coin to be used many times over. The accumulations made by previous generations are thus maintained, with little lost in amount. It is also not easily lost to wear and tear like (say) leather. Gold can, therefore, be expected to remain in circulation for a long period of time. Its homogenous nature allows it to be divided into parts and, unlike sheep, each part is exactly the same in properties as the whole. Gold is gold; it's the same irrespective of where it comes from. The gold from Africa is the same as the gold from Australia. The rarity of the metal and its high density permits a large weight (value) to be carried in a small volume. A smaller quantity of gold serves for the exchange of a vastly larger quantity of goods than would be required if a cheaper material than gold, like iron nails, were used as money. This also makes it convenient for transport across long distances. Gold will not tarnish or lose lustre even after 5,000 years. Gold will not dissolve in most acids and will not evaporate or burn in a fire like diamonds. Finally, nature has made gold scarce but not too scarce; platinum for instance is too scarce (and the Russians abandoned plans to coin it in the early decades of the 1800s) whereas a metal like iron is too easily found. It is this controlled scarcity of gold, by nature itself, which ensured a fine balance between supply of and demand for gold; world supply of the metal limited by the ability to find the metal in nature and the gradual increase in demand for gold for use as money (and its other industrial applications). It is as if God created gold to serve as money and thereby make exchange convenient. And as nature itself controls gold (money) supply, God separated the state or the ruler from nature's 'central bank'. If money supply in a medieval economy was entirely in the hands of a person or institution, it would be no surprise at all if too much of it was found circulating, quite like the villagers who would make iron nails instead of growing peanuts and weaving blankets.

Silver too possesses many of the features of gold. It might react with the atmosphere to form a thin blackish layer but this is often taken to be proof of its genuineness. And its distinct metallic ring distinguishes it from speculum metal (copper-tin alloy) and other metals. The lower value of silver, due to the greater abundance in which it was found made it ideal for transactions of small value.

Consider a situation where a person wants to buy a kilogram of tea. The cost in terms of gold may be just a fraction of a gram of gold. Such small units of gold would be rather inconvenient to deal with. Silver being less in value than gold, a more convenient quantity can be used to purchase a gram or two may necessary for a kilogram of tea. In fact, in most societies, the need for convenient coins for small transactions made it necessary to use silver, copper and even shells as money along with gold.

Over and above all these characteristics, the single most essential feature that money must possess is the trust and confidence that all others in society will accept it. Only then will I, like all others, accept money in exchange for the goods and services I give up. In other words, money in circulation must be recognized as an authentic claim on society by everyone, everywhere. Gold and silver, by virtue of their usefulness as money command a price in the market; receipt in the form of a gold or silver coin is therefore like receiving a commodity that has its own intrinsic (market) worth thereby making their acceptability as money easier. In other words, the metal itself possesses value irrespective of the stamp on it. When I sell a cow, I take in exchange a certain quantity of a commodity (say gold), which is equal in market value to the cow. Such commodity money like gold or silver coin is called *standard money*.

For smooth exchange and trade, it is crucial to ensure that the content of gold or silver coins, both in terms of purity of metal and weight, is fixed. The objective can never be to fix the price of gold or silver, i.e. the market price of gold or silver can never be held constant. Nevertheless the supply of gold and silver being controlled by nature instills a confidence that the market price of the money circulating will not crash on account of an over-supply. This assurance in the value of gold or silver makes it easier for money to command network externalities; as more people begin to use money, the more useful it becomes to all users. Such was the trust in gold and silver that they were accepted as money across the world. International trade and exchange in goods and commodities flourished on account of the acceptability of gold and silver as money across continents and cultures. The trust in gold and silver is so strong that even today, when people began to lose faith in other currencies (like the US dollar), for reasons we will return to later in the book, they fall back on these precious metals as a store of value. This is simply because we believe that even if the local shopkeeper refuses to accept paper currency, she will accept a small piece of gold or silver in exchange for a loaf of bread. And that's only because she is sure that someone else will accept that gold or silver for a cup of coffee anywhere in the world. This in turn has prevented gold and silver prices from plummeting due to lack of demand.

To those familiar with some basic tools of economic analysis, we graphically illustrate why supply is a crucial factor in determining which commodity makes good money and which does not. In Figure 1.1, iron nails are considered money. Initial (relative) price of nails is P_0, given demand as D_0 and supply S_0. As the economy grows, with a gradual increase in demand from D_0 to D_1 to D_2, the price of nails would increase. The ease of manufacturing nails, however, leads to increases in supply at a much faster rate from S_0 to S_1 to S_2 so that the price of nails, in spite of increases in demand, crashes. A kilogram of nails may be worth a kilogram of peanuts today, but only half tomorrow. When iron nails are used as standard money, this fall in its price as a commodity, will make people reluctant to accept it.

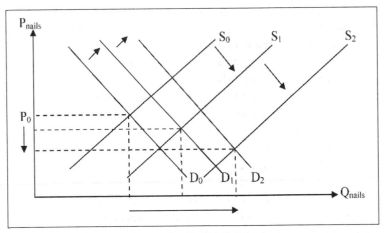

Figure 1.1: The Falling Relative Price of Nails as Currency Money

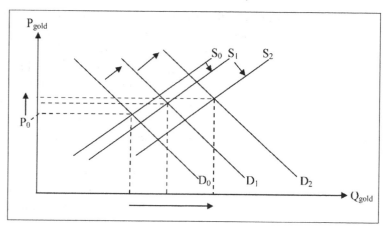

Figure 1.2: The Steadily Rising Relative Price of Gold as Currency Money

In Figure 1.2, gold coins are standard money. Economic growth leads to the same shift in demand for money. However, given the natural constraints on supply of gold, its price remains rather stable with a more likely increase in its price over time.

If the search for perfect money engaged societies over centuries, it is pertinent to ask, why did they take all this trouble to find money? Money allows us to overcome the limitations of barter and by doing so makes exchange easy, simple and smooth. But why is exchange so important? Any society if it must gain from specialization and the division of labour must allow exchange. And it is through specialization and division of labour that we are able to enjoy such high standards of living as we do presently. A world without exchange would, on the contrary, be quite unpleasant. Each of us would have to do all tasks required to keep us alive; a very partial list includes growing our own food, collect oil for lighting, cut wood for cooking, draw water from a pond, weave cloth, and so on. Obviously, there would be no time left, let alone the capability, to even begin thinking of building a concrete house or a motor car or a computer. With specialization all that changes. A software engineer who spends her life working on a programme embedded in a washing machine chip has access to almost everything in the world from food to clothes to movies to cars to holidays in the Antarctic . . . all this only because exchange allows specialization. Barter is no doubt a system of exchange but a rather sloppy one. Money, by lubricating the wheel of exchange, has spread and deepened specialization to such an extent that we no longer even care or need to care to understand its importance unless we specialize in economics.

It is also difficult to conceive of exchanges through barter in a world where a large number of services are rendered without any physical output. What would happen to a clerk or an accountant working in an office? What can she offer to a shopkeeper in exchange for her daily groceries? The same dilemma exists for the worker who hammers rivets into a car's body, lays railway tracks or ploughs the fields for a farmer, a locomotive driver or the captain of a ship, an actor or a singer, a doctor or a teacher, and thousands of other similar jobs. What do all these people take to the market to exchange for what they want? It would, however, be incorrect to say that specialization never existed in a world without pervasive use of money. In medieval India, for instance, occupational specialization was based on caste and the division of output was predetermined by norms that found basis in religion, tradition, culture and customs. When passing through Agara, a small village, now a suburb of Bangalore, Francis Buchanan (1807 I) reported on how the farmer divided grain produced by him.

> There is first set aside from the heap,
> For the gods; that is, for the priests at the temples . . . 5 seers
> For charity; that is, for the *Brahmans, Jangamas,* and other mendicants . . .
> 5 seers
> For the astrologer, or *Panchanga* . . . 1 seer
> For the poor *Brahman* of the village, whose office is hereditary . . . 1 seer . . .
> (pp. 265–6).

The list goes on to include the barber, pot-maker, carpenter, washer man, and other important village functionaries. Finally the state took its share of about 50 per cent from the farmer. The question then is not about division of labour but the degree to which it took place. While in medieval society, division of labour was broad and limited, in a complex and highly advanced industrial society the division of labour and specialization becomes narrower, more detailed and more concentrated on specific tasks or products. Exchanges across space and time become ubiquitous, omnipresent and all encompassing, and can only be organized through the market system. In a market system, signals as to what society needs are transmitted through prices. Specific tasks then get done accordingly and must then be exchanged. But exchanged for what and for how much? We would need a list like the one (a very long one though) Buchanan recorded in Agara. Instead, everything is exchanged for money and then money for goods. Money makes market exchange possible, exchange enables division of labour, and specialization ultimately gives us a better quality of life.

This discussion has sought to shed light on the question we began with: what is money? By elaborating the functions of money it is easy to see why gold and silver were ideally suited to serve as money. But if you thought that this was the end of the history of money you would be woefully off the mark. Gold and silver were remarkable metals as money, but not perfect. Although minting of coins authenticated the weight and fineness of metal in a coin, cheating was still possible and happened frequently and widely. Imagine a gold coin weighing 10 grams and stamped on one side with the symbol X. Suppose I could buy 100 blankets with this coin. But before doing so, I decide to rub some gold off from the unstamped surface, clip the edges of the coin and maybe drill small holes in the coin and fill them up with a little copper. I gather all the gold so obtained and get another coin of 2 grams minted. I can then buy 120 blankets with a coin of 10 grams. When everybody begins to do this, people would lose trust in the actual value of the coin. Any exchange may need re-verification and re-certification by agents or goldsmiths of the actual gold content in the coin. The cost of day-to-day trade and exchange would become exorbitant, ultimately reducing commerce to barter.

Apart from common people, there could be another, more sinister 'cheater'; the mint or the state itself. Suppose the mint decides to mix a little more copper while making the 10 gram gold coin or reduce its size by a small fraction. By doing so suppose it saves two grams of gold. The king, however, orders that this new gold coin of 8 grams be considered equal to the old 10 gram gold coin. In this way, the king could increase his wealth by 20 per cent. This was especially critical in times of war when he needed money to pay soldiers. People, however, would soon come to accept the 10 grams coin as an 8 gram gold coin, raising prices of all other goods and services by 20 per cent so that they would effectively get back the same amount of gold as they did earlier. In this way, debasement of currency led to a corresponding rise in the price of all other goods, or what is commonly known as inflation.

Throughout history, kings and queens cheated nature (which controlled the supply of precious metals) and people by debasing currency. But as Nicole Oresme cautioned Charles V of France in the fourteenth century, falsifying the *value of currency*, the gold content of a coin, would reduce him to a liar, guilty of perjury, and bearing false testimony. Sir James Steuart (1772) captured the problem of currency debasement most eloquently: 'To reduce the Winchester bushel³ to the contents of a drinking-glass, and to call a glass of wine a bushel of wine, is not more absurd, than to call by the term pound, what does not contain one ounce. From this abuse has been introduced the confusion which prevails everywhere in questions concerning money' (p. 4).

Not only was there a problem in verifying the purity of metal and other forms of debasement but there also existed a more overwhelming difficulty in the use of precious metals as money; either their scarcity to satisfy the needs of growing trade and commerce or at other times an oversupply of these metals. As we have shown graphically, like all other commodities, prices of precious metals fluctuate with demand and supply. In a situation of scarcity of these metals for currency, their price rises. Since money is the common denominator in whose terms all other exchange values are quoted, the increased price of gold or silver implies a fall in the relative price of other goods and services. Going back to Table 1.1, an increase in the price of sheep implies a fall in prices of all other goods, i.e. one sheep would command more than 2.4 blankets in exchange, more than 0.14 cows, and so on. This fall in prices would affect output as people began deferring their purchase in view of their expectation that price will continue to fall. The deflationary spiral of falling prices and output was a great cause of concern given its repercussions on employment and growth of the economy. On the other hand, a spurt in supply of precious metals would drive down their prices implying a relative rise in price of all other commodities. A moderate rate of inflation may not cause as much concern as deflation but it does have its own costs, especially when it's too high. Although the limited supply of gold and silver controlled inflation from getting out of hand, sudden increases in supply of gold and silver immediately after discoveries did cause concern over inflation.

The change in price of precious metals and their consequent impact on the value of money has been a recurrent concern throughout the histories of almost all nations of the world. The critical interrelationship between these parameters was succinctly articulated by one of the oldest economic theories, the Quantity Theory of Money (QTM). The QTM continues to be relevant even today although the scope of money has undergone incredible qualitative and qualitative changes, extending itself beyond a currency system based on precious metals.

The QTM begins with the following identity (a relationship which always holds true), the 'equation of exchange':

$$M.V \equiv \Sigma\, P_i.Q_i \equiv P_1Q_1 + P_2Q_2 + \ldots + P_nQ_n \equiv P.Q \qquad \ldots (1.1)$$

where M = amount of money in circulation, V = velocity of circulation of money or the average number of times that money changes hands, P_i = price of the ith good and Q_i = quantity of the ith good. This is a tautological relationship implying that it is always true. In an economy where all transactions take place with money, the total monetary value of all n goods produced and exchanged must be equal to the total quantum of money in circulation. Suppose there are only two goods, 1 and 2. Let $P_1 = 50$, $Q_1 = 100$, $P_2 = 10$, $Q_2 = 500$ then $\Sigma P_i.Q_i = 10,000$. This quantum of exchange would be possible when the total quantum of money in circulation is also equal to Rs. 10,000. But this does not mean that we need Rs. 10,000 in currency. If on average each rupee changes hands 10 times or V = 10 then for exchanges of Rs. 10,000 to take place, Rs. 1,000 of currency in circulation (M) would suffice.

Thus far equation 1.1 is an identity and is not of much signifi-cance. If, however, assumptions are made about the nature of each variable in equation (1), we have a theory. For instance, if we argue (i) that the velocity of circulation of money depends on prevailing institutional structures and can therefore be taken as constant at a point of time and (ii) that the economy is operating at full em-ployment level of output and is fixed, then we have:

$$M.V = \Sigma\ P_i.Q_i = P.Q \qquad\qquad \dots (1.2)$$

where V and Q are constants. Any change in money supply (M) or the amount of money in circulation would lead to a proportionate increase in the price level, P.

This textbook algebraic treatment of QTM leaves a lot unsaid. It leads to the simplistic understanding that money does not mat-ter in determining the level of output or that a decrease in M would merely bring down the price level. Instead, with some ab-straction, a more analytical account of QTM can describe the subtle relationship between the quantity of money, prices and output. At any point of time, a society, given the state of its technology, com-munications, transport networks, customs and practices, institu-tions like banks, etc., can produce a certain 'maximum' amount of goods and services such that all its resources are 'fully' employed, where 'fully' implies that specialization has reached its optimal level. This can only happen when there is sufficient money[4] in circulation to allow all necessary exchanges to take place. Consider our small, primitive village where there are just a handful of occu-pations, say, A to F. Let's begin with a situation without money in this village and exchange was solely on the basis of barter. Total output of all goods produced is as given below in Table 1.2. After the villagers agree to nails as money, the problem of double coinci-dence of wants is overcome and exchange becomes easier and more efficient so that a greater degree of specialization becomes possi-ble. Output produced is now as shown in Column 2 of Table 1.2. The quantum of nails introduced into circulation is one ton. How-ever, given the prevailing commercial customs and practices in this village, money does not circulate fast enough (say, the velocity of circulation of money is low because the houses are too far apart and the village market takes place only once a month) so that its

TABLE 1.2: SECTORAL OUTPUT WITH DIFFERENT AMOUNT OF MONEY IN CIRCULATION

	Column 1	Column 2	Column 3
A	10	12	15
B	3	4	9
C	32	47	77
D	1	3	4
E	76	83	98
F	2	8	11

(output) potential is not fully realized with just one ton of nails. Keeping its customs and practices (and all other parameters stated above) constant, let us suppose two tons of nails are just the right amount of money necessary to realize its full potential, shown in Column 3 in the Table 1.2.

This amount of money, two tons of nails, with a given velocity of circulation of money ensures that all exchanges (across space and time) that must take place to achieve 'full employment' of its resources do take place effectively and efficiently. In quite the same way, every village or society, however complex, requires a certain quantum of money in circulation so that it can achieve full employment of all its resources. This is the point at which we consider Q to be fixed at $\bar{Q}$. What the QTM then means is that any further increase in money supply cannot increase output or in other words, by simply putting more nails (or money) into circulation, this village cannot increase its output beyond Column 3 for these are limited by real parameters like technology, communications and so on. The QTM argues that once this potential is realized to the fullest, Q becomes a constant, $\bar{Q}$. It is important to reiterate that *until* this level of full employment or full potential output is reached, increase in money supply does influence the level of output as illustrated in Table 1.2. Only then does a *further* increase in the quantity of money lead to a proportionate increase in the price level, given $V = \bar{V}$.

Although not seen algebraically from equation 1.2, inadequacy in money supply can have equally significant repercussions. As we have described above, starting from output Q in Column 2, a decrease in the quantity of money could cause real output to fall. This could happen directly when exchanges are constrained by the lack of money or indirectly by causing deflation. If the same volume of transactions has to take place with a lesser amount of money (with *V* fixed), this can only happen if P were lower. As seen above, deflationary expectations then result in a fall in price and put the economy in a vicious downward spiral. Prices and output begin to fall in succession, with consequences that are considered even more dangerous to an economy than inflation. It is not surprising then that central banks in many parts of the world have an inflation target at + 2 per cent.

The modern analysis of the QTM has focused on using money supply as a policy instrument in controlling prices and influencing output and employment. In this case, what is most important is not the determination of the optimum amount of currency at any point of time but how changes in money supply could cause changes in prices and output. Here, the nature (its stability and predictability) and magnitude of the velocity of circulation plays a critical role in formulating monetary policy in capitalist economies. QTM as a guide to macroeconomic policy is of critical importance; however, our focus is on its historical implications where changes in money supply were caused by the flows of bullion into and out of the country. More often than not, when the world monetary system was based on metallic currency, it was the consequences that arose from a shortage of currency due to economic growth, trade and war that lead to economic contraction and with it strong reactions from people. The solution to the problem was, however, sometimes even bigger than the problem itself and remained a burning issue right into the nineteenth century.

One way to overcome currency shortages was to allow coins in more than one metal to circulate as money. In the normal course of trade when people trusted more than one metal with the requisite properties of currency, these metals began to circulate as money. The question, however, is whether coins in two metals can circulate simultaneously in an economy and on what terms? One option was to have either metal as the accepted unit of account and then allow coins in different metals to circulate simultaneously but with *the rate between them determined by the market*, a currency system called a parallel standard. But this system had a limitation; in a market with constant fluctuations in the exchange rate between gold and silver one could end up incurring losses unless the variations were fully known. The more appropriate alternative it seemed was bimetallism where both metals could circulate as coin but with the government fixing the rate (or ratio) of exchange between them.

Using Irving Fisher's (1912) articulation of gold and silver money as 'substitutes, but have no natural ratio of substitution' (p. 377) I have tried to describe these currency systems graphically using a simple demand-supply model. While supply of money is considered fixed at a point of time, the demand curves will typically be downward sloping. This is because as price of one metal falls with respect of the other it will be substituted for the other at least in the arts (non-monetary usages). Whether it will also be substituted for the other as money depends on whether a parallel standard or bimetallism is in existence. Consider Country C_P on a parallel standard where both gold and silver circulate as money at an exchange rate determined by the market. The gold and silver bullion markets are at equilibrium with demand equal to supply at (say) G/S = 15, i.e. 1G = 15S or S/G = 1/15 as shown in Figure 1.3(a) and 1.3(b) respectively. Suppose gold supply increases from S_G to S_G'. This would put pressure on the silver price of gold to fall from 15 towards (say) 14 as the excess supply gets absorbed for non-monetary purposes. But will substitution of silver money by the cheaper gold take place? Suppose a cup of tea had cost 1G = 15S before gold prices fell to 14S. If gold is the accepted unit of account, then the price of tea remains at 1G so that you pay either 1G or 14S for it. If instead silver is the unit of account, the tea price remains at 15S so you must pay either 15S or 1.07G (as per the new rate of 1G = 14S) for it. Gold will not replace silver as coin. However, as shown in Figure 1.3(a), the fall in the silver price of gold would result in an increase in quantity demanded of gold from G_0 to G_1 on account of its use in the arts (non-monetary usage).

At the same time, as the silver price of gold falls towards 14, the

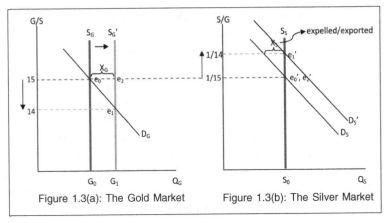

Figure 1.3(a): The Gold Market   Figure 1.3(b): The Silver Market

Figure 1.3: Exchange Ratio Fluctuations under a
Parallel Standard

gold price of silver increases from 1/15 to 1/14. What happens to the demand for silver? As seen in Figure 1.3(b) there may be some decline in the demand for silver for use in the arts as it becomes more expensive than its substitute, gold. The demand curves for gold and silver, although downward sloping, may not be highly elastic given that a change in relative price does not lead to a withdrawal of either metal from circulation.

Now the cheaper gold absorbed in the arts automatically means that there will be some excess supply of costlier silver in the market shown as X_S in Figure 1.3(b). The equilibrium e_0 is therefore an unstable one; an increase in gold supplies will cause a downward pressure on gold prices and consequently an upward movement in silver prices. This leads to an excess supply of silver that induces silver prices to fall or gold prices to rise. The situation will therefore be reversed; silver prices drift towards 1/15 and gold prices rise back to 15. This would then leave Country C_P with an excess supply in gold (X_G) and a new bout of price fluctuations.

It is possible for the markets to reach equilibrium at G/S = 14 or S/G = 1/14 provided there is an increase in the demand for silver (from within the country or from exports), shown as a shift in the demand curve form D_S to D_S' in Figure 1.3(b). Other possibilities exist too; however, any equilibrium ratio will mean an increase in demand for either gold or silver or both. Meanwhile, the instability in the price ratio triggered by changes in supply hinders exchange and trade by increasing the cost of obtaining information or procuring the services of a moneychanger.

A fixed price ratio between the two metals or bimetallism, with both gold and silver as legal tender, is therefore considered a superior alternative as the risk and uncertainty over not knowing the precise market ratio is eliminated. But can bimetallism ensure this? Unfortunately, all through medieval history, all across the world, the seemingly simple policy of bimetallism had disastrous consequences. Finding an explanation to this problem even engaged great minds like those of Nicolaus Copernicus and Isaac Newton. Consider a situation where the *bullion* (or market) value of silver and gold is G/S = 20, i.e. 1G = 20S. If, however, the legal ratio of coins *is fixed* at 1G = 15S, what will be the consequence? Silver as coin (i.e. legally) has been overvalued, gold coins undervalued. If a person has to settle a debt of, say, 1G, would she choose to do so using gold or silver coins? Suppose she holds 1G. With one unit of gold she can get 20 units of silver in the market. She can use 15S to settle the debt legally and still hold 5S. Gold coins would flow to the market to be melted into bullion, and silver bullion would come to the mints for coinage. The 'bad' or overvalued silver coins would soon drive out the 'good' undervalued gold coins *from circulation*; gold will end up in markets, even overseas, or hoarded as bullion but not used as currency.

Let me attempt to graphically illustrate how bimetallism works. Since the ratio between the coins of the two metals is fixed, declared and known to everyone, the elasticity of demand for them will now be close to infinity over the range of the monetary requirements of the economy. A small deviation in the market price from the legal ratio would cause a significant change in the quantity demanded of either metal for monetary purposes as people substitute the legally undervalued coin with the overvalued one. In Figure 1.4(a), with an increase in supply of gold the market rate deviates from the legal ratio. The substitution of silver will commence as soon as the costs of switching are covered; these costs include 'seigniorage charge, the cost of melting coins, delays and

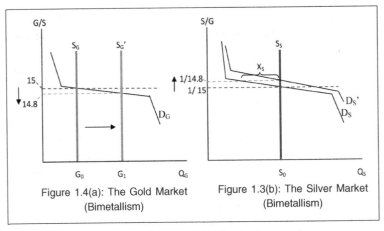

Figure 1.4(a): The Gold Market
(Bimetallism)

Figure 1.3(b): The Silver Market
(Bimetallism)

Figure 1.4: Exchange Ratio Fluctuations under a
Bimetallic Standard

associated loss of interest, insurance fees, and so on'. (Friedman, 1989, p. 8). Moreover, there could also be uncertainty and risk associated with knowing the 'exact' market ratio (it could also fluctuate) so that people might defer their decision to melt silver until the gap between the legal ratio and market ratio is substantial and unequivocal. When this point is reached, large volumes of gold will be coined and silver melted. It is even possible that all the silver coins are melted. But for this to happen the excess silver has to be drained from the system. If not the market ratio will oscillate between (say) 14.8S = 1G to 15 = 1G in Figure 1.4(a) or between (1.14.8) to 1/15) as in Figure 1.4(b). The knife-edge characteristic of bimetallism is evident in this model; small changes in supply could cause significant volumes of silver coins to be substituted by gold coins. Without it being drained out of the system, an excess supply of silver would result, causing its market price to fall, triggering a new bout of price fluctuations.

The principle that bad currency (gold in the above case) drives out good currency (silver) from circulation has come to be known as Gresham's Law. To reiterate the nature of this phenomenon, take a situation that you could confront; you have two currency notes of the same denomination, one soiled and the other new and crisp.

Wouldn't you want to dispose the worn out note first, keeping the new one? Since both notes command the same amount of goods and services in exchange, we prefer to put the 'bad' note in circulation, retaining the 'good' one. Just one last example to drive home the point; suppose you have Rs. 5 (paper) note and an old Rs. 5 coin made from silver but now worth Rs. 1,000 in the bullion market. If you were to buy a pencil priced at Rs. 5, which would you use as currency, the note or the coin? Obviously the note; you would either hoard or melt all the coins in the bullion market and get a thousand Rs. 5 notes in exchange, buy the pencil with one note and still have Rs. 995 with you.

The origin of Gresham's Law can actually be attributed to Oresme. In the mid-fourteenth century, when the debased coinage of France adversely affected foreign trade of the country, Charles V, called the Wise, believed the only way to restore prosperity was to change the denomination of the coin. He referred the matter to Oresme, who in his famous treatise, *Traictie de la Premiere Invention des Monnoies* argued that such a proposal would, without a doubt, fail. He noted something of critical importance; the consequence of debasements of coin would lead to gold and silver in the country being exported to other places where they command a higher value. In other words, people in the country would have their bullion minted elsewhere rather than in a country where bullion is (coins are) undervalued (overvalued). Moreover, by such debasements of the coin, foreign merchants would cease to bring their goods into the country, because what they get in exchange for their goods is nothing but overvalued coins which are less than the bullion value they claim to be. Such tampering with the money would destroy all confidence, throwing trade and commerce into a state of confusion.

The same conclusion was reached by Copernicus *c.* 1526 when Sigismund I, King of Poland, sought to redress the issue of debased Prussian (then part of Poland) coins with issue of a new currency. Copernicus explained the futility of this strategy in restoring order to the currency system. The overvalued Prussian currency would drive out the undervalued new currency as the goldsmiths and bullion dealers culled out the best pieces of currency, new and old, melting them down and selling the silver, leaving nothing in circulation but the worst coin. On the other hand, if the debased Prussian currency was allowed to circulate, all gold and silver would be exported from Poland with nothing but copper remaining. Which foreign merchant would exchange his wares for copper money? Import of foreign merchandise would cease, ruining all commerce. To restore order, as new money is issued, the old must be demonetized, totally forbidding its use after exchanging it at the mints at its market value. Good and bad money cannot circulate together for only one would remain in due course—the bad. And just as a bad debased coin will drive out a full-weighted good coin, a 'bad' overvalued coin of one metal will drive out the 'good' undervalued coin of another metal. Oresme and Copernicus had perceived the impossibility of bimetallism, i.e. the keeping gold and silver coins in circulation together in unlimited quantities, at a legal ratio differing from the market ratio of the metals.

In medieval England too, the instant disappearance of good coins as soon as they were issued from the Mint proved to be an enigmatic puzzle. Some financiers and statesmen even believed that people were inspired by the Evil One to prefer the bad coin and to reject the good. It was only in the mid-sixteenth century that Sir Thomas Gresham explained to Queen Elizabeth why good and bad coin cannot circulate together. In spite of his clear economic reasoning, nations continued to repeat the mistake made by earlier medieval rulers. In the early eighteenth century, Isaac Newton as Master of the Mint faced a situation of diminishing quantum of silver currency on account of, amongst other reasons, exports of bullion to India. Newton recommended a bimetallic currency system, fixing the price of the (gold) guinea at 21 (silver) shillings. Unfortunately, at the rate specified by Newton, the gold guinea was overvalued as coin by more than 1.5 per cent. People immediately converted shillings into silver bullion, purchased gold bullion in the market and minted it into guineas. The 'unexpected' happened; the full-weight silver coin was withdrawn or exported and the 'bad' guinea gold became the only practical measure of value.

The solution to bimetallism as we have seen is a parallel standard. John Locke and William Petty proposed that only one metal be adopted as unit of account, making coins of any other metal/s subsidiary to it with its/their value fluctuating in accordance to the market price of bullion. Coins of gold and silver must bear the same ratio to each other as the metals do in the market (as bullion). Such a system had in fact been in operation during Mughal rule and worked well in medieval India (as we will see subsequently). Unfortunately, the East India Company's skepticism over adopting it as India was slowly being transformed into a cash (from a feudal-in kind) economy caused several cataclysmic upheavals in the eighteenth and nineteenth centuries, with pernicious consequences.

These concerns over the scarcity of metallic money and of bimetallism led to the development of different forms of money; for instance, claims embodied in token money or a monetary instrument with an intrinsic worth less than what it is stipulated to be like lead or copper coins. Token money circulates as legal tender whereby people *have to* accept it by law against discharge of a debt of certain value. A copper coin intrinsically worth (its metal value) 1/10th of a rupee could legally be used to discharge a debt of, say, Re. 1. In other words, copper commands more value as coin than metal. Given copper's lower market worth, the coin remains in circulation. It is important to reiterate here that although the intrinsic worth of the copper coin is less than the actual value of debt it should in principle not affect acceptability as money; as long as people agree (or are compelled to as in the case of legal tender) that it is a valid token of claims. Token money then serves the same function as coins made from precious metals. Token money was, however, not coined freely at the mint or in other words, it was not possible to take copper to the mint and get it coined. Instead, the state would procure copper from the market and mint coins only at its own discretion.

Physical constraints in availability of precious metals, the inconvenience of physical transport and disorder that arises from bimetallism compelled the evolution of money into other complex and heterogeneous forms. Paper money is perhaps the best example of the latter, but its ascendance has been neither simple nor painless. In most countries of the world, paper money replaced gold and silver coins. Its acceptance in discharge of debt has been made compulsory with the state making it legal tender. Without this, unlike standard money, it has no intrinsic value; a currency note without the stamp on it is merely a worthless piece of paper that people might be reluctant to accept.

I have so far attempted to explain the key facets in the development of money, or rather currency, and the functions that it must fulfill in a given society. But just as money enables smoother exchange and specialization in any closed economy it could also perform the same functions across economies, or in other words, internationally. Let me return to our village which had agreed to use nails as currency. Suppose another village had agreed to use only shells as currency. If exchanges between people of the two villages were to take place, what would be the medium of exchange used by them for their inter-village transactions? All foreign trade would have to be reduced to barter if they are unable to agree on a common commodity as currency. But barter, as we have seen, would limit exchange, specialization and consequently, standards of living in both the villages.

Once again, it was the general acceptance of gold and silver not just within but also across countries as a means of exchange and store of value that made them the closest equivalent to a world currency. In medieval times, the world had pure gold and silver currencies wherein the metals, and nothing but these metals, served as money. Standard coins of one country could then be shipped to another country for the purchase of goods. The country receiving the coins could melt them for bullion and have them re-minted into domestic coins or even let them circulate in their original form (just as Roman coins circulated in India). If, however, gold were used as standard money in one country while silver was more acceptable in another, then gold coins of the former country would have to be melted, exchanged for silver in the bullion market and then be shipped to the other country. Apart from the cost of melting, transport and brassage, there would be no significant loss of value in this operation. But an additional concern over the rate of exchange between gold and silver might have still existed since relative prices of gold and silver were determined by and fluctuated with changes in demand and supply. Differences in relative prices of these precious metals across countries also induced their international movement; in sixteenth century Europe after the inflow of silver from America, the gold price of silver fell to about 1:12 while the demand for silver in India on account of its widespread usage as currency raised the price of silver (in terms of gold) to between 1:9 and 1:10. The higher worth of silver in India as compared to Europe, as we see in the next section, made it attractive to ship silver from Europe to India where the same quantum of silver commanded a greater quantity of goods.

It is also pertinent to mention that the flow of precious metals and their use as currency across countries, propagated through war, plunder and trade, began many centuries before colonialism. The world's craving for Indian silks, cottons, spices and jewels and India's desire for precious metals had continued unabated over thousands of years. Daniell (1884) tells us that Alexander the Great, *c.* 3 BC. in his invasions of Persia and India obtained a treasure valued at more than £50 million (p.11). In the first century AD some £3 million was annually exported by the Roman Empire to India, in spite of the restrictions imposed on such exports. And in the three hundred years after the East India Company begun trade, some £160 million of gold and £440 million of silver were exported to India.

I had mentioned earlier why bimetallism within an economy is prone to failure. Nonetheless, bimetallism was also adopted in the international arena with its supporters asserting that fixing a legal ratio between gold and silver by international agreement in a few countries would establish a stable exchange between several countries using different metallic currencies. But if it is impossible for one country to maintain a fixed ratio between gold and silver that differs from the ratio of their market price is it possible for all the governments in the world to do so? If the whole world were to agree to undervalue a coin below its market value it would disappear from circulation with only the overvalued coin remaining in circulation for the simple reason that coins are only received in foreign countries according to the market value of the quantity of bullion they contain. The truth is, however, not as simple as it seems; we will defer a more complete study of how the rejection of international bimetallism led to a complete transformation of the monetary system in the late nineteenth century. For now, I go back in time to a period with its own share of fascinating episodes and one in which the history of the rupee begins.

1.2: CURRENCY IN MEDIEVAL INDIA

The greater part of the gold and silver of the universe finds innumerable channels by which it may enter Indostan, and scarcely a single one for escaping from it.

SIGNOR MANOUCHI, 1708

Like in most other economies of the world, currency in India developed from objects like beads and cowries to metallic coins in gold, silver and copper. Gold, in the form of gold dust panned from river basins and tied in bags was used as currency in ancient India. Though there is evidence of gold being mined in India, it was done on a very limited scale. Silver, which was the preferred metal for currency in many parts of India, was, however, not found in India. Even though India did not look at the rest of the world as a source of commodities and goods for consumption, its only source of precious metals depended on acquiring them through international trade. India consistently ran trade surpluses with the rest of the world that were settled through imports of precious metals, used for currency as well as a store of value in the form of jewelry and/or bullion. In fact, as a feudal economy where many transactions were conducted in kind (not cash) the function of money as a store of value was equally if not more important for both the aristocracy as well as the common people.

It is therefore not surprising that Indian monetary history has been inextricably tied up with international trade even though the latter was *per se* never a large part of the country's total domestic product. What made international trade even more critical was the elasticity of supply of precious metals for currency, or the supply *at the margin*, which depended on the volume of foreign trade each year. In other words, while the stock of precious metals was important, additional quantities of these metals to enable greater domestic circulation of goods and services, could be obtained only through 'current' net exports.

Of the two metals, silver was more widely demanded for coinage as it conformed well to the prevailing price levels of commodities and services. This demand for silver as currency meant that its price relative to that of gold in India was higher than in Europe. For instance, in Akbar's time, *c.* 1550, the silver price of gold was about 9.4:1 in India while in Europe it was as low as 12:1, sometimes even lower at 15:1. This price differential sustained the inflow of silver into India from foreign countries making it commonly available for use as currency.

In the previous section we saw the impact of bimetallism on flow of bullion from the market to the mint and vice-versa. Differential purchasing power of coins across countries can cause a similar movement. Consider two countries, England and India with gold-silver exchange rates given as below:

England: 1G = 15S or 1S = 0.067G
India: 1G = 10S or 1S = 0.1G

Two direct possibilities arise to take advantage of these differential exchange rates.

I. Bring 15S from England to India, procure 1.5G in India, and take back 1.5G to England. This gives a profit of 0.5G (less transactions costs).

II. Take 1G from India, procure 15S in England, and bring back 15S to India. This gives a clear profit of 5S (less transactions costs).

Suppose, however, that bullion is not easily available in foreign markets, pure bullion trade is restricted between countries or transport of bullion across countries is too risky. In such a situation, trade in goods can substitute for direct bullion flows to take advantage of differential exchange rates. Consider, for sake of simplicity, that tradable goods are equally priced in England and India. Possibilities for trade then arise purely on account of differential exchange rates as follows:

III. Bring 15S of silver from England to India. Suppose good X costs 1G in England and India. Then with 15S we can get 1.5G in India which can be used to buy 1.5 of X in India. Take X to England and sell it for 1.5G. Once again there exists a clear gain of 0.5G (less transactions costs).

IV. Take 0.1G from India to England. Suppose good Y costs 1S in England and India. Then with 0.1G we can get 1.5S in England (because with 0.067G we can buy 1S) which can be used to buy 1.5 of Y in England. Bring Y to India and sell it for 1.5S. We have a clear gain of 0.5S (less transactions costs).

Historically, option III was exercised by most European trading companies, including the English East India Company. Moreover, apart from exchange rate differentials in the price of silver and gold, there were also large differences in price of goods as well as availability (spices) and quality (textiles), which the trading companies took advantage of.

The Indian metallic currency system developed since ancient times from these inflows of gold and silver as well as network externalities that precious metals offered in the development of international trade. A complex monetary system with a multiplicity of coins evolved over centuries. One of the noteworthy elements in the Indian system was the possibility for purchasing power of currencies to fluctuate with their market price. This *parallel standard* never seemed to have posed a serious problem to trade for perhaps two reasons, the first being limited monetization of the economy. Although gold and silver flowed into India much of it was hoarded as a store of value with only a portion of it used for coinage. Even here, the use of silver and gold coins was restricted to high-value transactions, others of a more routine nature were carried out either through barter, copper coins or to a large extent with low-valued cowrie shells whose denomination was a mere 1/6000th of a rupee. Second, nearly every village had traditional moneychangers or *shroffs* who converted different coins into locally acceptable and usable currency. An average man knew very little about the fluctuations in the rate of exchange so the necessity of specialized money changers was critical. As recorded by the famous French traveler Tavernier (1640–65) the shroffs not only provided the service of exchanging rupee 'for paisa and the paisa for these (cowrie) shells' (Tavernier, 1676, p. 24) but they were most adept at their profession. As he pointed out, 'all the Jews who occupy themselves with money and exchange in the empire of the Grand Seigneur[5] pass for being very sharp; but in India they would scarcely be apprentices to these Changers'. (ibid). At the same time, the force of custom and social pressure ensured conformity by shroffs to their trade and financial obligations. There are accounts of a shroff at Madras and his two bazaar colleagues having received severe punishment when they were found to have abused public confidence by putting into circulation bags containing pagodas of inferior value under their seals. The two bazaar subordinates were sentenced to banish-ment and a fine of 2,500 pagodas while the shroff was fined 3,500 pagodas that had to be spent on the improvement of the native part of the town. In another instance, two town shroffs of Madras who were guilty of sealing inferior *pagodas* were committed to a *choultry* (public rest house) and their houses sealed up (Wheeler, 1862, p. 242).

Medieval India had to contend with another issue—large surpluses in current account (excess of exports over imports) with the rest of the world that led to massive inflows of gold and silver bullion (or foreign coins melted into bullion). I will present more accurate estimates of these inflows in the next section; for now it suffices to mention that precious metals to the tune of some 20–50 tons of silver came into India every year over centuries. From an economic perspective, however, there is an important question that must be raised; the impact of these bullion inflows (that could be minted into currency) on the price level. Fortunately, no destabilizing effect on the price level as might be expected from the Quantity Theory of Money can be found. Several factors could have impeded price inflation in India. As explained above, the actual quantum of money percolating to artisans and cultivators at the local level may have been a fraction of the whole. Goods for exports to the foreign traders from India were usually supplied by relatively few and concentrated family business houses like Virji Vora, the Jagatseths and Arjunji Nathji (more about them and their activities are described later in the book). The bullion that flowed into India on account of her trade surpluses was appropriated by these large trading houses and by the nobility. The question then arises as to why it was not monetized so as to cause prices to rise. The answer once again lay in the hoarding habit of not only the nobility but across all sections of Indian society who drained the excess money supply from the system. Buchanan (1807 II), for instance, narrates the spending and hoarding habits of *goalas* or cowherds: 'His clothing, being a blanket, costs a mere trifle; and part of the money he expends in the mar-riages of the younger branches of the family, and in religious cere-monies; the remainder is in general buried, and a great deal of money is in this way lost; as when the men get old they forget where the treasures are hidden, and sometimes die without divulging the secret' (pp. 13–14).

At the other end of the hierarchy were the nobility and rich traders whose habits were not dissimilar. The Nawab of Oudh, it is said, hoarded more than half a million sterling every year. During their territorial expansion post-*diwani* in 1765, the East India Company laid claim to some of these vast hoards across the country; in 1781 more than a quarter million from a collector of revenue in Benares, £330,000 from the Scindias, some £900,000 in Bharatpur, and more than a million sterling was found in Srirangapatnam. This habit of Indians to hoard gold and silver, which worries policy makers even today,[6] would have drained large surpluses of currency from the system and controlled the possible impact of currency inflows on prices.

Theoretically speaking, if we look at the equation of exchange [Equation (1.2)], increases in M should have had a direct and positive impact on P.

$$M.V = \Sigma \ P_i.Q_i = P.Q \qquad \qquad \ldots (1.3)$$

The dampened impact on price level in spite of these increases in money supply is possible when we relax the assumption of a constant V. Irving Fisher (1918) explains how hoarding slows down the velocity of circulation of money.

Hoarded money is sometimes withdrawn from circulation, but this is only another way of saying that hoarding tends to decrease the velocity of circulation.

The only distinction between 'hoarding' money in a stocking or safe and 'carrying' money in a purse is one of degree. The money remains in the stocking or safe longer than in the purse. In either case it may be said to be in circulation, but when 'hoarded' it circulates much more slowly. In the case of individual hoards, as of misers, it is convenient to consider them as in circulation. (p. 197)

Fisher then makes one additional comment, which may also be of relevance to the Indian context where the nobility were large hoarders. 'Only in the case of the larger government hoards is it worthwhile to consider them as excluded from "money in circulation"' (ibid).

Apart from hoarding, the non-monetization of the economy also prevented the occurrence of inflationary pressures from the inflow of bullion. The division of labour in medieval India was not only limited but also predominantly based on tradition, custom and caste. In the previous section, we mentioned some of Francis Buchanan's observation from Agara near Bangalore where many of the local exchanges were made in kind, not cash. In another survey of the province of Bareilly in British India with a population of 66,000, only about 100 different trades were found, with very little subdivision of labour within them (*Asiatic Journal*, 1827, p. 466). A low degree of division of labour allowed for a greater number of exchanges through barter; the influence of money in day-to-day transactions was, therefore, limited. Even wages of farm servants and labourers were often distributed in grain and cloth and only partially in cash. The standing military force kept and regularly paid in currency by the government was also very small. The bulk of the troops consisted of foot soldiers maintained by zamindars and feudatories. These soldiers were supported predominantly on the grain and other supplies furnished by the territories in which they were located. The hereditary revenue and other administrative officers were compensated by land grants and a share of taxes collected in kind. Taxes too, as Buchanan observed in Agara near Bangalore, were collected in kind. Moreover, in many parts of the country, these taxes were not paid directly to the government by cultivators but through the zamindars and village moneylenders who would make advances in the form of money, grain, seeds or cattle to agriculturists on the security of the produce or movable or immovable property or even personal security. The zamindars were responsible for paying land revenue on behalf of the cultivators and received grain from cultivators in lieu of their paying revenue.

In spite of these factors inhibiting inflation, some historians do believe that money supply had increased significantly in medieval India, enough to impact the price level. Evidence of steep increases in price of food grains as well as commodities like sugar and indigo in the fifteenth and sixteenth centuries has been estimated by Irfan Habib; the annual rate being about 1.93 per cent. Such sustained inflation over a period of 150 years should have had an impact on the economy. In the West it did. Positive inflation rates, without a corresponding increase in wage rates, had meant a gradual accumulation of capital by the merchants, thereby sowing the seeds for capitalist development. Such a fall in real wage rates should have provided the basis for capital accumulation in India too. Unfortunately, this did not happen. Not only were the benefits of falling wages appropriated by the feudal nobility but the hoarding habits of the merchant class may have also dampened productive investment (see Habib, 1982, p. 376). In spite of this feature of medieval Indian history, it is important to appreciate the relative stability of the currency system.

It is sometimes argued that the positive side of India's hoarding habit was that it drained the world economy, especially the West of its surplus currency. If not for this, the discoveries of precious metals and inflows from the plunder of the Americas may have caused high rates of inflation in medieval Europe with the possibility of destabilizing the economy and society. Trade with the East provided a vent for their surplus currency. At the same time, the hoarding habit of Indians prevented inflationary pressures from developing in India. It is relevant to quote Keynes' (1913) remark on this point;

It is interesting to reflect that India's love of the precious metals, ruinous though it has been to her own economic development, has flourished in the past to the great advantage of Western nations . . . always ready to absorb the redundant bullion of the West and to save Europe from the more violent disturbances to her price level . . . From its very short period point of view the City is sometimes cross when this Indian demand shows itself in an inconvenient week; but if we take a longer view the Indian demand is, at a time of plentiful gold supply like the present, a true friend to the City and the enemy of inflation. (pp. 99–100)

1.3: CURRENCY IN MEDIEVAL NORTHERN INDIA

It is to be observed that the Silver Money of the Great Mogul is finer than any other, for whenever a Stranger enters the Empire, he is made to change the Silver he hath, whether Piastres or Abassis, into the Money of the Country, and at the same time they are melted down, and the silver refined for the Coyning of Roupies.

TRAVELS OF MONSIEUR DE THEVENOT, 1665

Our historical narrative begins with a specific coin that originated in the year AD 1542 during the reign of Sher Shah Suri; the rupee or *rupiya*. While the Mughal emperors, Babur and Humayun struck their own coins called *shahrukhis*, foreign coins like the Arabic dirham and dinar, Greek drachma (silver), and Roman denarius auri (gold) and follis (copper) also circulated as currency in the region. Suri, who usurped the throne from the Emperor Humayun and ruled for a period of just five years, reformed the currency system by abolishing use of mixed metals for coinage and issuing well struck coins of uniform weight and fineness. The rupee, which means silver, weighed about 176 grains troy (each grain troy, a measure of weight, equal to 64.79891 mg so that the rupee weighed ~11.40 grams) or close to a hundred *ratis*; a *rati* being 1.75 grains, the weight of *Abrus precatorias*, or the wild liquorice seed. The purity of the metal was maintained at close to 96 per cent.

Mughal coinage proper, however, began in the reign of Akbar and continued in circulation for almost 300 years. The currency system can be said to be of standard money with the rupee coin as essentially a small piece of silver, certified for its weight and fineness by a sharp and clear impression on its surface. The purchasing power of the rupee equaled the price of silver in the bullion market, except for the mint's cost of coinage. This is an important aspect of metallic money that must be noted; strictly speaking, the *value* of the coin is fixed with respect to weight and fineness while the *purchasing power*[7] varies with market price of the metal. This piece of silver, like sheep in the previous section, was also the monetary unit of account against which all other prices were expressed, including gold. If the price of silver bullion fluctuated in the market there would be a corresponding change in the price of all other commodities relative to the rupee. For instance, if the market price of silver were to rise (all else constant) then the purchasing power of the rupee would increase too or in other words, each rupee could be exchanged for a greater quantity of cows, nails, peanuts and even gold.

The Mughals also allowed circulation of gold as money and minted the *mohur*, a gold coin of 170 to 175 grains (about the same weight as the silver rupee) equivalent to 9.4 (silver) rupees in Akbar's time, *c.* 1550, stamped on both sides with inscriptions in Persian. A large number of other gold and silver coins, varying from a few kilograms to a few grains in weight were also minted and were in circulation. The Mughals managed the simultaneous circulation of gold and silver coins effectively by adopting a 'parallel standard'. Under this standard, the rupee was the single legal tender and unit of account, with the silver value of gold mohurs fluctuating according to the market price of gold or silver. The gold mohur was neither considered legal tender of payment in any public or private transaction, nor was the number of rupees for which it could pass in exchange ever fixed by the government. People could, however, transact in either coins, at their discretion, at ratios varying according to the market values of the metals.

The demand for and supply of gold and silver depended heavily upon factors like the people's preferences for jewelry or hoarding, on the requirements of merchants who wanted to send money over long distances, and on the occasional large disbursements of money by the Mughal and European armies. The government would sometimes also influence the rate between gold and silver in its bid to attract the kind of money desired. For instance, in times of warfare, gold was in greater demand than silver, because, for a given value, it occupied less bulk and could be more easily hidden and transported. By overvaluing gold at the mint, they could attract gold into the exchequer from the bullion market. The foreign trade of the English, French, Dutch and Portuguese also affected demand and supply for the precious metals. Sometimes silver flowed into the country, sometimes gold and sometimes gold was shipped out in payment for goods.

As we have seen, for objects or materials to become currency, they must be easily recognizable and universally trusted as evidence of claims by all members of society. This was in fact the purpose of minting coins by the state, which involved weighing and assaying the purity of metal, and certifying them by marking the piece of metal with some unique pattern or symbol. However, once the coin came to be recognized and trusted for its weight and purity, there was always the temptation for the mint or the ruler to cheat. Mints could buy bullion in the market and circulate rupees with just (say) 160 grains of pure metal while people presume them to contain 175 grains of silver. The difference of 15 grains could be pocketed by the ruler. Common citizens too could cheat by clipping edges of coins, drilling holes and filling them with other metals or rubbing its surfaces for a little gold or silver dust. Debasing currency was prevented by the artistic design of coins like, for instance, patterns along the edge of the coin and well embossed symbols on the surface. Table 1.3 shows the adherence of Mughal coinage to the standard weight of 175 grains pure; an indication of their credibility, authority and ingenuity of the rulers.

Table 1.3 also tells us of the responsibility with which the Mughals minted their coins from several locations spread across their geographical domain. Akbar's known mints numbered seventy-six; silver in thirty-nine while copper was struck in fifty-nine. Aurangzeb's conquests in the Deccan raised the silver mints to seventy, whereas copper mints fell to twenty-four. It is estimated that over two hundred mints may have been operated by the Mughals although perhaps only few of them like those at Agra, Delhi, Lahore and Ahmedabad struck coins continuously all through their reign. During Akbar's rule, a small charge of about 6 per cent during was usually made for assaying the metal and process of coining. When we consider the control exercised over geographically distributed mints, the high standard and purity of gold and silver maintained over three hundred years, the variety and the artistic merit of some of their coins, the smooth operation of a parallel currency system with gold and silver coins, the influence exerted on subsequent coinages and the continuing identity of its standard coin the rupee

TABLE 1.3: ADHERENCE TO WEIGHT DURING
THE MUGHAL ERA (IN GRAINS TROY)

Name of Rupee	Weight in Pure Grains
Akbari of Lahore	175.0
Akbari of Agra	174.0
Jehangir of Lahore	174.6
Jehangir of Allahabad	173.6
Jehangir of Kandhar	173.9
Shehajahani of Agra	175.0
Shehajahani of Ahmedabad	174.2
Shehajahani of Delhi	174.2
Shehajahani of Delhi	175.0
Shehajanhani of Lahore	174.0
Delhi Sonat	175.0
Delhi Alamgir	175.0
Old Surat	174.0
Murshidabad	175.9
Persian rupee of 1745	174.5
Old Dacca	173.3
Muhamadshahi	170.0
Ahmadshahi	172.8
Shah Alam (1772)	175.8

Source: B.R. Ambedkar, *History of Indian Currency and Banking*, Thacker & Co.,
    Bombay, 1947, p. 4.

to this day, the Mughal currency deserves to rank as one of the most exemplary coinages of the world.

In addition to gold and silver currency, copper coins based on Sher Shah's *daam* of 320 to 330 grains also circulated in north India. During Akbar's reign the daam circulated at a rate of about 40 *daam* to a rupee. Even though it was not the standard unit of account, its usage was widespread;[8] prices of several day-to-day commodities and even computations of Imperial land revenue and expenditure were made in terms of the *daam*. In the first half of the seventeenth century, due to a rise in price of copper, the weight of the *daam* was reduced to 220 grains, which then became the accepted standard for many mints. Given the importance of the daam as currency, many historians have termed the Mughal currency system as trimetallism. This is technically incorrect since the exchange rates between coins in the three metals were never fixed.

Apart from metal coinage, the cowrie-shell brought from the Maldives was commonly seen in many bazaars and in shops of the smaller moneychangers even as late as the nineteenth century. At a rate of close to 6,000 cowries for a rupee, the shells were essential currency for petty trade. Francis Buchanan (1833) reported from Bengal *c.* 1800 that moneychangers would arrive in markets and bazaars with cartloads of cowries, which they would exchange at a rate of some 5,760 to a rupee in the morning, taking back cowries in the evening at a rate of 5,920 for a rupee. This meant a clear margin for the moneychanger of about 3 per cent per day (p. 321).

As mentioned earlier, foreign coins too circulated in medieval India. Large hoards of Roman coins, imitations of the originals and even evidence of minting Roman coins locally have been found in southern India. In 1600, Queen Elizabeth coined 'portcullis pieces of eight' with her own portrait for circulation in India. She insisted that these coins be used by the East India Company rather than the Spanish silver ryal that had the portrait of the king of Spain. Her reason for this was simple: that her name and effigies might be recognized and respected by the Asians, and she would be known as great a ruler like the king of Spain. The merchants, however, were opposed to the idea since their Indian counterparts were not familiar with the English silver coin. The Company began minting its own coins in India only in the last quarter of the seventeenth century. One of their earliest coins minted in India was the silver 'Rupee of Bombaim' of 1677, weighing 167.8 grams. James Douglas (1893, p. 310) provides a rare sketch of this coin.

1.4: CURRENCY IN MEDIEVAL SOUTHERN INDIA

The Romans, when they wanted to get the products of the Malabar coast, had nothing but gold to pay for them, for they had no acceptable manufacture to offer in exchange.

COLONEL SYKES, 1864

In southern India, gold was the metal used for currency probably on account of its long history of trade with the Roman Empire. Coins were struck in two denominations: the *varaha, hun* or *pagoda* weighing approximately 50 to 60 grains and the *panam*[9] or *fanam,* a rather small coin, weighing approximately five to six grains. These weights corresponded to those of two seeds respectively, the *kalanju* or molucca bean (*Cazsalpina bonduc*) and the *manjadi* (*Adenathera pavonina*).[10] With foreign trade being an important component in the economy of the Vijayanagar Empire (AD 1336–1646), the weight of the varaha or pagoda was almost identical to that of the Egyptian dinar, the Portuguese cruzado, Venecian ducat and sequin, and the Florentine florine. Locally, circulation of gold coins was carried on chiefly by its fractional part, the fanam. Day-to-day dealings in bazaars and markets as well as collection of the revenue were generally made in fanam. Given the labour and trouble of reckoning large sums in such small currency, cashiers and money-changers would use wooden boards, their surface studded with 100 or 1,000 cavities, the exact size of a fanam. The board would be plunged into the heap of coin, and with a little manual dexterity, the exact sum would be taken up and thrown aside.

Silver coins were rare except in the south-western region of Travancore where the silver *chakram* was in circulation with its weight equal to that of the fanam. The gold coin had an independent development in the south from the earliest spherules (small globules) of plain gold with a minute punch-mark on one side to the cup-shaped *padma-tankas* stamped with punches, first on one side only, later on both obverse and reverse, and finally the die-struck pieces, of which the small thick Vijayanagar pagodas were the typical form. In Madras, at the end of the eighteenth century, the standard coin was the government pagoda, which bore the 'star' and contained by law 42.048 grains of fine gold. This star pagoda was reckoned to be of 10 per cent less value than the earlier and finer coin with a crescent and three figures, one of which represented Swami (or Lord Krishna) and hence was given name *swami-pagoda*. Other coins that circulated were the Pondicherry and Porto Novo pagodas. All these varieties of the pagoda were familiar at the beginning of the present century throughout the Indian currency area, which then included not only Ceylon and Mauritius, but also the Cape and St. Helena. Even in New South Wales in 1800, the pagoda was proclaimed legal tender. Irfan Habib contends that following Aurangzeb's annexations of the Deccan in the late seventeenth century, the rupee was issued from a number of mints in southern India thereby supplanting the pagoda as currency (Habib, 1982, p. 362).

In South India, copper coins too were also extensively used as currency. It was called *kasu*, from which comes the English word, cash.

1.5: THE COLLAPSE OF THE MEDIEVAL INDIAN CURRENCY SYSTEM

Medieval princes conceived that it was part of their inalienable Divine Right to alter the weight and name, and debase the purity of their Coin as much as they pleased, and to compel their subjects to receive the diminished and degraded and debased Coin at the same value as good full-weighted Coin. This was termed 'morbus numeric'.

HENRY DUNNING MACLEOD

In the early decades of the eighteenth century, changes in India's political landscape began to adversely impact her monetary system. When the weak Mughal emperor, Farrukhsiyar (r. 1713–19) faced a resource crunch, he chose to adopt a convenient but fatal policy of farming out his mints. This reduced minting into a private trade by licensed individuals. In Bengal, minting was exercised by the house of Jagatseths who had *de facto* control over the mint at Murshidabad. It was not the profits from minting that were a cause for concern but compulsion on people to re-coin their currency often that was a real danger to the system. By virtue of their office as Treasurer of Bengal, the Jagatseths insisted that annual revenues were paid in coins of *the current year* only. This practice was prevalent even under the stronger Mughal Emperors who treated coins of different years as different species of coins. Coins of earlier years were accepted only at a heavy discount. It became a lucrative occupation both for the shroffs and the mint to receive older rupees at discount and re-coin them. In the year 1746, the Jagatseths gave 201 sicca rupees for 240 rupees weight of silver offered to them, a profit of close to 20 per cent. It is not surprising why the Jagatseths protected the privilege over the mint so zealously. When English merchants made efforts in 1721 to secure the right of minting from the Nawab they were informed by officers that 'Fatteh-chand is so great with the Nawab, they can have no hopes of the grant let alone having the sole use of the mint nor any other shroff dare buy or coin a rupee's worth of silver' (quoted from Chaudhury, 2006, pp. 5–6). On another occasion when English merchants at Calcutta began to import Madras and Arcot rupees and use them for payments to Indian merchants, the Jagatseths obtained a *firman*[11] from the Nawab making these rupees receivable in public or private payments at much lower value. Shortly afterwards, a duty of 2 per cent was levied on all foreign rupees tendered to the government. It was not till 1757 that the Company got the right to establish a mint at Calcutta. Even then the mint was of little use as the Calcutta rupee, notwithstanding its weight and standard in every respect being as good as the Sicca Rupee of Murshidabad, was not widely accepted. Ultimately, a *firman* had to be obtained from Mir Kasim, ordering the rupee of the Company to pass current, forbidding any person to demand discount on it.

In southern India, the splintering of the Vijayanagar Empire in the second half of the sixteenth century into separate kingdoms de-centralized the currency system. Minting was undertaken by several, if not every successor-power; the Nayakas of Keladi, Madurai, Thanjavur, and Gingee; Haider Ali, Tipu Sultan and the Wodeyars of Mysore; the Nizam of Hyderabad; and even the East India Com-pany. Unfortunately, many of these independent sovereigns abused their authority to mint coins and resorted to wanton debasement of their currency. Stamping meant very little and in such a situa-tion, the only means of avoiding loss and fraud was to weigh and assay each coin. The role of the moneychanger gained even greater importance; in any transaction the weight of coins had to be ascer-tained with balances which were so sensitive that they would turn by a hair of the head. The coins had then to be assayed by them using touchstones and a gold bar of the royal standard of purity. The elaborate process meant that currencies began to lose their most important property: their general and ready acceptability as a medium of exchange. With currency reduced to merchandise or mere bullion, the system regressed into what Stanley Jevons termed as 'currency by weight'.

The situation worsened over the years so that by the time of Francis Buchanan's *Journey* of 1800–1 we find that in Bangalore, 'almost every coin of India is current' (Buchanan, 1807, p. I. 194), but many of the coins were 'much adulterated' (ibid) and passed off for more than their true intrinsic value. In Srirangapatnam, Buchanan reported the values of 13 different types of coins, which had to be assayed or converted by *sarrafs* (shroffs), who would charge a *batta* or commission of 2.5 per cent for their services. This was in Srirangapatnam alone; in north India it was recorded that some 139 kinds of gold mohurs, 556 kinds of silver rupees and 214 types of foreign coins were circulating. Across India the currency system had degenerated into confusion with hundreds, if not a thousand or more, gold and silver coins circulating, with different weights and fineness.

To make matters worse, people had to contend with fluctuations in the exchange ratio between gold and silver. Without a bimetallic currency standard where the legal rate of exchange between gold and silver currencies was fixed by ordinance, sudden fluctuations in the gold price of silver or vice-versa meant that the gold and silver currency rates oscillated concurrently. While a parallel standard had given the Indian currency system a great amount of stability in the past, it now proved to be equally damaging. Combined with debasement of coins and multitude of currencies, fluctuating prices of metals made the professional moneychangers indispensable in trade. Unscrupulous moneychangers could deceive them given the difficulty for an ordinary person to find out the true rate of exchange existing at any point of time. Unaware cultivators, the ignorant public and even foreign traders were constantly exposed to being cheated by exorbitant *batta* or commissions. The sufferings inflicted by the disordered state of currency prompted Dr. William Roxburgh to remark in 1791, in his letter to A. Dalrymple, 'You may be able to correct the evil, by which you will certainly go to heaven, if the prayers of the poor avail, and I may get a step nearer paradise' (quoted from Ambedkar, 1947, p. 5).

The constant weighing, valuing, and assaying the bullion contents of coins was, however, only a part of the problem. With the decline of the Mughal Empire there ceased to be such a thing as an imperial legal tender current all through India. Certain coins commanded a premium in districts where they were accepted as legal tender. A double coincidence of wants problem was developing with respect to currency itself—to find mutually acceptable currencies in which exchange could take place. At the same time, the transaction cost of using currencies and possibility of fraud by the moneychangers was slowly but surely reducing trade in India to barter. The choice between vitiated money and simple barter is not unequivocal. As Ambedkar pointed out, 'diseased money is worse than want of money' (ibid, p. 8). The production of gold and silver for use as money utilizes valuable capital; with no money society would at least save the cost of producing these precious metals. Bad money may not be the 'second best' solution to good money; barter could well be the better alternative. The 'first best' solution though was to have good money and it was now in the hands of the East India Company to make sure of that. Unfortunately, it did not turn out to be as easy as they may have imagined. Gresham's Law states that bad money drives out good money but the question that the Company had to confront was how do you get *good money to drive out bad money.*

1.6: INTERNATIONAL CURRENCY INFLOWS INTO INDIA

In 1717 the East India Company had exported near three millions of ounces of silver, which far exceeded the imports in that year; so that large quantities of silver specie must have necessarily been melted down, both to make up that export and to supply silversmiths.

PHILIP HENRY STANHOPE, 1838

Even as the Mughals continued their reign over a large part of India in the early decades of the eighteenth century, a momentous episode in world history had begun more than a century earlier: the rise of the English East India Company. The Company began operations to Asia in 1600 and by 1612, under permission from the Mughal Emperor Jehangir, had set up a factory at Surat with warehouses, offices, chambers and refection-rooms (cafeteria). The factory was the nodal point from where the goods imported from England were distributed through public auctions and also the place where Indian merchants (*bania*) would bring cotton goods, silk, tea, pepper, indigo and other native products from the interior parts of the country. The imports into India were limited to primarily broadcloth (woolens) and hardware like glass and cutlery, sword-blades, lead, copper and quicksilver. The Company's exports from India consistently exceeded their imports necessitating import of coin and bullion to meet the deficit.

After establishing a base in Surat on India's western coast, the Company expanded their operations from Masulipatam (Machalipatnam) to Madras, followed by Calcutta and Bombay.[12] While the Company expanded trade and strengthened its presence in India, concerns were being raised in England on the outflow of coin and bullion from England on account of trade deficits with India. In the very first charter granted by Queen Elizabeth in 1599, a ceiling of £30,000 in coin and bullion was imposed on the Company. The Company's bullion export on its first voyage in 1601 was 80,000 troy ounce (t.oz.) or approximately 2.48 tons priced at £0.27/t.oz. (£8.7/kg), totaling to £21,000. By 1618 the Company was authorized to ship about 12 tons annually but just five years later objections were raised in the English Parliament on this account; 'The East India trade was pronounced to be injurious to the national interests, on the plea of its draining the nation of treasure of which it was said they exported to the amount of £80,000'. (Milburn, 1813, p. xxi) At the turn of the eighteenth century, annual bullion exports had touched £550,000, i.e. about 58 tons at £9.35/kg. These figures in isolation do not give us a picture of the relative magnitude of bullion exports to India. Inflows and outflows for Spain and for Europe as a whole provide us with useful benchmarks; official silver imports into Spain from the Americas between 1600 and 1660 had totaled 303.7 million t.oz. or about 9,446 tons, i.e. 157 tons/annum, which alone was more than half of the total imports of silver into Europe. Table 1.4 shows bullion outflows between 1500 and 1800 from Europe to Asia and the rest of the world at about 40 per cent of their imports.

The import of bullion into Europe, however, exceeded exports

TABLE 1.4: AVERAGE ANNUAL BULLION FLOWS TO AND
FROM EUROPE, 1501–1800

(tons of silver equivalent per year)

Year	Imports	Exports	Net Balance
1501–25	40	x	x
1526–50	105	x	x
1551–75	205	x	x
1576–1600	205	x	x
1601–25	245	100	145
1626–50	290	125	165
1651–75	330	130	200
1676–1700	370	155	215
1701–25	415	190	225
1726–50	500	210	290
1751–75	590	215	375
1776–1800	600	195	405

Source: Ward Barrett, 'World Bullion Flows, 1450-1800', in James D. Tracy (ed.), *The Rise of Merchant Empires: Long Distance Trade in the Early Modern World, 1350–1750*, Cambridge University Press, 1990, pp. 224–54.

so that we find the net balance retained in Europe steadily increasing. As expected from the Quantity Theory of Money this would have had an impact on the price level. In Spain costs of production, depending on the region, rose by three and even five times during the seventeenth century. In England too, costs had increased by more than 250 per cent between 1500 and 1650.

Although figures specifically for England were not found, we do have estimates of bullion exports to India by the East India Company in Table 1.5. From Table 1.4 and Table 1.5 we can see that bullion exports to India were about 10 per cent of total imports into Europe and about 25 per cent of total exports out of Europe in the early decades of the eighteenth century. When we consider England alone, bullion exports by the Company would have accounted for a significant percentage of England's bullion imports. It is therefore not surprising that concerns of a currency shortage in England were being raised as the quote at the beginning of this section reveals. But caution must be exercised in reaching a final conclusion without taking into account the inflows of gold into England during this period. We will return to this point in a subsequent section.

TABLE 1.5: ANNUAL BULLION FLOWS TO ASIA, 1601–1800
FROM EAST INDIA COMPANY

(tons of silver equivalent per year)

Year	Tons of silver/year
1601–25	x
1626–50	10
1651–75	10
1676–1700	32
1701–25	42
1726–50	56
1751–75	50
1776–1800	40

Source: Ward Barrett, 'World Bullion Flows, 1450-1800', in James D. Tracy (ed.), *The Rise of Merchant Empires: Long Distance Trade in the Early Modern World, 1350–1750*, Cambridge University Press, 1990, pp. 224–54, esp. pp. 249, 251.

TABLE 1.6: POPULATION GROWTH IN ENGLAND
AND WALES, 1500 TO 1600

(in millions)

Year	Tons of silver/year
1500	2
1541	2.8
1550	3.2
1600	4.4

Source: 'Population of the British Isles', www.tacitus.nu/historical-atlas/population/british.htm

The per capita availability of precious metals for currency was further stressed by the growth of population by more than 100 per cent in the sixteenth century as seen in Table 1.6.

While the Quantity Theory of Money is today often quoted to explain the phenomenon of inflation, it is the shortages of currency and its impact on output and employment that have often led to violent reactions; in the seventeenth century the exports of silver to India and the consequent shortages of currency triggered off a wave of anti-Company public opinion in England.

1.7: THE INDIA TRADE AND CURRENCY OUTFLOWS FROM ENGLAND

Why should we send the money to employ the poor in India, when we have great numbers of poor at home?

THE WEAVERS' TWELVE QUERIES ANSWERED, *c.* 1700

Concerns over bullion exports that developed in England on account of silver exports must be understood in the context of the dominant economic philosophy of those times; bullionism or the idea that accumulation of precious metals within a country is of utmost importance for the prosperity, prestige and strength of a nation. Large outflows of money were considered as a loss of the nation's wealth with only 'useless' Indian goods coming in return. A series of counter-arguments made by supporters of the East India Company developed into a school called mercantilism—the means to increase the wealth and treasure of a country is by foreign trade, wherein a nation's total exports must exceed total imports *across all markets*. One must look at the total balance of trade position, not vis-à-vis any single country, in order to understand the benefits of the Company's India trade. For instance, the total exports to India including bullion between 1600 and 1620 was £840,376, while the imports from India cost £356,288. However, these goods were re-exported to other parts of Europe for a sum of £1,914,600. By 1624, there was widespread recognition of mercantilism by a number of economists who argued that more than 'four-fifths parts of the commodities imported are again exported into foreign parts . . . by the returns of which more than treble the bullion is imported . . . saves the kingdom . . . £500,000' (Scott, 1812, p. 457). The earnings from re-export of goods imported from India had been overlooked by the bullionists. To the mercantilist foreign trade in fact became the only means by which England could acquire treasure and the East India trade was the principal instrument that made it possible. Although mercantilism proved a valid attack on bullionism it is nevertheless important to understand that to the mercantilists' trade remains a zero sum game enhancing national wealth by enabling nations to acquire treasure with the ultimate objective of using it to establish colonies and take control of natural resources.

Mercantilism had provided a valid justification of the Company's trade. However, intense competition between the English East India Company and other foreign trading companies, especially the Dutch, dampened profitability of their enterprise. It was only after the Restoration of the monarchy with Charles II in 1660 (after the death of Oliver Cromwell in 1858) that a revival of the India trade took place. By 1675–6 ships to India were carrying a disproportionate amount of bullion as compared to merchandise; Table 1.7 shows a three-fold increase in outflow of silver to India from the early days of the Company. And from 1680 onwards the East India Company was once again at the receiving end of popular antipathy against its activities.

TABLE 1.7: BULLION EXPORTS BY THE COMPANY TO INDIA

Year	Bullion (£)	Year	Bullion (£)
1620	62,490	1667–8	1,28,605
1621	12,900	1668–9	1,62,394
1622	61,600	1669–70	1,87,458
1623	68,720	1670–1	1,86,149

Source: William Milburn, *Oriental Commerce*, vol. I, Black, Perry & Co., London, 1813, pp. xxii, xxxiii.

This time the attack on the Company was far more vociferous, even violent, centering on the more direct consequence of the India trade on specific sectors of English industry. By the end of the century English weavers had organized a systematic opposition to the import of Indian calicos and silks. 'It has been proved that many poor manufacturers being destitute of work, owing to Calicos, have been found dead in the streets and fields where they have perished. An infinite number of us are already reduced to great misery' (Khan, 1923, p. 175).

These voices of protest from protectionists across England were repeated in a number of pamphlets calling for nothing less than an import 'Prohibition Act'. The import of Indian goods was asserted to have adversely impacted employment of 250,000 manufacturers and to the consumption of 16 or 18 thousand packs of long fine wool in one year. The decline in woolen manufactures triggered off a chain reaction; landlords too grew increasingly concerned that competition from foreign articles was adversely affecting land rents. They prohibited French and Irish woolens and opposed sale of Indian calicoes in England. Traders and dealers in woolen manufactures too voiced their opposition to calicoes. Along with labour employed in the woolen industry, these opponents to the India trade called upon the state to protect them from the attacks of the East India merchants, linen drapers and other rival manufactures.

The first decisive piece of action was taken on Indian silk; in 1696, a bill prohibiting the wearing of East India silks was ordered and passed. This was followed by an act in 1701 stating that from 1 January 'the wrought silks, bengalls, and stuffs mixed with silk and huba, of the manufacture of Persia, China or East India, and all calicoes painted, dyed, printed or stained, and which are or shall be imported into this kingdom, shall not be worn or otherwise used within this kingdom of England, Dominion of Wales, or town of Berwick on Tweed' (Hamilton, 1919, p. 103). The weavers were determined to enforce their will, compelling the House of Commons to pass the bill. They, along with their wives, invaded the House of Commons and threatened the members who had voted against the Bill. Soon afterwards a mob of 3,000 weavers attacked the magnificent mansion of Sir Josiah Child, Governor of the East India Company. The Company's premises too was attacked and their treasure nearly taken possession off.

A new economic defense was needed to legitimize the activities of the East India Company; eminent personalities of the Company like Sir Josiah, justified silver exports with strong arguments on the basis of the valuable things they brought in exchange. Accordingly to him the wine, oil, tobacco, cloth or goods that are brought with silver and goldare no less than the precious metals and may in many cases be exported to national advantage as any other commodity. Child emphatically argued that 'no nation, ever was, or will be, considerable in trade, that prohibits the exportation of bullion' (Scott, 1812, p. 456). The East India Company, which once supported mercantilism, now repealed it in favour of the free flow of precious metals rather than its accumulation. It was the consumption of goods and services that ultimately constituted the wealth of a nation, not the stock of treasure it possessed.

There is one corollary to this story that makes it relevant even today. Mercantilism continues to live on. Countries like China, Japan and India accumulate treasures in the form of trillion dollar foreign reserves, sustain the price of their currencies at artificially low levels to increase exports and then utilize the accumulated dollars to gain access to natural resources across the world. And then there are the 'English weavers' too, who believe the multinational and foreign corporations are exporting their jobs to third world countries and lobby their States to prohibit imports or outsourcing.

1.8: THE IMPACT OF CURRENCY AND BULLION EXPORTS ON ENGLAND

Whilst they promote what Indians make.
The Employment they from the English take,
Then how shall Tenants pay their Rents,
When Trade and Coins (are) to India sent?
How shall folks live, and Taxes pay.
When Poor want work, and go away?
Such cargoes as these ships bring over.
In England were never seen before.

ANON. (1700)

The preamble to the Act of 1701 articulated the close relationship between the impact of bullion exports on the coin (money supply) of the realm and the destruction of English industry. 'the continuance of the trade to the East Indies, in the same manner and proportion as it had been for three years last passed, must inevitably be to the great detriment of this kingdom, *by exhausting the treasure thereof, melting down the coin,* and taking away the labour of the people' (Anderson, 1787, p. 646). Recourse may be taken to the Quantity Theory of Money as a possible justification of this argument. When there is a contraction in money supply, price level falls. If deflation persists, expectations of continually declining prices results in postponement of expenditure and a contraction in income and output set in. Simultaneously currency shortages inhibit exchanges and trade, causing production to slow down. But it is unlikely that silver exports by the Company could have caused an economy-wide contraction; the adverse reactions to the India trade were more likely sectoral outcries to competition, especially of English weavers, than on account of a general, economy-wide contraction.

It was also not clear whether the outflow of silver to India and other parts of Asia and Europe had indeed caused a net decline in England's money supply, or was it substituted by an inflow of gold? A passage from Kemmerer (1944) indicates an affirmative response to the question. 'In the recoinage of 1696 to 1699 the gold-silver ratio was raised from about 15 to 1 to 15½ to 1, making it unduly favorable to gold and thereby stimulating a heavy importation of foreign gold coins into England and their minting into British money; likewise stimulating a heavy exportation and melting down of the undervalued British silver coins' (p. 37).

The export of silver then perhaps did not affect money supply in England as much as the composition of money supply. But even the change in composition turned out to be painful. Silver had always been the accepted standard of value and also required for transactions of smaller denominations in England. Its exit caused severe hardship especially for the working class and the masses, and hence the antagonism against its export.

The discovery of America had lowered the value of silver in terms of gold in Europe to about 14 or 15:1, while in China and India it fluctuated steady between 9:1 and 12:1. The relatively cheap silver in Europe, as we have seen, was used advantageously to buy goods in Asia. Unfortunately, the decline of piracy on which England depended for her supplies of precious metals coincided closely with the formation for the Company in 1600. As the chief source of fresh bullion declined, the pressure of silver exports fell upon the English (silver) shilling which was steadily debased over subsequent decades. By the time of the Glorious Revolution of 1688, the gold guinea, which, from its first issue in 1662 had exchanged for twenty shillings, actually sold in the market for thirty shillings; a devaluation or debasement in the (silver) *shilling* by 50 per cent. 'This diminishing and counterfeiting the money was at this time so excessive, that what was good silver was worth scarcely one-half of its current value, whilst a great part of the coins was only iron, brass, or copper plated, and some no more than washed over' (Ruding, 1840, p. 35).

The severity of the debasement had reached such serious proportions that a number of steps were taken to check it. Clipping of coins was made a capital felony and dozens of people were given the death sentence by the Old Bailey, the Central Criminal Court in London. Men were hanged with the formalities of old treason laws and women burnt. However, with people making fortunes by clipping coins, even this proved to be an insufficient deterrent. Debasement of silver coins continued and so did the punishments. With bullion becoming dearer than light coin taken at its legal value, the temptation to clip and melt coins was irresistible. The metal was then exported to Asia where it commanded a higher price. One such place from where it was smuggled out was a secluded area, Romney Marsh, on England's south coast, by a group of smugglers called 'owlers', previously well-known for the smuggling of wool. Several new penalties were imposed to check these malpractices; a penalty of £10 for every 20 shillings on persons who sold unclipped coin for more than it was coined for, a £500 fine on any person who casted ingots or bars of silver, any person who bought, sold or had in his possession clippings would be branded on the right cheek with a capital R and imprisoned until a fine of £500 was paid. No person was allowed to transport bullion unless it was stamped at Goldsmiths' Hall, an oath had to be made that it was not produced out of English coin. In 1695, sheriffs of counties were instructed to pay £40 to anyone who procured the conviction of a clipper, the informant being permitted to sue the sheriff if he delayed to satisfy the claimant of the reward. Any unstamped bullion could be seized and confiscated by the Custom House. Goldsmiths alone were allowed to deal in bullion. The Warden with two assistants of the Goldsmiths' Company, or two Justices of the Peace, were given permission to break into and search any house for bullion, and if were to be found, the owner of the house had to prove that it is not the product of melted coin or of clippings. Unfortunately, men who were most zealous and active in searching houses were often clippers themselves who could not resist the temptation of robbing the houses which they searched.[13] The export of bullion continued unabated.

Box 1.1: A Satirical Poem, 1698

On Clippers and Coyners

The love of *Money* is so prevalent,
Some Men and Women are so fully bent
In quest of it, that they will undertake
To spoil the current Coin for Lucre's sake,
Clip, round, or wash, diminish or impair,
Or falsifie, all which offences are
Treason by Law, and such as are descry'd,
And guilty thereof found when they are try'd,
Must suffer Death with scandal and disgrace;
On Sleds the men are drawn unto the place
Where they are ignominious Exit make;
And Womens Doom is burning at a Stake.
Money such Persons surely does enchant
Whose Minds and Thoughts these Terrors do not daunt:
Her charms are wonderful that can require
Men to be hang'd, Women to burn i'th' Fire.

To an extent, the shortage in bullion and metallic currency was relieved by issue of paper notes. Medieval banking until then had gone no further than the establishment of reserves of coin, to serve as a medium for clearing bills of exchange. The English, however, took the great step of accelerating the circulation of their money, by using this reserve as a basis for notes. The Bank of England was incorporated in 1694 and their notes were made payable, not to any particular person, but to the bearer, *on demand* and for the amount of notes, the Bank was liable to be sued in the legal coin of the realm. We will return to a discussion on note issue later; here it suffices to mention that the effect of this step by the Bank was impressive and had a positive impact on reversing the prevailing deflationary trend.

With the price level rising slowly in the seventeenth century, it seemed that the issue of bank notes had given a certain degree of relief to England domestically. However, given that bank notes were convertible on demand to silver, there remained concern over the shortage of silver at a more fundamental level and also to meet the requirements of foreign trade. Moreover, the coins in circulation were mutilated by continual debasement. In 1699 under William III, a complete re-coinage was completed; almost £7 million worth of new coins were put in circulation at a cost of more than £2.7 million to England, i.e. the difference between the old and new currency. But this did not stop the drain of silver from England, and with it debasement of coins continued unabated. According to an account laid before the House of Commons over the period 1698–1703, bullion exported to the East was £3,522,797 out of which silver amounted to £3,392,158 (400 tons) and gold, £128,229 (*Journals of the House of Commons*, 1803, p. 677). The Company frequently gave 3d. an ounce, or a premium of about 5 per cent, for exportable silver above its value in coin, which was sufficient to tempt not just the English but also the Irish to melt down their own coins and send bullion to London

Bimetallism was contemplated as a way out of the currency shortage. In 1717, Sir Isaac Newton as Master of the Royal Mint recommended to the Treasury that gold was overvalued and its legal rate must be lowered. Consequently the legal ratio of silver was raised from 15½:1 to 15.21:1; however, in spite of the gold price of silver being raised, with the market price of silver between 15:1 and 14½:1,[14] silver remained undervalued by 1.5 per cent. The silver shilling continued to disappear from circulation and flow into the bullion market while gold flowed out of the market and into the mint as illustrated in Figure 1.5. This may have been

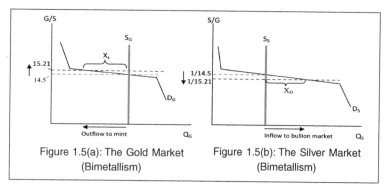

Figure 1.5(a): The Gold Market
(Bimetallism)

Figure 1.5(b): The Silver Market
(Bimetallism)

Figure 1.5: Flow of Metal to Mint and Market with Overvaluation of Gold and Undervaluation of Silver under a Bimetallic Standard

just a simple case of Gresham's Law in action but one underlying cause of the shilling's fate, though not the only one, was the Company's export of silver to India, which far exceeded the imports of the bullion in that year so that vast quantities of silver specie was melted down, both to make up the export and to supply the silversmith. Silver gradually disappeared from circulation in England, with gold and paper taking its place. The India trade had played an important part in the proliferation of bank notes in England as well as her transition to a gold currency.

1.9: THE CURRENCY DRAIN FROM BENGAL

Gold is a treasure, and he who possesses it does all he wishes to in this world, and he succeeds in helping souls into paradise.

CHRISTOPHER COLUMBUS

1765; the year in which the *diwani*[15] of Bengal (which then included Bihar and Orissa) was granted to the Company by the Mughal Emperor Shah Alam II. The acquisition of *diwani* was the culmination of a phase that began a few decades earlier in the conflicts of the Carnatic and Bengal, reaching a high point with the Battle of Plassey in 1757. With acquisition of diwani, the character of the East India Company underwent a complete transformation; from merchant to merchant-ruler. The disintegration of the Mughal Empire in the early decades of the eighteenth century had led to a crisis with a multiplicity of currencies but without adequate control over their value (weight and fineness). The only saving grace during that period was the steady inflow of bullion into India. While hoarding kept check over its impact on the price level, the inflows prevented any possibility of shortages in currency from developing that could worsen the severity of the already developing crisis. But the grant of *diwani* triggered off a series of events that fundamentally altered the course of Indian history, if not world history. While the political and military history of this period is intriguing and important, our focus will be on the transformation of India's monetary landscape that had in fact begun soon after the Battle of Plassey, in particular on two aspects; first, the decrease of net inflows of bullion into Bengal and second, the increase of net inflows into England on account of a sharp increase in the Company's as well as private remittances from India.

On 23 June 1757, Colonel Robert Clive with some one thousand English and two thousand Indian *sipahi* (sepoys) encountered and crushed the sixty thousand strong army of the Nawab Siraj-ud-Daulah. The conquest of Murshidabad, then capital of Bengal, placed a sum of £800,000 in coined silver in the hands of Clive, which was sent down the river Hooghly to Calcutta in a fleet of one hundred boats. In gratitude for his services, the treasury of Bengal was thrown open to Clive and it is said that 'he walked between heaps of gold and silver, crowned with rubies and diamonds, and was at liberty to help himself' (Macaulay, 1896, p. 55); and he did, taking between two and three hundred thousand pounds. See Box 1.2. When the news of Clive's success reached England, the Directors at once appointed him Governor of the Company in Bengal. And with this, the newly installed Mir Jaffer was reduced to merely a nominal Nawab of Bengal, Robert Clive its real sovereign and the Company its true proprietor.

Box 1.2: Robert Clive's Loot of Bengal

The second Charge against me is a Monopoly of Diamonds. And this also I shall get rid of in a few words. There are only two channels by which a servant of the Company, can, with propriety, remit his fortune. The one, by paying the money into the treasury in INDIA, and receiving bills upon the Company, payable in ENGLAND; the other by Diamonds.

By the acquisition of the DUANNEE (diwani), and the successful endeavors of the Select Committee, the Company's treasury was so rich, that we could not have been justified in drawing bills upon the Company. It was necessary I should, in some mode, remit the amount of my Jaghire. For this purpose, and for this only, I sent an agent into a distant and independent Country to make purchases of Diamonds. Those Diamonds were not sent home clandestinely, I caused them to be registered; I paid the duties upon them, and these remittances, upon the whole, turn out three per cent, worse than bills of exchange upon the Company—This is all I know of a Monopoly of Diamonds.

Source: Lord Clive's Speech, London, 1772, p. 9.

The access to Bengal's wealth was not restricted to the top; corruption and oppression was widely adopted by the servants of the Company who took full advantage of their newly acquired powers. They were driven by temptation of immediate gain and the possibility to acquire fortunes within a short span of time in India and return to England to enjoy their accumulated wealth. Plunder was a viable option and was indeed unleashed across Bengal: 'They seized and appropriated all. They monopolized the grounds, claimed the very products of the soil, rented out the land on terms and for purposes prescribed by themselves, seized the manufactures and placed them under the control of their servants, monopolized the entire trade of the country . . . (*The National Magazine*, 1857, p. 427).

The Company in its official capacity also extracted large amounts of money as compensation and tribute for the support given to Mir Jaffer. Concessions for trade and commerce that were previously not conceded to them were now acquired. The new order unsettled the whole country and many Indian chiefs rebelled against the puppet Nawab, control over whom was *de facto* with the British. Even though increases in expenditure on military and fortifications reached what may seem an alarming level of £9,069,684 between March 1751 and March 1766,[16] they were more than offset by the collection of revenues. A problem that remained was how the Company's and individual wealth of its servants could be remitted out to England; the means of remittances of wealth as well as the consequences of the drain of wealth from Bengal will be studied later, for now it suffices to mention that trade and commerce was the chosen conduit. In other words, since the bullion could not be shipped out from India, loans were taken by the Company from its own servants to buy goods in India and repaid from the sales proceeds of these goods in England.

While the issue on whether trade was subsidizing the Company's territorial expansion or vice-versa turned into a raging debate, we turn our attention to another fascinating claim that arose from the drain of wealth from Bengal. The staggering quantities of riches which arrived in England triggered off a revolution; this, however, was not just a revolution but in fact *the Industrial Revolution*. William

Digby (1901) in his book *Prosperous British India* asserts that between Plassey (1757) and Waterloo (1815) a thousand million pounds were transferred from Indian hoards to English banks (p. 33). Hamilton, however, in his study of trade relations between India and England refutes Digby's claims as sheer nonsense. His scientific estimates are as follows; by the treaty with Mir Jaffer in 1757, the Nawab undertook to pay the Company a sum of £2,394,000 in compensation for the public and private losses sustained. It was supposed that the treasures of former Nawab Siraj-ud-Daulah would amply suffice to meet these payments. This was based on an estimate by a Mr. Forth that Siraj-ud-Daulah's treasure at Murshidabad was more than Rs. 680,000,000 (£68,000,000). Though there is no information what happened to it, Mir Jaffer was compelled to negotiate compensation to the Company to be paid in installments, partly in jewels and partly in bullion. The Company's demands did not cease here. Further payments were made on the occasions of Mir Kasim's appointment as Nawab in 1760, of Mir Jaffer's restoration in 1763, and on the accession of Najam-ud-Daulah in 1765. The total payments made between 1757 and 1766 were calculated by the Select Committee of 1773 to have amounted to £5,940,498, of which £2,169,665 represented presents to private individuals while £3,770,883 was received into the treasuries of the Company (Mill, 1826, p. 329). But once again this could not be taken to mean that they actually were exported to England; most of these receipts by the Company were actually used in the presidencies at Madras and Bombay. This can be inferred from the fact that in 1771 the accounts of the Company in London showed a deficit of £1,293,000 and £600,000 was borrowed from the Bank of England. The latter amount was insufficient to meet their needs and applications were made to Government for a loan of £1,000,000. Clearly the silver had not found its way into the coffers of the Company, at least officially.

Do the large sums mentioned above seem reasonable? Here, it is appropriate to mention that the English themselves claimed the notoriously infamous conqueror Kouli Khan, more commonly known in India as Nadir Shah, returned to Persia with treasure worth £125,000,000 after massacring some 120,000–150,000 citizens of Delhi (Milburn, 1813, p. xlix). As an order of magnitude figure, Digby's estimates then cannot be dismissed off as bizarre. Moreover, it is not just the official flow of money through the Company that one must look but also the 'unofficial' export of bullion from India.

The Battle of Plassey took place in 1757 and the industrial revolution, 'began', if there is indeed such a moment, in 1760. Was this a mere coincidence? According to an early twentieth century historian Brooks Adams, definitely not. The wealth that flowed into England post-Plassey not only enhanced the flow of credit but also transformed the banking sector; critical elements that made what would have been just a scientific revolution into an industrial revolution. Inventions, by themselves, are a necessary but not sufficient element for economic transformation. The latter requires that inventions be put into production in factories for which the availability as well as the cost of credit becomes critical. Furthermore, the revolution if restricted only to industry would not have been sustainable unless it extended to agriculture so that food surpluses became available to support the growing urban population at a reasonable price. Once again, the flow of credit across the sectors of the economy sustained the momentum of the industrial revolution in England.

Box 1.3: The Loot of Bengal and the Industrial Revolution

Very soon after Plassey, the Bengal plunder began to arrive in London, and the effect appears to have been instantaneous, for all authorities agree that the 'industrial revolution', the event which has divided the nineteenth century from all antecedent time, began with the year 1760. Prior to 1760, according to Baines, the machinery used for spinning cotton in Lancashire was almost as simple as in India; while about 1750 the English iron industry was in full decline because of the destruction of the forests for fuel . . . Plassey was fought in 1757, and probably nothing has ever equaled the rapidity of the change which followed. In 1760 the flying-shuttle appeared, and coal began to replace wood in smelting. In 1764 Hargreaves invented the spinning-jenny in 1779 Crompton contrived the mule, in 1785 Cartwright patented the power-loom, and, chief of all, in 1768 Watt matured the steam-engine, the most perfect of all vents of centralizing energy. But, though these machines served as outlets for the accelerating movement of the time, they did not cause that acceleration. In them-selves inventions are passive, many of the most important having lain dormant for centuries, waiting for a sufficient store of force to have accumulated to set them working. That store must always take the shape of money, and money not hoarded, but in motion.

Thus printing had been known for ages in China before it came to Europe; the Romans probably were acquainted with gun-powder; revolvers and breach-loading cannon existed in the fifteenth and sixteenth centuries, and steam had been experimented upon long before the birth of Watt. The least part of Watt's labour lay in conceiving his idea; he consumed his life marketing it. Before the influx of the Indian treasure, and the expansion of credit which followed, no force sufficient for this purpose existed; and had Watt lived fifty years earlier, he and his invention must have perished together. Considering the difficulties under which Matthew Boulton, the ablest and most energetic manufacturer of his time, nearly succumbed, no one can doubt that without Boulton's works at Birmingham the engine could not have been produced, and yet before 1760 such works could not have been organized. The factory system was the child of the 'industrial revolution', and until capital had accumulated in masses capable of giving solidity to large bodies of labour, manufactures were necessarily carried on by scattered individuals, who combined a handicraft with agriculture. . .

. . . Extending his works, he built the famous shops at Soho, which he finished in 1762 at an outlay of £20,000, a debt which probably clung to him to the end of his life. Boulton formed his partnership with Watt in 1774, and then began to manufacture the steam engine, but he met with formidable difficulties. Before the sales yielded any return, the outlay reduced him to the brink of insolvency; nor did he achieve success until he had exhausted his own and his friends' resources. He mortgaged his lands to the last farthing; borrowed from his personal friends; raised money by annuities; obtained advances from bankers; and had invested upwards of forty thousand pounds in the enterprise before it began to pay.

. . . Agriculture, as well as industry, felt the impulsion of the new force. Arthur Young remarked, in 1770 that within ten years there had been 'more experiments, more discoveries, and more general good sense displayed in the walk of agriculture than in an hundred preceding ones'; and the reason why such a movement should have occurred seems obvious. After 1760 a complex system of credit sprang up, based on a metallic treasure, and those who could borrow had the means at their disposal of importing breeds of cattle, and of improving tillage, as well as of organizing factories like Soho. The effect was to cause rapid centralization. The spread raised the value of land, but it also made the position of the yeomanry untenable, and nothing better reveals the magnitude of the social revolution wrought by Plassey, than the manner in which the wastes were enclosed after the middle of the century. Between 1710 and 1760 only 335,000 acres of the commons were absorbed; between 1760 and 1843, nearly 7,000,000. In eighty years the yeomanry became extinct. Many of these small farmers migrated to the towns, where the stronger, like the ancestor of Sir Robert Peel, accumulated wealth in industry, the weaker sinking into factory hands. Those who lingered on the land toiled as day labourers.

Possibly since the world began, no investment has ever yielded the profit reaped from the Indian plunder, because for nearly fifty years Great Britain stood without a competitor. . . . In some imperfect way her (Britain's) gains may be estimated by the growth of her debt, which must represent savings. In 1756, when Clive went to India, the nation owed £74,575,000, on which it paid an interest of £2,753,000. In 1815 this debt had swelled to £861,000,000, with an annual interest charge of £32,645,000. In 1761 the Duke of Bridgewater finished the first of the canals which were afterward to form an inland water-way costing £50,000,000, or more than two-thirds of the amount of the public debt at the outbreak of the Seven Years War. Meanwhile, also, steam had been introduced, factories built, turnpikes improved, and bridges erected, and all this had been done through a system of credit extending throughout the land. Credit is the chosen vehicle of energy in centralized societies, and no sooner had treasure enough accumulated in London to offer it a foundation, than it shot up with marvelous rapidity. From 1694 to Plassey, the growth had been relatively slow. For more than sixty years after the foundation of the Bank of England, its smallest note had been for £20, a note too large to circulate far from Lombard Street. Writing in 1790, Burke mentioned that when he came to England in 1750 there were not 'twelve bankers' shops' in the provinces, though then, he said, they were in every market town. Thus the arrival of the Bengal silver not only increased the mass of money, but stimulated its movement; for at once, in 1759, the bank issued £10 and £15 notes, and, in the country, private firms poured forth a flood of paper. At the outbreak of the Napoleonic wars, there were not far from four hundred provincial houses, many of more than doubtful solvency. Macleod, who usually does not exaggerate such matters, has said that grocers, tailors, and drapers inundated the country with their miserable rags. . .

. . . At the close of the eighteenth century, many causes combined to make money plentiful, and therefore to cheapen it. Not only was the stock of bullion in England increased by importations from India, but, for nearly a

> generation, exports of silver to Asia fell off. From an average of £600,000 annually between 1740 and 1760, the shipments of specie by the East India Company fell to £97,500 between 1760 and 1780. . . .
>
> *Source*: Brooks Adams, *The Law of Civilization and Decay: An Essay on History*, The Macmillan & Co., New York, 1895, p. 259–66.

The truth as to the actual amount of plunder and their flows to England are difficult to ascertain and would remain a mystery. Nonetheless it is interesting to see what some modern day historians think of the claims made by William Digby and Brooks Adams. Cain and Hopkins (1980) argue that 'Plassey Plunder did not start the Industrial Revolution, but it did help Britain to buy back the National Debt from the Dutch' (p. 471). But according to Arrighi (1994) it did much more than that. By enabling Britain to start the Napoleonic Wars nearly free from foreign debt, it facilitated the six fold increase in British public expenditure in 1792–1815 that had a decisive role in shaping the capital goods phase of the Industrial Revolution (pp. 210–11). Even if the link between Plassey and the Industrial Revolution cannot be established without a doubt, one thing is certain; since the world began, no investment had ever yielded the profit reaped from the Indian plunder and its subsequent colonization, because, as Adams put it, for nearly fifty years after Plassey, Great Britain stood without a competitor.

The inflow of specie to or reduction in outflow from England and its consequences on the money markets in England was only half the story, the other half was, however, most disconcerting caused by the drastic reduction in inflow of specie into and the simultaneous outflow from India. And it is to this crisis in Indian monetary history that we turn to in the next section.

1.10: CURRENCY FAMINE

The lack of money is the root of all evil

MARK TWAIN

For centuries, perhaps millennia, India had always received a steady inflow of precious metals from its commodity trade surpluses with the rest of the world, which was converted into money or hoarded as jewelry and ornaments. The Romans, Venetians, Portuguese, Dutch, and English were all at one point of time or another concerned over the export of their bullion and coin to India in exchange for oriental luxuries. In the seventeenth century Surat alone is said to have received from its trade with the Persian Gulf about half million sterling per annum in specie. The export of bullion from England, as we have seen, became the most scathing weapon in the hands of the bullionists against the East India Company. Nonetheless, as long as the Company was a mere merchant, it had little option but to conduct its trade on the basis of bullion and coin.

The Battle of Plassey and subsequent grant of diwani to the English East India Company changed all this. Post-1765, there was a sudden increase in the outflow of bullion from India to England along with a sharp decline in silver exports to India. Table 1.8 gives us a quantitative picture of a dismal story. From an average of around £500,000 annually in the mid-eighteenth century, shipments of specie by the East India Company to India collapsed to a trickle between 1772 and 1785; they rose gradually thereafter and was especially high during 1802–3 (£1,772,085) and 1804–5 (£1,952,651) when it became necessary for Marquess Wellesley to import specie to fund the Company's aggressive territorial expansion plans in India.

TABLE 1.8: EXPORTS BY THE EAST INDIA COMPANY OF BULLION TO INDIA, 1708–1810

(*in £ sterling*)

Years	Bullion (£)	Average per Annum
1708/9 – 1733/4	12,189,147	420,315
1734/5 – 1759/60	15,239,115	586,119
1760/1 – 1765/6	842,381	140,396
1766/7 – 1771/2	968,289	161,381
1772/3 – 1775/6	72,911	18,227
1776/7 – 1784/5	156,106	17,345
1785/6 – 1792/3	4,476,207	559,525
1793/4 – 1809/10	8,988,165	528,715

Source: William Milburn, *Oriental Commerce*, vol. I, Black, Perry & Co., London, 1813, pp. xlviii, liii, lxvi.

This decline in the last quarter of the eighteenth century was not because exports from India were not in demand in the West. Rather it was because the right of diwani ensured that the revenues of Bengal passed into the Company's hands. It then became possible for the Company to utilize the large annual revenue surpluses for purchase of commodities to be exported (called investments), doing away with the necessity of importing specie.

W.W. Hunter (1868, p. 304) tells us on how revenues were channelized to investment; in Birbhum district, out of £90,000 collected through taxes and duties, the Council took care that not more than £5,000 or £6,000 were spent in governing it. An additional £10,000 went towards general civil expenses and about the same for the maintenance of the army. The net surplus of some £60,000 were then employed for the purchase of silks, muslins, cotton cloths, and other articles to be sold in Leadenhall Street, the headquarters

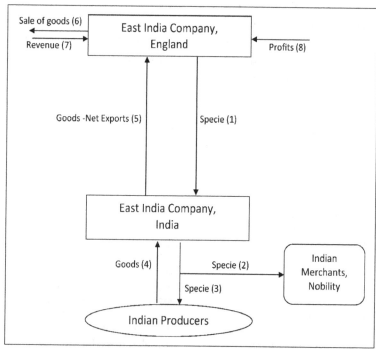

Figure 1.6: Liquidity in the Pre-*diwani* System

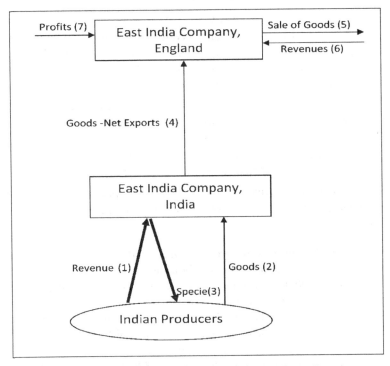

Figure 1.7: Reduced Net Inflow of Liquidity Post-*diwani*

of the Company. In short, the revenues of Bengal supplied the means of providing the expenditure for purchases in Bengal, reducing the net annual influx of specie to a pittance. The situation both, pre- and post-*diwani* has been illustrated in Figures 1.6 and 1.7 respectively.

James Steuart (1773) cites several other reasons that further fueled the scarcity. The relatively undervalued silver in Bengal proved a profitable source to finance the growing tea trade with China. Within a span of just three years some £720,000 of specie was sent out of Bengal to China. The widespread corruption and plunder by the servants of the Company not only transferred the wealth of the country to these individuals but was also sent out of the country by ingenuous means. These included the purchase of diamonds (which was not always available in Bengal) and the private funding of the China tea trade of the English Company and even of other foreign trading companies. The French and Dutch who would earlier bring in a large quantity of specie were now able to borrow funds in India from Company servants to finance their trade with China. The servants looking for ways to remit their wealth were repaid in Europe by the foreign companies from the proceeds of their sales. The annual tribute paid to the Mughal Emperor in Delhi also added to the specie outflow from Bengal. Finally, the necessity to fund expenditures (including military) in the other Presidencies of the Company, namely Madras and Bombay, also meant substantial export of specie out of Bengal.

The Governor of Bengal, Harry Verelst (1772) summarized the reasons for the deficiency of the import of precious metals into Bengal for the years 1757–66, which he estimated to be about £8 million.

> Between 1757 and 1765 the French, having lost their settlements, ceased to trade in Bengal. Previously they had brought into the province silver to the amount of £200,000 per annum on the average. The English Company after Plassey discontinued sending bullion to Bengal. This had previously averaged £250,000 per annum. The Dutch, who were the chief importers of silver, used largely for the purchase of opium, the trade in which was chiefly in their hands, sent no bullion to Bengal for more than four years after the capture of Chinsura. They had previously imported £300,000 per annum. Further, Bengal had enjoyed an export trade to Persia and the ports of the Red Sea which brought in a balance in specie of some £180,000 per annum. To the interruption of this normal inflow of specie from the various sources referred to there was added the abnormal export to China and to the other provinces of India. (p. 86)

When other forms of remittances from Bengal were added to this, including the King's tribute, the actual outflow of specie could have touched some £13,000,000; 'a sum so immense as will scarce gain credit with those who have not been at the trouble of examining the particulars' (ibid, p. 86). While a combination of easy money and scientific discoveries set off the industrial revolution in England in the second half of the eighteenth century, Bengal was at about the same time, receding into misery; the shortages in specie import added to the woes created by the vitiated currency system that had begun in the beginning of the eighteenth century with the decline of the Mughal Empire.

In the year 1770 a massive famine struck Bengal, claiming some 10 million lives or a third of its entire population. It was called the Great Bengal Famine. Descriptions and records of this catastrophe are heart wrenching:

All through the stifling summer of 1770 the people went on dying. The husbandmen sold their cattle, they sold their implements of agriculture, they devoured their seed-grain, they sold their sons and daughters, till at length no buyer of children could be found, they ate the leaves of trees and the grass of the field and in June 1770 the Resident at the Durbar affirmed that the living were feeding on the dead. Day and night a torrent of famished and disease-stricken wretches poured into the great cities. At an early period of the year pestilence had broken out. In March we find smallpox at Moorshedabad. . . . The streets were blocked up with promiscuous heaps of the dying and dead. Interment could not do its work quick enough even the dogs and jackals, the public scavengers of the East, became unable to accomplish their revolting work, and the multitude of mangled and festering corpses at length threatened the existence of the citizens. (Hunter, 1868, p. 26)

There may have been several root causes for the Great Famine of Bengal. Utmost of course was the East India Company's ruthlessness in collection of land taxes and that too in cash. But the one definitive factor which exacerbated the destruction wrought by the Bengal Famine of 1770 was the prevailing confusion in the currency system along with an absolute shortage of currency for trade and commerce. Currency for day-to-day transactions became scarce. In rural Bengal, rupees alone had amounted to about two-thirds of the currency. Money became so dear that prices of all other goods slumped; the scarcity of money was accompanied by deflation. Artisans, weavers and workers were thrown out with the slump in demand. The credit market collapsed; creditors fearing that they would be repaid in overvalued gold. Without credit and in the absence of traders, equalization of supply and demand became difficult and destabilizing. 'At present the distress is so great', wrote the English inhabitants (*Calcutta Review*, 1860) in 1769, 'that every merchant in Calcutta is in danger of becoming bankrupt, or running a risk of ruin by attachments on his goods' (p. 27). Merchants deserted their trade and began 'locking up their fortunes in their treasure-chests' (Hunter, 1868, p. 308). A petition of the Armenian merchants settled in Calcutta put their situation even more forcibly: 'the necessity of coin now felt in this capital, amongst the many intolerable evils arising from it, affects every individual to that degree, that the best houses, with magazines full of goods, are distressed for daily provisions and that not only a general bankruptcy is to be feared, but a real famine, in the midst of wealth and plenty' (Verelst, 1772, p. 423). As one historian put it, 'The Famine of 1770 was a simple famine. The British had removed a large fraction of the coinage, evidently, which destroyed the mechanism of the exchange of goods. It is difficult to buy food when there is no money' (Stevenson, 1943, p. 55).

While we tend to take for granted the availability of money in a modern economy, the scarcity of a circulating medium of exchange sometimes raises its ugly head. In the aftermath of the 2008 banking crisis, the lack of lending not only from banks to business but also between banks send almost all markets across the world into a tizzy and triggered off the Great Recession from which the world is still struggling to recover.

1.11: SALT CURRENCY

In Roman society, salt was used as currency, and soldiers were paid in salt. The Latin word 'sal' is the root for the English word salary. Based on this, we have the familiar phrase that a person is 'worth their salt', meaning worth the wages they receive.

MINERAL INFORMATION INSTITUTE

As seen in the introduction to this chapter, money is nothing but an instrument that can be used for the settlement of claims over a certain quantum of goods produced in a society. Surprisingly one of the most common and essential goods, salt, qualified as such an instrument and claims over it came to be used as money in post-diwani Bengal.

The East India Company acquired a monopoly of the salt trade in Bengal in 1772 and over the next couple of decades developed a system to sell salt at public auctions. The salt was stored in warehouses called *golahs*. The local merchants could buy the salt for which they issued a bill or receipt called *char* (delivery order) and *rowannah* (certificate from the collector of customs to cover cargoes of goods). These chars and rowannahs were sold in the market at a premium to retailers who could redeem the salt bills for salt at the golah before the stipulated date.

Given the scarcity of coin, salt bills began circulating as money amongst traders. But with price of the underlying asset, i.e. salt in the warehouse, open to fluctuation, an opportunity for speculation in the value of the bill simultaneously arose. This was realized in the year 1795 when something interesting happened; the salt sold through auction was about 3,400,000 maunds but the quantity physically cleared from the golahs were only 3,020,000 maunds. The difference remained undelivered. A question arose as to the cause for the undelivered stocks. A Report to the Secret Committee discusses one possible explanation which accused merchants of attempting to manipulate the market supply by not clearing stocks. It was felt this would put pressure on the Company to restrict supply in the following year and thereby push up the price of salt. However, with the government not doing so meant that the strategy, if at all adopted by merchants, would have entailed great losses upon them. Contemporary historians like Sayako Kanda (2010) instead believe that a speculative trade in salt bills may have been developing. When salt prices fell due to an oversupply from other parts of India, salt purchasers would have been unable to sell their salt bills and instead of taking delivery simply opted out. Could this speculation in salt bills have elements of the speculative trade in derivatives, with the underlying asset in this instance being salt?

In the 1820s another concern arose over the salt bills as money when forged bills began circulating in Bengal. The Company promptly took several steps to ensure credibility of the bills so that the salt trade remained profitable. The following extract from H.C. Hamilton's Notes on Salt Making in Bengal published in the *Calcutta Review* of 1854 narrates in greater detail the complexities which arose in the salt trade and in its use as money.

Box 1.4: Salt Money in Bengal

As soon as any golah is filled, the mass of salt is adulled or stamped all over with the Intendant's audul, after which the agent's guy or check audul is fixed thereupon. The golah is then closed in the presence of the Agent or his assistant, the doors, one at either end, are sealed with the Agent's seal and fastened with two padlocks; the key of one lock, together with the audul, remaining in the Intendant's possession, and the key of the other locks, together with the seal and check audul, remaining in charge of the Agent.

The whole of the salt stores at Ghaut Narainpore, are under the exclusive charge of the Intendant, who received a salary of Rupees 250 per mensem, a wastage allowances of 2½ per cent, to cover deficiencies arising from atmospheric causes, being also granted to him. Some years since, this allowance was considerably exceeded, but of late, the average deficit on the out-turn weightment of each golah, has not been above a few maunds, so that neither the Government nor the Intendant have lost anything.

. . . When any merchant is desirous of purchasing salt, he pays into the General Treasury the amount of his contemplated purchase at the above rate. In return, he obtains a receipt, which he presents with a written application at the Office of the Board of Revenue, and in exchange, he receives a document called a char tunkha, or delivery order on the salt Agent of Tumlook, to deliver over to the merchant the quantity of salt he has purchased and paid for, a rowannah or pass to protect the salt, (after delivery) in transit through the Salt Chowkies or Preventive limits, being simultaneously granted to the purchaser by the Board of Revenue.

Source: *The Calcutta Review*, vol. XXII, January–June 1854, p. xx.

1.12: EXPERIMENTS WITH A BIMETALLIC CURRENCY SYSTEM IN INDIA

Thus all the assertions of the bimetallists are melted into thin air, leaving not a rack behind.

HENRY DUNNING MACLEOD

The Company was at once both, the cause of the problem and also the only one in a position to alleviate the severe shortage of currency in Bengal post-*diwani*. A series of experiments were undertaken but with disastrous consequences. In Bengal, a plan was drawn up to make gold mohurs legal tender in addition to the rupee based on the belief that gold was in abundance and held by people in the form of ornaments and hidden treasures. With the (silver) rupee becoming scarce, it was hoped that mohurs coming into circulation would enhance the quantum of money into circulation. But how could the Government 'draw this precious metal from its lurking holes' (Steuart, 1772, p. 27) to the mints?

By Article 7 dated 2 June 1766 the government ordered a gold mohur to be struck of fineness 20 carats or 10/14 fine, weighing 179.66 grains at a legal ratio of 14 Sicca Rupees:1 gold mohur.[17] The latter was to be considered as legal tender that had to be accepted by all persons in all payments with severe penalties against those who disobeyed. Bimetallism had arrived in India, perhaps for the first time. But unfortunately, Gresham's Law soon followed. As the council minted more and more gold mohur, the silver (Sicca) Rupee kept disappearing from circulation. The reason for this was obvious but, as usual, difficult for the authorities to accept.

Let me begin with the relevant ratios:

- Legal ratio *mohur:rupee* fixed at 1:14
- Legal ratio of *gold:silver* was 1:16.45 (if the coins were melted)
- Market ratio in bullion market of *gold: silver* was, however, 1:14.81

While one unit of gold was legally valued at 16.45 units of silver, in the bullion market this unit of gold could exchange for just 14.81 units of silver. In other words, the gold in the newly issued mohur was overvalued in terms of silver by more than 17.5 per cent of its market value. Equivalently, the silver rupee had been undervalued. In terms of our analogy in Section 1.1, the mohur was the soiled note while rupees were the new crisp ones. Both could be used to settle a debt, i.e. 1 mohur or 14 rupees. Which one would be used as money? The soiled mohur, obviously. To put it differently; suppose I had a debt of 1 mohur or 14 rupees. With rupees in my possession, I could melt the fourteen rupee coins and divide the total quantity of silver in it into 16.45 equal parts. The sum of all these parts would be equivalent to one part of gold (a mohur), legally. However, if I take these 16.45 parts of silver to the market I could get 1.175 parts of gold at the market ratio of 1:14.81. I would settle the debt with one part of gold (a mohur) and keep a balance of 0.175 part of gold. Or I would use 14.81 parts of silver from the melted rupees, get a part of gold (for a mohur) in the market and keep the balance of 1.64 parts of silver. This is what happened. People rushed to the mint with gold to be minted into coin, while (silver) rupees were melted down or simply taken out of circulation and hoarded.

In Figure 1.8 we illustrate the impact on the gold and silver bullion markets respectively when gold is overvalued as coin, say, at the rate of 16.45S = 1G (or 1S = 1/16.45G) while the bullion market rates stand at 14.81S = 1G or 1S = 1/14.81G.

To bring silver back into circulation, the government in 1769, in desperation, threatened to prosecute all who held silver and would not give it in exchange for the gold coins at rates fixed by law. At the same time they fixed the legal ratio at one mohur of 99.64/100 fineness to 16 Sicca Rupees of 175.92 grains of fine silver. But even after this revision, the gold mohur remained overvalued by 5.25 per cent. The silver rupees continued to disappear from circulation. With the prevailing uncertainty, only small quantities of gold coins were issued from the mints. Commerce

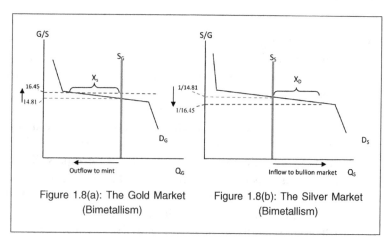

Figure 1.8(a): The Gold Market   Figure 1.8(b): The Silver Market
(Bimetallism)   (Bimetallism)

Figure 1.8: Flow of Metal to Mint and Market with Overvaluation of Gold and Undervaluation of Silver under a Bimetallic Standard

was seriously affected in Bengal. The credit market was also severely affected; native bankers refused to advance sums in silver fearing that repayments would be made later in artificially overvalued gold coins. Bimetallism, as predicted, led to an empty treasury and at the same time, a dearth of money in circulation. These events happening in Bengal were essentially the working of Gresham's Law; bad (overvalued) gold money driving out good silver (under-valued) money from circulation.

Bengal's experiments with bimetallism and currency reforms were, however, not the first by the British in India. Decades earlier, in 1742, the East India Company having obtained permission of the Nawab of Arcot began coining rupees in imitation of those struck at the imperial mint as gold was the preferred for currency. As one 1745 despatch of the East India Company (Dodwell, 1920) put it, 'Owing to great demand for mohurs, it is difficult to sell silver . . . gold is scarce. . . . Though little silver has been imported yet the price is low' (p. 18).

To overcome the shortage of currency the Company sought to increase the circulation of silver rupees in the Presidency, the Government of Madras in 1749 overvalued silver and fixed a legal rate of 350 Arcot Rupees to 100 gold pagodas while the market rate was closer to 400 Arcot rupees to 100 gold pagodas. No sooner had this artificial ratio been fixed, Gresham's Law began to operate. The undervalued gold pagodas began to disappear and the shortage of currency worsened. A despatch of the Company in the same year expressed concern that: 'Gold and pagodas being very scarce, and the value of rupees falling daily, have made rupees current at 350 per 100 Pagoda at which rate payments and receipts have been made since 1 May' (ibid, p. 90).

In 1750 the government sought to surmount the shortages in currency, not by an adjustment of the legal ratio to prevailing market rates, but instead through the import of gold and lowering its market price. For a short while it seemed that the strategy paid off but with the market price of gold escalating, or silver depreciating, we find from a Company dispatch that by 1752, the crisis from a currency shortage may have actually become even worse. 'Want of gold checks investment. Merchants are advanced in rupees to the

Company's loss. With the greatest difficulty have procured Madras Pagodas for Northern settlements' (ibid, p. 136).

The sharp fluctuations in the market price of gold and silver made it difficult for the Government to align it with the legal ratio. The continual undervaluation of the gold pagoda ultimately drove it out of circulation in southern India with silver rupees replacing it by the end of the eighteenth century. For sake of completeness, I have illustrated the possible sequence of events in the silver and gold markets in Figure 1.9.

In Bombay, the Company's experiments with bimetallism was initially satisfactory given that the legal and market ratio between the rupee and mohur were almost in sync; however, by the later part of the eighteenth century a problematic situation developed. The Old Bombay rupee was slightly lighter than the Sicca rupee, but contained a fraction more fine silver. By an agreement with the Nawab of Surat, the (native) Surat rupee of the Mughal Emperor was also adopted as the currency of the Bombay Presidency. The rupees coined by both, the Nawab and the Company, were to circulate at par, under a mutual pledge to preserve its standard. The Nawab's rupees, however, were soon found to contain 10, 12,

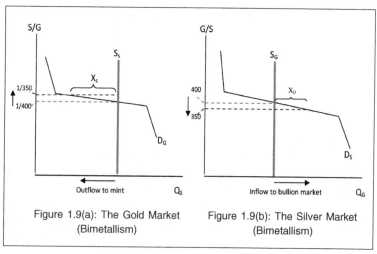

Figure 1.9(a): The Gold Market   Figure 1.9(b): The Silver Market
(Bimetallism)   (Bimetallism)

Figure 1.9: Flow of Metal to Mint and Market with Undervaluation of Gold and Undervaluation of Silver under a Bimetallic Standard

and even 15 per cent of alloy. At once Gresham's Law became operational; the Bombay rupees were melted down and re-coined at Surat. Not only were Bombay rupees driven out but with the devalued Surat rupee in circulation, gold mohurs too disappeared. The coinage of silver and gold in the Bombay mint was suspended for twenty years, and the debased Surat rupee was alone seen in circulation. Finally in 1800 the Company ordered the then Surat rupee to be struck at Bombay, and thenceforth it became fixed at 179 grains weight, 164.74 pure. The mohur too was equalized in weight.

India witnessed great turmoil in her currency system in the second half of the eighteenth century. But to an extent, the Company government had managed to bring about two major changes by the turn of the nineteenth century; first, to get rid of the large number of debased currencies in circulation and second, rejecting bimetallism as a means to overcome currency shortages. The stage was set for the introduction of a monometallic standard with the silver rupee as the standard of value.

1.13: CURRENCY CONSOLIDATION

Be it enacted, that from the First Day of September, 1835, the under-mentioned Silver Coins only shall be coined at the Mints within the Territories of the East India Company—A Rupee, to be denominated the Company's Rupee—a Half Rupee—a Quarter Rupee —and a Double Rupee.

ACT NO. XVII OF 1835

The East India Company's experiment with bimetallism was just one in a series of measures they implemented in order to consolidate the rupee as standard currency in the Presidencies they had come to acquire. I explore some other measures they adopted, beginning in the period preceding grant of *diwani* to the Company when it was merely a merchant and had not ascended to the position of merchant-ruler. At that time in Bengal, the minting of money was a monopoly privilege of India's largest indigenous bankers, the house of the Jagatseths. Although the mint mastership was not officially vested with them, nobody but the Jagatseths had the effective use of the mint at Murshidabad. As early as 1717-19, the English merchants made efforts to secure from the Nawab the right of minting. But, as mentioned earlier, they were informed by the officers of the Nawab that given Fattehchand's influence over the mint, the Company had little hope of getting a grant. In 1736 when English merchants at Calcutta began to import Madras and Arcot rupees and use them in payments to Indian merchants, the Jagatseth obtained a firman from the Nawab making these rupees receivable in public or private payments at much lower value. Shortly afterwards, a duty of 2 per cent was levied on all foreign rupees tendered to the government. In 1757 the Company acquired the right to establish a mint at Calcutta but this was of little use, as the Calcutta rupee notwithstanding that its weight and fineness was in every respect as good as the Sicca of Murshidabad, remained at the mercy of the Jagatseth who 'could make it fluctuate in such a manner as he seems fitting and convenient for his purpose' (Muranjan, 1952, p. 20) by insisting that it could be accepted only at a discount. A firman had to be obtained from Mir Kasim, Nawab of Bengal, ordering the rupee of the Company to pass current and forbidding any person to demand such discounts on it.

The stake of the Jagatseths and with them, of the banking community in maintaining the Sicca rupee as the sole rupee of the realm was a very peculiar one. As we have seen earlier, in virtue of their office as the Treasurer of Bengal revenues, the Jagatseths prescribed that the revenues of the current year had to be paid in coins of the current year. Meanwhile, coins of earlier years were accepted by their mint only at a heavy discount. Not only the Jagatseths but the shroffs found it a lucrative occupation to receive such rupees at discount and re-coin them. The profit of ordinary minting itself was not small. In the year 1746, the Jagatseths were giving 201 Sicca rupees for 240 rupees weight of silver offered to him; it is, therefore, not surprising to see why they strove to protect these privileges at any means.

After the bimetallism debacle, the government of the East India Company with its growing political power made several attempts at currency reforms in Bengal. In 1773 Warren Hastings abolished the earlier system of indigenous rulers discounting coins of the previous year by 3 per cent and those of two years by 5 per cent. This system had forced people to re-coin good coins every year and thereby incur charges of the mint. The most common silver rupee that circulated in Bengal at that time was the Sicca Rupee of 98/100 fineness and weighing 179.511 grains troy, first minted in the year 1773 and stamped 19 San Sicca, i.e. 'struck in the nineteenth year' of Shah Alam, the last of the Mughals. Hastings enacted a law that no deduction was to be on coins whatever their date of issue unless deteriorated or debased and furthermore ordered that all future issues of coins would have only one date imprinted on them, 1773, i.e. 'the nineteenth year of the auspicious reign of Shah Alam'.

However, it was the bold measures taken by Lord Cornwallis that gradually stabilized the currency situation in Bengal. In 1788 he put a stop to the minting of gold mohurs, returning to monometallic silver currency. In 1789, an order was issued preventing treasury officers from using any discretion in taking or rejecting coins on the ground of short weight. If a rupee was the genuine product of a recognized mint, no matter to what extent it had been clipped or drilled, the treasury officers were compelled to receive it by weight according to fixed rates hung up in the collector's office. By a single stroke the arbitrary discount which provincial treasurers had exacted on almost all coins was put to an end. Another order soon followed; treasurers were to register not just the net sums received, but details of the actual coin in which it was paid and the rate at which it was received. An invoice had to be forwarded to the Presidency mint along with the coin itself. With this the lucrative business of deducting any *batta* (commission) by treasury officers ceased. This business had been so profitable that many people had invested a fortune in bribing their way up to the post of treasurer, a post which in those days yielded a salary of £40 per annum but gave an opportunity of making £4,000 more.

In 1790, a shortage of currency on account of the Deccan wars forced Cornwallis to bring back gold into circulation but in 1791, after the currency shortage waned, he returned to the 'parallel standard' whereby the sale of gold and silver coin was free and unrestrained and their price in terms of each other were according to the rates prevailing in bullion markets. In 1793 a third attempt was made to introduce bimetallism in Bengal. A new mohur was issued in that year, weighing 190.895 grains troy and containing 189.4037 grains of pure gold and made legal tender at 16 Sicca rupees. This corresponded to a gold: silver ratio of 14.86 to 1. However, this was once again not equal to market ratio and so the third attempt to establish the gold mohur in Bengal failed as did the ones made in 1766 and 1769. Bengal again returned to a parallel standard. In 1794, Cornwallis decided that the time had come to get rid of the old defaced coinage by compulsory measures. The public had been allowed opportunity until the first day of the Bengali year 1200 (10 April 1794) to change old coins for new without any charge whatever. Thereafter the Sicca rupees of the 19 San became the only coin acceptable as legal tender. A further twelve month grace period was given, and in the year 1795 a new and uniform currency had at last completely replaced the debased currency which had afflicted the people for almost than four decades.

In 1805, Charles Earl of Liverpool published a letter to the King entitled, 'A Treatise on the Coins of the Realm' (1805), advocating a monometallic gold standard for England implying that only gold coin would be legal tender. In the light of its important recommendations, the Court of Directors of the East India Company in 1806 decided that a monometallic standard should be the basis of the future currency system of India. However, the government in India was still in favour of bimetallism or at least a parallel standard wherein although the standard of value would be one metal, coins of another metal could also circulate at the market rate. After a period of almost ten years, the East India Company decided on the latter and proposed a new coinage for India:

The Board have referred particularly to the letter from the Honorable Court, dated the 25 April 1806, which contains the ground work of all their subsequent orders concerning it. In that letter the Honorable Court explained their object to be to establish a general currency for the whole of India. They stated that the standard currency forming the money of account ought to be of one of the precious metals only, but not to the exclusion of the other; that the metal ought to be silver; and that no ratio ought to be fixed between the standard silver coin and the gold coin, but that gold should be left to find its own value. The Court further desired that the gold coin should be denominated a gold rupee, and that the gold and silver rupees should be the same in weight, fineness, form and inscription. They also desired that half and quarter gold and silver rupees and annas should be coined, and stated that a copper coinage of six-pice, three-pice, and one-pice pieces would be sent from England. (Thurston, 1890, p. 51)

Madras Presidency was the first to act upon the Court's proposal and a proclamation from Fort St. George, 9 December 1817, stated that the Madras silver rupee would replace the star pagoda. But the transition to the rupee and abandonment of other coins was easier ordered than put into practice. Difficulties soon appeared; in the year 1817, Collectors were directed not to receive Pondicherry rupees in payment of revenue, but this had to be rescinded on the receipt of a letter from the Collector of South Arcot to the effect that the old Pondicherry rupees, fanams and kasu had always been received into the district treasuries of that division, and that, if they were not received, it would tend to impede the collections. Moreover, non-acceptance of 'old' currencies would fall very hard on the cultivators as they would be obliged to pay a certain *vuttum* (commission) in order to get the village shroffs to exchange the Pondicherry coins for the Company's. The ryots (cultivators) would once again be at the mercy of the village moneychangers. It was accordingly resolved that the old Pondicherry rupee should be received in payment of revenue until they were found to deviate from their par value in weight and fineness.

Bombay followed Madras six years later with a proclamation on 6 October 1824, which declared a gold rupee and a silver rupee of the new Madras standard to be the only units of currency in that Presidency. The government of Bengal had a much bigger problem to handle. It had three different principal units of silver currency to be reduced to the standard proposed by the Court. It commenced its work of reorganization by a system of elimination and alteration and by the end of 1833 a uniformity of coinage was by and large accomplished. The final step remaining was to bring about the currency system envisaged by the Court of Directors—to demonetize gold and move on to a monometallic silver standard.

At this point, however, a conflict arose between the Court of Directors in England and the three governments of Calcutta, Madras and Bombay in India; the latter were opposed to demonetization of gold. The local governments preferred a bimetallic system of double legal tender at a fixed ratio prevalent in each territory. Rather than demonetize the gold mohur, they proposed to alter pure contents so as align the legal set ratio with market prices and to re-establish bimetallism on the basis of the ratio adopted by Madras in 1818. There was another point of contention between the Court in London and local governments in India. The Court was in favour of a 'uniform' currency, i.e. each Presidency coined its own money and the money coined at the mints of the other presidencies would not be legal tender in its territories except at the Mint. On the other hand, the Presidencies favoured a 'common' currency system, i.e. a single unit in place of a uniform currency. The reason for the governments' was their dependence upon one another for the finance of their deficits even though each had their own fiscal system. The surplus in one was constantly drawn upon to meet the deficits in others. Moreover, not being able to use the money of other Presidencies as legal tender meant that each was obliged to lock up, to the disadvantage of commerce, large working balances in order to be self-sufficient and meet contingencies. At the end of 1833, therefore, the position was that the Court of Directors in England desired to have a uniform currency with a single standard of silver, while the authorities in India wished for a common currency with a bimetallic standard.

The Charter Act of 1833 turned the tables in favour of a common currency albeit a monometallic one. Under this Act, not only were the Company's trade monopolies removed and all its commercial functions revoked, but more importantly, an imperial system of centralized administration was introduced whereby the Governor-General in Council had full power and authority to superintend and control the Presidency governments in all civil and military matters. Moreover, the Imperial Government set up by Parliament no longer saw itself as part of the Dewans or agents of the Mughals and therefore did not think it fit that coins should be issued in the name of the defunct Mughal emperors who had ceased to govern. 'It was anxious to throw off the false garb and issue an Imperial coinage in its own name, which being common to the whole of India would convey its common sway' (Ambedkar, 1947, p. 20). By Act XVII of 1835 of the Imperial Government a common currency was introduced for the whole of India, a silver rupee weighing 180 grains troy and containing 165 grains fine as the common currency and sole legal tender throughout the country. Coins of different denominations would bear on the obverse the head and the name of the reigning sovereign of the United Kingdom of Great Britain and Ireland, and on the reverse the denomination of the coin in English and Persian, and the words East India Company in English. The Indian mints would be open to the 'free coinage' of silver in quantities of not less than 1,000 *tolas* (of 180 grains each). The coinage charge was 2 per cent (in addition to 1 per cent melting charges) for silver of the Indian standard (91.6 per mille). On delivery of silver at the mints for coinage, the owner would receive a receipt which entitled him to a certificate from the assay master for the net produce of such bullion or coin payable at the general treasury. Copper coins would be legal tender only for fractions of rupee. Gold coins were, however, no longer legal tender. In 1835 India was placed on a silver monometallic basis with the rupee as legal tender and standard coin.

Box 1.5: Proclamation on India's Monometallic Silver Rupee

Fort William, Financial Department, 2 September 1835.

PROCLAMATION

The Honorable the Governor General in Council has resolved that the Device of the New Rupee, Double Rupee, Half Rupee, and Quarter Rupee, to be issued from the Mints of India, from and after the 1 September 1835, in conformity with Act XVII, of the same year, shall be as follows:

On the Obverse, the Head of His Majesty William the Fourth, with the words,

---

WILLIAM IV, KING

On the Reverse, the denomination of the Coin in English and Persian in the centre, encircled by a laurel wreath; and around the margin the words,

EAST INDIA COMPANY 1835

The new Coin shall be milled on the edge, with a serrated or upright milling. For the information of the public, an engraving of the device adopted for the Rupee, is hereunto annexed.

Source: The Canton Register, 22 December 1835.

1.14: DALHOUSIE'S CURRENCY LEGACY

Self-interest can generally find a reason, whenever it has the power of enforcing its own laws

THE BUSINESS HISTORICAL SOCIETY, 1864

By Act XVII of 1835 of the Imperial Government a common mono-metallic silver currency was introduced for the whole of British India. The Indian mints were opened to the free coinage of silver in quantities of not less than 1,000 tolas[18] (of 180 grains each). Copper coins were accepted as legal tender but only for fractions of a rupee. Gold coins were demonetized and no longer accepted as legal tender. However, the government continued coining of gold mohurs and even allowed them to circulate but at a rate that was to be fixed from time to time by the Governor-General in Council and announced in the *Calcutta Gazette*. They would be received and issued at public treasuries in lieu of silver rupees. At that time the rate was fixed at 15 rupees to a gold mohur.

The year 1835 marked the culminating-point of a long and arduous process of monetary reform that had begun soon after the rise of the East India Company as merchant-ruler, placing India on a silver monometallic basis with the rupee as legal tender and standard coin. Some commentators like Naoroji (1870, p. 16) argued that 'an artificial increased demand was created for silver by the Act of the Indian government which prohibited gold as legal tender, and by the demand for China'. Silver worth some £75 million had been exported between 1847 and 1867 by Britain alone to India and an additional £41 million had gone to China. India, Naoroji claimed, had purposefully been put on a silver currency so that its buoyant demand for silver prevented silver prices from falling and possible instability in international gold-silver parity.

The view that the 1835 proclamation for a monometallic silver currency was to keep India away from gold and at the same time sustain the price of silver was, however, not endorsed by others like Ambedkar (1947, pp. 24–6) who pointed out that the gold standard, at that time, had not found universal acceptance even in England. After the commercial crisis of 1825, questions were raised as to whether or not the gold standard was too narrow a basis for a currency system and then again in 1844, Sir Robert Peel had even contemplated the possibility of abandoning gold and moving on to silver or a bimetallic standard. In light of these arguments, it is not appropriate to see the adoption of a monometallic silver standard in 1835 as one implemented with an ulterior motive to keep India away from gold.

Ambedkar's line of argument is supported by the subsequent proclamation of 13 January 1841 wherein Indian treasuries were instructed to also accept gold coins in settlement of dues. Why was gold received by the government? In fact, in 1844, there is evidence that the government even encouraged the coinage of gold in Madras and Bombay as it reduced seigniorage on gold to 1 per cent while it continued to be 2 per cent on silver (Nolan, *c.* 1878, p. 380). The reason for this policy is, however, not surprising because between 1840 and 1850, the market gold-silver ratio remained above the legal ratio of 1:15;[19] in fact, gold had appreciated a few basis points from 1:15.62 in 1840 to 1:15.70 in 1850 (Statistical Abstract, 1955, p. 432). In spite of this undervaluation of gold legally, which should have been a disincentive to make payments in gold, there were instances when treasuries received locally available (gold) currency. This was primarily because silver coins were sometimes in short supply and rates charged by local moneychangers for conversion of gold into silver, exorbitant.

But this inconsistent and impractical policy of issuing coins, accepting them in discharge of claims of the government and, at the same time, not accepting it as legal tender, could apparently create a serious problem for the government. If the market price of gold exceeded its legal value, i.e. gold was undervalued as coin, then no gold would be received into the treasury at all. On the other hand, if the market price of gold was lower than the legal ratio, the government would end up receiving all its dues in gold while it would not be able to re-issue it in discharge of its own liabilities as it was not legal tender.

Tremors that shook confidence in the fixity of the par rate between gold and silver began with the gold discoveries in California in the late 1840s. However, the full impact of these disturbances in the market for precious metals reached India with the news of gold discoveries in New South Wales, Australia. A supply shock if followed by a fall in the silver price of gold would mean gold's overvaluation as coin (at the statutory rate of 15:1). Going by the proclamation of 1841, an inflow of gold into the government's coffers would have become inevitable, a fearsome situation for the government; '. . . we have reason to believe that speculations are already in progress for forming connexions with Australia for the express purpose of bringing up gold when the direct line of steam communication is open next year, in order to take advantage of the Government proclamation of 1841, by which gold is still receivable at 15 rupees to the so-called gold piece; and in this case we run the risk of being seriously inconvenienced by an excessive stock of this metal' (Copy of Financial Letter, 1852, p. 46).

The government clarified that the proclamation of 1841 was not understood by the Indian treasuries correctly. Their policy was not to receive gold when it was overvalued as coin relative to its market value thereby giving undue profit to the merchant at the expense of the state. It is true that the government of the Company could have used some of its gold reserves to meet its requirements back in Britain; however, the accumulation of gold reserves would take place not in adjustment of balance of trade but only because it was no use as coin in India. This, the Council considered, was an unsound argument in favour of allowing gold currency as legal tender.

Ultimately on 1 January 1853, Lord Dalhousie, Governor General of India in Council, withdrew and cancelled the amendment made in the proclamation of 1841, the Act of 1835 was reinstituted; although gold would continue to be minted by the government, the gold mohur was demonetized and no longer accepted in discharge of the public's liabilities in the Indian territories of the East India Company. See Box 1.6. India had followed in the footsteps of Holland, which had suspended the circulation of gold Guillaumes in 1850 out of the same fear that a fall in the silver price of gold would lead to an overvaluation of the gold coin and settlement of government dues in this lower valued coin. By the end of the first half of 1851 some £5 million equivalent of gold coins had flowed into the bullion markets of France, Germany and Britain from Holland (Faucher, 1853, p.37). The action of Holland was soon followed by Belgium. Other countries including Portugal, Russia and Spain followed suit by prohibiting the export of silver.

Box 1.6: Notification on The Termination of Gold Currency in India in 1853

Fort William, Financial Department, 22 December 1852.

NOTIFICATION

By Section 9, Act XVII, of 1835 of the Government of India, it was enacted, that thenceforward no gold coin should be legal tender of payment in any of the territories of the East India Company, and accordingly gold ceased from the date of the passing of the Act to be legal tender of payment in the Company's territories in India. But by a proclamation issued on the 13 January 1841, officers in charge of public treasuries were authorized freely to receive gold coins struck in conformity with the provisions of the same Act (XVII. Of 1835), at the rates indicated by the denomination of the pieces until they should have passed certain limits of lightness, set forth in the table published with the proclamation or until further orders, and gold coins have been thus received in liquidation of public demands up to the present date.

Notice is now given, that so much of the proclamation of the 13 January 1841, as authorized the receipt of gold coins into the public treasuries of

Government, will be withdrawn and cancelled from the 1 January 1853, and that on and after that date no gold coin will be received on account of payments due, or in any way to be made, to the Government in any public treasury within the territories of the East India Company. Gold will continue as heretofore to be received into any of the mints within the territories of the East India Company for coinage under the Act and rules at present in force for the coinage of gold; but mint certificates for gold coins will be discharged in gold only, and no such certificates for gold will be accepted in any public treasury in liquidation of public demands, or on account of any payment to the Government whatever.

Source: *Calcutta Gazette*, 25 December 1852.

India had transited from silver to a bimetallic and back to a monometallic silver standard in the beginning of the second half of the nineteenth century; copper coins circulated in denominations of only less than a rupee.[20] Gold had been demonetized and was no longer accepted at the treasuries, although the government continued the coinage of gold brought to mint. In any case, the authority to receive gold coins at Public Treasuries was rescinded. On account of this notification some £120,000,000 worth of gold currency was withdrawn from circulation and hoarded away.

The repercussions of this move on the economy were serious. In the states newly annexed by Dalhousie, the system of revenue collection *in kind* had been replaced by a new system wherein all revenues were collected only in cash, particularly, silver coins. The massive increase in demand for silver coin at the time of revenue collection meant an increase in the price of the rupee or its purchasing power. This increase in the price of the rupee was reflected in a corresponding decline in price of all other goods including agricultural produce. The latter led to widespread discontent amongst the rural population. Moreover, an enormous shortage of and difficulty to obtain silver coin soon developed across India. Everything had to be sacrificed to get that silver coin, but the problem was only for a few weeks after which the demand for coin once again subsided and prices returned to 'normal' levels. Meanwhile, the cultivator incurred substantial losses in selling grain at low prices in exchange for the temporarily overpriced silver coin. The sudden spike in value of silver coins, however, proved profitable to the receivers of revenue. The wealthy merchants, both Indian and European would buy up the produce when prices had depreciated and resell them whenever prices returned to their normal levels. Dalhousie's policy of aligning the government's interest to those of the moneyed class in India could have proved beneficial to the British but for another step that proved counterproductive. By the mid-nineteenth century, a new class of purchasers of government securities had developed—wealthy native capitalists. These securities provided them with an opportunity to earn a steady return and at the same time provide liquidity to the government. The issue of a 4 per cent bond was almost immediately followed with another issue of a 5 per cent bond. This was a disastrous strategy because it immediately led holders of the first bond to incur a capital loss of 20 per cent. In other words, with the initial issue a Rs. 100 bond would yield Rs. 4 per annum but now with a 5 per cent bond a Rs. 80 bond would suffice to yield a return of Rs. 4. As seen from Box 1.7 Dalhousie alienated and destroyed the confidence of the native capitalist class in the wisdom and integrity of their British rulers. Amongst the several possible reasons that led to the Mutiny of 1857, this one remains the least explored.

Box 1.7: Lord Dalhousie's Financial Blunder

'Lord Dalhousie's conversion of the Five per Cent. Stock into Four per Cents., followed as it was, almost immediately, by a Five per Cent. Loan, at once deprived these Securities of the only value that in the eyes of this class they had possessed. They found that, having purchased Four per Cents., they were unable to sell them again, except at a sacrifice of a fifth of their capital so employed; for the measure sent down the whole Funds of India from 97, at which they stood at the time, to 80, at a stroke'. (*quoted from the Press newspaper of 28 November, 1858*).

Great loss had been inflicted upon the moneyed class of the Natives, causing their previous confidence in the wisdom and integrity of their British Rulers to be considerably shaken.

Source: James Taylor, *The Mystery of Money Explained*, Walton and Maberly, London, 1863, p. 229.

1.15: TOWARDS A COMMON CURRENCY

A single currency would in some respects be like a world language, improving communications around the globe. It would eliminate the present problems of speculation, instability and uncertainty and would provide a strong foundation for the growing world economy. It would reduce a significant cost and risk of doing business internationally.

ONE COUNTRY,
THE ONLINE NEWSLETTER OF THE BAHA'I COMMUNITY, 1999

Early modern Indian monetary history overlooks the position of the native states during the period of colonial expansion. In this section we go back to the 1830s when the East India Company actively pursued strategies to bring about a common currency across India. This is an important episode in Indian monetary history which in some ways is a precursor to a contemporary process that we are all familiar; with—the European Monetary Union.

As the Company made progress its their territorial expansion, the need and priority to establish a common currency grew. In the 'Minutes of Evidence before the Select Committee of 1832', the benefits of a common currency were articulated in much the same way as were expected from the European Union; the eliminations of transaction costs from currency conversions and commissions, a standard unit of account making inter-regional comparisons of prices easy, a reduction in risks and uncertainty that arise from fluctuating currencies and the integration of the region into a single market.

Box 1.8: The Benefits of a Common Currency

28 February 1832
Holt Mackenzie, Esq.

312. In a financial point of view, what is your opinion with regard to the currency in India; do you think it should be one currency for all the Company's possessions in India, or that each presidency should have its peculiar currency?—I certainly think it should be one currency for all India.

313. Will you state the advantages to be derived from that?—The saving to government of the expense of re-coinage, in the case of a remittance,

---

which frequently happens, of money from one part of the country to another; and the loss and inconvenience to private merchants and others who have to make remittances in like manner, would be obviated; whereas now the rupees of one place are received merely as bullion in the other, and excepting at the mints, are not legal tenders at all. The troops when moved from place to place are particularly subject to inconvenience and loss from this cause; and Government has been occasionally embarrassed in providing the funds locally required, with the promptitude necessary to the public service. The pay of troops being calculated in coin not current in Bengal, there is occasional trouble in the conversion of accounts; and officers and serpahees (sepoys) complain when they receive a less number of rupees than their stated pay, though the intrinsic value be even greater. Probably if we had but one currency the mint expenses might be reduced. I think it likely, indeed, that we might discontinue the mint at Madras; but on that point I have not been able to form a conclusive opinion.

314. Exclusive of the profit to the Government, you think that the trade universally would be very much benefitted by such a change?—I do; the unnatural distinction of currencies must aggravate the fluctuations of exchange, and by the charges of recoinage frequently occasion a burthen to commerce that would not otherwise exist.

Source: Extract from the *Minutes of Evidence Taken Before the Select Committee on the Affairs of the East India Company, II. Finance and Accounts*—Trade Part I. Finance, House of Commons, 16 August 1832, p. 37.

In addition to these economic benefits, currency union is a critical step in the movement towards political union. Although the Company justified the economic basis for a common currency across India, the adverse reaction of Indian princes in losing a symbol of their sovereignty is hardly surprising. A solution to the problem was conceived; while the mints of Indian states would not be abolished, the British would take control over the mints and ensure issue of currency uniform in weight and fineness as that of the Presidencies. Further, one side of the coin would be like the Company's coin while the other could carry the name and emblem of the state to which it belonged. But there were technical issues that needed to be sorted out for this plan to be implemented;

special dies had to be procured from England or Calcutta for this purpose. In case coins and paper were produced at a centralized mint it was proposed that the states would be compensated with the average return made by the mint over the last ten years. Apart from ensuring uniformity and standardization of currency, another major concern that had to be dealt with was the mechanical capacity of the Calcutta mint to supply the whole of the country's requirement of silver currency.

Quite coincidentally, just as I was writing this section an article from in the *Wall Street Journal* (reprinted in Livemint, 9 December 2011) caught my attention. It spoke about how Ireland and Greece lacked printing presses to churn out currency in case they abandoned the Euro and moved back on to their old currencies. This report bore an uncanny resemblance to an East India Company report that is shown in Box 1.9.

Box 1.9: The Physical Capacity of the Mint

The die and the stamping machine would be sufficient for every purpose, all other processes being performed by native means and appliances as at present. These chiefs are all ready to close their mints whenever they are ordered to do so; but they represent that now that there is no mint at Saugor to supply the wants of the country with the Company's rupee, that it would be a great hardship upon the people were they compelled to do so.

In Madras steam power is not employed in all the departments of the mint, while at Bombay it is said to be impossible with the present machinery to work in silver and copper at once, and the inability to do so frequently leads to much loss of time. Great improvements might we think, be made in both these mints, at a comparatively small charge, which, if your Honourable Court see fit to authorize, will enable them to forward to the General Treasury at Calcutta, supplies of coin as occasion requires.

Source: *Accounts and Papers: Thirty-Five Volumes*, Session, 24 January– 28 August 1860, vol. XLIX, 1860, London, p. 77.

NOTES

1. In general if there are n goods in an economy, there would be $[n(n-1)]/2$ relative prices. In an economy with just 100 goods and services, 4,950 cross price ratios would be necessary.
2. I use the words money and currency interchangeably. Note, however, that money is a broader concept than currency.
3. A Winchester bushel is about 35 litres.
4. Money here would imply not just currency but also credit so that exchanges across time are also possible.
5. The Ottoman Empire
6. India's previous Finance Minister, P. Chidambaram was contemplating a duty on gold imports to curb the excessive flow of money into a non-productive asset (3 January 2013).
7. Throughout this book (and in the literature too) we do not abide in the strict use of these terms. Generally speaking, the term value is used to imply purchasing power of currency.
8. Even today *daam* is used in colloquial Hindi to mean the price of a good.
9. In Tamil, *panam* and *kasu* are now used to mean money and do not refer to a particular coin.
10. In south India these seeds are referred to as seeds from the 'money plant'.
11. *Firman* means an official order or decree issued by the government.
12. Given the historical context, the former names of cities have been retained. For information, Madras is now Chennai, Calcutta is Kolkata and Bombay is Mumbai.
13. The harsh rules governing possession of bullion and more have been vividly described in Burn, 1797, pp. 429–40.
14. The legal ratio of silver shilling to the gold guinea was fixed at 21:1.
15. *Diwani* is the right to collect revenue.
16. Urban, 1783, p. 342.
17. The Sicca rupee weighed 1 Sicca or 175.927 grains of fine silver. The Sicca rupee was equivalent to 2s3.84d.
18. A *tola* is approximately 11.6666 grams.
19. 1 gold = 15 silver was the legal ratio for conversion of silver into gold in India.
20. Copper coins circulated in denominations of only less than a rupee. Note that the amount of copper to be coined was regulated by Government. No private individual could bring copper to the mint and demand copper coins in exchange; otherwise the country could have been inundated with copper money. Moreover, copper coins were issued at a much higher money value than their actual weight would warrant (Ballard, p. 14).

CHAPTER 2

Remittance Money

Considering the great circulation of Bills of Exchange and Promissory Notes in this Kingdom, and the loss to which parties are subject, if they neglect to observe the rules affecting these securities, together with the frequency of litigation respecting them, there is no law so important to the merchant, as well as to the lawyer, as that relating to these instruments.

JOSEPH CHITTY, 1799

When money satisfies its three functions effectively and efficiently, the system of exchange functions smoothly, enabling a greater degree of specialization and higher standards of living. There is no doubt that metallic money in the form of gold, silver and copper coins facilitated commerce and exchange; however, there were limitations in their use. Amongst others, the physical transport of precious material entailed high costs and security risks that arose from piracy, theft and sinking of ships on the high seas. The search for more convenient means of payment across person, place and time (or any combination of the three) has been the driving force in the development of financial technologies over centuries. New monetary instruments and institutions reduced costs involved in moving metallic currency thereby increasing the velocity of circulation of money and at the same time releasing resources for more productive purposes. However, there has been a downside to these innovations; elevated risks and new types of risks from default or inability to settle claims. Transactions in coin might entail costs of transport and storage but the risks are generally low (apart from the possibility of counterfeit or debased coins) while other instruments like credit cards, cheques, bills of exchange and bank-notes may be far more convenient but do involve greater risks in terms of possibility of default. A whole set of instruments, commercial laws and institutions (payment systems) have evolved over centuries to address concerns over these risks in the use of new instruments so that a greater number of transactions at lower costs across people, place and time are possible. Nonetheless, when at times people *en masse* become concerned as to whether their claims will in fact be honoured there will be an adverse reaction to accepting these forms of money. When this happens, a contraction or a slowdown in growth of the real economy is inevitable, leading to a crisis. Once again, this is a question of balance; we need monetary instruments to make transfer of claims across space (and time) easy so that trade and exchange is facilitated. At the same time, an excessive growth of such instruments and its abuse could have adverse repercussions on the economy.

In this chapter, I explore bills of exchange, an instrument that was used to settle claims across space, eliminating the need for the transport of bullion. While bills of exchange facilitated trade enormously, their abuse in history is not uncommon. At times such abuse affected not just a few individual traders but led to economy-wide crises. As mentioned in the preface, to find an instrument that satisfies the three functions of money efficiently and effectively is not as simple as it seems. The history of bills of exchange in India tells us why this is indeed the case.

2.1: THE ECONOMICS OF REMITTANCE MONEY

There can scarcely be any regular commerce between two merchants at a distance from each other, without bills of exchange becoming in some form, and to some extent or other, the necessary means and instruments of carrying it on.

JOHN MCVICKAR, 1829

Apart from currency, there are other media of exchange that could be considered as money. Such 'non-currency' money includes (i) bills of exchange representing goods (ii) bank notes and credit paper, which are not universally acceptable such as cheques and drafts, representing bank deposits and (iii) securities representing property. In this chapter, I focus attention on the 'bill of exchange', an instrument widely used to economize on the use of precious metals in the discharge of debt and settlement of claims across space, eliminating the necessity to physically transport bullion and coin. Once again it is best understood as a receipt or an acknowledgement of claims and so long as parties agree to the rules governing its use, there is no reason why bills of exchange are not equivalent to money in a fundamental sense.

Let me explain with a simple illustration the fundamental nature of bills of exchange. Suppose A buys goods from X. X draws a bill on A, which is accepted by the latter. The bill of exchange acknowledges the fact that X has given A goods and is therefore entitled to goods or services of the same value in return. But from whom? If this bill is universally and generally recognized by everyone in a society it becomes currency. If, however, it is recognized by only a smaller community (say of traders) within a society it is a bill of exchange. X can use this bill to settle a claim that another trader J might have on him (X). J would then settle his claim with A or use the bill to settle a claim that F might have on him (J). In the latter case, F would then settle his claim with A. At the end of the cycle the bill must return to A for payment or final settlement. But *en route*, by settling claims, it has served as money amongst members of the community.

Bills of exchange called *hundi* were widely used in India since medieval times for domestic and, to a limited extent, even in international transactions. However, the use of foreign bills of exchange increased exponentially with trade and commercial expansion by the East India Company, particularly in the eighteenth and nineteenth centuries. But like bank notes there were risks associated with the use of bills of exchange, especially failure to settle claims due to default by the acceptor. Innovation through bank and broker intermediation reduced default risk although this came at an additional cost. Unfortunately, sifting through the archives on the use and evolution of bills of exchange in India might leave readers confused. I, therefore, present a brief exposition on the economics and operational mechanics of bills of exchange so that its use and abuse in Indian history can be more easily understood.

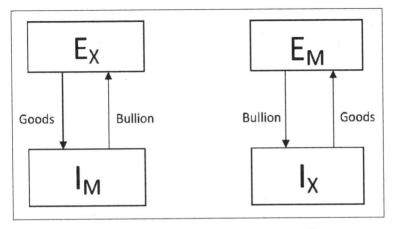

Figure 2.1: International Exchange with Bullion Flows,
Without the use of Bills of Exchange

Figure 2.1 shows the pattern of bullion flows without the use of bills of exchange (from here on also referred to as B/E) or any other instrument apart from metallic currencies and bullion. E_X refers to an English export firm and E_M an English import firm while the Indian counterparts are I_X and I_M respectively. Bullion flows to England from India and also from India to England in settlement of all claims. This, however, entails huge transport and insurance costs.

In their simplest form, B/Es would have arisen from the possibility to avoid these transactions costs in transport of bullion. In Figure 2.2 we attempt to understand how B/Es do so. Let's begin with a situation where no brokers and/or a market for B/Es exist. I_X then draws a B/E on the drawee, E_M (commonly stated to as 'draws a bill on England'). But to be useful, we need an 'equal and opposite' transaction, i.e. export of goods to India by E_X who then draws a 'bill on India' with I_M as the drawee and in favour of I_X. On presentation of the B/E by E_X to E_M, the amount would be paid by E_M to E_X. On completion of the export transaction, I_X would present the B/E to I_M for payment. Given the rate of exchange as (say) £1 = Rs. 10, in effect then I_M settles his dues with E_X by paying Rs. 100 to I_X and E_M settles his dues with I_X by paying £10 to E_X.

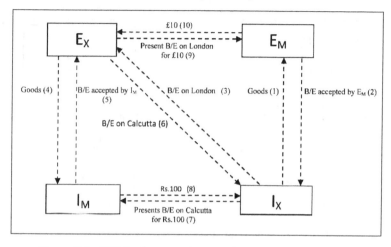

Figure 2.2: B/E Settlement without a Market or Bank-Brokers

Although B/Es do away with bullion flows, the need to locate a specific person or firm in another country (even if there were adequate trade volumes between the countries) who would buy B/E to settle their debt or remit money across place was the key to a making the transaction happen. This problem actually existed in the past as revealed by the following report from the early nineteenth century;

The usual way in which merchants settle their exchange operations in Bombay, and I believe it's the same all over the East, is by sending a notice to each house, intimating that A & Co have £10,000 to draw for England; A & Co. are called sellers. B & Co. want to remit £5,000 to England are called buyers, and offer for that amount of A & Co. bills; C & Co. are also buyers, and offer for £5,000 more, so that the whole transaction is completed; and unless a bank is prepared to buy up all the bills offered for sale, at the same, or more favourable rate than a merchant can offer, it cannot carry on its exchange operations profitably, the merchants buying and selling among themselves, save all the bankers' charges. This, I imagine, has been the case in all countries before the system of banking operations was clearly understood; and I have no doubt, but that in a short time we shall see all exchange business done by the banks. (Gilbart, 1849, p. 588)

The difficulty in locating buyers and sellers of B/E led the way for the development of B/E markets typically organized by a bank acting as a broker and also providing the service of accepting bills (or guaranteeing payment to make the bill more acceptable). In this market exporters could locate importers (and vice-versa) to receive and make payments. But before bringing in the bank, it is useful to understand the working of the B/E market with just traders in the market who buy and sell bills. In Figure 2.3 the development for a market in Calcutta for B/E on London is shown. I_X draws a B/E on London for £10 with E_M as drawee, and gets it accepted. He then sells it in the Indian (Calcutta) market for Rs.100 to I_M, who endorses it in favour of E_X in settlement of his debt arising on account of his imports from E_X. E_X presents the B/E on London to E_M for £10 in settlement of his dues.

Another possibility exists. In the Figure 2.4, E_X draws a 'B/E on Calcutta' for Rs. 100 with I_M as drawee, and gets it accepted by the latter. E_X then sells it in the London market for Rs. 100 to E_M, who endorses it in favour of I_X in settlement of his debt arising on account of his imports from I_X. I_X presents the B/E on Calcutta to I_M for Rs. 100 in settlement of his dues. In this case, a 'bills on Calcutta' market develops in London.

Consider the first option discussed above in Figure 2.3 where a market for 'bills on London' develops in Calcutta. Depending on the demand for and supply of B/Es, there would be a price for

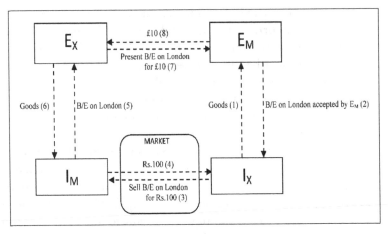

Figure 2.3: Market for B/E on London in Calcutta

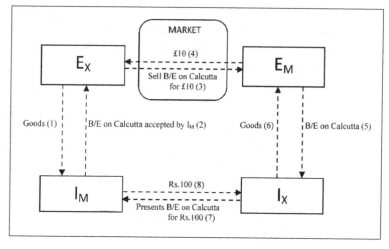

Figure 2.4: Market for B/E on Calcutta in London

them; this price was termed as 'exchange' or the 'exchange rate'. Suppose initially the exchange rate is exactly equal to the *par rate* or the rate corresponding to the gold/silver content (weight and purity) of the coins in the countries. As assumed above this is given as £1 = Rs. 10. As can be seen from Figure 2.5, Indian importers in Calcutta buy (demand) B/Es on London to settle the claims of London exporters while Indian exporters sell (supply) B/Es on London in Calcutta to Indian importers in settlement of their claims on London importers. The demand curve is downward sloping because as the rupee appreciates (say from Rs. 10 to Rs. 9 to the £), imports into India become cheaper and are stimulated. The same appreciation in the rupee, however, dampens Indian exports and the supply of B/Es on London. This gives us an upward sloping supply curve for B/Es. The equilibrium rate is when demand is equal to supply, initially equal to the par rate.

When total supply of B/Es exceeds total demand for B/Es it implies that (Indian) exports exceed imports. This will have repercussions on the exchange rate as well as bullion flows. If exports exceed imports then there being an excess supply of B/Es on London in the Calcutta market, the rupee will tend to appreciate to (say) Rs. 9 = £1 from the original level of Rs. 10 = £1. In other words, the Indian exporter receives only Rs. 90 for a B/E of £10. This

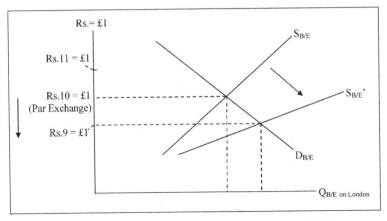

Figure 2.5: Demand and Supply for B/E on London in Calcutta

dampens exports as I_X gets only Rs. 90 for a £10 export order while it stimulates imports as I_M has now to pay only Rs. 90 for his £10 import. In Figure 2.5 the increase in supply of B/E (shift in the supply curve for B/E from $S_{B/E}$ to $S_{B/E}'$) due to a sudden surge in export demand causes the exchange rate for B/E to appreciate towards Rs. 9 = £1, the new rate at which supply is equal to demand.

There are, however, limits to the movement of exchange rates on B/Es. Suppose Indian exports exceed imports and the exchange rate appreciates to Rs. 9 = £1. A further appreciation may not be possible. Once again, let us begin with a par exchange rate of Rs. 10 = £1 in accordance to gold (or silver) content of the coins and assume that the cost of import of bullion is 10 per cent, i.e. Re.1 or £0.10. The £-s-d system refers to pounds-shillings-pence respectively where 1s = 12d. and 1£ = 20s. If so, the rupee cannot appreciate beyond Rs. 9 = £1 because if it were to, Indian exporters would insist on payment in bullion or coin instead of B/Es. Why would I_X want to settle a £1 debt for only Rs. 8 through a B/E when it could instead import gold itself for Rs. 9 (i.e. net of import costs)? Point m in Figure 2.6 is the so called 'gold import point' (into India) beyond which appreciation of the rupee is not likely. Similarly, there exists a 'gold export point' (from India), x, beyond which the rupee cannot depreciate. Here English exporters would insist on payment in bullion or coin from India rather than accept depreciated rupees.

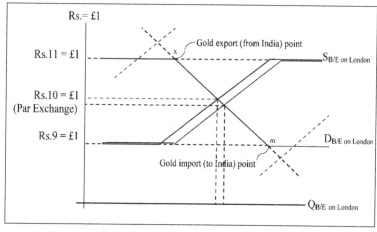

Figure 2.6: Gold Export and Import Points in the
B/E on London Market

The same logic would apply if we consider the 'B/E on Calcutta' market that develops in London as in Figure 2.7. If English exports exceeded imports, the pound would appreciate from Re. 1 = 2s. to (say) Re.1 = 1s.9d. This will dampen exports in England (decrease supply of B/Es on Calcutta in London) and encourage imports (increase demand for B/Es on Calcutta in London). If England's imports exceed their exports, the demand for B/Es would exceed supply and sterling would depreciate to (say) 2s.3d. This will dampen imports (decrease demand for B/E on Calcutta in London) while stimulating exports from England (increase supply of B/E on Calcutta in London) until equilibrium is restored. But as in the above case there is a gold export point (x') from England and a gold import point (m') into England. When sterling depreciates below 2s.3d to the rupee, England's importers will ship gold to India rather than buying bills on Calcutta in London at this rate. Similarly, if the sterling appreciates to anything above 1s.9d., English exporters will insist on gold being imported into England from India rather than accepting bills on Calcutta.

Leon Walras (1877) in his classic treatise, *Elements of Pure Economics*, believed that exchange rates for bills of exchange are an efficient way in which equilibrium in real markets is attained;

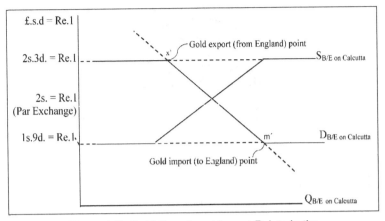

Figure 2.7: Gold Export and Import Points in the
B/E on Calcutta Market

Thus the world market for bills of exchange serves as a vast clearing house where the transactions of all countries are liquidated by the mere payment of differences. And this result is obtained purely and simply by the automatic operation of the mechanism of free competition. The law of supply and demand regulates all these exchanges of commodities just us the law of universal gravitation regulates the movements of all celestial bodies. Thus the system of the economic universe reveals itself, at last, in all its grandeur and complexity: a system at once vast and simple, which, for sheer beauty, resembles the astronomic universe. (p. 374)

The market for bills of exchange was further strengthened with the entry of banks. The banks not only took on the role of a broker for bills so that the search costs of traders fell but with their correspondents or other independent reputable banks across the world they were in a position to act as 'acceptor' of bills of exchange. By accepting a B/E the broker-bank assumes future payment obligations of the debtor (importer) so that an exporter (say I_X) could easily sell in Calcutta a B/E drawn on E_M. The service of accepting bills of exchange (acceptor) on behalf of the drawee, provided the drawee deposited a certain sum of money with the broker-bank, was carried out by the London merchant banks that developed into a 'bills on London' market, a reputable form of payment in international trade. In Figure 2.8, the broker-bank offers to purchase 'B/E

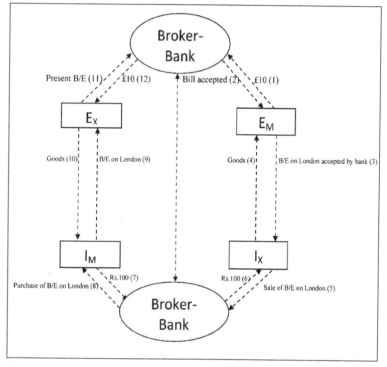

Figure 2.8: Bills of Exchange Markets with Broker-Bank Intermediation
(Commissions, Fees, etc. not included)

on London' from firms like I_X, for sale to firms like I_M in Calcutta. However, it must be kept in mind that that although the broker-bank acts as a guarantor, there was still the possibility of default by the importer at the time of final settlement.

The broker-bank in England would also buy 'B/E on Calcutta' from exporters like E_X which could then be sold to E_M. Given that the acceptor is an English bank rather than an importer in India, the B/E on Calcutta becomes more easily saleable in London markets. Consequently this buying and selling generates a market for B/E on Calcutta in London.

In this section we have discussed the use of bills of exchange as an *instrument of remittance*; bills of exchange also developed into an *instrument of credit*. I defer the study of this aspect to a later chapter.

2.2: THE HUNDI

The bulk of its work, for it was a thriving district, was hoondi and accommodation of all kinds. A fool has no grip over this sort of business; and a clever man who does not go about among his clients, and knows more than a little of their affairs, is worse than a fool.

RUDYARD KIPLING

Bills of exchange called hundi were widely used in India for domestic and, to a limited extent, even in international transactions since medieval times. The hundi business was in the control of a community of indigenous bankers who would issue and discount them to facilitate the transfer of funds from place to place. In Figure 2.9 we illustrate how hundi worked through a process of cancelation. The deliverer deposits money with a bank-broker in Place X for which he receives a B/E or hundi in exchange. This is sent by post to the merchant's client or the payee in Place Y who will submit the hundi to the drawee (the bank-broker's correspondent) in exchange for cash.

Hundis were usually payable on a specified date, according to convenience. For instance, 41 days at Benares, Bombay, Mirzapur and Lucknow, 61 days at Fatteghar and Faruckabad, 121 days at

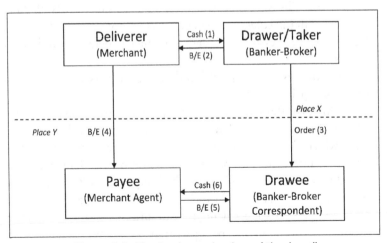

Figure 2.9: The basic mechanism of the *hundi*

Lahore and Multan. Some hundi were drawn as sight bills, sometimes known as *darsani* bills, with the first of three copies known
as *khoka*, the second known as *penth* and the third as *parapenth*.
The rate of discount was known as *hundiyana* and varied with the
state of trade and standing of the party. In Bombay, for instance,
the Multani bankers' main line of business was to deal in hundi
from which their annual profits amounted to several lakhs of rupees.
The hundi was transferable by endorsement and changed hands
like bills of exchange (Rau, 1922, p. 114). Given that local customs
and traditions governed this business that was carried on by specific
communities only, dishonouring of a hundi was very rare. Foreign
observers have noted with wonder how these hundi passed unquestioned not only across the length and breadth of the country but also
outside India in places like the erstwhile Constantinople (Istanbul).
With each adaptation to meet special circumstances, a large variety
of them came into existence under names like Shah Jog, Name
Jog, Dhani Jog, Jababi, 'bandyemudet' (*band-i-mudat* = fixed period
of settlement), etc. To avoid circulation of fake hundi, codes between
the drawer and drawee existed. Figures were expressed as fractions
of larger sums or multiples of small sums, the number of lines in
the bill was scrupulously stated and the name of the scribe of the
hundi appended. The transactions costs of the hundi system were
so low that bills were even issued for sums as small as Rs. 9. Apart
from avoiding needless movements of currency, etc., the hundi enhanced in a high degree the safety of financial operations and investments.

A sample text of a typical hundi along with its English transla-
tion is given in Box 2.1.

In this case Ram Bihari Lal of Ujjain was the drawer or taker,
Messrs. Ala Baksh and Madho Lal of Indore was the drawee or the
party which owed the money, the hundi was drawn in favour of the
Bank of Indore, or the payee. The name of the deliverer is not
available here. The date given on the hundi is sudi 8 in the month
Bhadwa of the year 1978 in the Samvat calendar (i.e. 9 September
1921 in the Christian calendar). The original bears the drawee's
acceptance, the signature being written across. Who could be the
buyer of this hundi, or in other words the deliverer? One possibility

---

Box 2.1: A Typical Hundi

USANCE HUNDI

To Sidh Sri Indore maha sulh sutank bhai Ala Baksh Madho
LaL likhi Ujjain se Ram Bihari Lai ka Ram Ram banchna.
Appranch Hundi 1 rupia 2,500 ankre pachis sau jiska nima rupia
sarhe bara sau ka duna pura athe rakha. The Bank of Indore Limited
pasmiti Bhadwasudi 8 se din 60 sath pichhe name sah jog Hundi
chalan kaldar dija miti Bhadwa sudi 8 Samwaf 1978.

LITERAL TRANSLATION

To the most propitious place Indore Messrs. Ala Bakhsh and
Madho Lal written from Ujjain Ram Bihari Lai sends greetings.
Furthermore one hundi for rupees 2,500 in words twenty-five hundred
and half of which is twelve hundred and fifty pay double of this to
the Bank of Indore Limited, from Bhadwa sudi 8 after 60 days in
current money with Emperor's head after due inquiry. Bhadwa sudi
8 Samvat 1978.

Source: Stanley H. Jevons, *Money, Banking and Exchange in India*,
Government Central Press, Simla, 1922, p. 312.

---

is a person wanting to send money to a relative from Ujjain to Indore.
Or it could have been a merchant who had imported some goods
to Ujjain and had to settle the claim of the supplier in Indore
(Jevons, 1922, p. 312). Like bills of exchange, the exchange rate of
hundis could also fluctuate; if the imports of Ujjain from Indore
were large as compared to that of Indore from Ujjain, the rates at
Ujjain for hundi on Indore would be higher than in Indore for
hundi on Ujjain.

Hundi exchange rates also fluctuated in response to market uncertainties; the following remark reflects these risks: 'These are today's rates. God knows tomorrow's.' (Muranjan, 1952, p. 12). Through
a wide-spread network of branches and agents, the indigenous
bankers maintained a system of intelligence and information to
mitigate these uncertainties. For example, the branch of the house
of Dixit-Patwardhan located at Bombay communicated with its

head office at Poona frequently, almost daily, on local developments that could impact the money markets. Details pertaining to the state of monsoon or the course of prices, the prices of precious metals, etc., were all carefully recorded. It is equally remarkable to record that as late as 1840 the British disaster in Afghanistan was known to Calcutta shroffs much earlier than the government. Again in 1844, the native *dak* beat the Government *dak* 'as usual' by some hours in conveying the news of the war fronts in Gwalior and the Punjab, causing fluctuations in the money market (ibid, p. 12). In fact, governments of the day often found it useful to use the information of these indigenous bankers as intelligence for their strategies and policies.

More than any other foreign power, it was the East India Company that aligned itself to the indigenous bankers, utilizing the latter's information network as well as their banking services for transfer of funds from place to place. At that time there were essentially three ways of transporting money into provincial districts for the purpose of investment (purchase of goods for export to England) that amounted to several million sterling by the early decades of the nineteenth century;

- carrying coin and bullion
- using government bills
- through hundi.

The transport of coin and bullion was by and large considered unsafe with dacoity and theft being a common phenomenon on Indian highways. The second alternative would be for a merchant to offer money to the Treasury in (say) Calcutta which would issue an order to the district collector of land-tax or customs. The collector's dues to the Treasury would be set off to the extent of payment made by him to the merchant. However, in situations where the collector was at a distance away from the location where payments had to effected, the merchant would prefer using the hundi. These means of transmission have been illustrated in Figure 2.10. While the cost of remittance through hundi was considered at about three times that of remitting funds within Europe, it was considered as perhaps the most perfect part of the indigenous Indian commercial

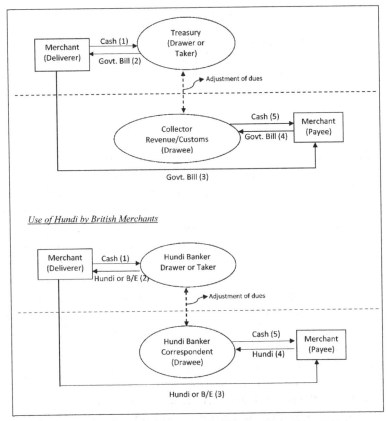

Figure 2.10: Use of Government Bills and Hundi by British Merchants to Transmit Funds Across India

system with non performance at the time of maturity being just about a fraction of a per cent.

Even today the hundi continues to be an important instrument in informal money markets across Asia, although they have often been used to effect illegal transfers internationally. In India, for instance, hawala transactions have become a cause for concern to the government. At the same time, the efficiency and reliability of monetary transfer between nations using these informal systems have been appreciated and considered as fitting competition to formal banking channels.

2.3: FACILITATING A CRISIS

This glimmering of hope set the busy ones to work, and when once the contagion took place, it spread like wild fire. Rich chiefs of provinces, collectors of the revenue, salt agents, fortunate soldiers, lawyers, doctors, tailors, barbers, and Undertakers ; all! all! became or employed, supercargoes and export merchants!

A FREE MERCHANT IN BENGAL, 1783

Bills of exchange were widely used in the seventeenth century by the Company's servants for remittance of their wealth acquired in India to England. This proved a mutually convenient arrangement; the Company was under pressure in England to minimize export of bullion while their servants in India were always eager, given the nature of the voyage, to find a safer alternative than to carry their savings from salaries and profits from private trade back to England in the form of bullion. The Company servants and/or private agents in India would deposit sums of money in the Company's treasury in exchange for B/E drawn on the Court of Directors in London. The Company could use the money so received for its investments (purchase of goods for export) in India, which would be realized in England after sales of cargo imported from India. The amount borrowed could then be settled by discharging their bills of exchange to the payee. Figure 2.11 schematically illustrates the remittance economy that developed in post-diwani Bengal using bills of exchange drawn on London. Although we do not have a clear picture on the exchange rate on bills during the early phase of the Company's history, we can infer that it may well have been stable and close to the par exchange rate.

In the post-diwani period the importance of bills of exchange grew rapidly. Unfortunately, the outcome of this development was rather paradoxical; though a new payment system should have promoted exchange, trade and commerce, the impact on Bengal was quite the opposite. This was simply because B/E facilitated the transfer of wealth accumulated by the Company's servants and private merchants in India to England. This caused a drain of currency from Bengal, which as we have seen aggravated the Great Famine in 1770. There was another route through which servants

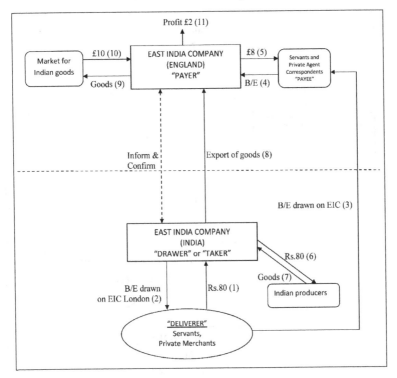

Figure 2.11: The Remittance Economy using Bills of Exchange

and private agents of the Company could remit their wealth to England using B/E. Foreign trading companies were keen to acquire silver in Calcutta for their China tea trade instead of procuring the metal in European ports like Cadiz, Spain. Sailing to Calcutta with nothing more than 'vile lumber' on board, the French, Danes and Swedes would sell bills drawn on Europe (say Cadiz) to the English subjects in Calcutta. With the silver acquired in exchange at Calcutta they would buy local articles like tin and pepper for sale in China. The proceeds would then be used for procurement of Chinese tea that would be sold in Cadiz, part of proceeds used to settle the bills drawn on Cadiz. By drawing bills on Europe, English subjects would be willing to give their silver (in Calcutta) in exchange for bills drawn on Europe. This scheme of transferring funds from Bengal to Europe is illustrated in Figure 2.12.

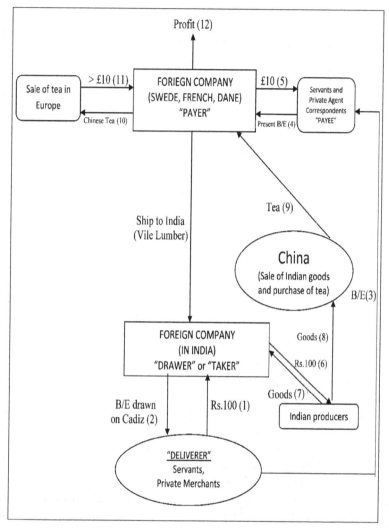

Figure 2.12: Remittances from India through China Trade

The remittance economy that developed post-diwani took a toll on Bengal's real economy, the implications of which extended far beyond the acute impact of the famine. A free merchant in his letters to the then Governor-General of the Company, Warren Hastings, tells us how trade turned from boon to bane.

Box 2.2: The Ruin of Bengal's Exports

These unnatural attempts to force back the dream of wealth to its fountain head had the same effect in mercantile polity, as the attempting to force a great river, with all its supplies and acquisitions of water, after a long course of running, back through the little channel from whence it took its rise: it overwhelmed the schemers with ruin. Had it ended there, it would not have signified much but its baneful influence extended much further. These new adventurers became rivals to the Company, and to one another. Their eagerness to buy up the manufactures of the country, raised the price, and sunk the real value: for the goods were so much debased, that though they cost more than thirty per cent, above what the same goods had formerly cost, yet at the markets to which they were carried, they would not produce anything like their prime cost, and many of them would not sell at all. At this unlucky period, the kingdom was visited by that most dreadful of all calamities, a famine, which swept away, perhaps, one fourth part of the labouring people: this increased the difficulty of obtaining wrought goods, and contributed still more to the debasing of their texture, which, by its effects, almost entirely annihilated the former great and beneficial trade of white cloth, from Bengal to the Gulfs of Mocha and Persia.

In the Asiatic section of the globe, the silk and cotton manufactures of Bengal, which were formerly so famous all the world over, had now lost their value, and were no longer sought after: others were found out which answered the purpose full as well, and came much cheaper. Yet the European nations still coveted the goods of this country. First, from a jealousy to one another; secondly, for the sake of the raw materials it produced; thirdly, from their having nothing to substitute in place of the coarse and fine cotton cloths of Bengal, which, inferior as they were, to those formerly manufactured still sold for a small profit in Europe; and lastly, the English East India Company had no other method of drawing home the tribute from their Indian subjects. The trade carried on in the country vessels, instead of being, as formerly, in favour of Bengal, was absolutely against it.

Source: *Five Letters from a Free Merchant in Bengal to Warren Hastings,* Esq., London, 1782, pp. 15–16.

Although one might be led to believe that alternative forms of money would have led to greater exchange and prosperity, bills of exchange had in fact assisted in the drain of silver bullion and coin from Bengal, causing its ruin from which it was perhaps never able to recover to its former glory.

2.4: TOO BIG TO FAIL

It is a description that means almost exactly the opposite of what it seems. 'Too big to fail' doesn't mean a financial institution cannot fail, but that it cannot be allowed to do so. Should that failure occur, it would bring catastrophe to the financial markets and the 'real' economy.

KNOWLEDGE AT WHARTON, 2009

The remittance economy also took its toll on the East India Company. To trace the sequence of events that sunk the Company into a crisis in 1772 we must go back to events that followed the acquisition of diwani. The euphoria of diwani soon translated into exaggerated expectations of the Court of Proprietors as well as the Crown. The former suggested a best of both worlds solution; an annual dividend of 14 per cent for the next 50 years and £900,000 to be paid annually into the exchequer. Some even suggested, basing themselves on the expected returns from the diwani, that a yearly dividend of 50 per cent might actually be a reasonable, perhaps an even conservative demand. As opposed to these claims the Court of Directors were, however, more realistic suggesting a dividend of just 12.5 per cent with the remainder of profits divided equally between discharging of accumulated debt and payment to the exchequer. Finally, after extended negotiations amongst the parties, an annual dividend of 10 per cent and payment to the exchequer of £400,000 was agreed upon. To meet these commitments, the Court of Directors had little choice but to enhance the investments in India (purchase of Indian goods for export to England) from £350,000 to £800,000 in addition to another £300,000 investment in China. The only issue was to find a source of money to pay for these investments. The answer was plain; the revenue from their territorial acquisition would be used to make purchases locally, the goods shipped to England and proceeds from their sales would become the Company's revenue. To ensure that revenues generated in India would be used for investment the Court of Directors prohibited their Indian governments from drawing 'Bills on London'. If they were allowed to do so, the governments in India would be able to raise loans in India but pass on the responsibility of payment on to the Company in London.

The effect of the ban on issuing B/E on London meant that private remittances had to be made via other foreign companies through B/E drawn by them on Europe. With this route being used for the transfer of wealth, inflow of specie by foreign companies from Europe to Bengal also ceased. By 1768, the sustained drain of currency from Bengal ultimately led the Court of Directors to relent on the ban imposed on issue of bills drawn on them in London. A nominal amount of about £200,000 was allowed in 1768 and again in 1769. These bills were drawn 365 days after sight and at an exchange rate of 2s.2½d to 2s.3d without interest in the event of payment being delayed.

At this point, the governments of Bengal and Madras acted surreptitiously; they concocted a plan to accumulate a fund of ten million rupees or £1,125,000 in cash to be used in case of wars and the consequent stoppage of territorial supplies, occasioned by Hyder Ali's visit to the Carnatic in 1768. To draw off remittances being made through other foreign companies, the Bengal Government on receiving orders from the Court of Directors opened its treasury for bills but not for £200,000; instead it accepted a sum £1,063,067. These bills on London were drawn at 365, 730 and 1095 days sight, bearing interest at per cent after the first 90 days, and at a rate of about Re. 1 = 2s.2½d. and 2s.3d. the current rupee (~Rs. 8.89 = £1) while the par rate stood at Re. 1 = 2s (Rs. 10 = £1).

Moreover, the governments in India unilaterally decided to restrict their investments in India to just about £500,000 or about one-half of their usual allocations. 'When intelligence of these proceedings reached the Court of Directors, it came like a messenger of death, as if to seal their future doom' (Rickards, 1832, p. 523). With the burden to settle dues of over a £1 million in bills on London and without the possibility for sales revenues, the Company was staring at bankruptcy. The governments in Bombay and Madras followed the defiant measures adopted by Bengal but to a far smaller degree. Meanwhile, the government of Bengal, as an ameliorative step, decided to purchase goods locally, called 'ready money goods' for export to the tune of close to £1 million; the money for this was raised not through bills but through sale of 8 per cent bonds. The 'ready money goods' were, however, of poor quality and sold below prime cost. Nonetheless, upon their sale in England, they provided some temporary liquidity to (Directors of) the Company. But the threat of default had only been postponed and not dispensed with; in spite of their condition, dividends of 12 per cent were declared. Finally, in July 1772, the day of reckoning arrived. To meet the payments between July and the end of October, the Com-pany needed funds to the amount of £1,293,000 but its coffers were empty. Just seven years after acquisition of diwani, by which the Company had become *de facto* ruler of one of India's most prosperous regions with access to some £3,000,000 in revenue, it was forced to petition Parliament and the Bank of England for a bailout package of £1,400,000. So disastrous was this revelation of the Company's affairs that its stock prices crashed from 220 to 139 in the span of a few months.

The logic for bailout of the Company would be quite familiar to most of us today; 'too big to fail.' An archival document provides an interesting summarization of this phrase that is both relevant to the Company's situation at that time but also in a contemporary context:

If the Company did not receive an adequate assistance, inevitable ruin was the attendant consequence; and the bankruptcy of a body of merchants so extensive in their concerns and of such importance in the opinion of all Europe, must necessarily give a very alarming blow to our national credit. On the other hand, though it was absolutely necessary to permit the acceptance of these bills, it would have been a measure deserving the severest censure, if the public faith had been pledged for their payment, without a previous examination into the affairs of the Company, and forming some plan for reforming their continuation. (Historical and Chronological Deduction of the Origin of Commerce, 1789, p. 512)

Several actions were taken by the British government following the bailout loan given to the Company,[1] including capping of dividends, presenting half-yearly accounts to the Treasury, restriction on issue of bills, fixing export targets and curtailing the manipulative practices of stock-jobbers. But it was one concession in particular made by Parliament to the East India Company that turned out to be a 'fatal boon' (Knight, 1870, p. 335); the granting of permission to the Company to sell stocks of seventeen million pounds of tea, valued at some £2,000,000 (Bowen, 1991, p. 122), lying in its warehouses in American ports with a duty drawback payable in England. This, as we know, triggered the Boston Tea Party and eventually the American War of Independence.

The Company's predicament became the focal point of fervent public debate. Report after report on mismanagement by their servants in India poured in, receiving a great deal of attention in several published works of that time including official documents, journals, books and magazines. And the Company responded to these charges with its own reports. The published reports on its debt are voluminous but rhetoric and counter-rhetoric in the writing, accounting and arithmetic confuses rather than clarifies the true state of the Company's finances. Critiques claimed that debt accumulated by the Company ever since acquisition of diwani in 1765 was on account of their commercial activities, not territorial expansion. In fact, revenues from territorial acquisitions had consistently yielded considerable surpluses over and above the charges incurred in this activity, which had been dissipated in remittances to England using the purchase of goods in India for export as a conduit. Trade and commerce, as intended and carried out by the Company was, therefore, the actual cause of the Company's bourgeoning debt and its consequent, albeit devious, debt management strategy. Some critiques like Richard Rickards (1832) even went on to assert that commercial activity of the Company was unprofitable and sustained only on debt, not just since assumption of diwani but ever since the first charter of Queen Elizabeth in 1600.

The Company's financial position, it seemed, changed for the better over the next few years. In 1776, the loan of £1,400,000 was reduced to £420,000 and fully paid off in 1777. By 1779, its bond debt was reduced to £1,500,000. From 1 April 1780, the (English) public was entitled to a share of surplus revenues accruing from India. Meanwhile, the Company was allowed to raise its dividends to a maximum of 8 per cent. Supporters of the Company also narrate with great pride two contributions made in 1779; a bounty to support 6,000 seamen for public service and three navy ships built for the king, each with 74 guns. In 1781, the Company reported a total surplus of revenues plus profits from trade at £688,025. After paying to the public the stipulated share of £400,000, the Company chose to retain the balance £288,000 in a *separate fund*. With conditions attached on the sharing of surpluses, the Company was able to procure an extension of its Charter preserving its exclusive trade and possession of Indian territories till 1791. But this was only the calm before the storm. Having incurred large expenditure on the wars with the Marathas and Hyder Ali of Mysore, the East India Company in 1782 was unable to settle its customs dues and other commitments on its territorial acquisitions. By 1783, the Company was once again close to bankruptcy.

Just as in 1772, a significant portion of the problem for the Company arose from drawing of bills of exchange on London and it was the 'too big to fail' argument that got the government to bail it out. But the bailout came at a cost; the intrusions by the government subsequently increased with the passing of William Pitt's India Bill of 1784 wherein a Board of Control was set up to supervise and control the activities of the Company. What is interesting in the debate over the bailout is the clear reference to the inherent 'systemic risk' associated with the closure of the Company, a concern that has made governments to bail out financial sector companies today.

From then onwards, the East India Company turned away from England and to India to raise loans. While their debt in England increased from £12,850,166 to £15,443,349 between 1772 and 1786, the corresponding debt in India increased from £1,850,166 to £10,464,955. As we will see in a later chapter, the indigenous financiers of the Company in this period came to be likened to the Rothschilds of England.

NOTE

1. Amongst these was the Regulation Act of 1773 which brought about many reforms in administration of the Company and in the judicial structure. It was also, as Buchan argues, a step towards separation of control and ownership (Buchan, 1994, p. 61).

CHAPTER 3

Commercial Credit

The subject of Credit is the greatest and most abstruse in Political Economy; what the Differential calculus is in mathematics, what Steam is in mechanics, that is Credit in commerce.

HENRY DUNNING MACLEOD

Like money, most of us might have an intuitive understanding of what credit is. However, if asked to articulate a definition, it is not as simple as it seems. Nonetheless it is common knowledge today that at the root of many crises is the over-expansion of credit. This makes it all the more important for us to cut through the jargon and get to its essence. By doing so we will be in a position to not only comprehend crises in a different light but also appreciate the critical role that credit plays in a modern economy.

3.1: THE ECONOMICS OF COMMERCIAL CREDIT

Credit . . . is the only enduring testimonial to man's confidence in man.

JAMES BLISH

Credit is to money what money is to articles of merchandise.

WEBSTER

We have seen how bills of exchange were used as money for the purpose of remittance; however, by the fifteenth century these bills increasingly began to be used as an instrument of *credit* in the trade between England and the Low Countries (which includes the modern states of Belgium, Netherlands and Luxembourg). The Staplers and Merchant Adventurers from England sold wool and cloth respectively in the Low Countries from where their monies had to be remitted back home. Another group called the Mercers imported silk and other fabrics into England. They needed money in the Low Countries to make their purchases before the goods could be exported to England where they would receive proceeds from sales. A system developed through the use of bills of exchange whereby the Mercers would reimburse the Staplers and Merchant Adventurers in England in exchange for money in the Low Countries. But this transaction went beyond the usual spatial transfer of funds; the Staplers and Merchant Adventurers ended up funding the Mercers through a system of credit, the latter conveniently settling their debt after completion of their sales transactions in England.

Figure 3.1 illustrates the mechanism for remittance of money using bills of exchange. The stepwise flow of goods and claims can be followed from the figure; what cannot be seen is the delay between the delivery of funds by the Staplers and Merchant Adventurers to the Mercers in the Low Countries and the return of the money by the Mercers to the former groups back in England. This delay between the time when funds were delivered and the time when it was returned was *credit* available to the Mercers.

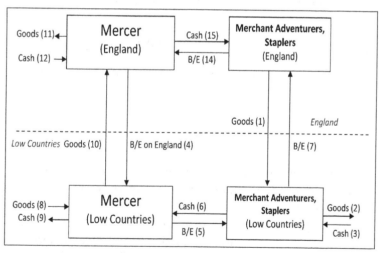

Figure 3.1: The Basic Mechanism of Credit Through
use of Bills of Exchange

Bills of exchange, although they began solely for the purpose of remittance, increasingly became an instrument to finance trade. Figure 3.2 shows how trade credit or trade finance between Firm A in location X and its correspondent in country Y, denoted as A_Y is raised without the use of bills of exchange. Here, the sequence begins with the A_X borrowing money in country X to finance its exports. The cash realized from sales by A_Y is then sent back to A_X from which debts would have to be repaid. Now suppose interest rates in country Y are much lower than in country X so that it may well be economical for A to borrow money in country Y to finance its purchase of goods in country X. How can trade credit be organized through bills of exchange? In Figure 3.3, A_X sells bills of exchange drawn on A_Y in X. From the cash received it would fund its purchases for export. The bills of exchange would be sent to A_Y for clearing at which time A_Y would borrow money in Y and honour these bills. The goods are sent by A_X to A_Y, the latter would carry out sales and pay off the debt in Y. Firm A has therefore managed to effectively borrow money in country Y to fund its exports instead of borrowing in country X where interest rates could be substantially higher. In this way, bills of exchange began to be used as instru-

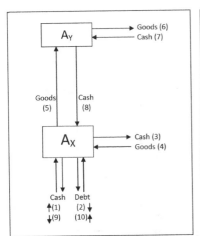

Figure 3.2: The Transaction Sequence of Exchange Without Bills of Exchange

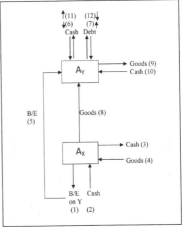

Figure 3.3: Bills of Exchange as an Instrument of Credit

ments of trade credit more than as instruments for remittance of money.

Bills of exchange were sometimes used exclusively as credit instruments. This method of raising credit, called 'dry exchange', was adopted in Venice many hundreds of years ago. As can be inferred from Figure 3.4, the time between issue of the bill on X by Y and the subsequent return of bill on Y for encashment is the period of the loan. Another method that could have been adopted to raise a loan could be through the refusal of X to honour the bill so that it would be returned to Y for settlement. In this case the transaction costs would be that of lodging or registering a complaint against X.

Although the analysis so far gives us a feel of how bills of exchange served as credit, it does not explicitly reveal the essence of credit. In attempting to get to this, I came across a fascinating work by Macleod (1863) which demystifies the notion of credit at

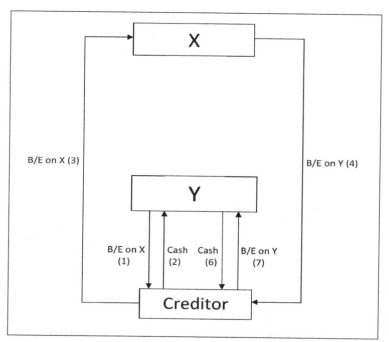

Figure 3.4: Bills of Exchange as Purely an Instrument of Credit

the most fundamental level. The remaining part of this section is based on his analysis.

Macleod introduces us to the essence of credit by drawing out the difference between Bills of Lading and Bills of Exchange. The captain of the vessel as the holder of a bill of lading does not own the goods, he is merely a *bailee* or trustee or safe keeper of the goods and is not entitled to do what he pleases with the goods. Possession of the bill of lading does not entitle him to dispose-off the goods. The bill of lading only represents goods, the document by itself has no value, and it cannot be exchanged independently of the goods it represents. Since only those goods or properties which can be exchanged have value, bills of lading have no value; it is not surprising that no one speaks of the *value* of a bill of lading. What about a bill of exchange? In the case of a bill of exchange, ownership of goods actually passes over *to the buyer* (of the goods) in exchange for a *bill* or *an order to pay* issued to him. This is the essential nature of *credit* as distinct from *bailment*; a bill of lading represents property while a bill of exchange does not represent goods at all (for the ownership of the goods has been passed on to the buyer of goods). It represents nothing but debt (an obligation), not even specific money. It is created as a substitute for money to transfer property, but it does not represent money any more than money represents it.

As illustrated in Figure 3.5 suppose B draws a bill of exchange on A or an order to pay on A (in exchange for goods sold by B to A). B then endorses it in favour of C in exchange for goods from C to B. Now C will neither have any claims over the goods sold by him to B nor over the goods sold by B to A. C could now send back the 'Bill on A' to A and get money in exchange. Or C could even buy goods from D by endorsing the 'Bill on A' in favour of D. Each of these endorsements represents nothing but debt and is neither claim over specific goods or over specific money.

From the example above it is evident that credit or debt is tradable, just as we trade any other commodity for money. There is, however, a crucial difference; trading with money is to trade with the earnings of *past* industry, trading with credit is to trade with the *expected earnings* of *future* industry. An illustration could help

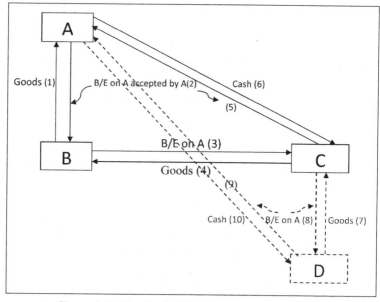

Figure 3.5: The Basic Bill of Exchange Transaction
to Raise Credit

in clarifying this statement. Suppose I had a silver rupee coin. Going back to Chapter 1, this means I have given *someone* in society goods or services worth a rupee and *anyone* in society must give me a rupee's worth of goods or services when I demand it. The rupee I posses is evidence of my past work and service to society. Consider a situation where I do not have a rupee coin at this moment but a possibility exists that I will have it a year later, from my future work. With credit I can get goods now from someone in society (say from B) in exchange for credit based on my future activity; in other words, I will have to give back the rupee plus interest to anyone in society at a future date, i.e. to whosoever holds the instrument of credit (say to C as the holder of the bill of exchange). Let me elaborate further; in exchange for goods, A creates a credit in B's favour promising him an equal amount of money on demand. The transaction is essentially an exchange or a sale wherein A buys the goods (or money) from B by selling him the right to demand an equal quantity of money at any time he pleases. A *new property is, therefore, created* by nothing else than the mutual consent of both parties, A and B. B may transfer this property to C or whomsoever he pleases, and it has value, because B or C (the owner of it) can exchange it for money, or anything else. It is called credit because B or C (as the owner of it) *believes*, but does not *know* (as in the case of a bill of lading), that he can obtain money for it. Moreover, unlike a bill of lading, in a bill of exchange there are no certain goods or specific money assigned to the credit. A is not the trustee or bailee of some specific goods; if he goes bankrupt then B or C may not get back the entire sum of money they are entitled to. Only a part may be received after liquidation of A's properties.

To put it simply, the debt or obligation of A has been traded by endorsement (which transfers the right to demand the money the debt is said to represent) just like money. A exchanges the bill of exchange with B, then B does so with C . . . and so on. Credit, therefore, makes the future productivity of an individual (or for that matter any productive unit), into an economic good that can be exchanged. Furthermore, although bills of exchange are exchangeable for commodities *in general*, it does not represent them. Credit is separate and independent exchangeable property. It is the *value* of commodities, but does not represent any specific or certain commodities. Money too is separate and independent of specific goods and may be considered as the highest and most general form of credit.

In Figure 3.5 although A has received goods from B, this kind of *commercial credit* is usually not expressed as a promise to repay goods but is invariably expressed as a promise to repay an equivalent amount of money. Sometimes commercial credit also entails loaning of money; when a person lends money to another, the loan is actually a sale. The property in the money passes absolutely to the borrower in exchange for the right or property to demand an equal (but not identical) sum of money at some future time. A commercial loan is therefore a sale and a new property called debt is created where the debt itself can be traded in a market like any other commodity.

By interpreting the algebra of signs in political economy, Macleod further argues that credit can be understood as a negative quantity, where the negative sign must be interpreted as expected or future earnings from an asset; the returns which are already realized being given a positive sign. Take for instance the purchase of a piece of land for Rs. 100,000. Into what specific entity has the value of your money gone? Does it consist of things in the land which have value at the present moment of time? Obviously not. When you buy the land you buy it with a *belief* that you will receive a stream of income in future, forever. This is the *credit* of the land and it is the present value of a future income stream. It is an abstract right that becomes effective as it unfolds into existence over a period of time. In the same way, a trader's credit is his promise to pay over and above his earned and previously accumulated wealth. This credit no doubt depends on the confidence people have in the trader's ability to earn that future income but credit is not the confidence *per se* but the right over the money itself. This potential income is something that can be bought and sold although it is not physically present. Since it is exchangeable it has value and anything that has value is wealth; credit is therefore wealth.

For exchange to happen it is, however, imperative that credit or debt is measurable and measured. The unit adopted in measuring credit is *the debtors promise to pay the amount of Rs. 100 one year hence*. The *price* of that unit is the discount; thus if a banker or a broker buys a trader's promise to pay Rs. 100 one year hence at a price of Rs. 97 today, the discount is 3 per cent. This is how the price of credit is usually expressed.

What are the limits to credit? Now every transfer of a bill of exchange gives rise to the creation of a new property. It is the number of transfers possible then which acts as the limit to the creation of credit. The problem begins when the numbers of transfers multiply too fast; based on their belief of expected future profits, speculators buy goods with credit hoping that prices will rise. However, when several speculators have the same belief there is a glut of goods thrown into the market, prices crash and the profits from which they were expected to settle their bills fall short, promises are broken and the market sinks into crisis.

Although excessive commercial credit creation in an economy can cause crisis, it is nonetheless important to appreciate that credit is *productive* capital. To Macleod production is to draw forth and credit is in this sense productive not merely in manufacture but even in commerce and trade. Take for instance a retail dealer (R) who buys goods from a wholesaler at Rs. 100 and sells it at Rs. 140. In this case he has used his capital productively. However, suppose he had no money to buy goods from the wholesaler and instead allows the wholesaler to draw a 'Bill on R' (i.e. on him, the retailer) in exchange for the goods. With this ownership of the goods passes over to the retailer in exchange for the right or property of wholesaler to demand payment in (say) three months. By the mutual consent of the retailer and wholesaler a new property has been created which has an independent existence from the goods and can be exchanged between the wholesaler and another party. It is likely that out of the total profits of Rs. 40 a slice of the profits has to be paid to the wholesaler as the price of credit. Nonetheless the retailer is able to use the credit as productive capital to earn a profit which otherwise would not have been possible.

In this section we have discussed *commercial credit* using bills of exchange or what is referred to as 'Orders to Pay'. I postpone the discussion of banking credit using notes or 'Promises to Pay' to a later chapter. For now we look at credit in the Indian context where a market for it grew more out of debt of the East India than from the commercial exchanges of merchants. The effort of the Company to raise loans through issue of Treasury Bills was wrought with challenges. After all they had to convince their creditors that they would be in a position to honour their debt through expected future revenues that were expected to accrue not just from trade but also from political rule.

3.2: THE INDIA ROTHSCHILDS

Give me control of a nation's money and I care not who makes its laws.

MAYER AMSCHEL BAUER ROTHSCHILD

Although commercial credit was prevalent in medieval India, it was limited to one-time transactions; no markets for credit existed. Such debts were usually locked up in the books of traders, moving only once from the purchaser to the vendor, but not coming into general circulation. Amongst the many borrowers of such credit money for trade was the East India Company which, in its early years, sought loans from its Indian counterparts for the purposes of trade. There are several references to Virji Vora, one of India's most prominent seventeenth century merchants, having lent money to the Company. As early as 1619, to one of the earliest voyages of the Company to the west coast of India, he 'lent 25,000 mahmudis' (Mehta, 1991, p. 53). In 1635 he 'lent Rs. 20,000 . . . at 12 per cent' and in 1636, 'Rs. 30,000 and Rs. 2 lakhs at 12 per cent' (ibid., p. 57). These loans were raised by the Company on account of the deficient funds to make purchases and then settled with bullion received in due course from England. The Surat merchants had over 50 ships trading overseas and Virji Vora's estate was alone valued at some Rs. 8 million in the mid-seventeenth century. The Company's correspondence and travelers' notes described Vora as 'prime merchant of this town', 'the greatest Bania merchant' and 'the greatest and richest general merchant that inhabiteth the vast kingdom' (Muranjan, 1952, p. 11). Other prominent bankers and merchants that figure in the Company's records include Champa Shah of Patna and Gopaldas Sahu of Benares. But it is in the post-Plassey period, when the Company began its territorial expansion that its loan requirements particularly for war funding burgeoned exponentially. And some Indian merchant-bankers once again obliged the Company with funds.

In a work by James Douglas (1893) I came across an interesting letter by one Jeverilal U. Yagnik to the *Bombay Gazette* of 1881 which tells the story of a native banker who was once well-known all over Gujarat and India as the Hon'ble Company's shroffs, Trawadi (Trivedi) Shri Krishna Arjunji Nathji. Arjunji supposedly financed the Company on a scale of magnitude which surprised even the agents of the Company. Long before the Company began its relationship with English merchant bankers like Sir Charles Forbes it was able to meet its financial needs through indigenous bankers like Arjunji Nathji. The memory of this house as the Company's principal shroffs still lived on in Surat and Gujarat at the time of Yagnik's letter, i.e. 1881.

The first recorded acknowledgement of the Company's obligations to this native banking house bore the date of the 23 November 1759. It was signed by Mr. John Spencer, Chief of Surat, and four of his assistants; it ran as follows: 'These are to certify that the house of Trawadi was employed in transacting the money matters at Delhi relative to the procuring for the English a firman for the castle and a sanad for the fleet, in which they acted with great punctuality and fidelity. This writing is therefore given them as testimony of their good behaviour, and to show that the house is deserving of the countenance of the Hon'ble Company in case of any oppression to them' (ibid., p. 470).

This testimony is confirmed by another letter from Mr. E.H. Boddam, who wrote on 4 December, 1783; 'I do hereby declare that since my residence here as Chief of Surat, Trawadi Arjunji Nathji has always shown great attention and diligence for the interests of the Hon'ble East India Company, and has, by the transactions of his house as shroff, rendered them every assistance and service in his power, which at various times have been very essential' (ibid., p. 470).

Before coming into close relations with the Company, the dealings of Trawadi Shri Krishna Arjunji Nathji were chiefly with Arab merchants. He gradually curtailed these dealings as his relations with the Company grew stronger. In 1804 when war broke out between Bharatpur and the English, the Company was desperately in need of money. Jonathan Duncan, in his letters to the Company's agents at Surat, described in pitiful terms the condition of the troops, who were left in arrears, and reduced to misery for want of supplies. Native bankers, seeing the fortunes of the Company trembling in the balance, withdrew from lending money to it at a time when funds were most needed. Duncan, knowing where hope lay for a loan, wrote to the Chief Agent at Surat to open negotiations with Trawadi Arjunji Nathji. Nathji consented to make an advance, and a sum of Rs. 3.2 million was sent out in hard coin. The story goes that carts loaded with rupee bags extended in long, continuous rows on the streets of Surat. The loans proved fruitful; the Company's troops returned victorious. The joy and thankfulness of the Company on obtaining a loan from Nathji was overwhelming. Trawadi's services were acknowledged with *khillats*, medals, and grants, and recorded in handsome terms for the information of the Company's Directors in England. Trawadi, it is said, was made a member of the Council at Calcutta and officially proclaimed as the Company's shroff in India.

In another instance, Duncan had earnestly requested Trawadi Arjunji Nathji to advance Rs. 300,000 to the Gaikwad of Baroda. And yet again, when war broke out with Nepal (1813) it was once again Arjunji Nathji who supplied the funds. The amount of advances he made to Company's Government has not been recorded but it is a fact that on the successful termination of the war, Trawadi was bestowed with a *khillat* for the joy of capturing Nepal and praise of his services was recorded: 'I have no hesitation in saying that the records of the Chief Office bear numerous and very decided testimony of the merit and services of Trawadi, and proofs of his fidelity and attachment to the interests of the Hon'ble Company (ibid., p. 472).

Trawadi died in 1822, at the age of 72 years. But Yagnik sadly reveals that the descendants of the one who was nothing less than 'the Rothschild of India' were reduced to penury and actually starving in Surat within a period of just fifty years.

Even earlier to Shri Krishna's rise to the status of 'First Shroff of Gujarat' is the story of another indigenous banking family in eastern India, the Jagatseths, also referred to as 'the Rothschilds of India' and whose operations Edmund Burke described as being 'as extensive as those of the Bank of England' with their fortune *c.* 1750 estimated at more than £10 million. Many members of this great Indian banking family met a gruesome end in the conflicts that arose post-Plassey.

Two other personages, who were financial, though sometimes also political intermediaries between the Europeans and the Indian Government *c.* 1750, were Coja Wajid, an Armenian, and Omichand. The former, known by the title of Fakhr-uttujjar, or the 'chief of Merchants' was a very rich trader who had extensive dealings with the French and Dutch, and was employed by Nawab Siraj-ud-Daulah in his negotiations with the chiefs of these nations. At first, he was inclined to favour the French in their quarrels with the British but he was an extremely timid man, and after his property at Hughly had been plundered by the British, he gradually changed sides. It was from him that the British learnt of the Nawab's intrigues with the French Chiefs. Another important financial personality in the eighteenth century was Omichand, an inhabitant of Calcutta. His proper name was supposedly Amir Chand, a Punjabi. Omichand was offered the Nawabship of Purneah in 1754 and received a *parwana* granting him the same privileges as Jagatseth. Omichand had for many years acted as the Agent of the English in regard to the annual investment or purchase of Indian goods in Bengal, but when this office had been unfairly taken from him by some Englishmen he instigated Nawab Siraj-ud-Daulah to attack Calcutta, so that he might prove his importance to the British by stepping in as their saviour at the last moment. Whether he intended to ruin or save the British was never known as the British put him in prison as soon as the Nawab approached Calcutta. Omichand was so enraged that he not only refused to write a letter to the Nawab in favour of the British, but even sent his servants to inform the Nawab of the easiest way to introduce his forces into the town.

In the banking activities of the South, Gujarati merchants and bankers were quite frequently referred to. About 1740, the largest banking house of south India was reputed to be that of Bukanji Kasidas, a fact well attested by the frequency with which he is styled as 'Sarkar's sowkar and the Chief Shroff of the province' (Sundara Rajan, 1955, p. 316). The Nattukotai Chettiars, however, had not risen to prominence at this point of time as they would eventually in the latter half of the nineteenth century.

Over two centuries—the seventeenth and eighteenth—Indian merchants and bankers had played a critical role in Indian political history by providing credit to the East India Company to wage war and acquire control over the country. This credit was based on pure trust and undertaken at great risk, at a time when instruments of credit had no legal sanction, and when the future of the Company was not only unknown but virtually non-existent. The implicit faith of the Indian merchants could have been only one; the Company would be able to consolidate its power, profits and revenue so that they would be in a position to pay off their debts, both principal and interest. It is not difficult to understand Arjunji Nathji's predicament had the Company been defeated by Bharatpur. The so called 'Anglo-Bania' combine, however, began to change in the later part of the eighteenth century as the Company began to look to the rising class of English merchant-bankers for its war funding.

3.3: DECLINE OF INDIGENOUS FINANCIERS AND RISE OF NEW CREDIT INSTRUMENTS

Charles Forbes, Esq.
Dear Forbes,—Poverty again begins to stare me in the face. I have only a balance of Rs. 3233, pray inform his honour.—Yours, & c.

P. P. TRAVERS, COMPANY OFFICER, 1804

The East India Company's territorial expansion plan required large amounts of money to fund its several wars; the consequence was a frequent and severe crisis in the availability of currency, making the need for credit inevitable. For instance, in 1798 and 1799, at the time of the Fourth War of Mysore, the exigencies of the Company's finances turned grave when large arrears were due to the army and sepoys. To overcome the currency crises, Lord Wellesley stopped ships at Madras *en route* to Bombay from China, and is said to have taken out huge sums of specie for public service. But taking of specie, if it had to be differentiated from robbery, had to be acknowledged with an instrument of credit in return. Wellesley therefore gave owners of the specie, government *securities* at very attractive rates of interest of about 10 to 12 per cent and also accepted a discount on the face value of these securities. The effective yield[1] on the securities therefore turned out to be much higher. In addition to securities, the Madras Government also raised money for the war against Mysore by issuing 'Bills drawn on EIC Calcutta'. With the rate of exchange at 100 pagodas to Rs. 365 it drew bills for 170,000 pagodas at the rate of Rs. 410 to 100 pagodas (or 89 pagodas = Rs. 365), working out to a discount on the pagoda of 11 per cent.

The readers interested in economic details may want to know

the reason for these exchange rate fluctuations. Using the analysis developed in Chapter 2, I illustrate the exchange rate adjustment process in Figure 3.6(a) and 3.6(b). Here the supply of Bills on Calcutta is on account of the sellers, the East India Company (EIC) in Madras who actually wanted money from Calcutta (they are equivalent to exporters of goods to Calcutta). The demand for Bills on Calcutta is from private merchants who imported goods from Calcutta and had to make payments to people or firms in Calcutta. Due to an increased supply (shift in the supply curve) of Bills on Calcutta (as EIC Madras needed cash), the exchange rate of rupee fell below par in Madras. In other words, the pagoda appreciated (because of the heavy demand for it) so that the government got only 89 pagodas for every Rs. 365 in Calcutta. The private importers in Madras were better off because an imported article which cost rupees 365 earlier (or 100 pagodas) now cost them only 89 pagodas. This would provide a stimulus to imports from Calcutta and a corresponding increase in the quantity demanded for Bills on Calcutta.

Figure 3.6: The Market for Bills of Exchange on Calcutta

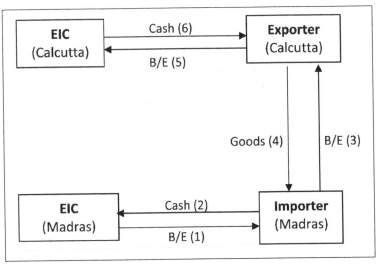

Figure 3.6(a): EIC Madras Issuing B/E on (EIC) Calcutta

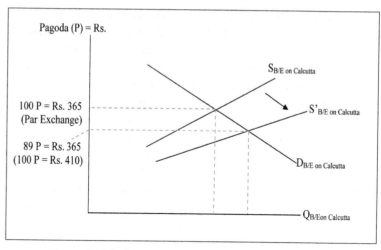

Figure 3.6(b): Discount on Bills of Exchange Drawn on Calcutta by EIC in Madras

In 1799, the Government of Madras opened a subscription for a loan against which bills of exchange on England for about 100,000 pagoda would be granted at 9s. to a pagoda (the par rate being 1 star pagoda = 8s.), at six months sight. For sake of completeness the exchange rate movements have been illustrated in Figures 3.7(a) and 3.7(b). These loans, raised in February 1799, at about 12 per cent, were called the War Loan. Funding the War of Mysore against Tipu Sultan had made it imperative for the Company to raise money in Bombay too. Securities bearing an interest of 6 per cent at a discount of 20 per cent on the face value were issued. Soon after another loan at 12 per cent interest had to be raised. The Government of Bombay also drew bills on England at 2s.10d. to the Bombay Rupee, at nine months sight. It was only after the War of Mysore ended on 4 February 1799 that the Company's financial situation improved.

The Company's tryst with bankruptcy in 1772 had brought it under increasing scrutiny of the Parliament and public opinion back home in England. This had compelled it to depend on India for funding its territorial expansion. But its sources here were limited to just two: indigenous merchants and shroffs, and English business

Figure 3.7: The Market for Bills of Exchange Drawn on London

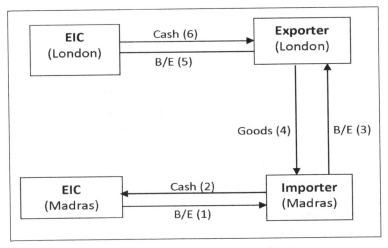

Figure 3.7(a): EIC Madras Issuing B/E on (EIC) London

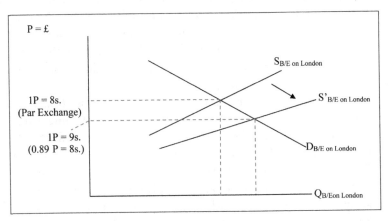

Figure 3.7(b): Discount on Bills of Exchange Drawn on
London by the EIC in Madras

houses. The government's keenness to lessen its dependence on individual indigenous bankers was possible only if a money market of wider appeal could be created. But good fortune was on its side; the English agency houses had by then accumulated a large quantum of loanable funds and second, the transition and consolidation of the Company as ruler or sovereign was becoming more real and convincing. The latter was critical for the Company's credit and its ability to raise money in the Indian market. Between 1785 and 1795 bonds of large and variable amounts like Rs. 100,000 gave place to bonds and certificates of fixed, standardized and convenient face values. Being made from engraved blocks, these bonds were better protected from forgery; they could be registered and were moreover long-dated instead of short-dated as before. The debt market was further widened from 1790 when arrangements were made for the public outside the metropolitan areas to receive interest from Revenue Collectors and Residents. From 1793, the non-metropolitan public was also allowed to subscribe to public loans.

It was becoming increasingly clear that the earlier personal Anglo-Bania[2] partnership was entering its last stages; a process that may well have been induced consciously by the emergent class of British merchant-bankers amongst whom one name stands out, Sir Charles Forbes. While Forbes shot into the limelight with the 'Northern Loan' of 1802, it was his advice and assistance to the Government of Bombay in times of crisis till about 1806 that not only ensured survival of the Company but also marked the beginning of the end of its dependence on indigenous bankers.

Once again, it was in the work by James Douglas, *Bombay and Western India: A Series of Stray Papers* (1893) that I came across a chapter entitled 'An Old Bombay Firm'. Writing towards the close of the nineteenth century, Douglas reminisces about the 'old Bombay' almost a hundred years earlier (*c.*1800) and how business was done not by 'persons' but by 'individuals'. But more importantly this chapter eloquently captures the pecuniary crisis faced by the Company and how it was resolved. The chapter also contains a collection of letters between the Governor of Bombay and Charles Forbes, which may be the only record of those letters.

'The following letters, relating to the preceding chapter, have been kindly placed at my disposal for publication, and now see the light for the first time, without addition or abridgement of any kind' (p. 253).

Towards the end of 1801, the Government of Bombay faced a severe scarcity of money. They signed an agreement with seven

Bombay merchants wherein the latter were to purchase 85,000 bales of the Company's cotton due for China at Rs. 10 per bale *cash down*. Armed cruisers accompanied the cotton laden ships as a convoy on their way to China. The merchants agreed to purchase no other cotton until this transaction was implemented. The estimated loan amount was £500,000 with interest to be paid by the government at the rate of 0.75 per cent per month, and at an exchange rate of 2s.6d. to a rupee on such amounts as might be repaid in England through bills of exchange drawn on London. These loans that extended over a period of two or three years were called the Northern Loan of 1802. This was perhaps the single largest contract undertaken till then but was the first instance of the 'new' commercial men of Bombay coming forward to assist the government with ready money. On the one side of this transaction was the Company and on the other side were Charles Forbes, just 29 years of age at that time, who represented the firm of Smith, Forbes and Co.; Henry Fawcett, who had been Accountant-General in 1792, who represented Bruce, Fawcett and Co.; Alexander Adamson; the Bomanjee Brothers; Hormusjee and Pestonjee; Ardaseer Dady Seth; and Sorabjee Muncherjee Readymoney.

The Northern Loan was probably used for the Battle of Assaye, fought in September, 1803. With money from traditional sources disappearing into secret hiding spaces, the Company's army was in a perpetual state of unrest, crying out for provisions and forage. An option was for the Government to raise loans from the public but having little credibility in the money market, access to ready cash was the question of questions. Writing on 15 June 1803, Forbes not only systematically articulated the causes of the government's liquidity crunch but also unveiled his plans for the Company to raise its finances. In doing this he subtly revealed how the indigenous financier could simultaneously be phased out from the position he had continued to occupy until the end of the eighteenth century.

To Forbes, the pecuniary distresses of government arose from only one reason; 'the present uncommon scarcity of cash'. He dismissed the impaired credit worthiness of the Company as a possible cause. In fact, according to him at that time their credit worthiness actually showed signs of improvement and was better than it had been at any time over the previous 10 years. This he reasoned from the declining yields on government loans. In the year 1793–4, at the different presidencies, the Government's 6 per cent notes were at a discount of 3–4 per cent, which, in the course of the six following years depreciated 20–25 per cent. However, from the year 1799 they gradually rose in value, and were once again back to the 1793–4 levels; in Bombay they sold at 5 per cent and in Calcutta at just 3–4 per cent discount. The 10 per cent decennial loan paper, which was issued in 1798–9 at par bore a premium of 7–8 per cent thereby lowering yield and the 8 per cent loan paper issued at a discount of 5 per cent was trading at par. Forbes further more believed that the crisis did not arise from any temporary increase in the expenditure of public money *per se*, which could have been managed were there sufficient liquidity in the market. The difficulty for the Government to borrow money was due to a lack of currency, which itself arose from several exogenous reasons, including:

1. Limited importation of bullion from China in 1800.
2. The necessity to send out specie from Bombay to pay their troops.
3. Large sums exported northward (now northern Maharashtra and Gujarat) and also to the Malabar for purchase of cotton.
4. The calamitous fire that broke in Bombay fort on 17 February 1803 by which individuals preferred to hoard rather than lend their money.
5. The shroffs, or indigenous financiers, who wanted to see the Company's distress for cash actually increasing so that the yields would rise.

Forbes then goes on to articulate a solution;

. . . until specie either becomes more plenty, or that some other efficient circulating medium be substituted, this general distress must be expected to continue. The issue of Government Treasury Bills has, therefore, contributed greatly to the convenience and advantage both of the Governments and individuals, and if carried on upon a regular and moderate system might still be rendered so; but the greatest possible caution ought to be observed in the mode of issuing them, and in avoiding any act that may in the smallest degree tend to depreciate them. (ibid, p. 254)

He suggested that the Government must not attempt to give currency to their paper by force but by securing the cooperation of 'principal European merchants and agents in the settlement'. The following measure was proposed: the merchants would agree to buy government treasury bills with all cash they could collect and spare. Contrary to what might be considered his selfish interests, Forbes insisted that these T-bills be issued at par only; offering discounts on par value or on exchange rates to shroffs was self-defeating for 'every new sacrifice would render a greater succeeding one necessary' (ibid., 255). In support of his claim he argued that it was when interest rates touched 12 per cent and the Bombay currency down to 90 per cent of its par value that the Company was most distressed for funds. In lieu of these discounts, Forbes suggested other ways in which the merchants ought to be compensated:

1. The merchants should be allowed to keep a running account with the government.
2. When merchants were in need of cash, they should be allowed to demand the same.
3. That merchants be given Bills on Bengal at 3 per cent under what merchants can negotiate on them in the market; i.e. if the actual market rate of Bombay Rupees is 5 per cent below par then the merchants should get them from the Government at 8 per cent below par. In this way they can make a profit of 3 per cent in the market less commission payable in Calcutta of 1 per cent; i.e. a net profit of 2 per cent. However, Forbes puts a lower bound on the exchange rate as the rate at which shroffs issue their own bills in the market.
4. That the accounts be drawn up on 31 December with the usual interest and a premium of 2 per cent added to the amount; merchants would be entitled to receive 9 per cent interest on the credit balance payable half yearly and the principal within 3–5 years as per the discretion of the government. The holders of the notes should, however, have been given the option of receiving the money in England at a rate of 1 Bombay Rupee = 2s.6d.

To prevent any possible sudden and severe depreciation of treasury bills, Forbes outlined certain precautionary measures; first, the bills must not be issued in too great an extent; second, means for their timely repayment would have to be ensured; third, there had to be no default in repayment. He further suggested that the bills must not be issued to persons who realize them into cash to procure their means of subsistence like subalterns of the army, servants on small allowances, contractors of any description but particularly those who will dispose of the bills to get cash to settle payments to labour. Great care had to be exercised in providing for the regular payment of treasury bills as they fell due. The government could also be open for receipt of treasury bills in payments of claims of the government except for bills on Calcutta, in which case only bills *when due* should be accepted. Forbes also made another recommendation to alleviate the currency crunch; the buying and stamping in the mint of Spanish dollars as there was a good supply of these in the market. Not only were these dollars easily acceptable in Bombay but also northwards in Surat where the cotton was sourced.

These measures, Forbes was confident, would bring a degree of stability into markets and also make credit available to the government at better terms than those offered by Shroffs like Manohardas Dwarcadas and Gopaldas Manohardas. Though Forbes was clear that the English merchants would not be able to meet the necessities of Government to their full extent and the government would necessarily have to make arrangements with the shroffs, or others, it is evident that the English merchants had articulated the need for the Company to lessen its dependence on indigenous finance that had thus far dominated India's financial landscape. It also shows the challenges of the Company in raising credit in a market through issue of Treasury Bills at a time when a question mark hovered above its own existence and before the establishment of an institutional support structure.

Although the Government adopted some of these measures, the situation deteriorated and by 31 October 1803, Forbes writes to the Governor; 'The pressure of demands on us in consequence of our exertions to assist Government (which have been carried far beyond the bounds of prudence) begin to be a little heavy, and what is worse they are likely to increase. Assistance we cannot look for at present, but I hope you will be able to repay us soon a part of what we have lent you, and as you know this is understood, for we have given you a great deal more than belongs to us' (ibid., p. 261).

By the end of 1803, Forbes once again made an offer for the 'last assistance'; he would move about 200,000 Rupees in gold and silver bullion imported from China for purchase of cotton from Surat. Although the cost to his firm would be significant given that premium on 'Bills on Surat' was already at 10–12 per cent and rising, he hoped this would at least keep the treasury going for as he was told, 'Mr. Travers . . . requires Rs. 35,000 tomorrow to pay interest due on 8 per cent notes . . . and his cash balance is only Rs. 2,000' (ibid., p. 262). Meanwhile, Forbes needed assurance that he would be repaid in bullion or Spanish dollars as soon as the ships *Essex* and *Anne* arrived from England.

Once again, for those who wish to understand why there was a premium on Bills on Surat a little economics would help. Here the supply of 'Bills on Surat' was on account of the sellers (merchants in Bombay) who actually wanted the money from Surat (they are exporters of goods to Surat). The demand for Bills on Surat was from private merchants who imported goods, mainly cotton from Surat. Due to an excess demand of Bills on Surat (as Bombay importers need to pay the Surat exporters of cotton), the exchange rate of Surat Rupees rose above par in Bombay. In other words, the Bombay importers would have to pay 110 Bombay Rupees for every Rs. 100 in Surat. The exporters of goods from Bombay were however better off since for every Rs. 100 of goods sold in Surat they could get Rs. 110 in Bombay. This led to an increase in exports from Bombay and a corresponding fall in quantity demanded for Bills on Surat. This is illustrated in Figure 3.8(a) and 3.8(b).

Meanwhile, the Northern Loans for purchase of cotton for export to China continued into the season of 1804 even as Indian commerce was about to make a new departure. 'England was no longer to use the chintzes, calicoes and muslins of India, but set herself in earnest—it was the dawn of mechanical forces in Lan-

Figure 3.8: The Market for Bills of Exchange on Surat

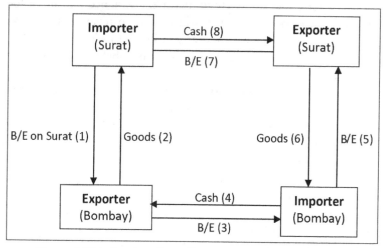

Figure 3.8(a) Bombay-Surat Trade Using Bills of Exchange

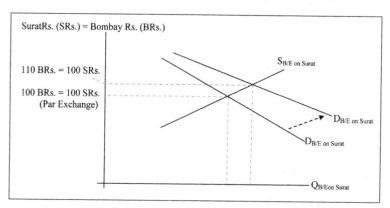

Figure 3.8(b): Premium on Bills of Exchange Drawn
on Surat in Bombay

cashire—to supply piece goods to clothe the millions of India's population, and the revolution was speedy and effective' (ibid., p. 250).

The exports from India to England which had reached some £2,000,000 in 1806, declined sharply thereafter. As the report (in Box 3.1) shows, this was certainly a significant period and a turning point in Indian economic history.

Box 3.1: The Decline in India Trade in the Beginning of the Nineteenth Century

PAPERS RELATING TO EAST INDIA AFFAIRS

Ordered, by the House of Commons, to be printed, 10 July 1813

Copy of a Financial Letter from the Governor in Council of Fort William, To the Court of Directors of the East India Company, dated 23 August 1809.

Exports	To London	To foreign Europe America
1805–6	60,99,065	84,83,608
1806–7	90,34,869	1,09,00,492
1807–8	84,24,199	97,18,968
1808–9	72,83,021	5,71,218

75. From this statement your honourable Court will observe, that the Exports to foreign Europe and America, which, so late as the year 1807-8, amounted to near a crore of Sicca rupees, were reduced in the past year, ending the 31st of May last, to the inconsiderable sum of Rs. 5,71,218.

76. Nor has any proportionate increase taken place in the Exports to London, on the contrary, they are not equal to the Exports of former years; and if the article of indigo be excluded, the Exports from hence during the past year will appear to be absolutely insignificant.

77. It has become doubtful whether this article will maintain its price in the London market; and if, from an excessive exportation, or otherwise, the trade in indigo should be materially affected, even for a season, the greatest inconvenience would be experienced, not merely by the manufacturer and merchant, but by the European capitalist.

78. The trade in piece-goods, which heretofore constituted the great staple of the country, has become comparatively trifling; and it is understood that cotton manufactures have been established in different parts of Europe, there is no reason to expect that this trade will revive.

Source: Papers Relating to the East India Affairs, Copy of a Financial Letter from the Governor in Council of Fort William, to the Court of Directors of the East India Company; dated 23 August 1809, 22 June 1813, p. 13.

3.4: CONSOLIDATION, CONFIDENCE AND CREDIT

The great change of circumstances is—that the public have now confidence in the Government; and that we have obtained a convenient medium of exchange; and the very debt of the Government, which, if unaccompanied by credit, would be the source and sign of general distress, is now what constitutes the capital—the wealth and prosperity of the community.

HENRY ST. GEORGE TUCKER

The Company's struggle to borrow money, or in other words, their credit in the Indian market was closely linked to their political legitimacy and people's confidence in their survival. When we look back in history we do so knowing full well the success of the Company in their territorial expansion; however, in *c.*1800 this was neither obvious nor could it be taken for granted. The uncertainty in the evolution of the Company must be recognized while studying the history of financial institutions. The recommendations of Sir Charles Forbes to the East India Company when seen in this light tells us that the ability of the government's to raise money, when their own credibility and ability to repay was in question, was fraught with challenges. Rising interest rates and discounts on the par value of treasury bills and notes, in other words rising yields, imminent of a debt trap and financial crises is not just a present day phenomenon; the Company's early history as merchant-ruler exposes this in a most transparent form.

Like Douglas' account of Forbes, another work by John William Kaye published in 1854 on the Life and Correspondence of Henry George St. Tucker, Accountant General and later Chairman of the East India Company, highlights the need and uphill task faced by a government to establish credit and borrow money through debt instruments during particularly hard times. Towards the end of the eighteenth century, as the Company was sinking into debt and there was increasing scrutiny of the British Parliament, the demand for money in India was burgeoning both for political purposes (war) and for economic reasons (investment). There was no such thing as Public Credit so that every time the treasury was empty, money had to be borrowed at high costs. The rates of interest were ruinous at about 12 per cent along with 3–4 per cent discount on the par value of treasury notes. Given the hostile environment in England to the Company's privileges and conduct, it had to turn towards local Indian sources as a primary source of funds but then, 'The native bankers of Calcutta, Moorshedabad, Benares, and other places, had no faith in Government securities, and either held back their capital or employed it in their private speculations' (Kaye, 1854, p. 105).

The Company's policy of bimetallism only made its own predicament far more complex. The receipt of revenues in gold while payments to the army and for investment that had to be made in silver meant a severe shortage of the right currency (see Box 3.2). It was in this dire context that Tucker proposed a strategy to establish Public Credit on a secure basis so that a reduction in interest rates and elimination of discounts would follow. But how was this to be done? He provided a solution that yielded immediate results—prop up the level of confidence. It was this fundamental element of credit that was successful in bringing down rates of

---

Box 3.2: Silver Currency Crunch *c.*1800

There was a scarcity of silver coin in those days. It was much needed by Government for the payment of the troops, for advances to weavers, molungeers, and others, and the native capitalists endeavoured to sweep the largest possible supplies of it into their own hands. The Revenue-payer was for the most part largely indebted to the native capitalist, through whom his payments were principally made to Government. The capitalist paid the amount into the Public Treasury in gold. But for the practical purposes of Government the gold coin was of little use. It was necessary, therefore, to convert it into silver, and the silver was in the hands of the native capitalist. It was only to be bought. The consequence was, that the gold coin was at a discount, sometimes as much as six or seven per cent., and large sums of money were lost to the State by financial operations which it was not in their power to control.

Source: John William Kaye, *The Life and Correspondence of Henry St. George Tucker*, Richard Bentley, London, 1854, p. 106.

---

interest into single digits along with elimination of discounts on par value of bills and bonds issued by the government. However, even as this confidence led to a growing impression that the Company was in a prosperous state and would be in a position to repay its debt, the reality was that it desperately required additional funds.

Tucker proposed that the government raise Rs. 75,00,000 at just 8 per cent. The operation was successful. Tucker was even personally congratulated by Lord Wellesley for improving the state of finances of the Company. At the core of the growing political power of the East India Company lay access to credit; individuals like Tucker and Forbes played a crucial part in lessening the dependence of the Company on indigenous merchant-bankers and making credit available to them using more innovative credit instruments and at a substantially lower cost.

There was another institution that Tucker proposed to Arthur Wellesley which at that time was flung into the 'great Hereafter'. It saw the light of day only five years later in the year 1806: the establishment of the Bank of Bengal. Tucker proposed a public bank that would effectively compete with private bankers and shroffs, to bring down the value of capital and the rate of interest to its 'proper' level.

3.5: THE ABUSE OF CREDIT

The race-course must be deserted. It is no honour to any place, and far less is it suitable in a trading community.

ANON, COMMENTATOR ON THE COMMERCIAL
CRISIS IN BENGAL, 1847–8

In the first half of the nineteenth century, colonial India, and in particular Bengal, was rocked by two major commercial crises; the first between 1829 and 1833 and the second, between 1847 and 1848. Both were caused by the abuse of credit; just as Macleod had reasoned, excessive speculation and overtrading could lead to a glut in production. When the bubble finally burst the repercussions on the real economy were severe and painful.

By the Charter of 1813, the monopoly powers of the Company were diluted and trade was opened to private merchants bringing the so called 'agency houses' into greater prominence. These 'great houses', as they were sometimes referred to, expanded their activities in India rapidly. They were also joined by many new merchants from England. Apart from the Bank of Bengal[3] which was closely associated with the Government of the Company and its requirements for resources to fund wars, these agency houses also set up their own affiliated banks. One of India's first banks, the Bank of Hindostan was set up by Alexander & Co., the Calcutta Bank was an affiliate of Palmer & Co.[4] while the Commercial Bank belonged to Mackintosh & Co. Many people, both Westerners and Indians deposited substantial amounts of their savings into these banks. In turn, the banks lent large amounts of money to indigo planters whose output was then exported by the agency houses to England. However, against all norms of prudential banking, the agency houses along with their affiliated banks took a stake in the planters' profits. This was akin to a situation in which banks were lending money to their own businesses. A glut in credit with a corresponding over production of indigo was soon followed by a crash in its price that resulted in default and non-repayment of debt to the banks. When the markets panicked over the fate of the agency houses, a simultaneous run on their affiliated banks was inevitable. By 1833, the net loss from the crisis was estimated at more than £10 million; on a capital of £15 million, dividends that had been paid out amounted to just about £4 million, the remaining £11 million being wiped out. Officers, salaried employees, pensioners, workers; the crisis beggared many living in England and in India. Not unlike what we often witness even today, many of the great merchants had personally not lost much and continued their lavish lifestyles. It is also pertinent to mention that even as I write about this episode which took place some 180 years ago, the Reserve Bank of India is in the process of considering the issue of licenses to some of India's largest business houses to set up banks. In spite of stringent norms that these banks would have to comply with, concerns remain on over-lending by such banks to affiliated businesses.

With consolidation of its political power in India, the ability of the Company to raise money locally eased in the early decades of the nineteenth century. However, by the 1840s the Company once again faced a challenge—remittance of surpluses from India to England. While trade had provided a convenient conduit for the Company to remit its territorial revenues from India, this became impossible after they were required to wind up all their commercial businesses in India under the Charter of 1833. The Company had now to find an alternative mode of remitting its surpluses to England. And it did, through an ingenuous combination of credit and trade. Instead of undertaking trade directly, the Company extended credit liberally to private merchants and collected the principal lent along with accrued interest back in England. But by 1847 this imprudent abuse of credit degenerated into severe 'commercial distress', particularly in Bengal. A glut in the produce of agricultural commodities including indigo, sugar, rice, silk, opium and cotton followed by the stoppage of production caused hardship to capitalists, workers and farmers. Some 22 large agency houses filed for bankruptcy. Once again, the mistakes of the 1829 crisis were repeated; the loans of banks being tied up with indigo factories, the crisis took its toll on banks too. The important and powerful Union Bank of Calcutta was forced to close down in 1847. More than a description of the crisis and its impact, the focus of this section is to demystify the nature of *financialization* in its most rudimentary form from a brief narrative of the 1847 commercial crises.

Every year, the Company had to remit a sum of some £3–4 million; these were surpluses from territorial revenues collected in India that had to be sent to England to meet 'home charges' and pay out dividends to shareholders of the Company. With trading rights revoked, the Company took on the role of an export bank that financed purchases in India of the agency houses and collected money in England on sale of exported goods by these firms. The method was rather ingenuous; the sale of 'Bills on Calcutta' in London and the purchase of 'Bills on London' in Calcutta. Figure 3.9 illustrates the mechanism adopted by the Company to effect transfer of funds.

The 'Bills on London' bought by the Company in Calcutta was

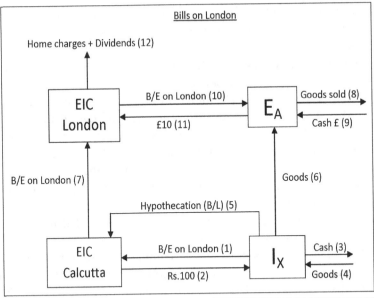

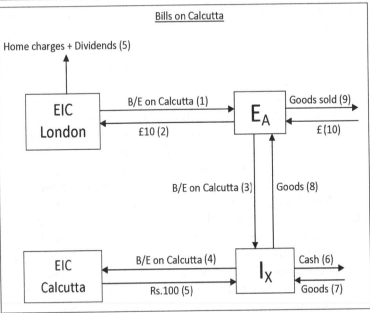

Figure 3.9: Remittance by the East India Company Through
Bills of Exchange and Credit

on the security of produce shipped through it to mercantile houses in England (E_A). More precisely, the goods were hypothecated to the Company as collateral security for the payment received by the Indian exporting firm. It was alleged that this system of advances made by the Company led to the development of low quality credit in carrying out the India business wherein the credentials and credit worthiness of the exporting firm and their British agents was not adequately scrutinized and assessed. In fact, the availability of easy credit was leading firms to avail themselves of the money to an extent far in excess of what they would otherwise have borrowed in the market and what would have been given to them after a thorough assessment of risk.

From the borrower's standpoint, the credit doled out by the Company was a strong temptation to seek quick gains that often led them to overlook the actual commercial profitability of the transaction from the sale of commodities in England. Opposition to the Company's scheme arose in Calcutta, their contention being the inducement to avail of easy credit for their 'investment' (purchase of goods for export) by the simple hypothecation of goods at 75 per cent of their value to the Company was corrupting the basis of trade. The East India Company, it was claimed, 'interfered' with the genuine British merchant's business and encouraged dubious ventures to proliferate from the availability of easy money and export trade. If the Company did not advance its money, trade would have fallen into the normal channel with prudent norms in the extension of credit. This would have entailed a scrutiny of the credibility of the drawer of bills as well as viability of the transaction itself. Fly-by-night operators and those in it for a quick buck would have been kept at bay. On the other hand, the Company was reckless in doling out loans, looking only at goods hypothecated to them as collateral security. Traders without adequate capital to make large purchases in commercial transactions were encouraged to enter trade, something which would not have been possible had the Company been more cautious in pursuing its objective. It was further argued that the system of hypothecation was altogether against the spirit of the Charter of 1833, which had prohibited the East India Company from all mercantile activities.

Apart from giving out easy loans to agency houses, the Company being wholly dependent on the export trade to remit money to England, resorted to an even more incongruous scheme—depreciating the rupee. This further distorted the export trade and some argued that it would perhaps have been better for the Company to simply export specie (although such a contraction of money in India could have had dangerous consequences). The concern over this strategy can be better understood from Figure 3.10; here the demand for Bills on London in Calcutta is on account of the Company wanting to get rid of its rupees in exchanges for pounds in London. On the other hand, the supply of bills on London would emanate from Indian exporters. Given the high demand for bills from the Company, the rupee's rate of exchange would fall from Rs. 10 = £1 to (say) Rs. 11 = £1, the gold export point. But the Company was desperate enough to accept an even more depreciated rupee rate (to say Rs. 12 = £1), 'pushing' private firms to undertake the export of goods. As the rupee depreciated, the sterling price of Indian goods fell, making them more competitive in English markets. This stimulated Indian exports of commodities like opium and indigo but the question was whether or not it was sustainable without the support of the artificial exchange rate.

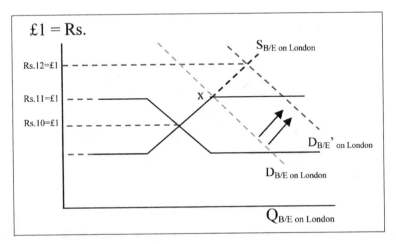

Figure 3.10: The Depreciation of the Rupee Beyond
the Gold Export Point

Apart from the 'unnatural' depreciation of the rupee beyond the gold export point, the system adopted by the Company introduced a great deal of uncertainty over exchange rates in the market. This was due to two associated reasons. First, the timing of Company's announcement was arbitrary; apart from the fact that the total transfer would be about £4 million, no one could say for sure when it would be raised. The element of arbitrariness is clear in a typical notification issued for purchase of bills: 'So far as is at present known, the sum to be provided in India by the purchase of bills will be £700,000, liable, however, to such modification or extension as may hereafter be demanded by the exigencies of the public service' (Sessional Papers, p. 112).

Second, the Company did not only raise money through purchase of Bills on London in Calcutta but also through the sale of Bills on Calcutta in London (see Figure 3.9). In Figure 3.10 we have seen the effect of the Company's actions on the exchange rate in Calcutta; the effect of their action through sale of Bills on Calcutta in London on the exchange rate in London is shown in Figure 3.11. Here the sale of Bills on Calcutta was executed by the Company in London while the demand for these bills came from English importers of goods from India, which were used to dis-

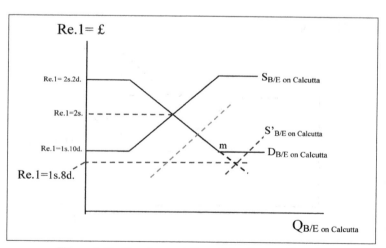

Figure 3.11: The Appreciation of the Rupee Beyond
the Gold Import Point

charge their obligations in India. Obviously the lesser pounds per rupee (depreciated rupee), the greater would have been the demand of English importers for these bills. On the other hand, the greater the number of pounds that the Company got from each rupee (appreciated rupee), the greater would be the supply of these bills. However, note that for any rate below (say) Re. 1 = 1s.10d. the Company should have rather imported bullion from India than sold bills of exchange and at any rate (say) above Re. 1 = 2s.2d. the importers should have rather exported bullion than meet their obligations through bills. Unlike the policy adopted in Calcutta where Bills on London were purchased at a depreciated rupee rate (below the gold export point in Figure 3.10), the Company adopted an aggressive posture in sale of Bills on Calcutta in London. While the private Bills on Calcutta in London were being sold at the market exchange rate of 1s.8d., the Company sold their bills at a rate of 1s.9d. claiming superior credit as the reason. The result of such an appreciated rupee is shown in Figure 3.12. The importer

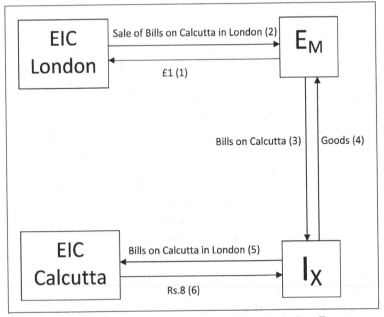

Figure 3.12: The Artificially High Rupee Hurt the Indian Exporter

in England would get only (say) Rs. 8 for every pound (instead of the market rate of Rs. 9, the par value being Rs. 10 = £1) only because the Company sold bills at this artificially high rupeerate. This often meant that the amounts raised by it were rather meager, amounting to less than 15 per cent of the total transfer.

However, there were times when the Company also resorted to selling of bills on Calcutta at a depreciated rate. The following testimony of one merchant, William Patrick Paton to the (Secret) Committee on Commercial Distress makes this argument clear: 'We buy bills (on Calcutta) in London, and we do not know at what rate they (the Company) may buy bills in India; they may be offering bills to the speculator in Calcutta in opposition to the bills that we send out there. For instance, I may buy a bill in London to-day, at the present exchange of 1s.9d; that bill goes to India, and by the time it gets there, the Company may have reduced their exchange on London to 1s.9½d. I should consequently be a considerable loser by such a transaction . . .' (Second Report, 1848, p. 109).

There was a complete lack of consistency in the Company's strategy that was driven more by its immediate needs for transfer of funds rather than market forces of demand and supply for goods. These arbitrary policies of the East India Company which were neither consistent nor predictable deranged the calculations of merchants; between 1845 and 1846 exchange rates fluctuated between 2s.3d. and 1s.10d. Instead of the hypothecation system along with simultaneous sale and purchase of bills by the Company in India and England, the merchants suggested a single policy of selling Bills on Calcutta in London *at market rates*. Merchants could purchase these bills, remit them to India, have them encashed in Calcutta, and use the proceeds as advances for their investments (which otherwise the Company would make by hypothecation).

Another cause for concern in the use of bills of exchange as a trade credit mechanism was their long date. Bills were drawn at ten month's date which attracted many traders without adequate capital, even mere speculators who had nothing to lose if their businesses failed but a lot to gain from rising international commodity prices. Overtrading was then a natural outcome. Several schemes of trading based on bills drawn with long dates emerged; two have been described below.

As illustrated in Figure 3.13, houses with good credit (I_X) issued bills in Calcutta drawn upon their houses in London (E_A) and made their investment in India with the money received from sale of these bills. The goods were then immediately shipped from Calcutta to their own houses in England (E_A) along with the Bills

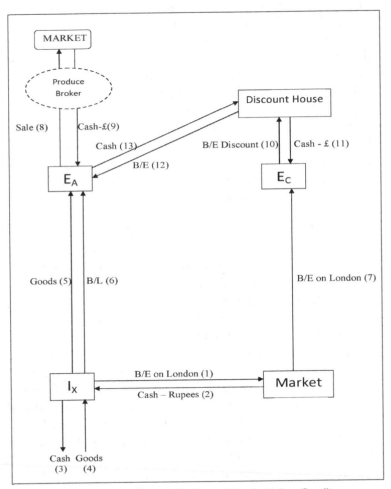

Figure 3.13: Financialization of Trade Using Credit
Through Bills of Exchange

of Lading (B/L). The purchaser of the bills of exchange in Calcutta at the same time transmitted the bills to London (E_C) for settlement. The bills had another eight months to run before they became due for payment. In the meantime, the bills of lading were handed over to produce brokers by E_A against settlement and the bills of exchange were discounted in Lombard Street by E_C. They would be presented to E_A for payment by the discount houses at the end of ten months by which time E_A had received cash from sale in the market with the intermediation of produce brokers. Carrying out trade by means of these long-dated bills furnished the credit-worthy trading houses with enormous amount of funds to transact business, when they had no real capital in hand, and only their credit in Calcutta. These houses exploited their standing in Calcutta to purchase, ship and resell produce in England. Little or even no capital was needed for this business, which could be carried out indefinitely as long as the firm was able to raise money in India through sale of bills. The critical question in this system was whether the purchase of produce was a matter of convenience for carrying out lucrative financial operations. Profits came easily from buoyant commodity prices and the long time gap between receipt of sale proceeds and the need to honour their bills.

An even more complicated scheme based on credit of both, sellers and buyers also developed. Four or five persons would get together, open a firm in Calcutta with a partner based in London (E_A) and begin correspondence with a London firm (L_F). The latter was at the centre of these schemes. They were a set of 'great houses' which had arisen from the dust of the commercial crisis of the 1830s, firms which once had capital but now had nothing but credit. Once an order had been received from manufacturers, the firm in Calcutta would draw bills either on E_A or, if E_A has no credit in the market, on L_F. Resources were raised locally through sale of these bills to advance money to the indigo factory for supply. Meanwhile, the bills on E_A or L_F were sent by their buyers to England by the bank. These bills were usually of long-date and were therefore discounted at the discount houses on Lombard Street. At the same time, the Bills of Lading would be received by L_F and sent to the produce brokers for encashment (Figure 3.14 illus-

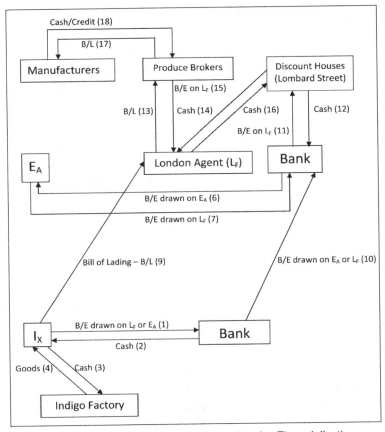

Figure 3.14: Another Scheme that Led to the Financialization of Trade Using Bills of Exchange as an Instrument

trates the scheme). It should be noted that neither the Indian firms nor L_F were really concerned about what they were trading in. Their remuneration being based on commissions, not on profit and loss, thrived as long as the commodity prices were rising and demand was good. The whole system operated on the basis of credit and grew rapidly. The problem arose when commodity prices began to fall and confidence in bills drawn on L_F declined. The bills could no longer be easily discounted and neither did these houses have the capability to discharge their obligations. The moment had arrived for the bubble to burst.

The toll taken by the commercial distress between 1847 and 1848 was heavy with several English firms going bankrupt on account of the East India trade. In fact, many argued that more than the hypothecation scheme, it was the long dated bills of exchange issued by many private firms that led to overtrading and the subsequent crisis. The passage below highlight this point:

A man with capital would hardly be likely to leave his home and his family to live as a colonial in exile. Consequently, Calcutta attracted more than its share of men who depended on the capital of others for their speculations. Furthermore, they were determined to make their fortunes quickly and return home, a tradition that began with the first adventurers to the Indies in the seventeenth century. The early European traders borrowed from the Indians and from the East India Company; the latter ones used the savings of civil and military officers of the company. In the 1830s and 1840s they relied chiefly upon bills drawn on ten-months' date on correspondents at home. (Kling, 1976, p. 227)

The suggested solution was (as stated above) for the Company to introduce market-based sale of bills drawn on Calcutta in London to firms who were desirous of transferring funds to Calcutta from England so as to make their purchases in India for legitimate and profitable trade. This would simultaneously provide a means for the Company to transfer their funds to England. Moreover, it was also proposed that a maximum limit be imposed on the duration of bills of exchange; a period of six months was considered adequate since by then, with the advent of steam ships, transport of goods from India to England took no more than two months.

NOTES

1. Yield = coupon/price of bond.
2. Bania here represents the Indian merchant caste/class.
3. We will deal with banking, bank credit and Indian banks later in the book. For now, the mention of banks may be taken as incidental to the subject of commercial credit.
4. See Webster (2007) for a fascinating account of Palmer & Co., the largest agency house of those times.

CHAPTER 4

Bank Money

What is the robbing of a bank compared to the founding of a bank?

BERTOLT BRECHT

The system of credit has two divisions: commercial credit and bank credit. In this chapter I study the latter and its development. Although the system of bank credit, or banking as we call it, has evolved differently across the world, it shares a common essence in economic terms. I have first attempted to draw this out. Before moving on to presenting its growth in India, I will briefly narrate its development in England for this had a bearing, although with important differences, on the evolution of modern banking in India.

4.1: THE ECONOMICS OF BANK MONEY

Banks lend by creating credit. They create the means of payment out of nothing.

RALPH M. HAWTREY

In Chapter 3, we discussed the progress of commercial credit whereby, through its principal instrument, bills of exchange, traders were able to buy commodities by creating debts, payable at some point of time in the future. Let us now explore the other principal component of credit: bank money. Once again, Macleod's (1863) work more than any other, brings out the essence of and differences between money, credit and banking. I have, therefore, drawn extensively from his work.

Banking is the process by which bankers buy money and commercial debts by creating their own debts, usually payable on demand. In other words, the banker buys the merchant's bills in exchange for its (the bank's) bills which it creates. These bills are usually called bank promissory notes. This is not a cancellation of debt but rather an exchange of valuable properties, both of which can circulate in commerce. Consider the simplest case where a customer deposits Rs. 100 in a bank against which the bank creates a debt for the same amount, namely a promissory note or a checking account against which the customer can issue cheques. Meanwhile, the banker also has Rs. 100 which is now his own property and which he can now trade for profit. Hence we now have two circulating and exchangeable properties circulating instead of a mere Rs. 100 in the customer's possession.

In this example the bank has bought money for debt; an obligation to repay the money on demand of its customer. The bank will therefore have to pay up a part of its property at the time of repayment of debt. But there is no *specific* property that it will have to pay up. In other words, no specific or certain property represents the money bought. The property (the Rs. 100 bought) is its own and it is are free to use all or some of it in any way that it pleases. In the extreme case it is even possible that it defaults, leaving the debt unpaid. When the banker is called upon to exchange some gold (money) for its liabilities (the Rs. 100 deposited by the customer) it must oblige. However, the business of banking is essentially based on the probability that a significant part of total liabilities will not be claimed at a single point of time. On any average day, the bank would know that (say) not more than 5 per cent of the total amounts deposited by its customers will be withdrawn by them. Nonetheless if a customer relieves the bank of some portion of debt, then this is essentially a destruction of debt, and therefore a destruction of property. By cancelling debt the bank cancels their future obligations to that extent.

From a macroeconomic standpoint, what is the implication of this exchange of debt for money? Consider a country with Rs. 1 million in circulating silver coins, which in other words, is the money in circulation. Suppose we now have banks where these silver coins are deposited. These banks then issue an equivalent amount of promissory notes while they, at the same time, lend out Rs. 800,000 in silver rupees, keeping only Rs. 200,000 for answering the occasional demands of their clients. The total money in circulation is now Rs. 1.8 million, or Rs. 800,000 in coin and Rs. 1 million in debt.

Credit is then simply circulating debt. While money is simply an order (on society) for goods and services, credit is an order (on society or at least a part thereof) for money. Furthermore, as we have seen, money is valuable property separate from the merchandize, representing no specific property. Credit then is also valuable property, separate from money and representing no specific money. From this we can say that payment of a bill of exchange in money is only an exchange of an instrument of general credit for one of particular credit.

It is now possible to understand the business of banking. It is the employment of their credit (trust) as capital on the basis of which banks issue notes, promising to pay the bearer of the note a certain sum of money on demand. Amongst people who are willing to accept these notes, it circulates just like money, becoming a powerful instrument of production. By providing such instruments of credit, banks add to productive capital in three ways; first, they economize on the use of metallic money and liberate resources for other uses. Second, by a system of issues or deposits they put into circulation capital which would otherwise remain locked up in vaults. And finally, by putting a new circulating medium out of their own debt that allows exchange and specialization they *bring forth* goods into the market or production. This makes bank money equivalent to productive capital. Banking therefore does not merely distribute existing capital; it adds to the existing stock of productive capital. Even if it does not create gold sovereigns or silver rupees (or for that matter currency notes today), it creates capital through instruments of credit. These deposits or issues are exchangeable or tradable property and perform the same functions that money does as long as society-at-large accepts them. Just as the railways reduce the capital expended for any supply to meet demand, in quite the same way banking reduces the capital expended in carrying out exchanges with actual currency. But one must never lose sight of a bank's most fundamental asset; trust or credit.

At a more specific level, credit is usually recorded on paper documents which then circulate more or less generally. These documents are of two types; orders to pay and promises to pay. The first includes bills of exchange, cheques and bank drafts while the latter includes bank notes, promissory notes and deposits. There are two classes of traders who specialize in the buying of commercial debt like bills of exchange. The first are bill discounters who buy debt in exchange for money. The second are bankers who buy debt in exchange for other debts payable on demand and created by them. Given that a bill discounter is limited by the quantum of money in his possession, the former is considered as a much less powerful instrument of commerce than bank credit. With a bank, however, the only limits (apart from regulatory norms) are those based upon their own judgement as to the amount that must be retained to meet demands made on them.

To Macleod, banks are akin to shops opened for the purpose of buying commercial debt. Banks do not lend money on the security of bills of exchange; they are not mere agents between people who want to borrow and those who wish to lend. They buy bills of exchange (under warranty when endorsed) and *issue 'promises to pay' in exchange*. Although we have seen in Chapter 2 the mechanism through which bills of exchange operate, we repeat the exercise with an emphasis on the role of the bank in the process. A schematic diagram of the credit system is shown in Figure 4.1. The producer (P) draws a bill on the wholesaler-dealer (W) who accepts it and returns the 'Bill on W' to P. W is now the principal debtor on the bill. P now takes the bill to a bank (B) for sale. By writing his name on the back of the bill, P sells the bill to B. The operation is called endorsement. But endorsement is not merely a sale of the debt; it also acts as a warranty of its soundness. In case of default in payment by W, P would be responsible for payment to B. To protect themselves the bank would retain some of the producer's deposit in the event of a default by a wholesaler. What does B give P in return for the property? B would create another instrument of debt which would typically be a credit into the account of P, called deposit or issue. This deposit or issue can be drawn up at pleasure and at demand of P. The banker B has bought

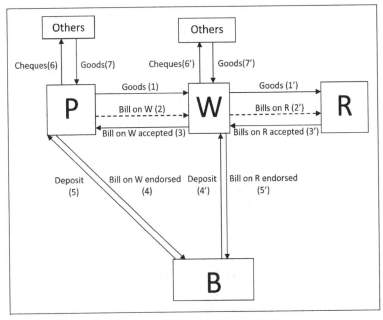

Figure 4.1: The Credit System with the Bank as a Dealer
in Commercial Debt

one debt with another debt. Both are valuable property and can be used in circulation just like money. This transaction is not a cancelation of debt; instead it creates valuable and exchangeable property based on credit (trust).

From here it is easy to see how credit is created and then multiplies in this system. A single producer like P would have several wholesalers like $W_1, \ldots, W_n$ as his customers. At any point of time they would endorse their 'Bills on W_i' to the bank in exchange for deposits, which they could then use for market exchanges or transactions. Each wholesaler like W_i would have several retailers $(R_1, \ldots, R_m)$ against whom they would draw bills (Bills on R_j) which would be duly accepted by R_j, and then sold to a bank by wholesalers with endorsements against deposits.

The role of the bank is to put into circulation the entire dead stock of commercial debt. Without the bank the producer's and wholesaler's capital would be locked up until the bills drawn upon their clients were discharged. With the bank they now have full command over ready money in the form of cheques against deposits, which they can use for any purpose they wish (say, purchase of goods from others as shown in Figure 4.1), thereby continuing the stream of production uninterrupted.

Bills of exchange can also facilitate circulation of goods through endorsements between traders and merchants. Suppose B draws a 'Bill on A', which is accepted by A. If B buys goods from C then C would draw a 'Bill on B' to settle his claim on B. Instead of drawing a new bill, B could endorse the 'Bill on A' which he possesses in settlement of C's claim on him. This could go on indefinitely. Macleod speaks of bills of exchange in Lancashire *c.*1860s having being endorsed 150 times. In effect then, just as the velocity of circulation of money effectively acts in carrying out several transfers of property, so could a bill of exchange.

Now endorsement of a bill of exchange does not absolve a trader's responsibility of payment. When a bill becomes due, payment must be made. This can be done through sale of property, which may be either; sale of commodities in the market or sale of debts due to them to bankers. When credit is good, and bankers are ready to buy debts, merchants could hold on to their commodities and sell debt to bankers in settlement of payments which have become due. However, when credit is weak, the system of credit can go horribly wrong. Banks will not accept debt from their clients in discharge of payments, fearing the possibility of default. Merchants will then have to sell commodities in the market. But when many merchants do this, a glut in the market (which can include commodity markets as well as stock markets and those for real estate) is inevitable and prices crash. Merchants who have adequate capital in their possession can tide through the crisis by making payments on due debts without distress sales of commodities. But when their capital is inadequate, ruin is inevitable.

Often what lies at the heart of commercial crises is the failure of confidence and the extinction of circulating debt on account of the banks' refusal to buy debt with issues and their insistence on settlement by currency. This invariably means that traders have to make forced sales of goods or their capital assets in the market, resulting in a glut in commodity and asset markets. This would result in prices of commodities and other assets crashing. To Macleod (1863),

It is, therefore, not the scarcity of money, but the extinction of confidence, which produces a pressure on the money market: and an examination of all great commercial crises in this country, will shew that they have always been preceded and produced by a destruction of this credit, which has usually been brought about by extravagant trading and over speculation'. (Macleod, 1863, p. 589)

With these fundamental notions in place on modern banking, we are now ready to explore the development of this vital institution in India. But before we do this, we make a short digression on the evolution of banking across Europe, in particular, England.

4.2: MODERN BANKING IN THE WEST

The introduction of credit, by means of a Bank, augments the quantity of money more in one year, than a prosperous commerce could do in ten.

JOHN LAW

The earliest banks in the world were 'Banks of Deposit' where people would keep their money for safekeeping. In return banks would issue receipts of deposits; such banks were found in Venice about eight hundred years ago, although Macleod believes they actually began only in 1587. At a time when the circulating medium consisted of a mixture of coins of many denominations, sometimes also clipped or debased, merchants had to weigh and estimate the fineness of each coin. This was costly in terms of time and expense. It therefore became a custom for merchants to deposit money in a bank where its value was accurately estimated, once for all, and placed to the credit of the depositor. The money placed to the credit of individuals in these banks was called *bank money* or *bank notes*; the amount of notes issued *corresponded exactly* to the value of bullion deposited with them. These notes guaranteed the bearer, bullion of certain purity on demand. The convenience of this service was so great that soon all bills payable on Venice above a certain value were enacted to be payable only in bank notes. In fact, given the benefits, notes commanded a premium corresponding to the average depreciation of coins. The transfer of bank notes between parties was, however, carried out through a cumbersome procedure. Holders of these bank notes would come to the bank at a particular hour and order transfers to be made in the bank's books. The money paid was thus always of full value, and all trouble in counting and valuing it was made redundant. To avoid the costs of being physically present to make transfers, banks began issuing cheques as a record of transactions between their clients. Although these monetary instruments reduced the transactions costs of using coin there were risks associated with them. Cheques could bounce and excessive issue of bank notes could end with the bank going bust in case of a bank run. The widespread counterfeiting of bank notes was also a challenge that banks and their clients had to contend with.

Amongst the other early deposit banks was the Bank of Sweden, supposedly established even prior to that of Venice. The currency of Sweden at that time was copper and given that large amounts of coins had to be carted for transactions of even moderate amounts, a public bank of deposit was set up to exchange copper money for bank notes payable on demand. The literature on banking history also makes mention of the banks of Amsterdam and Hamburg. These too were established for the same general purpose; a one-to-one exchange for notes in return for bullion and vice-versa. But these banks were not 'modern banks' that we think of today; it was in England that this important commercial institution developed.

Macleod (1863) asserts that 'banking, in the modern sense of the word, had no existence in England before the year 1640' (p. 78); it arose from Charles I's desperate need for money to maintain a standing army. Taxation, granting of monopolies, approaching other monarchies and the church, personal loans and debasement of coin were possible answers to the problem but had already been resorted to extensively. In an act of final desperation, the king seized £130,000 in bullion held in the Tower by the city merchants for safekeeping. The merchants were horrified; in a single stroke, Charles I had ruined the bullion trade that had flourished in London. In reconciliation, the king returned the bullion but only after the merchants agreed to grant him a loan of £40,000. Later, when civil war broke out in England, the merchants turned to the goldsmiths for safeguarding their wealth rather than the Tower, with whom all confidence had been destroyed.

These goldsmiths would receive gold for safe keeping and issue notes in exchange for them, payable on demand. After careful observation of how many notes would come back for repayment and once confident of these numbers, the goldsmiths could issue notes in excess of the reserves held. They were effectively creating money and can therefore be called, 'Banks of Issue'. Unlike Banks of Deposit, which played an important role in reducing the transactions cost of using bullion by merely substituting it with notes, the Banks of Issue actually *increased* the quantity of money in circulation. To Macleod this creation of money was equivalent to the enhancement of capital; 'a species of capital, no doubt, of a somewhat dangerous character, and one that was liable to be destroyed, but yet, as long as it did exist, it was equivalent to so much bullion.' (ibid., p. 70)

But concerns also arose over the goldsmiths' practices; they would export good gold coins out, putting only the debased ones into circulation. Further, and more dangerous, was the possibility for goldsmiths to actually debase the coins themselves. In spite of these concerns, and lack of other alternatives, a considerable sum of money was deposited with the goldsmiths who seeing that the whole of the deposits were never called up at once, began to trade with them. It has been said that the London goldsmiths received deposits, collected the moneyed capital of the community into larger volumes and on the credit (trust) they gradually came to possess, issued 'goldsmith notes' that passed as money thus building up a machinery of credit that enlarged and extended the usefulness of the actual moneyed capital deposited with them. This was, as we know today, is essentially the process of money creation through fractional banking.

But doubts grew and so did resentment against this emergent class of wealthy capitalists. Apart from debasement, the goldsmiths were charged with demanding exorbitant interest rates on loans disbursed, taking inadequate security from their borrowers and over-lending to the government. In the reign of Charles II, when people became suspicious of the government's inability to return their debt to the goldsmiths, London witnessed a run on the banks. A few decades earlier in 1672 when the government's debt had increased to £1,300,000 it ordered suspension of all payments from the national exchequer; this was nothing but an admission of national bankruptcy. Panic spread through London and some 10,000 people went bankrupt; a *coup de finance* as Macleod put it. But in the end the 'Banker's Debt' was never repaid, and people's losses amounted to some £3,000,000.

The need for a national bank was growing in England, bringing down interest rates and issue of paper currency were the needs of the day. But it was the political imperative, more than economic, that actually led to the formation of the Bank. When William III needed over £5,000,000 to meet expenses of his wars with Ireland, Scotland and France, neither taxes nor loans were adequate. As last recourse he adopted William Paterson's plan to set up the Bank of England. Paterson's idea was simple and can be summarized in his own words: '. . . if the proprietors of the Bank can circulate their own *fundation* of twelve hundred thousand pounds without having more than two or three hundred thousand pounds lying dead at one time with another, this Bank will be in effect as nine hundred thousand pounds or a million of fresh money brought into the nation' (quoted in Andreades, 1909, pp. 66–7).

The Bank of England began its operations by lending its capital to the government against which were issued securities. In turn, these securities became the asset against which the bank was allowed to issue treasury notes. This made it possible for the government to withdraw money from the markets without causing a shortage of money in the market; local commerce was therefore left undisrupted by the government siphoning off money. However, this also made the banking system especially vulnerable to government defaults. The basic model of Paterson's scheme is illustrated schematically in Figure 4.2. The bank's initial capital of £1.2 million raised through subscriptions was entirely lent to the government. Notes were issued to an equivalent amount and an interest of 2d. per day was paid on them. Initially, these notes were not used for transactions but instead attracted the patronage of the goldsmiths. They were issued with a promise to pay gold or

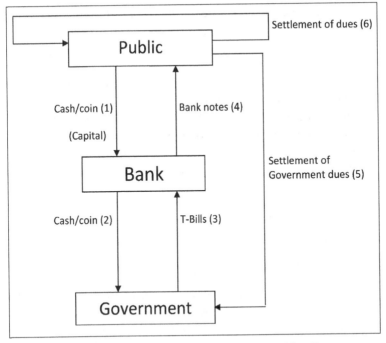

Figure 4.2: The Emergence of the Modern Banking System

coin to the bearer on demand, for the specific amount of deposit received, handwritten on Bank paper, (i.e. the receipt bore the name of the bank and not the account holder) and signed by the cashier. After the re-coinage of 1696, notes were issued only for amounts of £50 and above. With the average income of the population being only about £20, these bank notes circulated only amongst merchants, bankers and the government. The demand for notes for transaction purposes amongst these classes grew steadily and by 1698, bank notes were circulating without interest payable. To safeguard against the king borrowing excessively from the bank, a clause was introduced into the law prohibiting lending money to the government without the express authority of Parliament. But a clear pattern was emerging; raise capital, keep a portion of it as reserves, lend the rest to the Government and issue notes against deposits to the public that circulated as money.

As confidence in bank notes of the Bank of England grew, it was able to issue notes against purchase of bills of exchange (purchase of debt) rather than against cash (bullion) deposits. Suppose the bank began with a deposit of cash amounting to £10,000. This would appear in the liability side as deposits and on the asset side of the bank's balance sheet as cash-in-hand. Now if another customer brought in bills of exchange to be discounted (an asset to the bank) then assuming no commission is charged by the bank, it would issue promissory notes payable on demand in lieu of the bills of exchange. The balance sheet of the bank would now be as follows:

Assets		Liabilities	
Cash-in-hand	10,000	Customer's deposits	10,000
Bills of exchange	30,000	Promissory notes	30,000

Many banks in London began issuing promissory notes and in 1709 a statute was passed conferring exclusive privileges to the Bank of England and prohibiting any other bank from *borrowing, owing or taking up money on bills, or notes, payable on demand.* This prohibition on persons creating currency was tantamount to prohibiting them from banking. For more than 30 years these orders had the desired effect; no competitor to the Bank of England came into existence that could create currency in the *form of promissory notes, payable to the bearer on demand.* This was set to change when bankers adopted a change in the form of doing business; and it this change in form that led to the creation of money by the banking system or what is today called 'fractional banking'.

By 1772, London bankers adopted a different form of creating liabilities. Instead of issuing promissory notes, which was prohibited, they merely wrote down an amount to the credit of their customer who had brought in bills of exchange, in exchange for which he was given cheques; these cheques could be filled up by their customer in favour of anyone they pleased and which were also payable on demand. Any person coming with cheques issued in their favour would be paid provided their customer had an amount to their credit in the books of the bank. Cheques were nothing but the substitute to bank notes. Macleod, however, argues that there was one big difference; the balance sheet now appeared as follows:

Assets		Liabilities	
Cash-in-hand	10,000	Customer's deposits	40,000
Bills of exchange	30,000		

In the modern form of banking the customers' deposits seem as if they arise from actual deposits of cash. But it is clear from the above that £30,000 of the deposits did not come from cash deposits but merely from purchase of debt. In the old system, these were visible in the balance sheet as promissory notes. Under the new one, they lost their identity. When customers drew cheques against their deposits it led to multiple expansion of credit through the system.

The banking system was, therefore, able to create an enormous super-structure of credit built upon a small amount of bullion. A merchant brings debt to the banker who with a flourish of the pen issues promissory notes or cheques which the client can then use to settle claims made against him/her. The debt given in exchange for debt is akin to the bank actually giving the client coins in exchange for the debt purchased.

Like we mentioned in the first chapter of this book, money is nothing but a receipt, a bookkeeping entry that establishes that the bearer has given someone in society for goods and services of a certain value and that s/he has a claim over anyone in that society goods and services of an equivalent amount. Just as gold and silver coins act as money, a cheque or promissory note establishes precisely the same fact, at a much lesser cost to society. Imagine the resources that would have to be spent on mining and stamping gold and silver coins if all transactions had to happen only with metallic money. The one necessary condition for such paper receipts to become money is their voluntary acceptance by society at large.

The benefits that banking brought to England were enormous;

Box 4.1: Banking and the Industrial Revolution

To show the enormous practical benefits that may be produced by Banking, even by a bad system, we have only to adduce its effects in England, in the second half of the last century. Burke says that when he came to London there were not twelve bankers out of London there were not twelve bankers out of London. But in 1769, the first patent for the steam-engine was taken out by James Watt, and the spinning jenny was invented, and soon after that the country woke up from its lethargy, and commenced those great engineering works, which have so pre-eminently distinguished it from that day to this. Now, to carry out these works an enormous amount of capital in the form of money was absolutely requisite, but it would have taken a long time to accumulate this necessary quantity, and it would have required an enormous expense, because the necessary amount of gold and silver could only have been acquired by the exportation of an equal quantity of manufactures. But this was the case—an innumerable quantity of bankers started up in all directions, who created promissory notes, which circulated exactly as actual money did, and performed exactly the same functions as money did and by means these great works were carried out.

Source: Henry Dunning Macleod, *A Dictionary of Political Economy*,
vol. 1, Longman, Brown, Longmans, and Roberts, London, 1863,
p. 77.

---

the 'success' of the Industrial Revolution is usually attributed to science and technology while the role of banking is unfairly consigned to the backburner. As we will see later, England's banking system was the envy of the world and something that other Western nations sought to emulate.

Although England encountered several monetary crises and bank runs over decades to come, a new way of money creation had been found. Perhaps indigenous banking in India never developed along these lines, particularly note issue, due to the nature of domestic trade and also because pre-colonial India may never really have faced a chronic dearth of coins (or even depended on currency and credit money) to meet the demands of the real economy.

4.3: THE RISE OF MODERN BANKING IN INDIA

Ideas shape the course of history.

JOHN MAYNARD KEYNES

A brief history of indigenous bankers before the rise of European banking in India has already been presented in Section 2.2. Apart from lending or financing by way of direct transfer of coin or what is simply 'money lending', indigenous banking developed an effective system to economize on the movement of precious metals from place to place. Wherever direct reciprocal exchange did not exist between two distant places and it became necessary to transmit metallic money it was discovered that the use of paper documents would economize, if not altogether render needless, the use of metallic money in such inter-regional trade. The transmission of money (coin) not only entailed loss of interest during the interval of transit, but also lead to expenditure on security measures with the possible risk of total loss. The substantial advantages from avoiding moving of coin, as seen in previous chapters, gave rise to a system of Bills of Exchange or hundi.

Apart from engaging in trade and the transfer of money through hundi, indigenous bankers also engaged in some other functions of banking amongst which was the business of safe custody and collection of revenues. In 1741, when an inventory of the effects of a Company's shroff was being made in Madras, local residents claimed the bulk of the effects in his possession were those given to him for safe custody. There is also mention that several hundreds of years ago indigenous bankers charged one-twentieth per cent per month for safe custody of gold and silver valuables if kept open, and one rupee per item if kept under a sealed cover. But this was a minor activity; their main business was discounting of bills and spatial transfer of money.

In many parts of the country, revenues were not paid directly to the government but through shroffs as 'farmers of revenue'. As the government installments fell due before they were collected, shroffs made the payments in bills of 15 or 20 days and thus became sureties for the revenues. Manikchand (Jagatseth) was the Treasurer-

General of Bengal and keeper of the Nawab's private hoards. In April every year zamindars and collectors of revenues assembled at Murshidabad and settled accounts with the treasurer. Entitled to receive 10 per cent on all payments to the Nawab, Jagatseth's profit from this source alone was estimated at 40 lakhs. In all parts of the country, revenues were transmitted to the headquarters by means of hundis supplied by the shroffs.

But it is not in these services that the roots of modern banking are found. It is in the economy over use of precious metals that banking developed in the West. Even the hundi, although it eliminated the need for transport of coin and bullion, was neither replacing nor creating money for people still relied on currency for exchange. Modern banking began its history in India only after the Company had established its rule over Bengal. And just like in England, the roots of modern banking in India developed from an acute shortage of coin that developed post-diwani, the chaotic situation that prevailed on account of the circulation of several debased currencies and the burgeoning needs of the Company for its territorial expansion. The crisis over currency and the consequent premium on loans induced the government to look for way out.

The immediate solution to the problem of a scarcity of coins was to introduce notes into circulation. Unfortunately, in *c.* 1770, in a desperate bid to overcome the problem, the Company began forcing unpopular notes into circulation. It is not clear whether the notes bore interest but several complicated and confusing rules were enacted to attain this objective. It paid all salaries or fixed disbursements exceeding £1,200 a year, half in notes and half in cash, thus saddling individuals in remote places with the Company's paper, which people had to get rid of at a loss. Often there was nothing in the treasury except paper with which to pay the officials. An old newspaper at that time once announced, as an extraordinary event, that Calcutta employees of the Company would receive a month's pay in silver. At a time when the Company had little economic or political legitimacy, it was obvious that its notes would not find general acceptance as money. Perhaps even the Company itself was not sure of its own future; although paper was made a legal tender from the government to the public, the public was not, as a matter of right, to offer it in discharge of government demands.

After this unsuccessful attempt by the colonial government at note issue, it was decided to encourage private agencies to do so. One of the first banks started in India under European auspices was the Bank of Hindostan, established *c.* 1770 as a branch (with distinct operations) of Messrs. Alexander and Co., one of the leading Calcutta firms of the period. Previous to this date the English merchant houses of Calcutta did carry out some banking functions as agents for the whole of the civil and military services, the planters, and smaller private merchants scattered over the Upper Provinces. The Bank of Hindostan was, however, one of the first banks in India to issue notes. These notes circulated in and around Calcutta but were not found in the interior parts of the country. The government did not agree to their acceptance as legal tender, refusing to allow them to be received into the Collectors' Treasuries. The quantum of note issue fluctuated widely, sometimes mounting up to Rs. 2–2.5 million and at others running down to as low as Rs. 200,000–300,000 according to the state of the market. The Bank faced a major run in 1819 when false rumours were spread that unless notes were brought in by a certain day, they would not be paid. The withdrawals amounted to some Rs. 1.8 million, but the Bank surmounted it without great difficulty.

The next bank that seems to have come into existence was Warren Hastings' 'General Bank of Bengal and Bihar' established in 1773 but dissolved within the next two years. The purpose of the bank was to ensure smooth remittances by bills of exchange with fixed commissions and rates of exchange. It had a branch in every collectorate and its two managers were Indian shroffs. More than a decade after the Bank of Hindostan was set up came the Bengal Bank in the year 1784. The bank had a limited circulation of notes amounting to less than Rs. 1 million, a copy of which is shown below in Box 4.2. However, on account of a run on the bank after alleged over-lending to fund the war with Tipu Sultan, it closed in 1791.

Concurrent with the Bengal Bank was the General Bank of India, which was also in existence in 1790. This bank appears, like the Bank of Hindostan, to have been started by one of the mercantile firms of the period but there is little further information on this bank. In Madras Presidency, one of the earliest banks was the

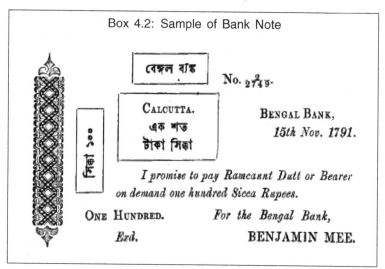

Box 4.2: Sample of Bank Note

Source: G.P. Symes Scutt, *The History of the Bank of Bengal: An Epitome of a Hundred Years of Banking in India*, Bank of Bengal Press, Calcutta, 1904, p. 2.

Carnatic Bank, which began operations in 1791. Nothing more, however, seems to be known about this bank.

The European system of banking had been introduced in India by the great agency houses in Calcutta like Alexander & Co. These houses combined their merchant business with banking; they were agents for the whole civil and military service, agents for planters and merchants in the interior, bankers receiving deposits, making advances for produce and trade, and issuing paper money. Between 1813 and 1833, when restrictions were imposed on the trading activities of the Company, agency houses received great impetus to extend their trade and banking activities. In 1829–30, as we have already seen, a commercial crisis developed in Bengal leading to the collapse of several agency houses. Since many businesses had borrowed heavily from their own banks, a run on the latter was inevitable. For instance, the bankruptcy of one of the largest agency houses, Palmer & Co., led to a withdrawal of some Rs. 2 million from the Bank of Hindostan. Other agency houses collapsed in quick succession including Alexander & Co., Colvin & Co., Ferguson & Co., Mackintosh & Co. and Cruttenden & Co.

In spite of the urgent need for currency in Bengal post-diwani, these initial attempts by private banks to introduce notes into circulation were not particularly successful. The time was ripe now to (re)consider Henry George St. Tucker's proposal to set up a large bank with sufficient credit as a permanent solution to currency problems; the first concerted initiative by the colonial government of the East India Company to introduce bank notes into circulation came with the setting up of the Bank of Calcutta in May 1806, which later evolved into the Bank of Bengal. The bank's capital was Sicca Rs. 5,000,000 in five hundred shares of Sicca Rs.10,000 each. The operational guidelines included:

- Loans were to be made against security for a maximum period of two months, and which allowed a margin of at least 10 per cent.
- The Directors were to be prohibited from advancing monies to any party who might previously have not punctually fulfilled his obligations to the bank.
- The rate to be charged for loans was never to exceed 12 per cent.
- No borrower was to be indebted to the bank for a greater sum than Sicca Rs. 5,00,000.
- The bank had to maintain a cash reserve of at least one-third of outstanding liabilities.
- Total liabilities of the bank could not exceed total capital of the bank.
- The bank was prohibited from engaging in trade or in buying/ selling of securities.

But it was the possibility for the bank to issue its own bank notes in exchange for government Treasury bills which made it a modern banking institution. This is the essence of bank money where a bank's credit is used to buy debts in exchange for debt. As shown in Figure 4.1, bank notes were to be receivable in payment of government dues at the general treasury, and at all the public treasuries and offices in the Presidency. The Bank was to hold an *equivalent amount* of interest-bearing treasury bills against all its notes in circulation. Notes were to be issued in sums not less than 10 nor exceeding Rs. 10,000.

More than the benefits to trade it was the Company's desperate need for specie to finance territorial expansion that led to the development of banks in Bengal. As we have seen, the movement away from indigenous merchant-bankers meant that the Company grew increasingly dependent on English private merchants and agents for hard currency. Treasury bills and notes were issued against loans raised by banks but the system did not gain the kind of acceptance that the Bank of England was able to secure. The absence of legitimacy of the new colonial government was obviously a key factor that restricted the acceptability of bank notes.

Right from their inception, banks in India had a close connection with the government of the Company, which subscribed a part of the capital and also ensured that it had a right to nominate some of the Directors. In return for these privileges accorded to the government, the banks were given some concessions including the right of note-issue although several restrictions were imposed on acceptance of notes at government treasuries as well as the quantum of issue. The Bank of Bengal was initially compelled to maintain a cash reserve of at least one-third of its outstanding liabilities on demand and its total liabilities were restricted by the bank's capital of Rs. 5 million. In 1823 it was allowed to issue notes up to Rs. 20 million or four times its capital. Nonetheless, the bank faced a series of crisis, including forgery cases in 1828 and the agency houses crisis of 1832. Owing to the inauguration of the government paper currency scheme in 1862 on the behest of James Wilson (to be discussed in Chapter 5), the bank lost its privilege of note issue in 1862. To compensate for this loss, the Bank of Bengal and other Presidency Banks were made the sole repositories of the government's balances, which they could then use for their businesses.

The Bank of Bengal was never able to increase the quantum of its notes in circulation beyond £1 million. At about the same time, the total of notes in circulation in England had reached (under a highly restrictive system) about £24 million and in Scotland, £9 million. The notes put in circulation by the Bank of Bengal were totally insignificant and far below the needs of the economy. The country had instead to rely on ponderous and costly metallic currency. No doubt caution had to be exercised on an over-issue but a limited issue did have its own downside.

Deposits were not popular in India for a long period because employees of the Company and other immigrants never looked at their stay in a foreign land as a protracted one. Their aim was to make a quick fortune in India and take it back home. Surpluses were therefore shipped out of the country at the soonest or at worst locked up in a government loan. Native Indians too did not believe in keeping his savings in banks. Landed property and hoarding were the preferred alternatives. One reason could have been 'doubts of the stability of British rule in India' (Cooke, 1863, p. 74) or the possibility to earn higher returns from their knowledge of local opportunities. Banks in India, in the early years, were therefore able to earn profits not through deposits but on account of the high rates of interest, principally induced by a certain degree of risk, and the difficulty in obtaining securities of an unquestionable character.

4.4: FORGERY AND FRAUD

Forgeries of Bank of England notes are so frequent, because they are so easy of imitation. They are of inferior workmanship to common engraved shop bills!

J.T. BARBER BEAUMONT, 1818

Just as 'adulteration' and 'debasing' of coins was a common practice, bank money would face a corresponding problem: forgery and fraud. There were many instances of such practices in the early history of Indian banking too. One well documented case was the Rajkissore Dutt forgeries in 1829. The scam began in 1828 when Dutt opened a Bank of India and circulated bank notes among the Indian community. In 1829 he borrowed money from the Bank of Bengal against forged securities of the East India Company. The bank had advanced some Sicca Rs. 350,000 upon the forged Company's papers tendered by him for loan. When the papers were taken in the usual course to the Secretary for the required advance, he noticed some peculiarity in the printing, which made him suspicious and prompted him to send the papers to the Treasury for examination. On their being returned with the assurance that all was right, the Secretary cleared them. But in course of time, duplicate numbers of the securities turned up. Only then did the bank realize that they were indeed forgeries. The exactness of the signatures was so perfect that H.T. Prinsep, the Financial Secretary to government, whose name was appended to the notes, when placed in the witness box in Court, declared that he could not swear that the signatures were not his own. Apart from forgeries and frauds, banks had to contend with several small technical hitches that had the potential of cascading into crisis. An interesting instance can be found in Box 4.3.

Box 4.3: A Bank's Issue over Ink and Copper

Destructive Action of Copper on Ink. The directors of the Bengal Bank lately refused payment of a number of bank notes, in consequence of their being without any signature. It appeared that they belonged to a Hindoo, who had kept them in a copper box. He asserted, that they originally possessed the signatures of the director, comptroller, cashier, & c., but that they had disappeared—he could not tell how. Prinsep, conjecturing that the ink had been acted on by the copper of the box in which the notes had been kept, placed a paper written upon with English ink between two pieces of copper. After a short space of time, he found that the copper had decomposed the ink, and that the writing was completely effaced. He concluded that the statement of the Hindoo was correct, and recommended the bank not to refuse payment. The same destructive action is stated not to take place when China ink is employed.

Source: The Mechanics' Magazine, 1837, p. 240.

The first half of the nineteenth century saw several banks coming up but many also going bankrupt. The Commercial Bank, the Calcutta Bank, the Agra and United Service Bank, the Union Bank, the Government Savings Bank and the Bank of Mirzapur came in existence while the Calcutta Bank failed in 1829 and the Commercial Bank along with several minor institutions, went under in the terrible agency houses' crisis of 1832–3. The Bank of Mirzapur collapsed in 1837 just two years after its birth. The Bank of Hindostan was resuscitated but failed a second time *c.* 1866. The Bank of Bombay commenced operations in 1840 but during the years 1848–51 it faced a crisis on account of several forgeries in which capital to the tune of almost Rs. 19 million was lost, that ultimately brought it down.

The Bank of Bengal too had its own share of problems; between 1829 and 1835 it had to write off bad debts to the tune of some Rs. 400,000, exclusive of that involved in connection with the Rajkissore Dutt forgeries. The bank had assisted Messrs. Alexander & Co. to the extent of Rs. 2.3 million even though the limit imposed by the Charter was just Rs. 100,000. Moreover, although the Charter prohibited security in the form of immovable property, the Directors had accepted collateral in this form, and on the failure of the agency house, it actually worked the indigo factories itself. The authority to engage in trade was, however, in direct contravention to the charter of the bank. The Government Directors had concurred to this without mentioning the fact to the Government. The Governor-General ordered that a new charter, adapted to the circumstances of the country, be drawn up wherein it became the specific duty of the official Directors to see that its rules were never violated. In 1839, after prolonged negotiations, a new charter was given to the bank. The Bank of Bengal survived all through the nineteenth century. It was later merged with other Presidency Banks in 1921 to become the Imperial Bank of India and finally the State Bank of India in 1955.

It is interesting to note that whilst banks were started in the Bengal and Madras Presidencies in the late eighteenth and early nineteenth centuries, there is no trace of any European Bank in Bombay until about 1840—nearly 70 years after Calcutta had seen her first bank open to the public. However, in a rare archival text, I found an account of a Western-style bank having been set up as early as 22 December 1720 in Bombay although there is little reference to it otherwise (see Box 4.4).

In 1836, a proposal came from England for a 'great banking establishment for British India'. There were several reasons forwarded as a basis for this proposal but the most important was that the bank and the government being one their interests were too closely aligned. In any crisis of the government it was only inevitable that this would immediately translate into a crisis for the bank. To overcome this it was proposed that a new bank be set up of adequate size with a large capital base and extensive credit so

---

Box 4.4: One of the Earliest Western Style Banks Introduced in India

It was proposed therefore that the improved system should be introduced into Bombay, and that an establishment in which Europeans as well as wealthy Natives of the increasing community might place confidence, should be instituted. Messrs. Brown and Phillips, being appointed a commission to obtain preliminary evidence and sound the opinions of Natives, reported on the 25 July 1720 that they had 'talked with the most eminent black merchants', whom they found so favourable to their proposal that, in consultation with them, they had prepared the scheme of a Bank. So pleased were the merchants with the plan, that they voluntary offered a tax of one per cent upon their property to defray the first expenses, and as a small commencement a capital stock of a hundred thousand rupees was raised. It does not appear that it was ever designed to be a Bank of issue; but it was proposed to open cash credits, receive deposits in money, to discount bills, and make advances on mortgages or hypothecation of goods. . . .

On 22 December business was opened by proclamation, but as after many efforts we have discovered little of the Bank's operations, we conclude that they were of no importance . . . this attempt at banking was premature, and that many years elapsed before the European system was effectually introduced into India.

Source: *The Bombay Quarterly Review*, vol. III, January and April 1856, London, 1856, pp. 46–7.

---

that it could afford pecuniary assistance to the government. When the Directors of the Bank of Bengal were asked for their opinion they felt that the Bank of Bengal could itself take over the management of government business, and it was quite willing to extend banking facilities in India without the assistance of London. This reply put a closure to an interesting proposal for a larger bank.

There are several benefits that accrue to a country from the issuance of bank money but as governments would come to realize, the issue of such money is beneficial to all parties only when it is conducted upon a sound method of regulation. If not, the consequences are apparent from our brief narrative of early banking in India and the series of scams and failures which followed.

4.5: BANK FAILURES

I look upon all that is past as one of those romantic dreams which opium commonly occasions, and I do, by no means, desire to repeat the nauseous dose for the sake of a fugitive dream.

Lord Chesterton

The abuse of credit by agency firms, using the instrument of long-dated bills of exchange, took their toll not only on the merchant but also the dealers in such instruments—the banks. As mentioned at the end of Section 3.5, the essential difference in the commercial crisis of 1830 and that of 1847 was that while the former used the savings of civil and military officers to fund the expansion of trade, the latter developed from the excessive circulation of credit through bills of exchange. Promises to repay amounts borrowed today, tomorrow, are fraught with risks and uncertainty. But the temptation and appetite for large gains leads speculators to indulge in it. Overtrading is the obvious consequence and with excess supply of commodities, a crash in their prices becomes inevitable. The bubble bursts and those who have lent their savings in the hope of receiving it back with interest and profit, lose heavily. While this simple truth underlies many contemporary business cycles, the more complex economic environment and multiplicity in instruments of credit makes it harder for us to see through. However, the relative simplicity of the economy in the 1840s, as we have already seen, lays bare the abuse of credit and commercial crises.

This section explores how banks were sucked into the whirlpool of commercial crises, ending with nothing less than total bankruptcy. The case in point was that of the Union Bank which from being one of the most prominent institutions in Bengal declined into oblivion in a matter of less than two decades, taking with it the hard earned money of individuals and the trust of many more. Once again, our narrative will be brief and focus on the economics of money and the abuse of credit instruments *per se* rather than being a description of events and actions of individuals that led to the bank's failure. The latter has been accomplished in minutest detail in a work by Blair Kling (1976).

At the core of the Union Bank's decline was the abuse of bank *post-bills*, an instrument recognized for their safety and facility of transmitting money spatially. Bank post-bills were instruments in common use by banks. They were drawn and accepted by a bank and payable to order a certain number of days after sight. When endorsed by the payee they became payable to the bearer, and were negotiable as other bills or notes, until ultimately paid by the bankers issuing them (Grant and Fisher, 1865, p. 432). Using this instrument of post-bills, the Union Bank had given liberal credit to several firms for the indigo trade. But the borrowers were no ordinary firms; they included prominent trading houses like Cockerell, Larpent & Co., which traded as if it was one of the wealthiest houses in England, on little or no capital except a very bad debt in India; the Fergusson Brothers & Co. and Gilmore & Co. which had £400,000 of the bank's capital when they failed in 1842; Carr, Tagore & Co. who also had their representatives on the Board of Directors of the bank and were liable to the bank to the tune of almost £1 million, equal to the entire capital of the bank.

As illustrated in Figure 4.3, in July 1847 when the bank faced great difficulties on account of the crash in indigo trade, its Director, W.P. Grant, drew bills on Cockerell & Co. for £45,000 (it is not clear whether this was to clear his own debts or to obtain funds for the bank) and sold them to two companies Jardine, Skinner & Co. and Kensalls & Co., taking bills on the wealthy London correspondents in return. The money for which the Jardine & Co. and Kensalls & Co. bills were sold was credited into the bank. As security to Cockerell & Co., Union Bank post-bills were sent to them in London. The same amount of security by way of post-bills was also given to Jardine & Co. and Kensalls & Co. by the bank in exchange for their Bills on London. Meanwhile, the collapse of Cockerell meant that their bills on London were dishonoured. Moresoever, Cockerell & Co. misappropriated the post-bills. Reacting to the collapse of Cockerell & Co. meant that both Jardine & Co. as well as Kensalls & Co. did not accept the bills drawn on them in London and returned them unaccepted to the discount house. Thus, in order to find temporary funds of £45,000

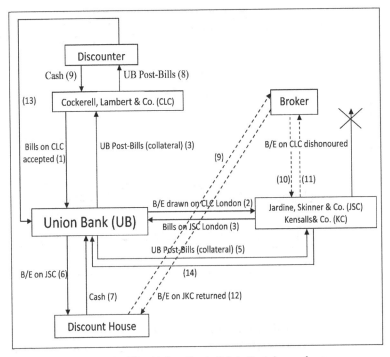

Figure 4.3: The Union Bank Crisis that Arose from
the use of Bank Post-bills

(either for the Bank or for Grant), the bank became liable for post-bills amounting to £90,000.

This was but one scam that the management of the Union Bank was accused of. The other one, perhaps more related to business than a scam, was the exchange business it had indulged in without realizing the risks and required quantum of liquidity. The bank's profit was the difference between the buying and selling price of the bills. The bills purchased in Calcutta were drawn at ten months' date. They may have reflected a good price on indigo when they were purchased but the prices (of indigo) could drop steeply so that the houses on whom they were drawn (E_M) could end up not being able to meet their obligations at the time when they were presented (Steps 7 and 8 in Figure 4.4). In such a situation, its bank in London, viz., Glyn, Halifax, Mills & Co. would refuse to

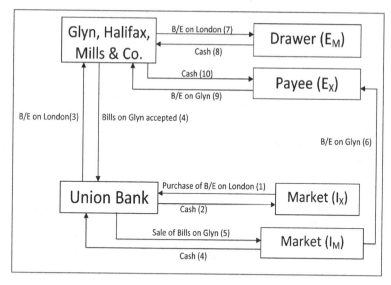

Figure 4.4: The Exchange Business of Union Bank

honour the bills drawn on them and presented by E_X (Steps 9 and 10 in the Figure 4.4). If the bank had sufficient funds to ensure that the bills on E_M were honoured, business could have been sustained. But its capital of just £1 million was insufficient to meet the contingencies arising from a decline in indigo prices.

The Union Bank had also invested heavily in indigo factories. By the mid-1840s, it had become a 'giant satellite of the indigo-exporting agency houses' (Kling, 1976, p. 210). This trend continued with disguised loans made to indigo cultivators. Indigo prices started falling in 1840 but the bank had to continue support to the planters and factories to keep them afloat, especially since large amounts had already been lent to them. The more prices fell, the more support was needed to bail them out. The crisis which began in England spread to Calcutta and by 1847 several agency houses went bankrupt. This was the beginning of the end of the Union Bank.

By the mid-nineteenth century, modern banking and with it financial crises had arrived in India.

CHAPTER 5

Paper Currency

Bankers own the earth. Take it away from them, but leave them the power to create money and control credit, and with a flick of a pen they will create enough to buy it back.

SIR JOSIAH STAMP, BANK OF ENGLAND

Paper currency has become so much part of the everyday lives of people all across the world that its usefulness is more or less taken for granted. Once in a while we might wonder if paper is convertible into gold or silver, but few actually go to their country's Central Bank to find out. So is your rupee note convertible into gold or silver? The answer is 'no'; meanwhile the purpose of this chapter is not to delve further into this question *per se* but instead to throw light on some of the fundamental issues that had to be addressed when attempts to introduce paper currency into an economy were made by governments. The Indian experience was particularly challenging because of the context in which the earliest proposals for paper currency were made. The political ferment that had grown from the Sepoy Mutiny of 1857 had thrown the finances of India in a deplorable state with accumulated debt of the British East India Company reaching a worrisome £50 million. In 1858, the decline and eventual end of the Company and the transfer of power to the Crown in the person of Queen Victoria brought India under direct British rule. Soon after India embarked on the introduction and use of paper currency—a landmark development in India's monetary system.

5.1: THE ECONOMICS OF PAPER CURRENCY

You have to choose (as a voter) between trusting to the natural stability of gold and the natural stability of the honesty and intelligence of the members of the Government. And, with due respect for these gentlemen, I advise you, as long as the Capitalist system lasts, to vote for gold.

GEORGE BERNARD SHAW

To understand the nature and essence of paper currency we must go back to the notion of money. As we have seen money is nothing but a receipt which certifies that *a* person has provided goods or services to *someone* in society and that *any person* in this society will have to repay the debt owed to the former, on demand. Recall, however, that this claim does not entitle the holder to any specific good or service. Macleod argues without debt there is no currency and it is essentially when goods or services *cannot be exchanged* for one another that currency intervenes. In this sense, currency abolishes exchanges rather than facilitating them. Money is called the circulating medium because it enables goods and services to circulate without an exchange of goods for goods. The quantum of money in circulation in an economy must then be equal to the quantum of debt in that economy.

Over time, societies vested their faith in precious metals as their primary monetary instrument. From this evolved the coin; a quantum of precious metal of a certain fixed value in terms of its weight and fineness (purity). A reliable coin did away with the need to weigh and assay the metal each time a transaction had to be completed. As network externalities from the use of precious metals and coins grew, so did their demand. Their limited availability in nature ensured that a chronic over-supply did not develop, which in turn ensured stability in their market price and consequently in their demand. The intrinsic worth of precious metals in the bullion market made coins from these metals easily acceptable; a virtuous circle that gave gold and silver their legitimacy as money and further as 'currency'. Metallic money being commonly used and generally accepted as the circulating medium began to be called currency although the term 'currency' actually refers to a particular action of money.

Having understood currency in its widest sense, we can look at it in a more narrow form; promissory notes issued by banks (usually a central bank or government bank) payable on demand which are generally acceptable amongst the public in lieu of coin in discharge of debt. As long as this receipt is accepted by one and all in a society it can be considered as money or currency; the form of promissory note whether metallic, paper or electronic blips on a computer screen is beside the point. It is worth reiterating that paper instruments including bank notes did not represent goods (like bills of lading do); they only maintain their value on the belief, confidence and trust (credit) that they can be exchanged for money at any (or some) point of time. If that trust or confidence fails or is destroyed, a colossal amount of property will be destroyed. This was a major concern in the introduction of paper currency. To prevent such loss of confidence it was agreed upon that the only sound basis for currency issue is to back it with bullion. This was called the Currency Principle; bank notes are to be issued exactly equal to the quantity of coin displaced from circulation. Those who adhere to this principle do believe that paper currency led to definite economic savings (for instance, the cost of transport) but arbitrary issue of paper currency should not be allowed. All paper currency in circulation should be representative paper money issued by banks or the government.

Such representative money has a long history. Ancient nations were unacquainted with the use of paper money simply because they had no paper. But it would be a mistake to suppose that they did not employ representative money exactly on the same principles as paper bank-notes. Even in times when skins were used as currency, small pieces were clipped off, and handed over as tokens of possession instead of the inconveniently bulky skins (money). It is however in China that the use of paper money was most fully developed in early times. More than a century before the Christian era, an emperor of China raised funds to conduct his wars using token money. The tokens were made of the skins of white deer, all of which he collected together at a single location. He further prohibited his subjects from possessing any animals of the same kind. Having thus obtained a monopoly of the material, reminding one of the monopolies of the Bank of England in watermarked paper, he issued pieces of white leather as money at a high rate. But it was in the middle of the thirteenth century that Marco Polo found a paper money in circulation in China, composed of the inner bark of a tree beaten up and made into paper, square pieces of which were signed and sealed with great formality. These notes were of various values, and were legal tender, death being the penalty imposed upon those who refused to receive them. Counterfeiters likewise incurred the same penalty. Another traveler, who visited China in the fourteenth century, gives a very similar account of the paper money circulating, and adds that, when worn or torn, it could be exchanged for new notes without charge.

Limiting paper currency to representative money (backed 100 per cent by bullion or coin) was a view not accepted by all. There are those who think that the Currency Principle is too strong and unnecessary. As long as banks notes are convertible on demand and prudential norms are adhered to, issue of bank notes would be kept in check. As discussed in Chapter 1, there is no way of knowing what the optimal quantum of money in circulation should be at any point of time. Take for example paper currency of Rs. 1 million replacing Rs. 1 million in coin; here the Currency Principle may not be effectively met since the velocity of circulation of paper and coin could well be different. The only way then to figure out whether paper currency issued is excessive is when the price level, the price of bullion and/or foreign exchange rates change. Of course, if the conversion rate between paper and bullion is fixed legally then as the price of bullion increases, Gresham's Law would be set in motion so that overvalued paper would drive away metallic currency from circulation.

The idea of inconvertible paper currency did exist too. Here paper money would consist of notes that were irredeemable on demand. These notes could also be issued by banks or the government. Although there were long periods of time in the Bank of England's history when notes were declared irredeemable they were not declared to be permanently irredeemable at the time of issue. When there exists no expectation on their convertibility, paper currency is called fiat money. Such paper money could be issued with or without security. In the former case, the security of land or of taxes may be assigned as backing for the note issue. In the latter, no backing exists at all and notes are issued under political authority and declared to be legal tender, forcing people to accept it in discharge of debt. Although the production of coins from precious metals takes away capital from its alternative productive uses, it more than compensates for this opportunity cost by creating additional value to the remaining capital as exchanges become possible. Nonetheless, any means by which use of coins in an economy can be reduced would release capital for more productive uses. There are additional savings that accrue to society from minimizing the use of coin including savings in operating mints, savings through reducing wear and tear of coins, and finally savings in transporting coins from place-to-place. Banking operations, through instruments like cheques, orders transferring funds from one account to another, drafts, bills of exchange and hundis, was the primary system by which such economy in capital was implemented. But perhaps the most cost-efficient money possible is paper money issued in the form of printed note, which reads as a promise to pay the bearer a certain amount of the standard money of the country on demand. With paper currency it would become possible for banks to immediately convert bullion acquired by merchants through exports of commodities into money. In Bombay, for instance, the delay in minting coins meant that merchants had to wait for a while before their bullion could be converted into coin. The advantages of paper money are many and well recognized; however, the disadvantage in terms of excessive issue and inflation are real concerns that could easily outweigh the benefits.

The Currency Principle became the norm in England after the Bank Charter Act of 1844 was passed by the Parliament under the government of Robert Peel. Until then the principle was not adhered to; the Bank of England as well as other private banks issued convertible bank notes based on their own judgement of necessary reserve requirements or what came to be referred to as the Banking Principle. During this period, bank runs were a common phenomenon, causing great hardship for the general public. Under the Bank Act of 1844, the power to issue notes was taken away from private banks and assigned solely to the Bank of England. Furthermore, the Bank of England itself was restricted to issuing notes only if they were backed fully (100 per cent) by gold and up to a maximum of £14 million in government securities.

The Bank Act restricted only issue of bank notes; it did not restrict the creation of new bank deposits. This meant that the system of commercial credit could still exist so that bills of exchange (debt) could be purchased against debt in the form of deposits (see Chapter 3). Bank notes were effectively and efficiently replaced by a system of deposits and cheques that provided an elastic supply of money to meet the demands of a growing economy. This system was perfected by England over the years and compensated an inflexible bank note system; to Keynes (1913) this system was 'more perfectly adapted for the economy of gold than any which exists elsewhere (in the world)' (p. 16).

For India though, the Currency Principle and the Bank Charter of 1844 provided the conservative backdrop against which its own paper currency system had to develop and evolve.

5.2: PAPER CURRENCY IN INDIA

Thus, our national circulating medium is now at the mercy of loan transactions of banks, which lend, not money, but promises to supply money they do not possess.

IRVING FISHER

We have seen how, in the last decades of the eighteenth century, India had to face a chronic shortage of metallic currency when, under Company rule, the import of bullion against its exports was substituted by revenues collected internally. The situation was relieved in the early decades of the nineteenth century with the gradual elimination in monopoly powers of the Company, the entry of free merchants into India's foreign trade and withdrawal of prohibitions in Europe for the export of precious metals to India. These factors allowed India to increase its exports so that a net inflow of bullion once again became possible. While a portion of bullion was minted into coin for circulation as money, a significant portion of it continued to be hoarded or converted into jewelry. In 1835 India opted for a monometallic silver standard; unfortunately, the gold discoveries between 1848 and 1850 led to an abundance of gold. Silver soon became the relatively scarce metal. This also coincided with a steep growth in India's external trade and commerce; in particular, cotton exports to England as a substitute for American cotton which had collapsed as a consequence of the Civil War. With India importing more than the annual production of silver, there was a growing fear that the increase in price of silver would permanently cripple her commerce. Calls for a switch to gold became louder while, at the same time, proposals for a paper currency also gathered momentum.

Dalhousie's monetary legacy, his proclamation of 1852, had further deepened the dependence of the economy on silver. With gold completely demonetized, silver was the only metal available for currency. This proved to be a severe constraint especially for larger wholesale exchanges. Decades earlier, from the 1770 currency crisis onwards, several private banks had issued notes in Bengal. The three Presidency Banks, established under government control at Calcutta, Bombay and Madras, were allowed to issue notes under their charter from 1809, 1840 and 1843 respectively. The notes of the Presidency Banks did circulate as money to a limited extent. As security an amount of government 'treasury notes' equal to one-fourth of the quantity of bank notes in circulation had to be held. However, the notes were not legal tender and therefore their circulation barely touched £5 million;[1] an insignificant figure compared to the quantum of silver coins in circulation, which may have been close to £100 million. The other banks in existence at that time like the Oriental Bank, Mercantile Bank, Agra and U.P. Bank, etc., had paltry sums of notes in circulation; the total amounting to just a few hundreds of thousands of pounds.

In addition to bank notes there were government-issued promissory notes and interest-bearing treasury notes; but these too were rather unsuccessful in alleviating the dependence on silver. The 'promissory notes' were drafts on the treasury for the payment of interest on public debt; the 'treasury notes' were a kind of treasury-bill, whose price varied materially from time to time. Their quantity in circulation in any given year between 1850 and 1856 never reached a million pounds. Apart from not being legal tender, a reason for their failure was that these notes lacked liquidity; they were not allowed to be received in payment of revenue for twelve months from date of issue, they were discharged only at their place of issue and their face value was too large. Moreover, the conversion of these notes being restricted to their place of issue meant that circulation of these notes never extended beyond the main towns as people usually needed small value coins for their dealings in the interior regions of the country. In addition to these technical deficiencies, one can easily appreciate the most fundamental problem in introducing a non-metallic currency; the lack of trust and confidence of the people in the very survival of the Company and its government.

As mentioned above, the shortage of currency in circulation opened up two important debates in India. The first was the necessity and challenges in introducing paper currency and second, on whether and how India could move on to a gold standard instead of silver given the plentiful supply in the world of the former. In this chapter we examine the deliberations that occurred over the former question, leaving the latter issue for the next chapter. The benefits that could accrue to society from non-metallic money were never really the matter of contention; it was the possibility of an over-supply that was the basis of opposition to them. To fully appreciate this debate, we must take support of the Quantity Theory of Money as interpreted in our introductory chapter. While a dearth of currency could actually mean that an economy is constrained from achieving its full potential on account of limitations on exchange, an excess of money in circulation would lead to inflation and a redistribution of wealth. As there is no measure of whether there is 'too little' or 'too much' of the circulating medium in an economy, the debate often remains a debate with no definitive answer.

These issues were all set to play out in British India. In a Financial Despatch dated 27 April 1859 to Rt. Hon. Stanley, Secretary of State for India, Canning, J. Outram, J.G. Ricketts and B. Peacock outlined a proposal for the introduction of a paper currency. This was followed by a note by the Financial Secretary, J. Lushington, on the extension of the paper currency across India. Charles Wood, Secretary of State for India, responded to these proposals on 4 November 1859, but not favourably. He wrote that although the economics of a paper currency was acceptable, the 'sensitiveness of the Indian money market was so manifest' that the time was not appropriate to introduce any measure which might worsen it. Meanwhile, James Wilson, a remarkable financier and an influential economist was sent to India in 1859 on a mission to tackle the financial condition of the government. On the 25 December that same year, Wilson drew up a minute drawing on the proposal of Canning et al. for a paper currency.

Although a new chapter had opened in Indian history with the replacement of the Company by direct British rule, the economic context at the time of Wilson's arrival for the issuance of paper currency still remained challenging. By examining his detailed and meticulous plans, many interesting and important facets of paper currency and of money in general, are revealed.[2] In a speech made by Wilson on the 3 March 1860 delivered in the Legislative Council, Calcutta, he outlined his plans to introduce a convertible paper currency in India. The advantages that would flow from this were the savings in using metallic currencies especially savings in the maintenance of coins, costs of transporting metallic currency from place to place on account of its weight and bulk, and losses due to theft and robbery.

Wilson's scheme for India was to introduce a convertible paper currency as legal tender; an inconvertible one that would simply be unacceptable to the public when, as mentioned above, the government's legitimacy was at a low, post mutiny of 1857. But even if the paper currency was backed by precious metals it represented, there was still an important choice to be made. Should the paper be backed 100 per cent by gold or silver or would it suffice if reserves were a fraction of this? The latter is akin to fractional reserve banking where, say, with Rs. 100 worth of gold or silver, notes to the tune of Rs. 400 would be issued. The reserves would be sufficient to meet the demand for convertibility of paper to metal at any point of time. In other words, the great practical question that had to be solved in the issuance of paper currency was how the government could ensure the maximum possible advantage at minimum risk, i.e. how much paper may be issued without reserving gold or silver to the full extent but, at the same time, renders its convertibility *absolutely* certain? Wilson scheme of leveraging precious metals to issue paper currency was based the principle that sufficient reserves must be maintained at all times to ensure the convertibility of paper into coin. Moreover, assets (or securities) of an undoubted and available character should always exist sufficient to represent the entire amount of such paper issues. Convertibility is ensured through reserves and ultimate payment of the notes by the balance held in government securities. If these conditions are met, the demand for actual conversion of paper into coin would in fact be minimal on account of the sheer confidence in the currency.

One of the most critical benefits from the issue of convertible paper currency was the possibility for the Government to raise public loans without interest. The operation happened thus; suppose a deposit of Rs. 30 million in silver coins was made in a bank against which notes of equivalent amount are issued. Out of this Rs. 30 million, Rs. 10 million was held by the bank as silver coin and the remaining Rs. 20 million was used to buy government securities (which could then be held as security for the issue of notes). This purchase disengaged a capital of Rs. 20 million of the government which was then used for alternative purposes, including repayment of old debt. This was especially useful given that the Company's debt at the time of its dissolution had crossed the £50 million mark. A significant profit accrued to the government from the interest avoided on such securities thus held against the portion of notes not represented by coin. Yet another advantage that accrued from the scheme is that the net supply of government securities in the market being reduced by this amount (that the government would otherwise have to sell to raise money), resulted in a higher price of the securities for a given market demand and consequently a lower yield or effective market interest rate. The lower market rates of interest also increased the demand for industrial and productive investment. Furthermore, reduction of debt and interest payments led to a reduction in taxation, giving a positive impetus to trade.

Implicit in Wilson's scheme was the belief that an increased supply of money would bring about benefits to the real economy; this

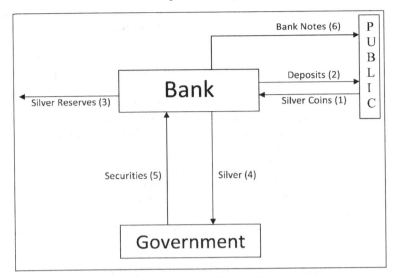

Figure 5.1: Issue of Bank Notes

would have indeed been the case if the Indian economy was operating with a sub-optimal quantum of currency in circulation. Given the scarcity of silver, and the demonetization of gold, leveraging available metallic currency with issue of paper currency could have stimulated trade and investment, resulting in higher real output. But there were others who saw a downside to this line of reasoning. Amongst them was W. Nassau Lees who accused Wilson's scheme of creating some £51 million in paper currency against £17 million in coins and bullion as being solely in the selfish interest of the government. He questioned whether it had the 'right to make use of its prerogative as a government to bring them about unnaturally for the purpose of reducing a debt incurred through its own mismanagement?—that is the question; and I venture to answer,— it has not' (Lees, 1864, p. 126). Unlike Wilson, Lee saw increased money supply translating into higher prices, with little impact on the real economy. He argued the consequence of the scheme would have been to inflate the currency of the country—to cause a general rise of prices; to raise largely the wages of labour; to reduce considerably the means of all persons living on fixed incomes; and to depreciate generally the property of all capitalists. The only

> ### Box 5.1: Bubbles for Children and Men
>
> The bubble, which for an instant sails majestically through the air, delights an admiring group of children, and, with wonder they gaze on the prismatic beauty of its colours, as they dance in the bright rays of the summer's sun. 'Look!' they cry, 'we have *created* it, how firm, how solid, how beautifully it soars aloft! higher! still higher! Yet higher still!—surely it will reach the skies!' But alas for the vanity of human wishes; bubbles *always* burst, and the deluded children are left—with so much soap-suds in their eyes! But if bubbles are fascinating to children, to grown men far more fascinating are dreams of prosperity based on paper issues which are not money, yet not a whit better fate awaits them; and awaits them; and with other schemes, however well devised, if inapplicable to the existing conditions and circumstances of things, it is much the same. Both, like bubbles, are destined to burst and vanish in thin air.
>
> *Source*: Nassau W. Lees, *The Drain of Silver to the East, and the Currency of India*, Wm. H. Allen & Co, London, 1864, p. 130.

beneficiary from Wilson's scheme then would have been the Government. Particularly interesting, and contemporary in his articulation, was Lees' analysis on how the increased money supply would result in a financial 'bubble' (Box 5.1).

Wilson's scheme also met resistance from the then Secretary of State for India, Charles Wood, who wanted notes to be covered rupee for rupee by an equivalent amount in metallic reserve; in other words, adherence to the Currency Principle. A very small fraction, however, of paper could be issued against securities instead of metal. Wood was following the conservative stance of Sir Robert Peel's Bank Act of 1844 that aimed at monetary contraction and repression of evils arising from over-issue and redundancy of currency. The prevailing situation in India at that time further contributed to anxiety over issue of a paper currency; the mistrust of the people towards the British government, the refusal and unwillingness of the people in receiving notes and the eagerness to government's conservative approach. Opponents to Wilson's scheme, which *per se* did not completely eliminate the danger of the government over-issuing paper currency, also saw an inherent moral hazard once a degree of confidence in paper currency had been established there was a greater likelihood of an over-issue.

However, Wood's conservative approach, unlike Wilson's scheme, made money supply inelastic in the extreme, incapable of expanding with the needs of the economy unless there was an equivalent amount of specie to back it. To Wilson, this constrained approach towards paper currency in fact defeated the very purpose of paper money and would, at the same time, ultimately circumscribe the profits of the issuing authority, the government. Moreover, his scheme had not called for the introduction of an inconvertible currency in which case some of the fears raised by the Secretary of State could have been well founded. Instead Wilson's scheme was a long-term initiative to substitute coin with paper currency by retaining and setting aside total security available at all times for the redemption of such paper, the whole of the valuable consideration it received in exchange for such notes at the time of issue. It was not a means of momentary relief from momentary pressure. By the end of 1859 Lord Canning felt that there was no need for apprehension on Wilson's scheme and on 29 December 1859, he forwarded the Minute by Rt. Hon. James Wilson to the Secretary of State for India, reiterating that it was perfectly safe for the introduction of paper currency. Public credit, trade and occupations were fast improving throughout the provinces that were disturbed by the Mutiny and mistrust for the scheme raised earlier was not well founded. Sir Charles Wood, however, did not relent and Wilson's scheme was not implemented as he had proposed.

But there are interesting historical lessons to be learnt from Wilson's Minute, which dealt with many aspects related to the introduction of paper currency. First and foremost, the big challenge was to ensure the ready conversion of notes in the interior parts of India (where large purchases of commodities had to be made), and at the same time provide adequate reserves against the possibility of too many notes being presented for payment at any one place and at the same time. Meeting these challenges simultaneously would force the government to maintain an inconveniently large amount of cash balance in district treasuries. To overcome this problem it was suggested that conversion should be allowed

only at a few large treasuries, conveniently located within demar-
cated circles of 300–400 km. in diameter. A typical district like
Oudh would be divided into three or four circles, and the batch
notes of one circle would be acceptable only in that district and
perhaps in the treasuries of a few neighbouring districts. Each circle
treasury would have to retain a cash balance of 25 per cent of total
paper issue; the figure was based on the experience gathered from
the Bank of Bengal. In this way it was felt that a large amount of
notes could be put into circulation in India without an increase in
specie.

The plan of using circles to minimize the necessity for smaller
banks to hold reserves and also transport of coin to the interior-
most parts of the country was at first glance a convenient solution
to these problems. The alternative, a uniform currency system, would
have put too high a monetary burden on the government; as a simple
example, consider a Bombay merchant wanting to buy cotton in
Nagpur. He would deposit silver in Bombay, procure notes and
take them to Nagpur where he would once again reconvert them
for coin to be used for purchase of cotton. In this way the cost of
transport of silver would fall on the government. If the bank in
Nagpur did not have the required amount of silver, there would be
a run on the bank. As this would have to be avoided, the bank in
Nagpur would have to be sufficiently well stocked with coin in
addition to transport cost. Given these limitations of a uniform currency, the alternative circle system seemed to be a practical option.

However, it was later felt that the circle plan was actually a limiting factor due to the simple fact that it rendered the paper currency practically inconvertible. A person travelling from Calcutta
to Lahore, after crossing the first circle would suddenly find that
his money lost its power of being legal tender; he would then have
to exchange it with a local moneychanger for local currency at a
considerable fee. While it was accepted that establishment of circles
instead of a uniform currency saved the government from incurring the cost and risk of transporting bullion, the scheme went to
the other extreme and in fact, as one critic put it, 'the knot had
been severed, not untied' (West, 1867, p. 687).

Without easy and ready convertibility, a vicious circle arises in the use of paper currency; why would cotton traders in Nagpur insist on silver instead of paper? Because paper was not current in Nagpur. But why was it not current? Because it was not convertible. The only way out then was to make convertibility of paper easy and convenient. Every district treasury would have to be made an office of issue and payment of notes. No doubt the burden of transporting bullion and coin would fall on the government, but in the longer term ease of convertibility would actually render paper current and reduce the actual need for conversion. Paper currency would become current.

Although it may not seem to be a matter of great importance, the decision on the denomination of paper currency was also a complex one. On the one side there were arguments for small denomination notes. Given that the transactions cost of conversion of small denomination notes would also act as a disincentive for frequent conversion it was suggested that such notes should be introduced first. Large denomination notes, on the other hand, were more likely to be converted into coin to engage in smaller transactions. Wilson, however, proposed that, as was done in England, higher denomination notes of Rs. 10 and above should first be issued in India. The reason for this strategy was that high-valued notes would take away little from coins in circulation; instead they would act as substitutes for bills of exchange and cheques. If for some reason, circulation of high-denomination paper currency was suppressed, the impact would be minimal on the economy as the shortfall would be filled in by other paper instruments. This, however, would not be the case with low denomination paper currency. Bills of exchange and cheques given their transactions costs rarely circulated in low denominations. In England, it was feared that one pound notes would drive a lot of gold out of circulation causing its price to fall (on account of decreased demand for gold as currency) relative to the rest of the world. This in turn would have lead to its export out of England. The consequences could then prove disastrous during periods of panics and crises when paper currencies cease to be negotiable. With gold exported and paper currency unacceptable, the dearth of money would accentuate crises. Wilson, however, following Ricardo's line of thought on this matter, argued that during a crisis there would usually be a surge in demand by domestic bankers for reserves. If there exists a well established paper currency in circulation in which the public has confidence and is also legal tender then paper could meet the demand for reserves. He also argued that it would be incorrect to suppose that the excess gold taken away from circulation on account of paper currency would actually be exported. If gold remained hoarded in the domestic economy, then as foreign claims for gold increased, the hoarded gold disengaged from circulation could actually be available to meet the demand from external claims. Finding the right denomination of paper currency was therefore a matter of great importance for the success of the scheme. Drawing upon the experiences of several countries, it was decided that notes would be issued in the following denominations in India: Rs. 5, Rs. 10, Rs. 20, Rs. 50, Rs. 100 and Rs. 500. The notes of higher denomination would be used mainly as remittance money and then exchanged for notes of lower denominations. Below Rs. 5, fractional payments would have to be made in silver and copper coins.

But there were still those who believed that the lack of low denomination notes would limit the potential success of paper currency in India. Chesney (1870) argued that a one rupee note was essential for India; given the number of transactions it would go through, in fact he even suggested that the note be made of card or leather. To him, notes of higher denominations would find comparatively little circulation and would constantly be brought to Calcutta for conversion into coin for making smaller payments. Unless these smaller denomination coins were replaced by paper there would be little net benefit accruing to society except as an instrument for spatial transmission of money.

Another crucial matter that had to be addressed in the introduction of paper currency was that of forgery. The innovations made by the Bank of England in this regard, and which the Indian Government could draw upon, were considered fool-proof, making forgery almost impossible. This included the quality and uniqueness of the paper and watermarks by which each denomination of note would be distinguished. There were also a series of checks in the numbering and lettering of notes; even if a whole note was destroyed except the number (say, 1789^A_B), bank cashiers would at once be able to ascertain the amount, date, place of issue and whether the note had been presented earlier for payment or not. 'However clever, therefore, Indians may be at imitating writing or printing, the paper used by the Bank of England, with the watermarks, which are visible to the common eye, would be a great security against even the attempt being made . . .' (Accounts and Papers, 1860, p. 104) to forge currency in India. The high fixed cost of setting up a printing press for forged notes was so prohibitive that it was unlikely to be set up in India. Apart from the cost, it would take a minimum of two years to set up, in addition to developing the technology for the watermark which at that time was confined to a single family in England. In fact, the effectiveness of the technology for printing of notes was considered so satisfactory that the Bank of England had not changed the plates for more than thirty years. Wilson also reveals that there existed at that time only three forged plates and the source of forged notes could be easily traced. In defense of his scheme, Wilson pointed out that in the United States, forged coins were a bigger concern than forged notes.

With forgery by and large ruled out, the next major decision that had to be made was the quantum of paper currency to be put into circulation. Between 1837 and 1860 some Rs. 1,050 million (= £105 million) of silver coins had been minted in India. The treasuries of the government itself held some £11–13 million in silver coin. The initial order of magnitude of notes in circulation proposed was around Rs. 100 million. This would mean a significant saving to the government as paper currency was considered to be similar to bank notes bearing no interest. There were, however, costs of producing notes that had to be considered. In London, notes were never re-issued; its average life therefore tended to be very short. The branches in the provinces, however, re-issued their notes several times over. In spite of this practice the Bank of England was able to register profits of close to £300,000 after paying an annual fee of £120,000 to the government for the privilege of printing paper currency. In India, it was suggested that notes could be re-issued and it was furthermore not expected that notes would come back for conversion as frequently as in London. After considering the costs of setting up and running the establishments for this purpose, the issue of paper currency was considered a viable and profitable decision.

Given the general nature of the scheme, Wilson then addressed another crucial question: whether management of the paper currency should be left to banks or assigned to the government. The concern with the latter option was the possibility of an over-issue of paper especially after a certain degree of legitimacy had been acquired by the British Indian Government. This was equivalent to debasement of coin by sovereigns, something that had been extensively resorted to throughout history. On the other hand, if public or private banks were to be given the responsibility of paper issue, two concerns remained; first, if the issue of notes backed 100 per cent by coin and public securities had not yielded additional dividends to the proprietors then they would at any time abruptly give up this activity; second, without any absolute guarantee by the state to convert paper into coin, it would become impossible to make paper legal tender, although in England, by the Act of 1844, paper issued by the Bank of England *was* made legal tender. But even in England there were some serious concerns over the practice so that the business of the Bank of England was separated into two parts; an Issue Department and a Banking Department. In spite of the Issue Department holding adequate reserves of bullion for convertibility of paper, a technical difficulty remained. In case of bankruptcy the bank could not set aside a part of its assets for conversion of its notes—the separation of the bank into two departments did not ensure the legal separation of its creditors.

But the biggest concern in India was that, unlike the Bank of England, no private bank in India possessed the kind of establishment that extended its activities across India. This made it all the more necessary for the Government of India to undertake such a scheme. Not only did the government possess the necessary reach, but it was through its operations including collection of land revenues and taxes, payment of troops, purchase of commissariat stores, and disbursement for public works that most of the monetary transactions of India took place. If the government had accepted settlement of its claims in paper, Wilson and his supporters were confident that paper currency could gain widespread usage with its credit-worthiness amongst users established. To address the problem of over-issue by the government, Wilson suggested that the issue of notes be kept as independent as possible of the Executive Government. Restriction by law on the issue of paper currency was therefore required; the law itself would have to be passed by Parliament (in England) and not the Legislative Council in India. A commissioner could be appointed by the Governor-General but not removable except by the Secretary of State and his functions would be defined by an act of legislature, to which he would be bound to adhere, under heavy penalties. Independence of the paper currency-issuing bank from government, which even today continues to be topical, was a visible concern in Wilson's scheme.

Wilson also outlined details as to where the notes would be manufactured, the numbering and dating of notes, printing of half-printed notes at their place of issue, as well as the operational aspect of the entire scheme. He suggested that all other notes in circulation, including the Bank of Bengal's notes be cancelled and replaced by government notes. A central bank of issue would be established in Calcutta attached to the Mint where notes for the whole of India would be half-printed and then distributed. The date of issue would be printed at the provincial banks. One of the first actions of the central bank would be to receive a large portion of the coin held by the public treasury against which notes would be issued. Banks too could exchange their coin for notes to supply to their customers. Thenceforth the Treasury would make all payments in notes, except small payments in coin. Holders of notes could, however, on demand and at will convert their notes into coins at the Issue Department attached to the Mint. Merchants receiving silver bullion for their exports could carry it to the Mint and exchange it for notes at once, without waiting for it to be minted into coin. These notes could be deposited into their accounts in banks, which could be freely withdrawn as notes and/or coin. This business of the Issue Department would therefore be self-acting; when notes were needed, silver would come in and when coins were wanted, notes would come back in. When silver is imported new notes would get printed and put into circulation.

Wilson further suggested that for a considerable period of time, till the system was firmly rooted, a sufficient amount of coin and silver would be retained for ready conversion of note into coin. As confidence grew, a significant portion of coin and silver could be used to purchase government securities but under no circumstances would reserves be allowed to fall below 33 per cent. Similarly, the provincial commissioners would remit their surplus silver and coin to Calcutta for purchase of government securities.

To secure the confidence of the public-at-large Wilson was categorical that full transparency was the key and all details of the notes in circulation, reserves held at in Calcutta and at each branch be published. Notes were to be issued only against coin and not against discounts, loans, or advances upon credit. The whole amount of notes in circulation would be represented in coin and public securities. The plan was to begin with Calcutta and take it to all parts of India in a period of two years. At the same he did not want this scheme in any way to be considered an alternative to the creation of a large banking corporation; the latter would be similar to the Banking Department of the Bank of England.

As we have seen above, Wilson's plan was opposed by Charles Wood who implicitly wanted to follow the Act of 1844 allowing for the issue of all paper in excess of a certain fixed minimum, *only* against coin and bullion. Meanwhile, Wilson's untimely death brought in Samuel Laing as successor. Laing's scheme bore little resemblance to Wilson's and instead adopted the Currency Principle exemplified by the Act of 1844 and followed by the Bank of England. The Indian Government would be at liberty to issue notes to the extent of £4 million against securities, i.e. the coin received in exchange for the notes would to this extent be invested *only* in government stock. All paper issues in excess of these £4 million would have to be covered by metal reserves. But Laing went astray from the views of Wood by proposing that note circulation should be developed through the agency of the Presidency Banks or chartered State banks. In exchange for some privileges to be accorded to them, these banks would establish branches throughout the country where government notes could be cashed on presentation. The banks would also be responsible for the transport of specie to meet the demands of their branches. Charles Wood who was still Secretary of State for India did not agree with the role accorded to the Presidency Banks by Laing. The matter remained in limbo except for the replacement of bank notes with government notes in the Presidency towns. Laing resigned from office and the matter was resolved under his successor, Charles Trevelyan, who combined features proposed by Wilson and Laing. The mode of regulating the reserves of bullion and securities were those proposed by Laing but the establishment of circle notes coincided closely with that of Wilson. However, one wish of Wood was not met; the lowest denomination of notes issued by the government was Rs. 10 and not Rs. 5 as he had wanted.

The results of the introduction of paper currency remained dismal in the years to follow. There are some reports from 1867 and 1870 which track the developments after the introduction of paper currency. Prior to the issue of paper, the three Presidency Banks had notes to the tune of some £3 million in circulation. By 1866, this had crossed £10 million. This threefold increase seems to be significant; however, caution needs to be exercised before reaching a conclusion. The paper of the Presidency Banks was notes held by the public, while the paper circulation of the government consists of notes held by the public, *including* the amount held by the state banks and different government treasuries. A very large deduction has therefore to be made from the nominal to arrive at the real or effective quantity of paper circulation, i.e. currency which actually makes exchange convenient to the public-at-large. Furthermore, since 1861 a great increase in trade and commerce had taken place. This leaves us with a counterfactual situation wherein even if paper currency had not been issued by the government, perhaps the Presidency Banks too would have been able to increase their notes in circulation on account of real economic growth.

Wilson's circle system also constrained the usage of notes in the interior regions. As a case in point, in a district like Waynad where a large number of employers required supplies of metallic money every week to pay their labourers, the inconvenience of not having a place within reasonable distance to convert currency notes into rupees became problematic. To overcome the problem, coffee planters would have an agent on the western coast, with whom funds would be deposited, and who were responsible for safe transmission of bags of rupees whenever required.

Going beyond the stipulated scope of Part I, it is interesting to see the usage of paper currency in India over the next few decades. Table 5.1 shows the relevant data for the nineteenth and early part of the twentieth century.

The key to the growth in use of paper currency in the third decade of the twentieth century was mainly due to the ease in the universal encashment of notes (Rs. 10, Rs. 50 and Rs. 100) into silver money. The last period also saw the issue of Re. 1 and Rs. 2-8a-0p[3] notes. It should be noted that in 1920 it was estimated that the rupees in active circulation amounted to some Rs. 2,700 million while the currency notes issued amounted to Rs. 1,860 million. The importance of introducing an efficient currency in India was seen as a way of exploiting its resources fully. We will return to the development of paper currency in this period later in the book; for now we have completed Part I of this book, which attempted to provide an economic insight into the various forms of money, their introduction and evolution in India as well as the periodic bouts of instability and commercial distress that arose in this process.

TABLE 5.1: GROWTH IN PAPER CURRENCY
IN INDIA, 1865–1920

Year	Value of Currency (Rs. million)	% increase in the period
1865	74.3	–
1875	11.24	51
1885	145.8	30
1895	307	111
1905	391.8	28
1915	616.3	57
1920	1745.2	183

Source: Jevons, 1922, p. 24.

NOTES

1. The exchange rate at that time was £1 = Rs.10 or Re. 1 = 2s.
2. Interesting details of the debate that took place in India and England at that time can be found in Ambirajan (1984).
3. The notation followed here is Rs. anna-paise (Rs.–a–p); an anna was equal to 1/16 rupee. It was subdivided into 4 paise or 12 pice (thus there were 64 paise in a rupee and 192 pice).

PART II

EXTERNAL AND INTERNAL STABILITY IN THE VALUE OF THE RUPEE, *c.* 1860–1971

CHAPTER 6

The New Wave of International Economic Integration

We must find new lands from which we can easily obtain raw materials and at the same time exploit the cheap slave labour that is available from the natives of the colonies. The colonies would also provide a dumping ground for the surplus goods produced in our factories.

CECIL RHODES

Although not commonly recognized, the period *c.*1860 to 1893 is one of critical importance in Indian monetary history, perhaps even internationally. The country was undergoing a qualitative shift from a medieval-feudal system to a modern-market based one, gradually transforming itself from a kind to a cash economy. This obviously meant that money began playing a more prominent role in the everyday lives of people. Furthermore, under British colonial rule, India's integration into the world economy as a supplier of important industrial raw materials was gaining momentum. Economic disturbances were no longer of mere local importance; disruptions in production of commodities would affect not just the lifestyles of a few wealthy Englishmen but could throw industrial manufacture half way across the world completely out of gear. And, as history had already shown, one of the most important causes for such disruptions in production could be small perturbations in money and credit markets. The early decades of the nineteenth century had already introduced India to the dangers of commercial distress; with monetary linkages rapidly extending to larger sections of the population, the effects of a crisis could now quickly percolate down to the masses and destabilize the economy.

At the international level, this integration of production across the world through trade and commerce also shifted the emphasis in international monetary economics from the search for instruments of money transfer to stability in exchange rates and price levels. And Britain was at the centre of these changes in the international economy; its exports rose eightfold between 1850 and 1913 and its foreign direct investment had touched 45 per cent of the world's total before the war. The variation in supply of precious metals with discoveries of mines across the world was becoming a major concern. Changes in supply and the relative price of gold and silver could have serious repercussions on production and trade. This led to the gold *versus* silver debate even as many argued in favour of gold *and* silver as the best solution to ensure stability; the latter refers to an international bimetallic system. But there was a definitive shift towards the gold standard in the last quarter of the nineteenth century and as countries one after another made the transition, silver prices crashed and with it the rupee. An era of rupee rate instability had commenced that ultimately culminated in the abandonment of the silver standard in India. New ways of maintaining exchange rate and price stability had to be devised, which I take up for discussion in later chapters of Part II. For now, I begin with debates and episodes that arose from concerns over instability in the relative prices of gold and silver in the final decades of the *silver* rupee.

6.1: THE COTTON FAMINE AND BOMBAY BUBBLE

It came with all the characteristic suddenness and swiftness and all the titanic force and velocity of the avalanche, sweeping away in its fatal course many an old institution and mercantile firm, and burying hundreds of mushroom monetary organisations which had enjoyed an ephemeral sunshine awhile.

Dinshaw Wacha on the Bursting of
the Bombay Bubble, 1865

Before I begin a discussion on the monetary events of this period, let me narrate an episode from the real economy that set the (shaky) stage for India's integration into the world production system.

Between 1840 and 1860, American production of raw cotton had increased almost 100 per cent while the demand from England's spindles had grown by almost 150 per cent; the demand-supply mismatch translated into higher cotton prices. The Cotton Supply Association, set up in 1857 over concerns of a possible crisis developing in Lancashire's textile industry from inadequate supplies of raw cotton prompted it to explore alternative sources. The potential in every tropical and semi-tropical country was investigated to meet an estimated supply gap of £30–40 million worth of cotton per annum. The Association outlined the need for close cooperation between industry, the government, development of public works and even the legal apparatus in order to ensure a reliable supply of cotton to England. But before all these plans could be put into action, the Civil War erupted in America; England was forced to turn to India to keep its mills running. The surge in exports of raw cotton from India can be seen in Figure 6.1. A great opportunity was now available for India to emerge as a long-term source for cotton but the sudden and unexpected windfall from its exports triggered off a massive speculative run that ultimately culminated in a bust that brought ruin to the economy.

In 1860 the proportion of Indian cotton consumed by England was 7 per cent, but by 1863 it reached 65 per cent. Until 1860 the annual exports of cotton from India were worth approximately

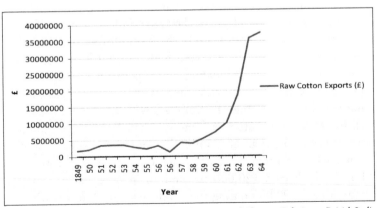

Source: DSAL, Digital South Asia Library (nd), *Statistical Abstracts Relating to British India from 1840 to 1865, First Number*, http://dsal.uchicago.edu/

Figure 6.1: India's Growing Raw Cotton Exports

£7 million annually. In the next three years, Europe paid more than £40 million annually to India for its imports of cotton, half of the amount being remitted in bullion. However, it is interesting to note that while the quantity of cotton produced had increased 2½ times it was the price increase that contributed even more to the rise in cotton revenues. In India, the beneficiaries of this ballooning wealth were not just urban traders; poor farmers were suddenly rolling in wealth, displaying their newly acquired bounty unabashedly. The literature speaks of people collecting fine breed of cattle and horses, riding bullock carts with silver-lined wheels and carrying bags of rupees on poles through local festive processions. A report mentions that in the Khandesh, traders were seen negotiating with peasants, bundles of cash in their hands, one with Rs. 30,000 and another with Rs. 40,000. Rural India too reaped the benefits of the cotton famine.

But more than these reports from rural India, scenes of the speculative frenzy from Indian cities, Bombay in particular were most vivid. The bubble was unequivocally set off by the sharp rise in the price of cotton that found recourse in excessive speculation on account of the lack of channels of productive investment except (as usual) land. Bombay was even then a city with scarcity of space; an island just eight miles in length and three miles wide. The growing trade and commerce accompanied by the burgeoning inflow of people into Bombay with the opening of the railways exerted immense pressure on land prices. The large inflow of money into the city on account of cotton trade therefore flowed towards investments in land given the expected high and quick returns from it. This contributed to the building up of speculative pressure on land prices while immediately reflecting on rental rates. Rents, even in normal times, were high in Bombay; with the boom, it exceeded all limits. House rents rose from less than Rs. 300 per annum to Rs. 1,000 in the span of months. The boom also spread rapidly to other parts of India. In Calcutta rents rose sharply; a mercantile house which paid £20,000 per annum in rents had to cough up more than £100,000 during the boom. Back in Bombay, with rents shooting up, schemes were proposed to reclaim land from the sea and alleviate the shortage of space. In a matter of just months, shares in the Colaba Land Company rose from Rs. 10,000 to

Rs. 1,20,000. Shares of the Back Bay Reclamation Company went up from Rs. 2,000 to Rs. 54,000. The share frenzy was not limited to land companies; even shares of press companies attracted speculators; the Elphinstone Press Company stocks went up from Rs. 40,000 to Rs. 1,35,000 and that of the Apollo Press Company increased from Rs. 12,000 to Rs. 20,000. An article by Charles Dickens captures the mood of the Bombay Bubble beautifully, with a touch of literary charm (Box 6.1).

Box 6.1: Charles Dickens' Account of the Cotton Bubble

The Rupee to the Rescue

There is an awful state of affairs in India now. People are making more money than there is money to make, and payment is becoming impossible. This, I believe, is the real meaning of the 'commercial crisis' which has some time past been threatened in the three presidencies. Trade never was in such a flourishing condition. Given, a pretext of any kind of plausibility, and a capitalist is at hand. You need not go for him to business haunts. He may be found anywhere—in clubs or hotels, encountered at street corners, or picked up at the band. Opium, tea, cotton, castor oil—native produce of all kinds, even to unfortunate indigo—nothing comes amiss to him. 'Europe goods', whose numbers legion is no name, find speculators equally abundant. And such has been the high pressure of transactions for many months past, that an explosion would have been inevitable long since, but for the safety valve of that glorious invention—limited liability . . . Your tailor, whom you have hitherto treated as an individual, sends you in your new bill, and your old too, it may be, not to mention your middle-aged too, as 'The Asiatic Clothing Company, limited', and instead of one creditor you have five hundred, with a collective capacity to be paid which there is no resisting. Your bootmaker—in whose small account there are some trifling items for saddles and silver-mounted harnesses—develops in a similar manner, and 'The Cape Comorin and Himalaya Leather Company, limited', reminds you of your past liability and solicits future favours. The livery-stable where buggies and horses are let out to the vehicleless and studlessensign, expands in a similar manner; and the other day there were in Calcutta companies to supply every possible want of the public, even the cutting of your hair and the shaving of your chin. . . .

Source: Charles Dickens, *All the Year Round: A Weekly Journal conducted by Charles Dickens*, no. 258, Saturday, 2 April 1864.

Like today, speculation on shares did not happen with hard cash; most of it was based on credit. This can be inferred from several facts that indicate that bullion inflows were not translated into an abundance of currency (coin). At a time when the coin of realm was the silver rupee, a significant portion of bullion imports into India during the cotton boom was actually gold. The gold imports in 1855–6 were about Rs. 25 million, which shot up to almost Rs. 100 million by 1864–5. Most of this gold went directly into hoarding and domestic consumption. The import of silver was also substantial, with a large part of it actually coined but then re-melted 'for bangles'. Between 1855 and 1860, the average silver imports were about Rs. 100 million, in 1865–6 it touched Rs. 180 million. But even at the height of the inflow of bullion into India Bombay was starving for the want of circulating medium; the Bank of Bombay's lending rate reached 23 per cent. If shares were not bought and sold with cash, then it could have happened only on the basis of credit and, as the case with many such instances in history, with the involvement of financial institutions. The Bombay Bubble was no different; speculative activity in land and shares was accompanied by the mushrooming of banks and financial institutions.

The bust came on 1 July 1865, bringing with it the downfall of many banks including the bank of Bombay. In fact, the ultimate cause of the Bank's failure was pinned to the Act X of 1863 which allowed lending of shareholders' and depositors' money to men of moderate means but out of proportion to their financial positions, without limit. Millions of rupees were given away or overdrawn without adequate guarantee. Concealment, cash credits with a single name, fixed loans and open loans with or without adequate securities at substantial premiums were rampant. Finally, it is important to note that most of the shares were actually bought and sold as 'time bargains' (or what resembles margin trading today) wherein no physical delivery of shares were taken; only the difference in purchase and sale price was settled. Initial purchasers bought shares on credit often taken from banks and promised to pay at a long future date, expecting to realize a huge profit as well as recover the original investment in the interim period. While the shares changed hands, profits were no doubt realized. However, by the time the original amount had to be repaid, share prices had crashed. Several investors pleaded bankruptcy and with it banks too faced the same disastrous consequences.

The cotton famine and Bombay Bubble are replete with stories of individuals, land reclamation companies and financial companies including banks with little or no track record that made large sums of money in a short span of time but lost all in an even shorter span of time. Amongst the most famous (or rather infamous) speculators was Premchund Roychund, who until the boom was a clerk earning £30 per year amassed a fortune of £2 million through daring speculation. Rustomjee, son of millionaire Parsee baronet Sir Jamsetjee Jejeebhoy, became a millionaire with capital estimated at £2.5 million. The nephew of Sir Jamsetjee Jejeebhoy, who from a vendor of old bottles became, at a point of time, one of the wealthiest men in the world. In 1865, however, he sought protection of the Insolvent Court; his assets were Rs. 1.3 million while his debts amounted to Rs. 5.5 million. He was sentenced to two years imprisonment for fraud.

Companies too were financially at an all time high; stock prices rising exponentially even before they had declared a single dividend. But there were stories of good companies like the Back Bay Reclamation Company which were also brought down by the hubris of a speculative bubble. Many people believed that it was a useful enterprise that could have been of the greatest use to society. The company was to engage in the first important public work by a private firm, which the government wanted to encourage by wise and liberal concessions. The company was to also set up the foundation on which Bombay's magnificent Port Trust was later built. It had commenced operations before the speculative bubble began but when the crash of 1865 came, the shares of the company also suffered. The shareholders who turned insolvent made distress sales of their shares in the market; shares of the Back Bay Reclamation Company fell as low as Rs. 400. Ultimately, the government decided to buy up the company, the shareholders being compensated with debentures.

Perhaps the most riveting account of the mania which gripped Bombay is the work of Dinshaw Wacha (1910); however, the account from the archives (Box 6.2) captures the mood at that time perfectly.

Box 6.2: The Bursting of the Bombay Bubble

It is not yet four months since an able writer, with peculiar means of information, described Bombay as a city has been enriched by an enchanter's wand. Every trader has become a millionaire, every wealthy trader a Rothschild; clerks were looking down with contempt at official magnates, merchants offering to prefects the fee simple of their pensions merely as an inducement to accept shares in their profits and their labours. Prices had risen till the wages of servants were multiplied by five, animal food was beyond the means of officers with fixed incomes, and the Government officially declared that unless salaries were increased by at least 30 per cent the Administration would be disorganized by want of men. Merchants held a speculation contemptible unless it promised 100 per cent, and peasants, unable to conceal, or use, or comprehend the sudden influx of wealth, jumped from tireless cart-wheels of solid wood to wheels bound round with silver tires. . .

At last the crash came . . . Paper property worth at least fifteen millions became for the moment absolutely worthless, and firms like the Camas, whose dealings cover the world, who believe themselves masters of millions, found themselves within an hour without a shilling. . .

There is not an industry connected with Bombay which will not feel the effect of the shock; there is scarcely a firm which will not suffer; there is not a family which will not for years to come have cause to remember the bursting of the great bubble of 1865. Of course Bombay will survive it all, for it has lost neither its original trade, nor the thirty millions accumulated out of its windfalls, nor the new industries those thirty millions must in the end develope, but the individuals who made up the Bombay world—they with new habits of luxury, new wants, new tastes, and new thoughts of life have to bear a return to deeper poverty than they thought they had escaped forever.

Source: *The Spectator*, no. 1928, 10 June 1865.

Most of the gains from higher cotton prices were captured by speculators, merchants and moneylenders. The returns were then invested in speculative businesses and hoarding; little was channelized into productive investment for improved cultivation. Only a few private companies installed cotton cleaning and pressing implements. The magnitude of benefits reaped by the ryots (cultivators) may have been only a small share of the total. India could actually have clothed the world but neglect in its cultivation rendered output short in staple and brittle. The want of proper transport meant its long exposure to weather, and the accumulation of dirt during loading and unloading meant that cotton exported was of inferior quality. It was not just the crash of the bubble that was the most important event; rather, it was India's missed opportunity for a larger market share of raw cotton supplies to the world in the years to follow.

6.2: A GOLDEN OPPORTUNITY

There is an awful state of things in India just now.
People are making more money than there is money to make. . . .

CHARLES DICKENS

Between 1814 and 1845, India's importation of precious metals had declined on account of a fall in its exports of cotton textile and the simultaneous increase in imports of cotton cloth from Britain. However, towards the mid-1800s, a relaxation in British tariff policy (which had earlier allowed import of British cotton and other goods into India at duties of just 2.5 per cent while preventing entry of Indian goods into England with duties of between 50 and 500 per cnet), and repeal of navigation laws gave a great fillip to Indian exports. The Crimean War of 1854 that cut off Russian supplies, particularly of oilseeds and fibers, and the silk crop failure of 1853 throughout Europe further benefitted India. But the greatest driver of Indian exports, as seen in the previous section was raw cotton. The outbreak of the American Civil War and the consequent disruption of supplies from America to England turned India into the primary source of raw materials to Britain's textile mills. Trade began flourishing like never before. The overall external trade of India increased from approximately £28 million in 1849 to almost £100 million in 1865. The burgeoning trade surplus was further supported by the inflow of large sums of money that came from borrowings to support the wars of the Company and later the British Government, the expenses incurred for suppressing the Mutiny and for carrying out large public works. The flow of precious metals began in full steam and from the beginning of the second half of the nineteenth century there was a sharp increase in imports of both gold and silver. As Coyajee (1930) put it, 'the increased flow of specie to India between the years 1855–6 and 1869–70 was indeed a remarkable phenomenon'. (p. 20)

At the same time, the numbers of British troops, railway engineers, contractors and workers, merchants and shopkeepers, speculators, port employees, new jobs and services all contributed to the increasing need for currency. Wages rose by almost 25 per cent while price level rose by almost 50 per cent between 1861 and 1866. Exports of opium, tea, indigo, castor oil, cotton—aided by the institution of limited liability and speculation, brought in an element of commercial fever in the three presidencies. To enable this larger volume of circulation of goods and services the currency requirements of domestic trade and commerce witnessed a simultaneous surge. The import of bullion and the coinage of silver rupees at the mints of the Presidencies show the growing currency needs of the Indian economy at that time (see Table 6.1 and Figure 6.2). With the supply of currency unable to keep up with rising demand, India was once again confronted with a problem that had haunted her on several occasions in the past—scarcity of currency. As mentioned above, the shortage of currency was evident in money markets where bank rates of interest rose up to 23 per cent. Government securities were trading at just Rs. 83 (par Rs. 100) simply because everyone wanted to sell for cash (demand for money was high) and there were few takers for bonds. Those who sourced their capital from England did so at a rate of 2s.3d. six months forward per rupee against the par rate 2s. per rupee.

While the scarcity in supply of silver for coinage was causing a currency problem for India, gold availability was increasing on account of the gold discoveries in California (United States) and New South Wales (Australia) in the mid-1800s. With demonetization of gold in 1853 having rendered silver as the only metal available for coinage, *ad hoc* arrangements soon developed across the country. In Bombay, gold bars stamped by the Bombay Banks began circulating in the market. In north-west India, people were exchanging mysteriously sealed bags each supposedly containing

TABLE 6.1: TRADE AND CAPITAL FLOWS, 1850–70

(in millions of £)

Year	Exports	Net Imports (Silver)	Net Imports (Gold)	Coinage (Silver)	Coinage (Gold)
1850–1	18.164	2.117	1.153	3.557	0.123
1851–2	19.879	2.865	1.267	5.17	0.62
1852–3	20.464	3.605	1.172	5.902	0
1853–4	19.295	2.305	1.061	5.888	0.145
1854–5	18.927	0.029	0.731	1.89	0.002
1855–6	23.038	8.194	2.506	7.332	0.167
1856–7	25.338	11.073	2.091	11.22	0.128
1857–8	27.456	12.218	2.783	12.655	0.043
1858–9	29.862	7.728	4.426	6.641	0.132
1859–60	27.961	11.147	4.284	10.753	0.064
1860–1	32.97	5.328	4.232	5.297	0.065
1861–2	36.317	9.036	5.184	7.47	0.058
1862–3	47.859	12.55	6.848	9.355	0.13
1863–4	65.625	12.796	8.898	11.556	0.054
1864–5	68.027	10.078	9.839	10.911	0.095
1865–6	65.491	18.668	5.724	14.639	0.017
1866–7	41.859	6.963	3.842	6.183	0.027
1867–8	50.874	5.593	4.609	4.385	0.021
1868–9	53.062	8.601	5.159	4.269	0.025
1869–70	52.471	7.32	5.592	7.51	0.078

Source: B.R. Ambedkar, *History of Indian Currency and Banking*, Thacker & Co., Bombay, 1947, pp. 31, 40.

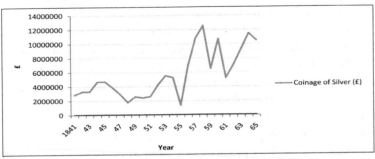

Source: DSAL, Digital South Asia Library (nd), *Statistical Abstracts Relating to British India from 1840 to 1865, First Number*, http://dsal.uchicago.edu/

Figure 6.2: Coinage of Silver (£)

Rs. 1,000, entirely upon the faith of the merchants. In Ambala, the government found counterfeit gold coins having extensive circulation. The trusted Jaipur gold mohurs were gaining widespread acceptance in many parts of the country. In south India silver had become so scarce in 1858 that the government had (once again like in the past) to accept gold sovereigns coming from Ceylon and Australia in settlement of taxes. But these were arbitrary responses and a more definitive course of action was required. With currency shortage constraining trade just when India's economic condition was showing signs of dynamism, calls for a gold currency by India's business community began to grow louder, especially in Bombay and to a lesser extent in Bengal.

There were several benefits that the pro-gold lobby articulated for India moving to a gold currency. By 1863–4 the average uncoined bullion accumulated in the mints was almost £3 million. This was simply because the working powers of the mint were insufficient for the job. This also coincided with the period when coin was in greatest demand to make purchases of cotton for shipment to English mills. The use of gold instead of silver would have surely alleviated the situation at the overworked mints as the value of a gold coin was manifold that of silver.

The adoption of a gold currency was also seen as favourable to enhance capital flows between Britain and India. With political rule passing from the East India Company to the Crown in 1858 after the sepoy mutiny, India attracted a massive amount of British capital to fund the building of the railways, irrigation works and telegraph (Figure 6.3 shows India's growing debt in England). Between 1856 and 1862, the railways alone absorbed British capital of some £50 million (Lees, 1864, p.49). With silver production slowing down at that time, along with the relative abundance of gold, expectations were that the gold price of silver would increase. Given its relative scarcity then, silver would not only be an inconvenient currency but more importantly an appreciation of silver would dampen capital inflows into India. At the same time, moving on to gold would bring down the costs of raising loans for India, enabling it to raise a greater amount of capital for its developmental needs. The process succinctly described by Hendriks (1870) is presented in Box 6.3.

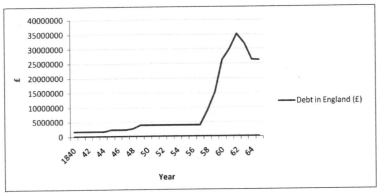

Source: DSAL, Digital South Asia Library (nd), *Statistical Abstracts Relating to British India from 1840 to 1865, First Number*, http://dsal.uchicago.edu/

Figure 6.3: India Debt in England (£)

Box 6.3: The Benefits of a Gold Currency for India

'It would be a means of consolidating, to some extent, the funded debt of India, and very probably of reducing the interest on future loans. . . . The interest on the latter (Guaranteed railway debt) is paid in sterling, half-yearly in London, whilst, although a power is given to the holders of Indian registered debt to have it enfaced for registration at the Bank of England, in London, the practical result is, that when the holder goes to receive the interest, it is not in sterling, but in the shape of a bill on the Treasury in India for so many silver rupees. This has to be sold to a bank or dealer in bills, at the fluctuating exchange of the day. The element of uncertainty is thus introduced. The recipient of interest has to face the inconvenience of the exchange market, the details and secrets of which he is quite unacquainted with, and wherein his loss is the buyer of the bill's gain on the transaction. Under these circumstances, it is not surprising that, out of the total of 628¼ millions of rupees of registered Indian debt, on 31st December, 1868, only 157½ millions of rupees were held in England. A much larger amount would be thus held, to the eventual advantage of the finances of India, if gold were made the standard in India, and 10 rupees made equal to one sovereign, either of its present weight, or of the weight of 25 francs, or 5 dollars of international coinage. On such a footing, interest might easily be arranged to be paid in sterling, or in rupees, ten to the pound, half-yearly in London or in India, just as the interest on many loans to the colonies is made payable there or in London. The result would be an increased holding of Indian registered debt in London, and the loss arising from the fluctuating, and, on the average, losing price of the interest bills, and from the liability to have the capital of the loan repaid in silver rupees, which, to the holder here, are bullion only, and not money, would be avoided.' (p.18)

Source: Frederick Hendriks (1870), 'Untitled Remarks', *Society for the Encouragement of Arts, Manufactures and Commerce, A Gold Currency for India: Report of Conferences held by the India Committee of the Society of Arts*, Bell and Daldy, London, pp. 16–23.

In quite the same vein as capital flows, common gold standard based currencies were also expected to bring down the transactions costs on trade, particularly hedging costs. A significant portion of India's trade and investment being inextricably linked to Britain (Table 6.2) a common currency would have been mutually beneficial.

Fluctuations in the rupee-sterling exchange rate[1] in spite of a relatively stable gold: silver par rate must be understood. While the intrinsic par rate based on the value of metal contained in each coin may have been stable, the commercial exchange rate could

TABLE 6.2: COUNTRY-WISE TONNAGE SHARES
OF IMPORTS AND EXPORTS

Country	% share of imports	% share of exports
United Kingdom	36	43
Ceylon	15	16
China	7	11
Straits Settlements	11	8
Mauritius and Bourbon	5	6
Arabian & Persian Gulfs	5	5
France	2	3
Suez	3	3
Others	11	6
Total tonnage	2,117,371	2,151,295

Source: DSAL, Digital South Asia Library (nd), *Statistical Abstracts Relating to British India from 1840 to 1865, First Number*, http://dsal.uchicago.edu/

still be volatile on account of seigniorage, a variable component between coin and country. Silver when taken from India to England had to be sold in the bullion market (the British mint would not accept it), exchanged for gold and then minted into sovereigns. Gold mohurs could be taken from India to England and would yield a fixed number of sovereigns; however, the silver price of gold (how many rupees would have to be melted for the gold) in India was not definite and depended on the bullion market. These fluctuations and costs were taken into account in the usage of bills of exchange. The exchange rate between the rupee and sovereign had indeed exhibited such fluctuations; at times the rupee had appreciated to 2s.2d. while at others it had sunk to 1s.10d. This amounted to a swing of around 16 per cent. The adoption of a common gold currency, it was argued, would have restricted these fluctuations to a maximum of 1 per cent (Smith, 1870, p. 10).

There was another advantage that supporters of a gold currency drew attention to; the convenient and cheaper access to gold from Australia. While Figure 6.4(a) shows the flow of goods and coin between Britain, India and Australia as it existed, Figure 6.4(b) indicates the possible streamlining in the flow of goods and money if India adopted a gold currency, in particular sovereigns and half-sovereigns that were already (since the early 1850s) being minted in Australia.

The adoption of a uniform currency between India and Australia would have further induced opening up of trade between the countries, which had until then been negligible. Cotton cloth which had to reach Australia from England could be manufactured in India and shipped to Australia at much lower costs, apart from the significant savings on transport. Samuel Laing, successor to James Wilson, while introducing the Currency Act of 1861 pointed out how an Australian merchant had to pay for a cargo of Indian rice by resorting to the roundabout and expensive process of sending his Australian gold to London, thence to France or Germany, to buy silver, and finally send that silver overland or round the Cape to India. A common gold currency would therefore bring in significant network externalities in international trade.

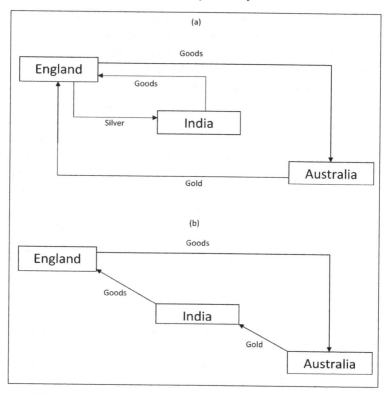

Figure 6.4: Goods and Money Flows between England, India and Australia with India on (a) Silver Currency and (b) on a Gold Currency

One of the principal advantages of gold was its higher density as compared with that of silver by which it packed in more value for a given weight. The pro-gold lobby in India categorically claimed that costs of transporting, handling and even counting silver rupees made it an inefficient currency. Rupees at that time worth £100,000 weighed about 11 tons whereas in gold it was just about 700 kg. The protection of government treasure during transport entailed the employment of some 30,000 troops. In addition to transport costs, a silver currency also meant a greater amount of time expended in counting, weighing and examining a large number of coins; this was akin to doing large business transactions with small change rather than high denomination notes. There was another important impact of this inconvenience with silver; the government often retained large and unprofitable balances in its various treasuries (to avoid the cost of frequent transportation) resulting in a loss of interest as well as restricting business operations. In Europe, the increasing volumes of trade along with the simultaneous increase in the value of transactions lent support to the calls for gold as a more appropriate currency. Although the average value of transactions in India may have been much lower than Europe, the commercial centres of Bombay, Madras and Calcutta witnessed rapid growth in the latter half of the nineteenth century. This obviously would have made them eager to replace silver with gold.

Another important, though an often neglected reason for the transition to gold was articulated by Lt. General Mansfield: the decrease of wastage and economy in mintage of gold coins. Circulating coins are subject to constant wear and tear of the metal amounting to a loss in national capital. Given equal mechanical properties of both gold and silver, it would seem that the loss of value of a coin (or the degree of wastage in percentage terms) would be the same for coins of either of the metals. This, Mansfield pointed out, was erroneous; coins of higher value are not subject to the same turnover as smaller coins and therefore escapes the same degree of wear and tear. Moreover, given a fixed cost of assaying and minting a coin of either metal, it is obvious that it would have been cheaper to mint a sovereign (or mohur) than a rupee. The production cost of coin was therefore in inverse ratio to the value of the coined medium. While both these factors gave gold a cost advantage, it was only half the story. As a means of transacting business, each metal as coin provided different degree of benefits. Ultimately, these benefits had to be provided at the lowest possible cost. If both gold and silver were allowed to circulate as legal tender then the metal with a lower net benefit would be driven out of circulation.

The gold lobby also believed that the adoption of a gold currency would dissuade people from hoarding precious metals—a habit which Indians were customarily 'infamous' for Gold could be obtained at a much lower cost directly from Australia rather than being shipped half way across the world to England where it had then to be converted into silver before being shipped back to India in settlement of claims (see Figure 6.4). On the other hand, silver received in India was so expensive that it was unable to find a market elsewhere when re-exported. Indians were in a sense *forced* to hoard silver. Transiting to gold would therefore not only have meant a significant saving in transport costs but also a fundamental change in India's position as a recipient of precious metals; as aptly put by the Bombay Chamber of Commerce (1864) in its memorandum to the Viceroy and Governor-General of India in Council, 'instead of being the last recipients and absorbers of silver, we (India) might become the first importers and the distributors of gold'. (p. 8). As first importers of gold from Australia and given the possible gains from its exportation there would have been little incentive in hoarding it. India would fall on the route through which gold traveled from Australia to Europe. This would not only give India the opportunity to become the largest distributors of gold but would, at the same time, release vast amounts of its hoardings for productive use.

There were also some small but audible anti-gold (pro-silver) voices[2] heard during this period. They came primarily from government servants (British in India) who received their salaries in silver. The appreciation of silver meant that each rupee would fetch a greater number of sovereigns back home. However, the arguments raised against gold went beyond this purely selfish motive and were sound and logical in their own right. Giving them due consideration provides a more complete understanding of transition to a gold standard.

The anti-gold commentators strongly contended that the masses of India were neither in favour of gold nor would its high value be suitable for the needs of a poor country. Gold may have circulated in ancient and medieval India but even then it was the metal preferred only by the aristocracy. In fact, it was the copper *daam* which circulated widely in day-to-day transactions. Moreover, in a country where cowrie shells still circulated at the rate of 6,000: Re. 1, it was argued that silver was more commensurate with the prevalent wage levels, price of goods, and general standard of living than gold.

An argument against a change in currency standard which attracted intense debate was the breach of faith that it would entail against public creditors. The monetization of gold (and the fall in demand for silver as currency) would have raised the silver price of gold (or reduced the gold price of silver). The British Government had accumulated a large amount of debt and repaying its creditors with depreciated silver for debt contracted in silver would mean the repayment of debt in a relatively cheaper metal. However, the pro-gold lobby argued that if public creditors were to be protected from a repayment of debt in a cheaper currency, the government and the public at-large would have to be protected from the repayment of debt in a currency of greatly appreciated value (i.e. repayment in silver that had appreciated relative to gold). One suggestion was that the government raise new loans in gold, purchase silver and payoff their existing silver debt; in effect this would mean a conversion of all their silver debt into gold, absorbing the loss at one go rather than constrain commerce of the country by an altogether inferior currency. Another alternative proposed was to announce that silver debt would be converted to gold at a rate to be decided by the government and acceptable to creditors. Objections to this rate could be received within a stipulated time period of, say, one year. Many, however, within the pro-gold lobby insisted that these measures were uncalled for; that there was really no breach of faith in the first place. It was perfectly just that the government adopt a different currency in the larger interests of the country and its progress.

Apart from these arguments, several other criticisms against a change in monetary standard can be found in contemporary discussions. More than currency shortage some commentators believed that there may well have been a glut of currency in India at that time. The general shortage of currency should have resulted in deflation; a fall in the general price level. Prices, however, held steady or as argued by some, the general silver price of all other commodities actually showed an upward trend. The paradox was explained by Cassels (1864, p. 14); according to him many traders instead of parting with goods for a smaller quantity of the circulating medium (silver), preferred to hold on to their stocks of goods.

Business was therefore almost entirely suspended in lieu of falling prices.

As far as stability in the exchange rate between India and Britain was concerned, this was considered to be inadequate in scope. Trade with other countries did matter. China, which was on a silver standard, was a case in point accounting for about 10 per cent of India's foreign trade (in tonnage terms—see Table 6.2). It was even pointed out that the effects were not just monetary; 'the established reputation of the *tola* weight must not be done away with, if we wish to keep up our reputation as honest traders' (Boycott, 1870, p. 212). Objections against the costs of exchange fluctuations were also dismissed for in fact, these not only generated activity and intelligence but also gave jobs to many people. This point may have actually been one of the key factors for the banking sector in Europe to resist the transition to a gold standard (Russell, 1898, p. 43; Einaudi, 2000, p. 294). Even the more mundane contentions against silver like the cost of escorting silver during transport were considered flawed; 'if the mass in one case had been lighter to carry, it would also have been lighter for robbers to carry off' (Campbell, 1870, p. 12). Finally, many contemporary authorities felt that a change of this kind in currency matters could prove disruptive especially if silver was driven out of circulation too abruptly. The poor whose savings were predominantly held in silver would have faced an erosion of their capital on account of a fall in its price. The British Indian government was still struggling for political legitimacy in India post-1857 and was concerned that a breakdown in the monetary system of the country could have dangerous political implications. On the other hand, silver was available in abundance and people were used to it. All-in-all, the benefits of a gold currency did not unequivocally outweigh the potential costs of transition.

While acknowledging the inconvenience of silver (due to low density as compared to gold), it was felt that paper (backed by/convertible to silver) would be the appropriate alternative; in other words, the ideal currency system for India was silver *and* paper. The gold lobby realizing that it was a paper currency that was the most significant rival to gold made a concerted effort to convince the government that paper was inadequate in making up the currency shortage.

In spite of the arguments made against a change in the currency system, by 1864 it seemed that the need for a gold currency in India was overwhelming not just amongst the urban Anglo-Indian community but also in every part of India. The only questions that remained to be resolved pertained to when and how. Technically there was no problem; as Ballard (1868), Master of the Mint in Bombay, pointed out, 'the mints exist, it is only the mint rules which require alteration . . .' (p. 5). Calcutta could mint about 500,000 coins/day and Bombay about 300,000; this was together roughly half the capacity of the Royal Mint.

Economic issues however remained in effecting the transition. Even the pro-gold lobby was against any attempt to impose a sudden change in the currency of India. If gold were made legal tender while silver was de-monetized, the shortage of gold coins would drive up its price with a severe deflationary impact on the economy. Sufficient time would be required for the mints to gear up in India to meet the demand. Moreover, the people's choice of currency would have to be respected for which both, gold and silver would have to be allowed to circulate at a relative price determined by their demand and supply. The gold lobby also argued against adopting silver as token coinage. The latter was required when silver was in short supply or had been exported out of the country. With India having large stocks of silver there was no real necessity of a silver token coinage. In fact, bank notes were likened to a silver token coinage; neither of them would find general acceptability in India amongst the masses. It was therefore felt that the transition to gold could only be made after a transitory period of a *parallel standard* with gold and silver as legal tender, their exchange rate varying with the market rate. But a parallel standard without a single unit of account would have meant utter confusion as the gold–silver ratio would be inherently unstable. Nascent expansion in India's trade and commerce would have been disrupted. This was unacceptable and the only viable option that remained was *bimetallism*.

The past experience of the Company in the late eighteenth century with bimetallism had been unfavourable. A deviation of the legal rate from the market rate would have led to the immediate exodus of the undervalued currency (silver) with potentially disastrous consequences as explained above. Nevertheless, an intermediate phase of bimetallism seemed indispensable in the transition to gold. The critical issue that now remained to be settled was the legal ratio between gold (sovereign) and silver (rupee). Many proposals were submitted, many rates proposed but the constantly fluctuating exchange rate between gold and silver made them redundant even before they were given serious thought. Finally, the scheme proposed by Charles Trevelyan (Finance Member) in 1864 was accepted by the Secretary of State for India; gold would not be made legal tender but accepted at the treasuries of the British Indian Government. This was a return to the situation that prevailed before Dalhousie's directive in 1853. But Trevelyan made an error of judgement on the people's willingness to switch to gold. He fixed the legal ratio of the sovereign at Rs. 10 when it could not be laid down in Bombay from Australia for less than Rs. 10–2a–9p.[3] But why? Trevelyan felt the discount on sovereigns would be acceptable to people transacting (especially) large sums of money (given the inconvenience of silver) and also assumed that Australia would reduce export duties to meet the Indian demand. Neither of these happened. Almost no payments were made in gold, only silver flowed into the treasury. The small amount of gold that accumulated in the government's treasury was either used as a reserve against the issue of notes or sent out to England; very little, if at all, came into circulation in India. Without possessing adequate reserves to push gold into circulation the government should have instead overvalued gold legally (at say Rs. 10–4a). In 1866, Mansfield did alter the rate from Rs. 10 to Rs. 10–4a. But by then the market rate for gold was Rs. 10–7a. Once again, the same question can be asked; why this deviation in legal and market rates? Mansfield had observed the rate for gold had been falling steadily from Rs. 10–12a to Rs. 10–7a. He simply assumed that it would fall further and touch the proposed legal rate of Rs. 10–4a. The fear of overvaluing gold and driving out silver led Mansfield to be conservative in fixing the legal rate. Unfortunately, the market rate never reached the legal rate and gold never entered circulation. Meanwhile, the demand for money in India slowly abated with the end of the US Civil War and decline in cotton exports.

India's failed attempt to transit to a gold currency in the 1860s gave rise to an uneasy feeling that the government clearly seemed disinterested in and unprepared for success. In a review of the government's actions, Hendriks (1869) clearly pointed out their indifferent attitude to the entire scheme.

Notwithstanding the unanimous decisions of the repeated commissions of inquiry in India, in favour of the speediest practicable introduction of a gold currency (referring to the reports of 1864, 1866 and 1869) . . . the questions has, more or less persistently, been put upon the shelf. It has, apparently, been placed aside for the advent of some more auspicious occasion, as was formerly the case with the well-conceived intentions in favour of a gold currency . . . No more seems likely to come of it than reference to the Secretary of State for India in Council, who, in turn, may probably relegate it again to India, and thus the matter may, for an indefinite term, be handed backwards and forwards, until the pressure of circumstances brings itself to bear upon it in England as well as in India. (p. 103)

But the proportion of 15 to 1 which that government has used in its calculation is *unreal, imaginary, and infected with error at the outset*[4] . . . instead of having been 15 to 1, it may be clearly shown to have been, and still to be, in the practical working, 15.15306 silver to 1 gold. . . . (ibid., p. 105)

After a series of events (as discussed in Section 1.15), India had virtually been prohibited from using gold as currency on account of Dalhousie's 1853 proclamation. Had gold been allowed to circulate freely along with silver, its lower price (overvaluation as coin) would have driven silver out of circulation, just as it had happened in France and the United States. But why would Britain have been against reintroduction of a gold currency for India? A critical question no doubt; however, an answer to the question takes us to what were perhaps the most significant events in the monetary history of the nineteenth century—the emergence of the gold standard and the decline of international bimetallism.

6.3: INDIA AND THE EMERGENCE OF THE INTERNATIONAL GOLD STANDARD

Gold still represents the ultimate form of payment in the world.

ALAN GREENSPAN

The only guarantee against the rise of prices due to inflation is an automatic system of currency in which the principal money used is convertible into gold. This may appear to be an old-fashioned view, but it is sound.

BRIJ NARAIN

The interdependence of world economies in the mid-nineteenth century was accompanied by a growing anxiety over instability in exchange rates arising from supply shocks in precious metals and their consequent impact on relative prices of gold and silver. It was therefore contemplated that all countries with strongly interdependent economies move on to a monometallic gold currency so that they would be free from the uncertainties that arose when currencies were based on dissimilar metals. The 'network externalities' emanating from a monetary system in which the standard unit of account of each country is a fixed weight of gold would greatly benefit trade and capital flows by curtailing risks emanating from currency fluctuations. Other arguments strengthened the desire for a changeover to gold across Europe; its higher density, greater availability and Britain (with its monometallic gold standard) as a role model to some of them.

Apart from England which had been the first country to adopt the gold standard in 1821, the wave of European changeovers began with Portugal in 1854, followed by a few smaller states in 1867, but gathered a more compelling momentum only after 1872. Outside of Europe, Japan made a transition to gold in 1897 while the United States officially converted to gold in 1900. *De facto* transition to gold in these countries had, however, begun in the mid-nineteenth century soon after gold discoveries had lowered the market price of gold relative to silver. But it is not the study of the emergence of the gold standard or an evaluation of its merits and demerits which is the objective of this section. Instead, my purpose here is to highlight the interrelation between India's failed attempt in transiting to gold (as seen in the previous section) and Europe's *de facto* transition to a gold standard in the 1860s (that set the basis for their official transition in the 1870s). Put bluntly, my argument is that for the (Western) world to have transited to a gold standard, India had to remain on silver.

It was not just the anti-gold voices in India but also the entire Western world that believed India should remain on a silver currency. This argument was based on a simple reason; if India had to move entirely to a gold currency then, given the rate at which India was already absorbing precious metals (gold and silver), a shortage in gold would arise in the West. Cassels (1864) drew attention to this possibility. In 1864 even when the annual production of gold was some £25 million he claimed that 'the present large production of gold would *not* be more than sufficient for the wants of the world, if Indian demand drew from it, as it now does of silver, so large a portion as £12,000,000 sterling' (p. 17). Figure 6.5 illustrates the narrowing gap between world output and India's growing imports of silver and gold. More interesting, is however Figure 6.6 which has been constructed to show the inadequacy of gold output (in spite of its increased production) if India were to substitute silver entirely with gold.

It was not merely the Indian import of precious metals that was the issue. The problem was that gold and silver once imported was hardly exported back or put into circulation; they were literally consumed in India, never to return back into circulation. In a world that was experiencing rapid economic growth, there was obviously the danger of an inadequate supply of currency dampening the trend. Even the issue of paper currency required adequate backing of precious metals. If adequate reserves of gold were imperative for the development of fiduciary money, India's demand for gold was particularly worrisome for as it was nothing but a fathomless abyss, a sink of precious metals.

At about the same time, a well cited work by Lees (1864) reiterated this fear in quantitative terms. While the accumulated hoarding of precious metals was estimated at a whopping £300–400

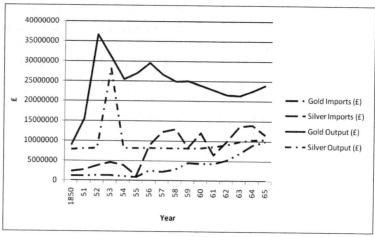

Sources: DSAL, Digital South Asia Library (nd), *Statistical Abstracts Relating to British India from 1840 to 1865, First Number*, http://dsal.uchicago.edu/ and B.R. Ambedkar, *History of Indian Currency and Banking*, Thacker & Co., Bombay, 1947.

Figure 6.5: World Output and Indian Imports
of Gold and Silver

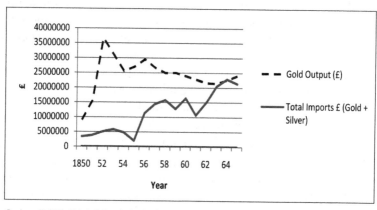

Sources: DSAL, Digital South Asia Library (nd), *Statistical Abstracts Relating to British India from 1840 to 1865, First Number*, http://dsal.uchicago.edu/and B.R. Ambedkar, *History of Indian Currency and Banking*, Thacker & Co., Bombay, 1947.

Figure 6.6: World Output of Gold and Total Indian Imports of
Gold if India's Silver Imports were to be
Substituted by Gold

million, Lees believed that India, given the rate at which it was growing since the early 1860s, would require another £400–500 million to meet its currency needs.[6] Although these figures may have been an exaggeration, it is not surprising then that there would have been apprehension in European money markets over India moving on to gold (and hoarding it). Britain obviously, being on a gold standard, would have been most weary of this fact. After all the impact of India's demand for precious metals on their real economy was already a matter of concern. 'The gold remains in the Bank of England until the Indian demand sets in, and then it is suddenly withdrawn to sweep the Continent of silver for transmission to India. In order to protect themselves, the Banks of England and France raise their rates of discount, and by their so doing, and by the violent oscillations on the foreign exchanges, every description of business is deranged' (Trevelyan, 1870, p. 74).

Meanwhile, coinciding with the Indian transition episode, a new chapter in monetary history was just about unfolding in Europe. In France, the increase in supply of gold had caused the *market exchange ratio* to fall from nearly 16:1 (that had remained almost constant till 1850) to less than 15.5:1 in 1851 (while the *legal ratio* in France was fixed at 15.5:1). As predicted by Gresham's Law, with gold overvalued legally silver francs soon began to disappear from circulation, the demand from the east absorbing them at the same time. They were replaced by silver coins with a lower fineness from Italy and Switzerland. To prevent a 'race to the bottom' amongst these countries, the Latin Monetary Union was conceived. Meanwhile, the surplus gold from the United States filled the vacuum caused by export of silver to the east. Addressing the problem with their silver coinage was only one part of the agenda in the LMU; its members, including France, were already contemplating transition to a monometallic gold standard (Box 6.4).

In 1866, the Latin Monetary Union (LMU) came into effect as silver outflows from Europe to the East reached their peak. While the demand for Indian exports abated from 1867 and with it outflows of silver too, representatives from Europe and the United States overwhelmingly voted in favour of moving towards gold monometallism at the International Monetary Conference held in Paris that

---

Box 6.4: The Latin Monetary Union and the Transition to a Gold Standard

... the delegates of the Belgian, Italian, and Swiss governments unanimously and earnestly expressed the desire that the principle of the gold standard should exclusively prevail in the formation of the union. Because France opposed the change at the time, it has been assumed to be another instance of her heroic devotion to and defence of the double standard. As a matter of fact, France did not defend the principle of the double standard at all on this occasion ... it was premature in Napoleon's programme. He preferred to let matters wait till he had assembled all the nations in a monetary conference, and then, in the face of a probable demand for the gold standard, seem to yield the double standard in consideration of the adoption of the French coinage as a basis for monetary unity. One prerequisite of success in negotiations is to have something to yield. .... The French delegates were at heart partisans of the gold standard. Parieu was one of the strongest gold monometallists that France ever had, and, as has been said, was the diplomatic manager of Napoleon's programme.

Source: Henry B. Russell, *International Monetary Conferences: Their Purposes, Character, and Results*, New York and London, 1898, p. 30.

---

same year. The West had overtly planted the seeds of a gold standard. This, however, was possible only because Europe (France, in particular) by then had drained off its excess silver to India. In other words, India's absorption of silver had been a necessary condition for France's and the US's *de facto* transition to gold.

The gold standard itself may have been a smaller part of something larger happening at that time; a political crystallization in Europe and to the embryonic development of *European federalist ideas* (Einaudi, 2000, p. 285). Could Britain then have purposefully preferred India to remain on silver to smoothen the transition to gold in the West? After all, given that their European market was relatively more important than India a common gold currency in Europe would have been more beneficial for their trade and investment flows (Table 6.3). But there is little real evidence to support such insinuations. The question, however, remains as to

TABLE 6.3: PATTERN OF BRITISH FOREIGN TRADE, DESTINATIONS AND ORIGINS

Imports

	1794–6	1854–6	1913
Europe	44	36	41
Asia	22	14	16
North America	7	24	23
West-Indies	25	6	1
Other	2	20	20

Exports + re-exports

Europe	38	40	37
Asia	13	11	23
North America	28	21	14
West-Indies	18	3	1
Other	3	24	25

Source: Jurriën de Jong, 'Great Britain, the Industrial Revolution and the World Economy, 1780–1914', *Leidschrift*, Jaargang 18, no. 2, September 2003.

why Britain did not take a firm decision on India's transition to a gold currency in the 1860s. When seen through the prism of 'real history',[7] it may have been Britain's measured ambivalence towards the movement for a gold standard more than a well thought out strategy that resulted in a missed 'golden opportunity' for India. This is evident when we closely study the remarks against a gold currency made in 1861 by a person of utmost importance in deciding India's transition to gold, Sir Charles Wood, Secretary of State for India: 'Silver is your (India's) standard. It is, in truth, the standard of the greater part of the World now. It was, near to the end of the last century, the standard of the whole word. Accident and some silly reasons made England adopt a gold standard' (quoted from Ambirajan, 1984, p. 95).

Sir Charles Wood also reiterated some of the points raised by the pro-silver voices in India, which included the political dangers of arbitrarily altering the standard from silver to gold as well as possible disruption of trade on account of bimetallism. Other important British-Indian government officials too raised similar concerns over a gold currency rather than articulating any strategic motives that consciously kept India away from gold in favour of Europe.

But why was Europe so keen on gold and not silver as metal for a common coinage? There are several economic reasons for this including its efficiency in higher value transactions, the abundant availability of gold that could meet the demands of their growing economies and the success of Britain. But there was an ideological angle too. Gold was considered as the currency of superior or civilized nations. These 'civilized nations' were not restricted to Europe. They included the United States, South America and even perhaps Australia and Canada (though not explicitly stated). The lines of demarcation for monetary standards were drawn not only in economic terms; the International Monetary Conference of 1867 contains several pointers that gold should be the monetary standard of the West/rich/civilized/Christian nations while silver belonged to the East/poor/barbaric[8]/pagan world. See Box 6.5.

To Morys (2012) the movement for a gold standard in Europe began for rather straightforward, almost trivial reasons; first, its density whereby gold 'allowed to encapsulate more value in the same volume than silver' (p. 7) and second, the increased inflow of gold into Europe after the Californian and Australian discoveries *along with the outflow of silver on an unprecedented scale*. Both, gold inflows into and silver outflows from Europe had therefore made the transition to a gold standard possible. But where was France's (and Europe's) silver going if their own silver standard countries were not absorbing the excess supply?[9] India; the answer though commonly known has not been explicitly highlighted in recent research as a fundamental trigger and a necessary condition for the emergence of gold monometallism in Europe. Contemporary literature saw this inter-linkage between India and Europe in the transition to a gold standard as a matter of fact. It was this massive drain of silver reserves to India that had put the United States and France on a *de facto* gold standard by 1864.

In the last nine years (prior to 1864) the silver imported into India alone, after deducting re-exports, has amounted to £89,638,792, or within half a

Box 6.5: The West and the East

Wisely limited by its own organic law to one common coinage between the two great oceans, the world needs only the assent of our own continental republic to give to the gold dollar and its multiples a free, unchallenged circulation, meeting no money changer or other impediment through the whole breadth of *Christendom*. The United States may alone complete the golden chain binding in one *common monetary civilization* the outspread lands and waters of America and Europe, stretching from the 'Golden Gate' of the Pacific over the auriferous 'Oberlands' of the wide interior, and across *Christian Europe* to the western bounds of the Ottoman Empire. To widen and extend still further this majestic belt, to embrace in the same great measure of *civilization* the residue of Europe with the wide extent of Asiatic Russia has been among *the leading aims of the international monetary conference.* (p. 17)

'Speaking the languages of Spain and Portugal, these 'Latin' races of the two Americas approach, to say the least, in general culture and intelligence, the Teutonic and Sclavonic races represented in the Conference (p. 89) . . . above all let us never forget that the two Americas are *Christian members* of the great family of nations, and that unification of money may be close akin to other and higher objects of *Christian concord* . . . (ibid., p. 94)

It appears that, in ignorance of the actual relative values of the two metals in our Atlantic world (of 15 or 16 to 1) . . . *these pagan Asiatics* had fixed the ratio at only 4 to 1 . . . the partial correction of the mistake by 1860 . . . shows an advance of intelligence in this distant region, inspiring the hope that, *in due time*, at least a portion of eastern Asia *may be brought* within a world-embracing and world-protecting belt of monetary unification. (ibid., pp. 87–8)

The world is divided in its monetary relation into *two considerable and very distinct groups*: on the one side the western states, where gold tends more and more to prevail; on the other, the countries of the extreme east, where silver continues to predominate. (ibid., p. 40)

Source: An extract from a letter by Mr. Ruggles (Index, 1868), Vice-President of the United States Commission at the Universal Exposition at Paris, written in July 1867, reprinted in Index to the Executive Documents, no. 14, Printed by the Order of the Senate for the Second Session of the Fortieth Congress of the United States of America, Washington, 1868, pp. 1–110.

million of the entire estimated production of the whole world for the same period. There were two great reserves of silver, the currencies of the United States and France. Both these reserves have been exhausted. The United States has been avowedly placed on upon the basis of a gold standard with a subsidiary silver token currency. In France, although the law remains unchanged, gold has been coined in vast quantities, and the only silver coins remaining in circulation are those which by wear and tear have become depreciated. (Levi, 1864, p. 403)

Between 1856 and 1862 India 'consumed' 15 per cent more than world production of silver. As seen in Figure 6.5 this increased to almost 50 per cent more than world production by 1863. India was draining Europe of its 'excess' silver.[10] The global demand-supply gap was even greater; the total demand was approximately three times the supply (annual net production). India absorbing silver may have been a necessary condition for the movement of Europe on to gold; however, it was also causing its own share of problems. A severe dearth in small token silver coins developed across Europe and the only silver coin which remained were the worn down and debased ones. Britain too came under threat. Even smaller monomentallic silver standard countries like the Netherlands which had chosen to abandon gold (in 1850) faced adverse consequences on their coinage from the spurt in Indian demand for silver.

At a more basic level, India's demand for silver had arisen from the phenomenal increase of its cotton trade with Britain. If trade with India were to continue at the same rate, and with it the absorption of silver, then there was only one option remaining; the total annihilation of silver currencies in Europe. The Indian gold lobby, sensing the imminent danger for Europe, cited it as an urgent reason for moving to gold. This would have had a stabilizing influence on the gold–silver parity by increasing the demand for gold and dampening that of silver. But the world was not listening. Like we mentioned above, silver had to be drained off the system and there was no country better than India to do that. At the same time, as seen in Figure 6.6, the inadequacy of gold would have become a critical constraint if India had moved onto a gold currency.

6.4: THE ABANDONMENT OF
INTERNATIONAL BIMETALLISM

But this (Gresham's) law will not always work, for were it a bald truth, without exceptions, that the bad money drives out the good, then a deficient penny would deplete a treasury.

JOHN ROSCOE TURNER

There was a cataclysmic change in the international monetary system that took place in the closing decades of the nineteenth century; the move towards a monometallic gold standard. But there was a corollary to this change and it was in no sense less significant—the relinquishment or abandonment of international bimetallism. And India in particular had to bear the impact of the crisis that arose from this event.

Gresham's Law explains why bimetallism *within* a single country is doomed to failure when the mint or legal ratio of gold and silver does not correspond exactly to the market ratio of the two metals. In such a situation, the overvalued currency will remain in circulation while the undervalued currency disappears from circulation, the latter being melted for other uses and/or exported as bullion. This argument has been more fully explored in Chapter 1. Although bimetallism popularly came to be known as an unviable system, when we look back in history we find that bimetallism actually was the rule rather than the exception. Prior to the nineteenth century no nation had really adopted pure monometallism. England was the first to do so in 1816, India followed in 1835 with silver; many of the other nations transited to a monometallic (gold) standard only in the 1870s. Bimetallism was workable essentially because, unlike what one may presume, the market price of gold and silver was highly stable (see Figure 6.7), and remained almost in a state of extraordinary permanence for years. In fact, an even stronger argument is that bimetallism had actually ensured this stability in the gold–silver ratio. If this was indeed true, then with the legal ratio fixed close to the (stable) market ratio, coins in both metals would circulate as if they were one, at a fixed exchange ratio.

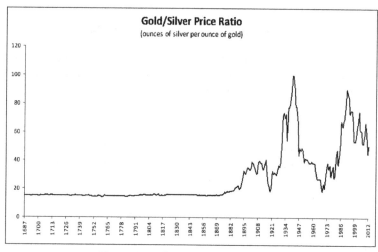

Figure 6.7: Gold–Silver Price Ratio

The question then is what had given rise to this extraordinary stability in the market ratio of gold and silver? The answer lies in what came to be called as the 'compensatory principle'. Both gold and silver were demanded for two important purposes: coinage, and industry or the arts (including jewelry). While the industrial demand curve for gold and silver would have been fairly inelastic, the demand for precious metals as coin was highly sensitive or elastic to changes in their individual prices. Such changes in price of one metal would immediately alter its purchasing power over all other goods and services making it either more or less attractive than the other precious metal in circulation. It is this elastic demand for precious metals as coin that prevented them from deviating significantly from their original price ratio. Stanley Jevons likened the compensatory principle to two tanks of water. Suppose these tanks were not connected, each tank having its own inlet. When water flows into any one tank, the level in that tank only will rise and with it, the ratio of water levels in the two tanks will undergo a change. Now if the two tanks were interconnected with a tube, then even if water is let into any one of the tanks, the water level in the two tanks will rise simultaneously, the ratio of their water levels remaining constant.

In Chapter 1, I had presented a simple graphical model of bimetallism in a single country and how adjustments in exchange ratios take place. I now extend this to the case of international bimetallism, illustrated in Figure 6.8. Consider three countries, one on a monometallic gold (C_G), another on monometallic silver (C_S) and the third on bimetallic (C_B) standard. For international bimetallism to work countries with all three types of monetary standards must exist simultaneously; in the Western world, Germany and the US were on a silver standard, Britain on gold and the crucial bimetallic standard was adopted by France which guaranteed conversion of silver to gold coin at the legal ratio of 1G = 15½S.

To illustrate the working of international bimetallism let us assume the legal ratio is set at (say) 1G = 15S. Suppose now there is an increase in supply of gold in C_G from S_G to S_G'. Gold prices begin to fall towards 1G = 14S in C_G [Figure 6.8(a)]. But price of gold will not fall below 1G = 14.8S as it is exported to C_B where gold prices are determined by the legal ratio of 1G = 15S. As the cheaper gold flows into C_B, silver coins are taken out of circulation (in C_B) and replaced by gold as a small deviation in the market price from the legal ratio would cause a significant change in the quantity demanded of either metal. As we had seen in Figure 1.4, the substitution of silver will commence as soon as the costs of switching are covered.[11] Moreover, there could once again be uncertainty and risk associated with knowing the 'exact' market ratio (it could also change) so that people might defer their decision to melt silver until the gap between the legal ratio and market ratio is substantial and unequivocal. When this point is reached, large volumes of gold will be coined and silver coin melted. As silver prices increase to 1/14.8 an excess supply of silver [X_{SB} in Figure 6.8(c)] is generated in the market on account of the melted coins. With the price of silver at 1/14.8, an excess supply of silver is also generated in C_S [X_S in Figure 6.8(d)]. This cannot be an equilibrium situation and price of silver must fall; the exchange ratio will therefore oscillate between 1:15 and 1:14.8 without reaching a stable equilibrium. One possibility of reaching an equilibrium of 1G=14.8S is if there is an increase in demand for silver in C_S from S_S to S_S' (=$X_{SB} + X_S$) in Figure 6.8(d). For the silver of France and

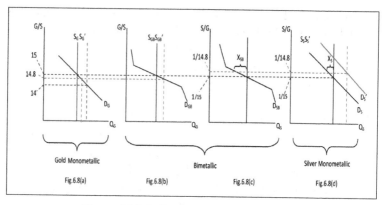

Figure 6.8: A Graphical Representation of International Bimetallism

Europe to drain, gold had to be continuously overvalued as coin, i.e. the legal ratio of 15S = 1G > market ratio of (say) 14.8S = 1G. This could happen if the continual increase in gold supplies were matched by shift in D_S so that price of silver was sustained above the legal ratio (1/14.8 > 1/15). The Indian demand for silver did this job efficiently for the West in the 1860s so that it was able to move to a *de facto* gold standard. If this had not happened, the excess supply of silver would have pushed silver (gold) prices down (up) so that silver would have once again come back into circulation. There is also a possibility for the market rate to return to the legal ratio of 1G = 15S. This would happen if for instance the D_G and D_{GB} were to shift upwards and intersect S_G' and S_{GB}' respectively at G/S=15.

A stable market equilibrium of 1G = 14.8S can be achieved under international bimetallism as long as there is sufficient quantity of silver going out of circulation in C_B. If, however, before G/S touches 14.8, the quantity of silver going out of circulation is exhausted, then gold would have fully driven out silver from circulation before equilibrium is reached. This is illustrated in Figure 6.9. The gold inflows into C_B drives G/S to 14.8; however, at S/G = 1/14.9 silver demand reaches zero. No further decreases in supply (and its export) are possible to raise its price to 1/14.8. We, therefore, cannot have equilibriums in both, gold and silver markets at G/S =

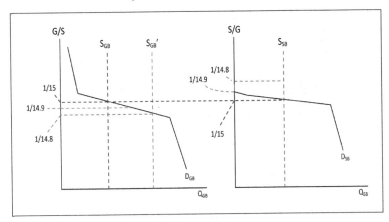

Figure 6.9: Gresham's Law in Operation with
International Bimetallism

14.8 and S/G = 1/14.8. Meanwhile, gold remains undervalued in the market at 1:14.8 as compared to its legal rate of 1G = 15S. If there is no increase in demand for gold as coin (shift in D_{GB}) to bring up the rate back to 1G = 14.9S or 1G = 15S then in such a case silver will not be able to return to circulation; Gresham's Law operates.

Apart from this possibility, international bimetallism was considered successful in keeping market exchange rates close to the legal ratio. However, what we have stressed here is the role of India in making the West's transition to gold possible with international bimetallism in place with its continually increasing demand for silver that absorbed the excess supply of silver. This prevented the gold price of silver falling and it returning to Europe in which case their *de facto* transition to gold would not have been possible. At the same time, as we will see in the next section, India had lost the battle in the search for a stable currency; silver prices crashed and with it the rupee too.

Meanwhile, some significant fluctuations in the market gold-silver ratio between 1858 and 1866 lend support to our graphical model as presented in Figure 6.8. In Figure 6.10 a sudden spike in gold–silver ratio from 15.30 up to 15.51 in 1858–9 can clearly be observed. This, as the data in Table 6.4 shows, coincides with the

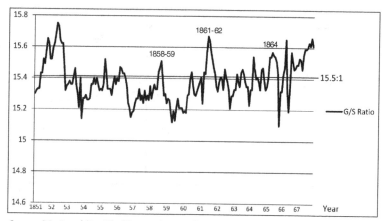

Source: J.L. Laughlin, *The History of Bimetallism in the United States*, 4th edn., New York, 1897, p. 294.

Figure 6.10: Gold–Silver Price Ratio, 1851–67

TABLE 6.4: INDIA'S GOLD AND SILVER
IMPORTS (£), 1850–65

Year	Gold Imports (£)	Silver Imports (£)
1850	1,159,548	2,235,792
1851	1,205,310	2,656,548
1852	1,338,778	3,713,280
1853	1,332,106	4,490,227
1854	1,078,708	3,770,643
1855	882,721	1,145,137
1856	2,508,353	8,792,793
1857	2,176,002	12,237,695
1858	2,823,484	12,985,332
1859	4,437,339	8,379,692
1860	4,378,037	12,068,926
1861	4,242,441	6,434,636
1862	5,190,432	9,761,545
1863	6,881,569	13,627,400
1864	8,920,440	13,974,400
1865	9,875,032	11,488,320

Source: B.R. Ambedkar, *History of Indian Currency and Banking*, Thacker & Co., Bombay, 1947, pp. 31, 40.

increase in India's gold imports by some £2 million with a simultaneous decline in silver imports by more than £8 million. This would mean an outward shift in the D_{GB} and inward shift in D_S that allowed for a higher G/S and lower S/G. In 1861 we once again observe a spurt in gold prices; a correlation with the sharp decline in India's silver imports is once again noted. In 1864 as India opened the doors to a gold currency, albeit cautiously and in a rather ad hoc manner, the trend in the falling price of gold was broken and instead the price of silver began to fall. From 1867, the price of silver began to show signs of falling steadily. Why did this happen when production of silver had not increased? The answer lies in India's absorption of silver, which declined dramatically from 1866 onwards on account of the slowdown in cotton exports and capital inflows. And when silver outflows to India further slowed down, almost immediately the minting of silver coins began returning to their old levels in France. While France minted only about 40,000 5-franc silver pieces in 1866, it minted 10 million in 1867 and 18 million in 1868. Table 6.5, which shows the mintage of gold and silver coins in France, bears a close relationship to India's trade pattern and inflows of precious metals. The reversal of the trend in France post-1867 also indicates that bimetallism had not yet lost its relevance. Nonetheless, the seeds of a gold standard were planted at a period when silver outflows from Europe to India were massive.

TABLE 6.5: MINTAGE OF GOLD AND
SILVER IN FRANCE

Years	Gold (million francs)	Gold (million francs)	Ratio of Value
1803–20	868	869	1-15.58
1821–47	301	302	1-15.81
1848–52	448	449	1-15.67
1853–6	1,795	1,796	1-15.35
1857–66	3,516	3,517	1-15.33
1867–73	876	877	1-15.62

Source: B.R. Ambedkar, *History of Indian Currency and Banking*, Thacker & Co., Bombay, 1947, p.127.

Post-1866, India's absorption of silver declined while that of gold continued at its prior levels. The sharp decline in silver imports was on account of the declining stocks in the West. If India's overall exports had to continue at their earlier levels, India would have been compelled to move on to gold; but the trend in exports did not continue and showed a sharp decline after 1866. Capital imports also showed a sharp decline. The demand for money slowly abated with India's exports stabilizing at lower levels.

If India had successfully shifted to gold and if India's growth had sustained, the story may well have unfolded differently in Europe, with perhaps a different ending too. Gold prices would have remained high, silver exports would not have taken place and the transition to a *de facto* gold standard in Europe and the US in the 1860s may never have taken place. Figure 6.6 starkly illustrated that simple fact; if India had substituted its silver imports with gold, there may well have been inadequate gold for the rest of the world to move to a gold standard.

While the answers to such conjectural hypothesis are difficult to 'prove' we have nonetheless raised them with the objective that the Indian experience and its failed transition to gold are at least (re)drawn into the recent[12] bimetallism-gold standard narrative, which has otherwise been rather tentative in discussing this significant episode in international monetary history; *'silver left France and the United States because a demand arose for it in India'* (Naoroji, 1870, p. 16).

Before I wind up this discussion, I return to some general issues surrounding the debate on whether international bimetallism ensured stability in exchange rates or was a monometallic gold standard a better alternative. The pro-bimetallists contended that when countries are on a monometallic standard changes in the market price of precious metals could have a destabilizing impact on the real economy. For instance, a shortage in a precious metal will lead to an increase in its price, or equivalently a fall in the price of all other goods. This deflationary effect will have several adverse effects; debtors lose as they have to pay back the principal that has more purchasing power than when the loan was taken. Investment is also adversely impacted when prices are falling; the firm will buy raw materials at higher prices but will have to sell final output at lower prices. Consumers in anticipation of further fall in prices will postpone their buying decision that will only further accentuate deflation. On the other hand, a gold or silver discovery could have inflationary effects as the price of the precious metal falls. Although a mild positive rate of inflation may not have the kind of negative impact as deflation, it could still have disruptive impact on the real economy through higher rates of interest and lower investment spending.

International bimetallism focuses on the relative price of gold and silver rather than the absolute price of just one metal. By keeping the relative price of precious metals stable by rapidly draining off excess supply or quenching excess demand it can maintain gold-silver parity. To reiterate what we have discussed above, suppose there is an increase in supply of gold, its price falls. If gold was the only material used for currency, there would be an inflationary pressure on price of all other goods. But under bimetallism, when gold price falls, it is automatically overvalued vis-à-vis the fixed legal ratio. The demand for gold as currency increases, while at the same time the supply of silver to the market increases. This will lead to an increase in gold price and a fall in that of silver. However, it is at this point that we have raised a doubt; stability in the market (equilibrium rate) can only be reached if there is an increase in demand of gold and/or silver. India provided this outlet for the excess silver to drain out of the system and for the market to reach an equilibrium that deviated within small and viable limits from the legal rate. The beneficial effects of this stability in gold and silver prices attained through international bimetallism were then immense; international trade and capital flows were greatly enhanced in an atmosphere of exchange rate stability. If we return to the situation immediately after the gold rushes of the 1840s, we find that throughout this period in spite of the great gold discoveries the ratio of gold and silver remained almost the same. But it is important not to forget that India was draining the world of silver. And the cotton famine had made that possible.

6.5: THE DECLINE OF SILVER AND
CRISIS OF THE RUPEE

I wish the Committee to bear this in mind, that right through the statement I have to make, the one difficulty with which the Indian Government have to contend is the fall in exchange—it has a blighting and withering influence in every direction.

LORD GEORGE HAMILTON, SECRETARY OF
STATE FOR (BRITISH) INDIA

The movement towards an international gold standard and breakdown of international bimetallism broke the gold–silver parity of 1:15½ which had been maintained for centuries. With this the gold price of silver went into free fall. From here on, a structural break in the fundamental notion of monetary stability can be articulated; stability now required both, *specific* stability in the foreign exchange rate possible only with external sector equilibrium and *general* stability in the purchasing power of the rupee possible only with domestic price level stability. As mentioned in the beginning chapter of this book, the search for money which is stable in 'value'[13] both *externally and internally* is a great challenge—this became a particularly complex issue for India when the gold-silver parity broke down. Till then international bimetallism had ensured that as long as the state did not take recourse to the physical debasement of their currency, the exchange rate of gold and/or silver currencies would not change. Concerns were then significantly focused on to domestic inflation or deflation in the price level as well as changes in output, if any. As we saw throughout Part I, such expansion and contraction in currency and other monetary instruments, did cause economic instability and crises.

With the abandonment of international bimetallism in the 1870s, the gold price of silver began to fall. Even as the West chose to embrace gold, India was compelled to remain on silver. It is important to emphasize that, during this period depreciation of the rupee was not caused by an endogenous disequilibrium in the balance of payments but rather by a set of completely exogenous events. These shocks then had serious implications for the Indian economy; I will, however, briefly begin by discussing the international reasons for the breakdown in gold-silver parity before presenting its consequences on the Indian rupee.

It was at the International Monetary Conference of 1867 that a move towards a common international currency was first propagated. Gold, which had become relatively abundant by then on account of its discoveries, was to be the basis of this international currency. The conference suggested that the multitude of silver coins in circulation around the world be substituted by a single gold standard currency with a mathematical unity of the coinage. Unfortunately these recommendations were not the outcome of rigourous deliberations but the appeal of gold-based currencies across the world was overwhelming. The idea caught on; universal gold monometallism somehow became the norm that would ensure stability in exchange rates and eliminate the fear of an unexpected disruption in gold–silver parity. By 1869, the monometallists were in majority even as those in favour of bimetallism vociferously argued that it would ruin the world monetary system and the stability in prices that been possible only because of at least one country maintaining a fixed legal ratio between gold and silver.

In 1854 Portugal turned to the gold standard. In 1871 Germany demonetized silver, which was finally carried out by an act of 1873. By 1875, Norway, Sweden and Denmark had adopted a gold standard. Holland adopted a double standard but free coinage of silver was suspended in 1875. Russia changed to a gold currency in 1876. Austria suspended silver coinage in 1879. Earlier France had stood between the great gold using state of England and the silver using state of Germany with a bimetallic standard assuring the world of converting gold to silver or vice versa at a fixed legal ratio. But when Germany adopted gold, it became inevitable that a glut of silver would cause gold prices to rise and silver to fall. At the fixed legal ratio, the falling gold price of silver would render gold undervalued in France and silver overvalued. Under normal circumstances this would have raised demand for silver as coin (raising the bullion price of silver) and increased supply of gold into the market (decreasing the bullion price of gold) thereby restoring gold-silver parity. However, in this case there was a danger that Germany's large-scale sale of silver would drive gold out from circulation from

France *entirely* before the market rate could return to equilibrium around the legal ratio; as described in Figure 6.9 above, Gresham's Law was coming into force and breakdown of bimetallism was imminent. Gold disappearing from circulation became a growing concern in France ultimately forcing them it to restrict the coinage of silver. This was the beginning of the end of international bimetallism. The gold–silver parity was soon broken and as can be seen from Figure 6.7, silver went into free fall.

At that time the world was not unanimous as to the cause of the falling price of silver; while bimetallists attributed it to the end of bimetallism, those who supported gold monometallism attributed the fall to the decline in costs of production of silver and to the decline in exports of silver to India with the end of the cotton famine. However, by 1881 gold monometallism was on the defensive. While the demand for gold increased with countries moving over to gold monometallism, gold production slowed down. The problems from the 'break of gauge' between gold and silver began to surface; the continual rise in gold prices led to a fall in the general price level, which developed into a deflationary spiral.

Table 6.6 shows the decline in gold price of commodities in England; this can be viewed as an appreciation of gold or equivalently, a fall in gold prices of (all other) commodities. Bimetallists considered this to be one and the same and interpreted it as arising from an appreciation of gold due to the increased demand for it with many countries opting for a gold standard. Figure 6.11 graphically reveals the rising silver price of gold (or falling gold price of silver) and the close relationship it had to the price level in England. The monometallists, however, argue that the above arose not from an appreciation of gold but due to changes in technology and methods of production that had significantly brought down the costs of production and transport. However, as any debate over index numbers goes, the evidence of this price deflation was disputed as it depended on which goods were chosen.

Even as these events were unfolding in Europe, India witnessed a major crisis in its monetary system with the decline in the gold price of silver. As we have seen, the 1860s had witnessed vociferous calls for a gold currency. But this did not happen; India remained

TABLE 6.6: INDEX NUMBER OF COMMODITY
AND SILVER PRICES

Year	Commodity	Silver
1874	102	95.8
1875	96	93.3
1876	95	86.7
1877	94	90.2
1878	87	86.4
1879	83	84.2
1880	88	85.9
1881	85	85
1882	84	84.9
1883	82	83.1
1884	76	83.3
1885	72	79.9
1886	69	74.6
1887	68	73.3
1888	70	70.4
1889	72	70.2
1890	72	78.4
1891	72	74.1
1892	68	65.4
1893	68	58.6
1894	63	47.6
1895	62	47

Source: Francis Walker, *International Bimetallism*, Henry Holt & Co., New York, 1896, pp. 260–1.

on a silver standard and the (silver) rupee continued to prevail as the medium of exchange. Meanwhile, the decline of international bimetallism that had supposedly maintained a stable parity between gold and silver came to an end and with it the dangers of a monometallic international standard brought in new concerns and dangers as Europe discarded its excess silver in the market. It was only inevitable that silver prices fell. The rupee being nothing but a fixed quantity (and purity) of silver, its value depreciated with a fall in the price of silver. The implications for India's exchange rates were, however, cataclysmic.

From the year 1873 India went through a distinctive phase of

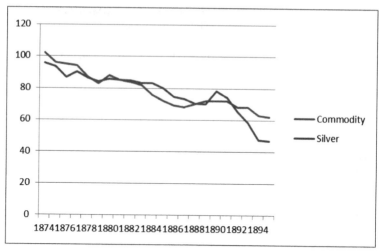

Source: Francis Walker, *International Bimetallism*, Henry Holt & Co., New York, 1896,
pp. 260–1 (based on data given in Table 6.1).

Figure 6.11: Gold Price Index of Commodities and Silver

exchange rate instability. Given that the rupee was a silver coin,
the depreciation in its value can easily be inferred from Figure 6.7
and Figure 6.11. In addition, in Figure 6.12 we specifically show
the depreciation of the rupee vis-à-vis gold sterling between 1835
and 1914. The periods 1835–73 and 1893–1914 were clearly
ones of relative stability in the rupee-sterling exchange rate as compared to the period 1873–93 in which the rupee depreciated by
almost 50 per cent. This exogenously induced disturbance in currency value affected several other macroeconomic elements, in particular, the quantum of home charges that had to be remitted annually
to Britain, government revenues and expenditure, debt and investment and foreign trade.

For two hundred and fifty years before the depreciation of silver
began the international gold/silver price ratio had fluctuated only
slightly, within a range of 1:13.75 to 1:15.25. This parity which
had been maintained over centuries was disrupted forever in the
1870s. In 1870–1, when the gold price of silver was about 60d.
per ounce, the Indian rupee was worth almost 2s. By 1893, the

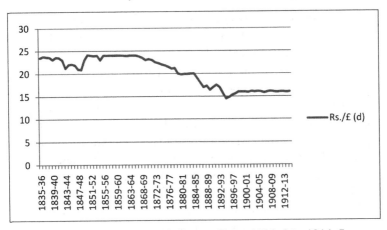

Figure 6.12: Rs./£ (d) Exchange Rate, 1835–6 to 1914–5

Source: B.R. Ambedkar, History of Indian Currency and Banking, Thacker and Co., Bombay, 1947.

gold price of silver tumbled to just 39d. per ounce, so that the Indian rupee was equivalent to just 1s.3d. Equivalently, the pound appreciated from Rs. 10 to Rs. 15 in just 20 years. The reasons for this change in exchange and parity rates were, in the first place, an increase in the production of silver relative to gold followed by the abandonment of international bimetallism and discontinuation of silver as money by the principal countries of the world. Efforts to re-introduce international bimetallism and stabilize the price of silver failed. Several international conferences were held, in which India too participated, but the final outcome at the International Monetary Conference held in Brussels in 1892 sealed the fate of silver when the U.S. decided to adopt a pure gold standard, giving up the pursuit of bimetallism.

Before we present the specific concerns raised on the impact of the depreciation of the rupee, the remarks reproduced below give an idea of the passion evoked by experts and commentators that seemed to be have imposed a hegemonic influence on the debate. MacLeod described it in the following terms: 'A monetary crisis of the most momentous gravity has arrived in the affairs of India . . . which have brought India onto the verge of bankruptcy. The Government themselves describe the state of the country as "*intoler-able*" (Macleod, 1898, p. v). In the Introduction to his book, George Monson stated that he had 'endeavoured to call attention to the great evil to the universe, and India and Great Britain in particular, caused by the depreciation in the gold value of silver' (Monson, 1914, p. 5). According to Shirras, who was on special duty in the finance department of the Government of India, 'No period of our currency history is so rich in literature as is the third period, 1874–93 . . . the currency machine was the master of man, not the man of machine' (Shirras, 1920, p. 114).

The primary cause for this sense of desperation over depreciation of the rupee was primarily remittance of 'home charges'. Every year the government had to reimburse the expenditure incurred in England by the Secretary of State for India called 'home charges' or 'drain'. Since it had to be reimbursed in gold, larger and larger amounts of rupees (silver) were required. As the gold price of silver fell year after year, the government's annual budgetary exercises began to go awry. Between 1873 and 1893 the rupee value of home charges increased from 147 to 270 million, more than the combined revenues from land and customs duties.

In hindsight one might suppose that the problem the Government of India was undergoing at that time was merely a depreciating currency. However, it is important to realize that an even greater problem was the *uncertainty* in anticipating the gold value of silver and therefore the extent and duration of the fall in the rupee, which in one particular year, fell by as much as 17 per cent. Sir David Barbour, Finance Minister to the Indian Government calculated that the additional burden imposed on the finances of India by the fall in exchange from 1s.6d. to 1s.5d. would have been more than Rs.10 million (Vakil and Muranjan, 1927, pp. 40–1). On the other hand, a small appreciation of the rupee could have left the government with a large unwanted surplus. The former was, however, more dreaded which put increasing pressure on the Government of India to raise revenues to provide for unexpected contingencies emanating from the currency depreciation. Table 6.7 shows how differences in anticipated and realized rupee-sterling exchange rates impacted the budgetary process, making budget calculations and arrangements nothing more than illusory.

TABLE 6.7: FLUCTUATIONS IN EXCHANGE AND
RUPEE COST OF GOLD PAYMENTS

Year	A	B	C
11874–5	1–10.4	1–10.2	1,591
1875–6	1–9.91	1–9.6	1,957
1876–7	1–8.5	1–8.5	–76
1877–8	1–9.21	1–8.83	3,843
1878–9	1–8.4	1–7.8	5,687
1879–80	1–7.0	1–8.0	–8,440
1880–1	1–8.01	1–8.0	424
1881–2	1–8.01	1–7.9	1,017
1882–3	1–8.01	1–7.53	3,746
1883–4	1–7.5	1–7.5	–362
1884–5	1–7.5	1–7.3	1,897
1885–6	1–7.0	1–6.3	5,682
1886–7	1–6.0	1–5.4	6,517
1887–8	1–5.5	1–4.97	7,190
1888–9	1–4.9	1–4.4	7,798
1889–90	1–4.4	1–4.6	–2,731
1890–1	1–4.6	1–6.1	–23551
1891–2	1–5.3	1–4.7	8,009

Source: B.R. Ambedkar, *History of Indian Currency and Banking*, Thacker & Co., Bombay, 1947, p.107.

Notes: A = Estimated Rate of Exchange on which the budget of the year was framed (in s-d) of the year was framed.

     B = Rate of Exchange actually realised on the average during the year during the year.

     C = Changes in the rupee cost of sterling payments consequent upon changes betweent he estimated and realised exchange rates.

     All figures indicate an increase in the necessary rupee outlay, except for those preceded by (-), which indicate a decrease.

With limited revenue sources available to the Government of India and an increasing and uncertain expenditure, a crisis in Indian finance was fast developing. Even as early as 1877, Bagehot (1877) observed, 'the whole interest of the debate on the Indian budget centered in the discussion on the value of silver' (p. 6). The home charge, moreover, was not the only outgoing in terms of (gold) sterling; expenses for European troops maintained in India, pensions and non-effective allowances payable in England, and stores purchased in England for consumption in India were other payments that had to be remitted abroad. With increasing rupee expenditure the government had to urgently look for ways to enhance its revenues.

While the impact on the budget seemed more or less but unequivocally negative, this was not as clear when it came to the issue of investment. Did a depreciating rupee have a net positive or negative effect on investment in India? Generally speaking, a depreciating currency has contradictory effects on investment decisions. On the one hand, when the exchange rate of country X's currency falls, foreign firms (from country Y) may increase investment in X because they can buy more of currency X per unit of currency Y. On the other hand, once they have invested, a continued depreciation of currency X would mean that profits, when repatriated in terms of currency Y, shrink. This is a disincentive for firms in country Y to invest in country X. MacLeod (1898) conjectured that reduced inflow of capital to India due to currency depreciation between 1861 and 1898 was more than £100,000,000 (p. 42). In 1892 Barbour (1892) similarly articulated the impact of the depreciation on the construction of the railways: 'The fear of a fall in silver, however, stands in the way of their construction . . . the small, though certain, profit which Indian railways are likely to return for the first few years the risk of investing capital in a country with a silver standard deters the prudent investor, while such railways have no attraction for the more speculative' (p. 5). The depreciation and instability of the rupee made the raising of capital increasingly difficult and expensive not only for private investors but also the Government of India, which had to guarantee minimum returns on the stocks of the railway companies. Since this capital was raised in England, a decline in the gold price of silver obviously meant an increase in the quantum of repatriation in rupee terms.

The development of other public works such as irrigation tanks and canals also suffered on account of the government's difficulties in raising capital. With inadequate domestic savings, the government had to tap foreign capital. As long as gold–silver parity existed, this was not problematic. However, when the gold price of silver fell the government had to increasingly issue sterling debt as foreign investors were not willing to hold rupee debt. This led to an increase in silver rupee expenditure in servicing sterling debt and outflows for repayment of principal on maturity, with the result that expenses on extraordinary public works were curtailed. The impact of this slowdown of investment in public works dampened agricultural expansion. At the same time, the depreciation presumably could have had a positive effect on exports and the spatial expansion of crop cultivation. The possibility of such impacts, ambiguous as they may be, is nonetheless important to recognize. Private business investment in India, though not guaranteed by the government like the railways and public works, may also have been affected by increasing risk from the declining sterling value of accumulated profits due to a depreciating silver rupee. The growth of the cotton, jute and tea industry may therefore have been impeded to some extent by the prevailing currency situation, though at the same time a greater purchasing power of sterling would have meant an incentive to invest in as well as export from India. According to Jevons, it is the latter trend that prevailed. Thanks to the falling rupee, merchants of Bombay and Calcutta made large fortunes in the export trade, which were reinvested in cotton and jute mills in India. The steady decline in rupee value may have also contributed to the overall growth in overseas demand for Indian tea and have been an incentive to invest in the tea industry. The depreciation further facilitated expansion of small-scale commodity production such as wheat, cotton, jute, tea and other primary products.

From a macroeconomic perspective an exogenous depreciation of the rupee should have increased exports and reduced imports. With an increased surplus in the balance of trade, silver inflows should have increased and with it, the domestic price level. But even here the outcomes were not as straightforward as one would expect. When it came to exports concerns were raised as to whether at all the rupee depreciation stimulated exports of goods and commodities and even if it did, who really benefited from this increase. Economists and economic historians of the early twentieth century believed that the depreciation of the rupee *per se* may not have had a significant impact on export. For instance, Vakil and

Muranjan (1927, p. 42) argued that the advantage of a depreciating rupee to Indian exporters was only transient; a benefit accruing to exporters only in the time interval between the depreciation of currency and the proportionate in crease indomestic price levels. Ambedkar (1947) moreover argued that the long-term impact of rupee depreciation benefited Indian producers but left labour worse off; the steep increase in price levels without a corresponding increase in nominal wages caused a fall in real wages (p. 105). In spite of the argument that domestic price increases would have nullified the benefits of a fall in the rupee, a continual depreciation of currency could have meant a sustained benefit to exporters, since price adjustments occurred with a time lag. Moreover, the increase in price level, although expected from a theoretical standpoint, may not have fructified. In India the habit of hoarding precious metals resulted in the non-monetization of silver into coins, so that price increases may not have been commensurate with the surpluses in the balance of payments. In this regard, Schmidt (1886) commented: 'Prices in the silver countries have admittedly not risen, and the equilibrium of trade has therefore not been reestablished in the manner which the text books lead us to anticipate. But I even doubt whether conditions such as would produce a rise in prices exist in the silver countries' (p. 34). Brij Narain (1926, p. 259) too concluded that although theoretically the fall in the rupee exchange should have led to a fall in the purchasing power of the rupee (vide higher domestic price level) this was not observable from a study of price indices available between 1874 and 1893.

Although it is difficult to pinpoint a specific causal link between rupee depreciation and export growth in the late nineteenth century, there is extensive evidence that India did witness growth in exports in this period. This, however, could have arisen from a multitude of factors including the opening of the Suez Canal in 1869, the replacing of sailing vessels with steamships, an expanding railway network within India, declining freight rates and the elimination of the middleman. In this changing global macroeconomic environment, the steady depreciation of silver-based currencies such as rupee against the gold based currencies of Europe and North

America could have kept Indian export prices competitive in the 1870s, 1880s and early 1890s.

On the other hand, a depreciating rupee should have meant a fall in India's imports. The rest of the world would therefore be weary of the unfair advantage gained by India (more competitive exports) and loss to their domestic industry (due to a decline in India's imports) may not have been entirely unfounded. But, quite to the contrary, the import trade from England to India had shown a marked increase as compared to the exports from India to England. This happened because higher demand for gold and a rise in its price caused the gold price of commodities to fall in England, which more than offset rise in exchange rates. Table 6.8, presented by Waterfield to the Gold and Silver Commission shows the trends in exports from and during the years of silver depreciation. The figures show that the concerns over any unfair advantage accruing to India may have been unfounded. After all, what needs to be kept in mind in reaching hasty conclusions of exchange rate depreciation is the elasticity of demand for exports and imports and

TABLE 6.8: DEPRECIATION OF THE RUPEE AND
TRADE FLOWS WITH BRITAIN

Years	Imports in India	Exports from India	India's % share of Britain total trade
1874–5	100	100	8.5
1875–6	96	101	8.5
1876–7	110	105	8.5
1877–8	132	110	8.9
1878–9	93	101	8.5
1879–80	108	99	7.8
1880–1	132	111	8.9
1881–2	127	125	9.2
1882–3	135	127	9.8
1883–4	145	132	9.9
1884–5	147	121	9.7
1885–6	146	124	9.8
1886–7	154	125	10.5

Source: H.L. Chablani, *Studies in Indian Currency and Exchange*, Oxford University Press, Bombay, 1931, p. 6.

there the concern has always been over the lack of it when it came to India's foreign trade.

Like the crisis of the 1860s there were once again calls for a change in India's currency system. At that time it was the fear of silver appreciating, this time it was the depreciation of silver. While there is no doubt that the gold–silver parity had been broken once and for all, many believed that there was an overreaction to the depreciation of the rupee. After all the external trade of India with gold standard countries was only 5 per cent of her total trade (external and internal). Moreover, for the twenty years ending 1892–3, India's aggregate deficit was just about Rs. 2.4 million (Chablani, 1931, p. 15), which was not really something to be overly concerned about.

The strongest lobby in favour of a change in the currency system of India was that of British officials working in India. A depreciated rupee meant a smaller number of sovereigns in exchange for their (fixed) rupee savings. Obviously they wanted the rupee to stop depreciating and if possible be revalued at a higher rate. However, there was little reason for British government officials in India to complain; the loss on account of silver depreciation was adequately compensated by the fall in gold prices of goods and services in England. Between 1873 and 1893 the purchasing power of gold had increased by almost 50–60 per cent in England over a range of some 45 commodities (see Table 6.6). If the rupee exchange had not fallen British officials would have gained even more, but to say that they lost purchasing power was incorrect. Questions were further raised as to whether it was appropriate to change a nation's monetary standard for the sake of a relatively meager number of government officials.

Perhaps the only argument then in favour of a change in India's currency seemed to arise not from the situation that prevailed between 1873 and 1893, but the future. The United States was at the verge of abandoning silver and if it did it would almost certainly have led to another massive bout of rupee depreciation. To what extent, no one could anticipate. But the apprehension was palpable. In spite of this there were those who insisted that concerns over India's budget could have been managed; austerity measures of the government rather than a change in monetary standard would have amply sufficed. The austerity measures could have come through cuts in military expenditure and retrenchment. And, with price levels falling in England, the government could actually have trebled the duties on Indian imports of British goods. But in case of the latter, reactions from Lancashire would have not been acceptable to the House of Commons. It, therefore, seemed that in the end, India's decision to change her currency system may not have been in her own interest but that of a few officials in the Indian Government.

Before I conclude this section let me once again return to the search for an instrument that is stable; the depreciating gold price of silver once again showed that precious metals *per se* are not the end of the road in finding a satisfactory solution to monetary problems. India, therefore, experimented with something different. But before I reveal India's new monetary system, I wish to share an interesting episode that may be treated as an aside in our narrative but one with important lessons nonetheless.

6.6: THE WYNAD GOLD RUSH

Gold, Gold, Gold, they just gotta have that gold
Gold, Gold, Gold, they'll do anything for gold.

OL' TURKEY BUZZARD, *MACKENNA'S GOLD*

Before we discuss the end of the silver rupee, I make two brief digressions; the first is about the search for gold in India and the second, a description of the monetary systems prevailing in the princely states towards the end of the nineteenth century.

The movement towards adoption of a monometallic gold standard was forcing gold prices up and setting off a deflationary spiral across many parts of Europe (see Table 6.6). Increasing the supply of gold to bring down its price became critical to sustaining the gold standard. The fever to find gold also gripped India, and the small towns of Wynad district in the present day states of Kerala and Tamil Nadu were soon the centre of fervent gold exploration. The Wynad gold rush has been vividly described in the works of Jennings (1881) and Francis (1908).

Wynad's gold mining industry preceded British rule by decades. However, it is only in the second half of the nineteenth century, when Wynad opened up to coffee estates that some British planters realized the scale of medieval operations that had already been undertaken to exploit gold reserves; sluicing works, channels, heaps of rubble, tunnels extending 70–100 metres into the rocks. They also learnt that the mines would have 500–600 Mapillah[14] labour working at a time. The industry declined when it became possible to find jobs with higher wages on the estates.

Given the growing demand for gold across Europe for coinage, and the need to prevent gold prices from rising, the British were keen to explore and exploit India's potential reserves. Surveys by the Geological Survey of India were positive on the prospects of gold. In 1874, the Alpha Gold Mining Company was set up with a nominal capital of Rs. 600,000. New companies soon followed. In 1879, an acclaimed expert from Australia, Brough Smyth made a favourable remark that 'gold-mining will be established as an important industry in South India'. This set off a massive mining effort in Wynad, but even before that could actually happen, it sparked off a speculative bubble.

The depressed state of markets in England yearned for such positive news; no verification was needed. In a matter of months 41 companies with a capital exceeding £5 million were launched in England. Companies with a capital of some £250,000 were also started in India. Shares were allotted to the tune of some £4 million. But most of the capital raised was used up to buy land which had shot up to more than £2600 per acre in Wynad. Very little capital was left for machinery.

The confidence in the companies striking gold in Wynad was reflected in their share prices; by 1880 the shares were quoting at a premium of 50 to 100 per cent even before machinery had been shipped let alone any mining having commenced. Cables (telegrams) kept streaming into England with fanciful claims: 'four feet of magnificent reef, exceedingly rich in gold', 'grand discovery; Needle Rock reef turning out very rich' . . . dividends of more than 60 per cent could be sustained for years . . . these reports kept the boom alive for well over a year. Plantation owners began to look at the possibility of mining gold and experts abounded in Wynad; one was reported to be formerly a baker and yet another circus clown. Attractive prospectuses were drawn up enticing the public to subscribe to the shares of companies. Two small towns, Pandalur and Devala were soon turned into booming mining towns, the former boasted of a church, post and telegraph offices, a hotel, a saloon and even a race-course. The companies even contemplated the necessity of bringing Chinese labour to work the mines.

By 1881 when crushing of mined rocks finally began at the mines, the mood slowly changed; optimism soon descended into pessimism. In the midst of the drooping sentiment, some good news came in. The Alpha Company mines had yielded 4 oz. of gold to the ton! Their share price shot up to £15 and others soon followed with increases of 400 per cent. Within a week, the share price of the Wynad companies had grown by more than £500,000 on the London Stock Exchange. But it soon became clear that the above report was true only for one ton; the subsequent yields were dismal. The bad news started pouring in; one company had expended £70,000 but produced only 7 oz. of gold. Like all other bubbles, the moment had arrived for it to burst. Share prices collapsed. Some dropped by 200 to 300 per cent in a single stroke, never to recover. Within a year some 15 companies passed into the hands of the liquidator. The Alpha Mining Company was the last to close in 1893. The government pursued several scientific surveys but by the turn of the century the gold-mining industry in Wynad was dead although they still continue to be worked in by local artisanal miners even today.

Box 6.6: The devastation of Pandalur and Devala

At Pandalur three or four houses, the old store, and traces of the race-curse survive; at Devala are a grave or two; topping many of the little hills are derelict bungalows and along their contours are grass-grown roads; hidden under thick jungle are heaps of spoil, long-forgotten tunnels used only by she-bears and panthers expecting an addition to their families, and lakhs worth of rusting machinery which was never erected; while along the great road to Vayitri, which now, except for the two white ruts worn by the infrequent carts, is often overgrown with grass, lies more machinery which never even reached its destination. Moreover, most of the numerous coffee-estates which formerly bordered this road all the way from Gudalar to Cherambadi were acquired by the gold companies and thenceforth utterly neglected; and now not a single one of them all is kept up. They have all gone back to jungle and are covered with such a tangle of lantana and forest that it is hardly possible to make out their former boundaries. That the coffee industry is dead and the mining industry which killed it is dead also; and this side of the Wynad is now perhaps the most mournful scene of disappointed hopes in all the Presidency.

Source: W. Francis, *The Nilgiris: Madras District Gazetteer*, Government Press, Madras, 1908, p. 19.

6.7: PAPER CURRENCY AND BANKING IN BRITISH INDIA AND IN THE PRINCELY STATES

There is no example in history of a lasting monetary union that was not linked to one State.

OTMAR ISSUING, CHIEF ECONOMIST OF THE
GERMAN BUNDESBANK COUNCIL, 1991

The pillars of the nation state are the sword and the currency, and we changed that.

ROMANO PRODI, EU COMMISSION
PRESIDENT, 1991

In this section I take a brief look at the developments in the country's progress in adopting paper currency and the monetary situation prevailing in the princely states. Ellstaetter (1895) divides the circulating medium of British India into three parts: (1) money coined by the royal Indian Government; (2) currency notes in circulation in British India; and (3) the coin circulation of the Princely States. While the first has received attention in discussion of the rupee crisis, the latter two aspects are often missing in narratives of Indian monetary history. It is useful to have a perspective on these aspects too so that we get a fuller picture of the prevailing monetary system.

To recap some of what we have already said, by Act XVII of 1835 the silver rupee became the standard coin of India. It contained 10.692 gm of fine silver. All silver brought to the mint up to June 26, 1893, was coined at a seigniorage of 2.25 per cent. Gold coins were also struck but only to a relatively small extent. Table 6.9 shows the net imports of gold and silver as well as coins struck in these metals for the period 1835 to 1892.

Most of the silver imported into India was struck into coins. However, it would be erroneous to reach the conclusion that all the coins struck were actually circulating as currency. A significant portion of it was often minted into coin but then hoarded or re-melted for jewelry. The import of precious metals into India was a function of people's purchasing power and their demand for savings, not always reflecting the need for circulating medium. The general economic situation prevalent in the country had a strong bearing on the import of silver; it surged during the mutiny of 1857 and the cotton famine in the 1860s while it fell drastically during the Mysore famine of 1875 and Deccan famine of 1876. Similarly the drought in northwest India the following year and the subsequent droughts and famines across India reduced silver and gold imports with a general fall in people's purchasing power. However, since 1880 the trend showed a marked reversal and as the economic condition improved in the country so did the import of precious metals.

The progress of banking in India during the nineteenth century

TABLE 6.9: INDIA'S IMPORTS OF BULLION
AND MINATGE OF COIN

(in millions of rupees)

Metal	Year	Net Imports	Coins Struck
Silver	1835/6–1884/5	263.8	275.1
	1885/6–1891/2	71.4	60.2
Gold	1835/6–1884/5	127.9	2.4
	1885/6–1891/2	27.9	2.3

Source: K. Ellstaetter, *The Indian Silver Currency: An Historical and Economic Study*, translated by J.L. Laughlin, University of Chicago Press, Chicago, 1895, p. 4.

was to say the least, tardy. The three Presidency Banks, viz. the Bank of Bengal, the Bank of Bombay and the Bank of Madras were authorized to issue notes. This right was withdrawn in 1862 and in lieu of this the government placed at their disposal, funds of the government, interest-free. However, when the government was in need for funds, the banks put up several obstacles on withdrawal of funds. The government then decided to set up its own treasury in 1876. Other restrictions were also imposed on the Presidency Banks including dealing in foreign exchange transactions, advancing long-term loans of more than six months and advancing loans on the basis of immovable securities. These measures were justified as necessary to prevent bank failures and the negative externalities on the banking sector on account of such failures, which could have retarded the overall development of banking in India by several decades. Another major issue arose between the government and the Presidency Banks in 1877; the denial of their access to London money markets. The main argument against allowing the Presidency Banks to raise money in London was that it would only increase the channels available for the flow of funds, not the quantum of funds and that it would force the Presidency Banks to deal in fluctuating exchange rates. But the most important argument in favour of such operations was the elasticity it would induce into the Indian monetary system during the busy seasons of the year. The government treasury resembled a Central Bank of deposit (with several branches) but one in which the government was the only depositor. This led to many rupees being swept away to government coffers just at the time when they would have been most useful in relieving the monetary stringency in the market. Market interest rates therefore shot up at this time. Keynes, however, argued that access to London money markets would not help since it would not make sense to bring in such short-terms funds from overseas. Instead, it would have been appropriate for the government itself to grant loans from its surplus reserves to the Presidency Banks. This was done but at the published bank rate leaving them with no margins and making it unattractive to go through the process. The Chamberlain Commission later reduced the Government's lending rate to 1 per cent below the bank rate.

Meanwhile, the main business of these banks in the last quarter

TABLE 6.10: GROWTH OF PRESIDENCY BANKS IN INDIA

(in millions of rupees)

Year	Capital & Reserves	Total Deposits (Public + Private)	Cash held
1870	36.2	118.3	99.7
1880	40.5	114	74.1
1890	44.8	183.6	129.7
1900	56	156.9	50.4

Source: M.L. Tannan and K.T. Shah, *Indian Currency and Banking Problems*, Ramachandra Govind & Son, Bombay, 1917, p. 210.

of the nineteenth century was re-ordained to receiving deposits, making short-term loans on security of goods or their titles deposited with them, and managing government debt. It had been suggested that the rupee crisis after 1873 was responsible for the slow growth of banking in India. But with hedging instruments at their disposal there was no reason why fluctuating exchange rates should have posed a major problem for banks. Moreover, there is little evidence available that fluctuation in exchange rates actually impacted export and import volumes. The capital and deposits of the Presidency and Joint-stock banks in India between 1870 and 1900 are given in Table 6.10.

Apart from the silver crisis, the slow growth of banking was attributed to (i) the general stagnation in the economy including severe and recurrent famines (ii) the decline in the price level, especially that of indigenous manufacturers, these being the most important customers of the banking sector (see Table 6.11). Such a deflationary situation was obviously not conducive to stimulate growth of deposits and banking, especially amongst businesses, and (iii) other factors including the hoarding habit of people, direct loans to trade and industry in the form of company deposits rather than through banks, the absence of the cheque habit of people, and the negative impact of bank failures in India.[15]

The growth of paper currency was also slow in India in this period. While the authority of note issue was granted exclusively to the government by the Paper Currency Act of 1861, the circle system constrained the quick expansion in the use of paper currency.

TABLE 6.11: GENERAL AND MANUFACTURED GOODS
PRICE LEVEL INDEX IN INDIA AND BRITAIN

Year	General (India)	Manufactures (India)	Britain (General)
1866	134	83	100
1869	101	81	93
1870	107	94	98
1871	93	96	98
1886	96	74	110
1893	121	92	100
1899	99	75	110
1900	112	84	110

Sources: S.K. Muranjan, *Modern Banking in India*, Kamala Publishing House, Bombay, 1952, p. 26; Safalra.com (nd), http://safalra.com/other/historical-uk-inflation-price-conversion/; data obtained from 2004 paper 'Consumer Price Inflation Since 1750' (ISSN 0013-0400, Economic Trends no. 604, pp. 38-46) by Jim O'Donoghue, Louise Goulding, and Grahame Allen.

Furthermore, the government was overly concerned that there would always be a temptation to increase printing of currency; a legitimacy crisis that could then trigger a run on currency, undermining the future of the system. The Mutiny of 1857 was an important reminder to the British that their status in India could not be taken for granted. It was felt that the penetration of currency had to come about slowly and had to progress along with a deepening of their political legitimacy in India. Concerns over the return of small denomination notes for conversion into silver prompted the government to introduce the five-rupee note as late as 1871, the ten-rupee note following a few years later. The gross circulation of notes in 1862 was about Rs. 37 million. In 1892 it had not even expanded ten times, reaching only Rs. 271 million; the notes in 'active' circulation (total notes in circulation less that held by government treasury and Presidency Banks) being just about Rs. 200 million (Keynes, 1913, p. 47). The extraordinary increase of currency notes in circulation from 1891 was on account of the great speculative shipment of silver to India. The silver which came to the banks was exchanged for treasury notes, on the basis of which new notes were put into circulation. See Table 6.12.

TABLE 6.12: NOTES IN CIRCULATION IN INDIA

(*in millions of rupees*)

Year	Note in Circulation
1871	104
1876	109
1880	124
1884	128
1885	147
1886	142
1887	139
1888	164
1889	158
1890	157
1891	257
1892	241
1893	264

Source: K. Ellstaetter, *The Indian Silver Currency: An Historical and Economic Study*, translated by J.L. Laughlin, University of Chicago Press, Chicago, 1895, p. 3.

Another reason for the slow growth of both paper currency as well as banking in India could have been the suspension of competitive note issue by private banks. This practice had in fact constituted the mainstay of banking in many countries (France, Germany and Belgium) rather than the cheque system, which was widely used in England. Competitive note issue could have led to a greater degree of confidence amongst the public and the more easy adoption of paper currency. The institution of monopoly issue of bank notes by the government may not have been the best route for the introduction of paper currency into a country like India. Overall one can only say that while the government recognized the importance of expanding note issue as a medium of exchange, it's over cautiousness in doing so probably restricted the expansion of paper currency.

Coming to the situation in the Princely States towards the close of the nineteenth century, a large number of them retained their right of coinage, zealously guarding it as a mark of their sovereignty. The rupee remained the primary coin of most states, although the standards differed from state to state. By Act IX of

1876, the British tried to bring about the acceptance of a common standard of money throughout the whole of India. It, however, failed because of the stringent terms of the act. The princely States had to agree that no coins would be struck for a period of thirty years; they would not allow any coins similar to British-Indian coins to be struck in their domains the coins would have to be of uniform weight and fineness as the rupee of British-India and they could not use the devices and machinery they previously used. Only if these terms were complied with would their coins could be circulated as legal tender throughout India.

Sparse data is available on the coinage undertaken by the Princely States. Ellstaetter (1895) provides some details of coins in princely states in terms of tola where 1 tola = 1 rupee = 11.664 grams:

I have also put down some trivia from Ellstaetter, which gives us a glimpse of what was happening in the Princely States with their currencies. In 1891, Baroda set up new machinery at the mint. At about the same time the mint of Kashmir stopped functioning. Mysore had no mint. The coins of the Holkars and in Travancore were unimportant. The best known coins, with perhaps the best reputation, were those of the Nizam from Hyderabad and Gaikwad from Baroda. Coins of Princely States circulated in the British provinces, especially in the border regions. They were accepted even by British mints, although appropriate discount was made.

TABLE 6.13: COINAGE IN SOME PRINCELY STATES OF INDIA

State of Hyderabad

1887–8	816 tola of gold	15,051 tola of silver
1888–9	784 tola of gold	1,776,421 tola of silver

Baroda

1883–4	800,000 rupees
1884–5	900,000 rupees

Source: K. Ellstaetter, *The Indian Silver Currency: An Historical and Economic Study*, translated by J.L. Laughlin, University of Chicago Press, Chicago, 1895, p. 2.

6.8: THE END OF THE SILVER RUPEE

Englishmen would not stand such a system for twenty-four hours, and yet this is what is seriously proposed by able people for the benefit of the Indians.

SIR DAVID BARBOUR, 1892

In the discussion of standards, to no country is more attention drawn than to India; and rightly, since the fate of silver is to be decided, above all, in India.

KARL ELLSTAETTER, 1895

In 1890 silver prices rose briefly when the US announced that it would purchase some 4.5 million ounces (127 tons) of silver every month. There was a fear that increase in silver prices and a return to its old rate would mean a fall in general price levels by some 30 per cent in silver standard countries. Although the purchases of silver by the US led to a short-term increase in price of silver in 1890 (a small drop in the silver price of gold in 1890 can be seen in Figure 6.7), this attempt to prop up the price of silver was rendered ineffective on account of increase in silver production during this period. The average yearly production during the period 1861–70 was 39 million ounces whereas it reached 161 million ounces by 1891–3. No scarcity of silver or a rise in discount rates was observed even as there was a small surge in the price of silver. In fact, just the opposite happened. Banks were flush with silver and the discount rates were at their lowest ever. The exchange rate of the rupee, however, fluctuated violently between 1s.9d. and 1s.5d between 1889 and 1890–1. After 1890, the gold price of silver began declining steadily, and the rupee followed suit.

Although the Indian government sought restoration of international bimetallism to stabilize the depreciating gold price of silver, it was evident that little would be achieved at the Fourth (and last) International Monetary Conference held in 1892 in Brussels. Moreover, restoration of the old gold–silver rates of 15½:1 would mean a strong increment in silver prices and consequently, as mentioned above, a massive general price deflation in silver standard countries. Options had now to be considered in light of the imminent failure to restore bimetallism. The Secretary of State for India appointed the Herschell Committee to study and make recommendations on the future of the Indian currency system. The committee heard several viewpoints, although only one Indian was called upon to present his views. It was upheld that the depreciation of the rupee had affected different sections of the population differently. The impact on the government was negative; its payments to England were in terms of gold and therefore the quantum of silver required for the same amount of payment in gold had increased. One option available was to raise the required quantity of silver through additional taxation; however, experts opined that the government had already reached the upper limit and any attempt at doing so would have political repercussions. Merchants were divided; importers found their prices in India increasing while exporters found their goods becoming more competitive internationally. Tea planters were particularly benefitted by the depreciations of silver; their goods sold at their usual sovereign (gold) price while their costs remained the same in terms of cheaper silver. Bankers in general were in favour of depreciation since many of their clients, particularly exporters, were doing good business. But it was the government officials who were personally anxious about the continued depreciation of silver. With fixed silver rupee incomes, the amount in terms of gold was declining. Since these officials would eventually return to Britain, their savings in terms of gold was adversely affected by the fall in silver.

The imminent failure of the Brussels conference to restore bimetallism and the possible repeal of the Sherman Act in the United States was expected to lead to a further and an even steeper fall in silver prices. The rupee could then further descend into free fall. In 1892 the Bengal Chamber of Commerce and the European mercantile community led by Sir James Mackay, later Lord Inchcape, argued for the need to maintain the value of the rupee at 16d. (= 1s.4d.), instead of its bullion value of just 10d. This would allow them to get 60 per cent more in England for every rupee earned in India. In the end, it seemed that the interest of the government and a section of Englishmen prevailed (and also perhaps the interest of some sectors of England's industry against further depreciation of the rupee); on 26 June 1893 the mints were closed to the free coinage of silver. India went off the silver standard to which she never returned. Instead, the government was directed to coin and issue rupees on demand in exchange for gold sovereigns or bullion at the rate of Rs. 15 to the sovereign (= 1£) or Re. 1 for 1s.4d. Gold sovereigns and half sovereigns would also be accepted by the Indian government in settlement of its dues[16] and would be issued for rupees at the same rate for international payments.

India for centuries had possessed a 'perfect' silver metallic standard, where the metal from a coin melted down would be equal in value to the coin less brassage. The closure of mints to new coinage meant that those coins already minted now possessed a monopoly value; the value of the coin as coin was now greater than the value of the silver it contained. The silver rupee coin was token money and possessed all the attributes of inconvertible paper with one important feature; the value of this money would remain steady in relation to the sovereign and thereby to the value of gold. The standard economic unit of account of the rupee was now fixed in terms of a certain number of sterling (Re. 1 = 1s.4d.), which in turn was fixed to a certain weight (and of a certain purity) of gold (£1 = 7.2 grams of gold or Re. 1 = 16d. = 0.48 grams of gold).

Before studying the implications of this recommendation, it is important to first articulate the reasons for closing of the mints to the free coinage of silver. As stated above, the rupee as coin had a value greater than the silver contained in it or, in other words, rupee as silver. It was, therefore, obvious that people would rush to the mint to have their silver coined into rupees. This would cause an increase in the supply of rupees, an increase in the general price level and consequently a fall in its value. An adjustment or more specifically depreciation in the rupee-sterling exchange rate would then be necessary. Preventing new coinage of rupees was possible with a closure of mints. The closing of the mints to silver also *delinked the rupee from silver and instead linked it to gold via the sterling.* As mentioned above, rupees were for all practical purposes like inconvertible notes printed on silver but had to find their value or exchange rate vis-à-vis the *gold* sovereign by the forces of demand

and supply. However, there were limits within which the exchange rate of the rupee could fluctuate. The upper limit was the ceiling rate of 1s.4d. = Re. 1. Once the rupee reached this upper limit the Government agreed to sell rupees in unlimited quantities (to meet any excess demand for them) in exchange for a fixed amount of gold sovereigns (Re. 1 = 1s.4d.), irrespective of the price of silver; the supply curve for rupees therefore becomes perfectly elastic at this rate. The demand curve for rupees is also perfectly elastic at this rate. This is because if the gold price of silver were to increase above 1s.4d. (to say Re.1 = 1s.5d.), the demand for rupee coins would fall to zero because coin as bullion would be worth more than coin as rupees. Coming to the lower bound, the only lower bound of the rupee would be its intrinsic worth as silver because if the rupee were to fall below the gold price of silver the demand for rupees would fall to zero as it would be better for people holding rupees to melt them and exchange it for gold rather than exchange the rupee (as rupees) for gold. We will return to a more complete description of the demand curve for rupees and its relationship to the silver bullion market in Section 8.1.

Meanwhile, what we have here in effect is a 'fixed' exchange rate system where the exchange rate of the rupee was fixed in terms of sovereigns, the latter itself being convertible into gold at a fixed rate. But the 'fixed' exchange rate was applicable only to the upper limit; while the rupee was not allowed to appreciate above 1s.4d. (for instance, 1s.5d. would mean more gold for each rupee or an appreciation of the rupee), it could depreciate freely. As seen above, although the government did not set or maintain the lower limit, the market price of silver would define the lower bound.

Although the rupee was free to depreciate below the rate of 1s.4d., it must be understood that the government did not want this to happen; the entire policy objective was to ensure that the rupee did not depreciate. It was the falling price of silver that was forcing the rupee to depreciate and not a fundamental disequilibrium in India's balance of payments. In fact, if depreciation of the rupee were to continue after the closing of the mints, it would mean that the policy was uncalled for and redundant. The government's payment of home charges would continue to increase in rupee terms. At the same time the full benefit of silver depreciation would not accrue to Indian exporters so that the entire exercise would be seen as one serving no purpose apart from dampening India's competitiveness in international markets.

The closing of the mints to silver was essentially to ensure that the price of the rupee was independent of or delinked from the price of silver and, given India's favourable balance of payments, the rupee could appreciate to a more realistic level of 1s.4d. This would enable the Government to buy gold on cheaper terms for remittance of home charges. At the same time this would also prevent the adverse effect of a fluctuating exchange on India's foreign trade, ensure that sterling capital invested in India (especially by banks) would not lose its value, protect English holders of rupee paper against losses on repatriation of their investment, and allow Anglo-Indian officials to purchase more gold for remittance back to England in exchange for their rupee salaries. The coinage of silver for rupees was furthermore considered important as it would sustain global prices, or at least prevent a complete crash in silver prices. London at that time was the centre of the world silver trade and rupee coinage in silver was looked upon as critical to silver traders. Many historians view the decision to delink the rupee from silver as one which, more than anything else served the interest of the British colonial regime. This may well have been true; the spirit of this book, however, is not to critically examine this aspect but rather to understand the 'positive economics' of these policies and their implications on the economy.

Let me now briefly point out some of the concerns raised on the closure of the mints to the free coinage of silver into rupees. We have already seen the danger of widespread melting of coins had the gold or sovereign price of the rupee fallen below the gold price of silver. The same situation could also arise if the gold price of silver increased above (to say, 1s.5d) the gold price of the rupee, i.e. 1s.4d. Once again, people would melt down rupee coins for more valuable silver bullion. Such an event would have a catastrophic impact on the availability of currency and thereby on the real economy. As we will see later, this in fact did happen. If, however, the rupee rate was higher than its intrinsic silver value, as hoped for, there was another danger—counterfeiting. Suppose the rupee was at 1s.4d. while silver was at (say) 1s.1d. This would induce people to 'mint' silver illegally into counterfeit (silver) rupee coins. After all, silver as silver would fetch just 1s.1d. whereas silver as rupees would fetch 1s.4d. This was, however, not a cause for great concern given the high cost of machinery and the risk of being caught. True enough, this particular problem did not arise.

Another objection to the closing of the mints was that silver as silver would continue to depreciate so that people who held their wealth in silver would be exposed to a decline in the value of their wealth and at the same time were unable to convert it into rupees. Since many poor people in India held small quantities of silver and fell back upon it at times of distress like famines, the impact could be disastrous if they were unable to convert their savings into a medium of exchange. Politically there was potential danger that the people of India would perceive that the 'sircar has taken our wealth away' (Barbour, 1892, p. 19), which could become a rallying point for the then nascent independence movement in India. But facts and figures told a different story. In earlier times, in spite of falling silver prices, Indians had continued to accumulate silver. In fact, the fall in price of silver had induced them to accumulate even more. Moreover, these arguments against the rupee-silver divergence had to be counterbalanced by the benefits which accrued to people from the greater purchasing power of the rupee (as opposed to silver) and also the fact that people would have hoarded rupee coins and not merely silver bullion. A final concern over the appreciation of the rupee was its adverse effect on India's international competitiveness since many Asian currencies, including China, continued to remain on silver. The only solution would be a fall in domestic price levels to counter the relative appreciation of the rupee. But this would bring with it troubles of deflation.

In any case, in the midst of a raging debate, the mints were finally closed in 1893 to the coinage of silver and a new chapter had begun in the rupee's history. India was now under what later came to be referred to as the *gold exchange standard*. The working of the gold exchange standard is illustrated in Figure 6.13. The demand curve for rupees is downward sloping because deprecia-

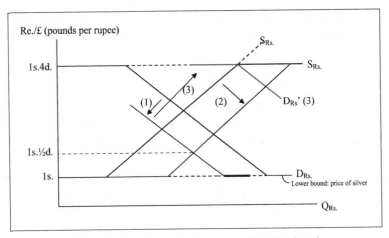

Figure 6.13: The Gold Exchange Standard and Shifts in D_{Rs} and S_{Rs}

tion of the rupee in terms of gold sovereigns (less sovereigns per rupee) would lead to an increase in Indian exports and therefore greater would be the demand for rupees. A shift in the demand curve for rupees could arise (say) due to a surge in demand for Indian commodities in foreign countries on account of positive growth in those economies. Consider now the supply curve of rupees in the foreign exchange market; an appreciation of the rupee from 1s.1d. to 1s.3d. would mean increased competitiveness of British exports and hence greater demand for sovereigns or a greater supply of rupees in the foreign exchange market to enable these imports from Britain. The government in 1893, however, effectively announced a ceiling exchange rate of the rupee at 1s.4d. by promising to give any amount of rupees in exchange for gold sovereigns at this rate. The market rate could not go beyond this since the government was obligated to give Rs. 15 for a sovereign or a rupee for 1s.4d. There was no need for anyone to pay 1s.5d. in the market to exchange sovereigns for rupees. As already mentioned, this could be represented as the supply curve becoming perfectly elastic at the rate of 1s.4d. At the lower bound of 1s. per rupee, the supply curve becomes perfectly elastic. No supply of rupees would be forthcoming at a rate below the bullion value of coin (presumed here to be 1s.). The closing of the mints to free coinage of rupees in India meant that any outward shift in the supply curve of the rupee was restricted (although it did happen when hoarded rupees, not silver bullion, came into circulation). The quantity of rupees in circulation could only be increased through an increase in (foreign) demand for rupees and a movement along the given supply curve S_{Rs}. And as emphasized in Chapter 1.2, *international trade continued to be (almost) the only source of rupees to the domestic economy.*

When the closing of the mints was announced in 1893, the actual market rate of the rupee opened below the ceiling rate and by 1895 fell as low as 1s.½d. A series of adverse events kept the rupee below the rate of 1s.4d.; widespread depression following the repeal of the Sherman Act and the imposition of higher import duties to raise revenues in India led to a decreased demand for rupees (inward shift in D_{Rs}). But the steep fall in the gold price of silver meant that, in spite of the fall in the rupee, hoarded rupees came back into circulation both from within the country as well as from outside India (because coin as rupees were worth more than coin as silver). The increased supply of rupees pushed the supply curve (S_{Rs}) outwards, causing further pressure on the rupee to depreciate. See shifts denoted by (1) and (2) in Figure 6.13. Fortunately, the declining gold price of silver in bullion markets kept the rupee at a higher rate than the gold price of silver or the lower bound below which rupee coins would be melted for silver bullion.

However, between 1896 and 1898 the Government had to incur heavy expenditures to counter the effects of the severe famines during that time and to meet war expenses in the northwest frontier provinces. For this it had to borrow heavily in India and in the London markets; these factors increased the demand for rupees and gradually pushed the rate up to 1s.4d. [see shift denoted by (3) in Figure 6.13]. In September 1897, the Secretary of State entered the money market in London as a purchaser of bills on India for which he offered a rate of $16^{3/}{}_{32}$d. (= 1s.$4^{3/}{}_{32}$d.) per rupee. This was for the purpose of remitting money to India to meet the contingency expenditures.

By 1899, with improving international trade, the gradual increase in the demand for rupees and the policy of 'starving the currency' by stopping the free coinage of rupees prevented any shifts in the supply curve for rupees (apart from dishoarding). This enabled the rupee to reach the ceiling rate of 1s.4d. Once the rupee touched a rate of 1s.4d., the government was keen to see that the rupee did not depreciate again. To ensure this it had to mop up any excess supply in rupees by purchasing it with gold. Figure 6.14 explains this scenario. With a decrease in demand for rupees (a shift in the demand curve from D_{Rs} to D_{Rs}'), an excess supply of rupees at the rate of 1s.4d. develops. The government can then ensure stability in the rupee exchange rate at 1s.4d. by buying the excess rupees with sovereigns (gold) at this rate. In other words, it would have to decrease the supply of rupees to S_{Rs}'.

For the purchase of rupees, it was proposed that the government borrow £20 million in gold, equivalent to Rs. 300 million, at the rate of £1 = Rs. 15. Rupees could then be bought in the market at the rate of 1s.4d., melted and sold as silver bullion in the market. This silver could however not be minted back into coin given that the mints had been closed for the free coinage of silver. At the going rate of silver bullion, the loss borne by the government was close to 38 per cent. This loss was the difference

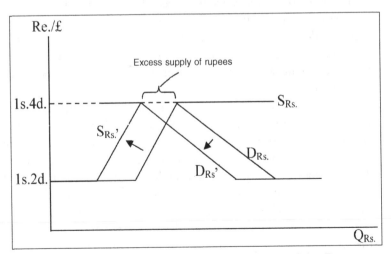

Figure 6.14: The Depreciation and Appreciation of the Rupee

between the rate at which rupees were bought (i.e. 1s.4d.) and the value fetched from the sale of silver in the bullion market on melting down the coins (lower rate than the purchase price of 1s.4d.). Therefore, the fund could be used for purchases of Rs. 800 million.[17] This, however, would entail a massive contraction in rupees available for circulation within India. Nonetheless, it was felt if the exchange rate of the rupee could be maintained at this level, India would soon be in a position to move on to the gold standard.

However, there was great concern over the policy of 'starving the currency' in order to maintain the exchange rate of the rupee at 1s.4d. To do this the supply of the rupee in circulation had to be restricted but to what level, no one could say. No rupees were coined between 1893 and 1899 except for small amounts to replace the currency of some native states in 1898. Furthermore, any increase in the quantum of rupees in circulation (hoarded coins and inflow from abroad) was drained off so that the rate of 1s.4d. was maintained. Not only would this mean that benefits from higher liquidity in the domestic economy were lost to Indian businesses but also that required gold reserves to 'starve the currency' (or buy the excess rupees) were simply not available. The government would incur huge costs to borrow gold necessary to buy out the rupees from circulation. This, as we have seen above, would entail further costs since silver bullion prices (or the rate at which the rupee coins would be sold by the government as bullion (i.e. at < 1s.4d) after they have been purchased (at 1s.4d.) would entail a loss to the government; a loss that would ultimately have to be borne by Indians in the form of additional taxation.

With the delinking of the rupee from silver a new challenge arose in the settlement of the balance of payments between India and Britain, between rupees and gold sovereigns. The basic mechanism of settlement of India's balance of payments is shown in Figure 6.15. The Exchange Banks bought council bills drawn on India in London for sovereigns and sent them to India for collection from the Treasury in rupees. This could then be conveniently used to discount the bills (of the Exchange Bank) drawn on the Indian branch of the Exchange Bank, purchased by E_M and sent to I_X against goods imported (by E_M). Meanwhile to raise more rupees in India, the

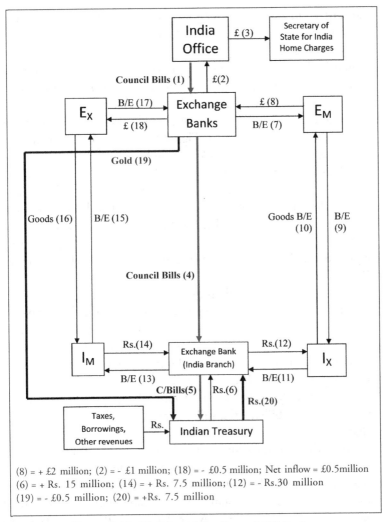

Figure 6.15: Working of the Council Bill System

Indian Branch of the Exchange Banks would also sell bills drawn on the Exchange Bank in London, which I_M would send to E_X as payment against goods imported by I_M. Now since Indian exports were typically greater than imports, the total quantum of rupees in India with the Exchange Bank would not have been sufficient for settlement of the claims by I_X. Gold sovereigns would have to be sent to the Indian treasury where it would be exchanged for rupees. Since the rupees had to be minted from silver, the silver would be bought in the bullion markets and sent to the treasury. It was only from this additional inflow of silver that new rupee coins were struck and put into domestic circulation.

Some contrived figures on the possible flow of sovereigns and rupees have been included in Figure 6.15. The total sovereign inflow into the Exchange Bank in London is £2 million which is equal to the total outflow of rupees from India (= Rs.30 million @ Rs. 15 = £1). However, monies raised through sale of bills drawn on London in India plus discounting of council bills at the treasury yield an inflow to the Indian Branch of the Exchange Bank of just Rs. 22.5 million thereby warranting shipment of gold sovereigns to the Treasury for conversion to rupees of £0.5 million = Rs. 7.5 million.

The use of council bills provided a convenient solution; without these gold to a much larger extent would have to be shipped to India to settle the claims of Indian exporters and at the same time silver rupee coins would have to be melted and exchanged for gold to settle the claims arising from the home charges payable by the Indian government. Prior to 1904 the India Office would issue council bills only to the extent of home charges; thereafter it began issuing council bills to the full extent of the demands of the Exchange Banks.

Since these inflows and outflows were fairly evenly matched, bullion movements were by and large avoided as they were cancelled out through bills of exchange or 'council bills'. On average, India had to make payments against home charges to a tune of approximately £20 million. After deducting the amounts raised by the India Office on account of Government of India borrowings in London, some £15 million had still to be remitted by India to England. However, given that India's net exports were greater than this amount, more than £2.2 million had to be paid by English importers to Indian exporters in rupees. While gold could be converted into rupees at the rate of 1s.4d., the silver could be bought in the bullion markets at a cheaper rate and shipped

---

Box 6.7: Council Bills or Drafts

Also termed 'council bills', 'India council bills', 'India council drafts', etc., these are issued in London and payable in India in rupees. The financial affairs of that country are managed in London by what is known as the 'India Council, which offers for sale Wednesday of each week to the highest bidders a certain amount of council bills, which are purchased by those desiring to make remittances to Calcutta and other points in India. The London papers give the prices at which these bills are sold, distinguishing between those which are sold for remittance by mail, and for what are known as telegraphic transfers; namely, where immediate use is wished for the money in India—the latter usually selling at a slight advance over the former. The reports always show the amounts disposed of, and the minimum rates obtained. Any sales made between the regular Wednesday meetings are referred to as 'specials'. India payments in London must be made in gold, whereas London payments in India must be made in rupees. All this is made possible by means of the India Council.

Source: Rollins, Montgomery, *Money and Investments*, George Routledge Sons Limited, London.http://chestofbooks.com/finance/investments/ Money-Investments/Council-Drafts.html#ixzz2443wvzJl, 1917.

---

to India.[18] From this silver, *and this silver alone*, rupee coins were struck and put into domestic circulation.

One important point remains to be discussed here; the rate of exchange in the council bill market. When the rupee began to fall after the closing of the mints in 1893 an attempt was made to raise the exchange rate in the council bills market; after all the whole purpose of the gold exchange standard was for the Indian government to obtain more sterling per rupee (than the silver rupee). The India Office withheld the sale of council bills in order to raise the exchange rate to 1s.4d. But at this rate the sales of council bills fell to just £9.5 million in 1893–4 as against £16.5 in 1892–3. Gold sovereigns were instead shipped by British exporters through Exchange Banks to India. These Exchange Banks with operations in Australia, Egypt, Ceylon and other countries were able to get better rates for sovereigns in India as compared to the (overvalued) rates offered by the India Office for rupees. This forced the latter to lower the rates to 1s.2.54d. in 1893–4. To an extent this was an acceptance of failure in the policy adopted to stabilize the exchange rate. But as the volume of council bills drawn on India slowly improved so did the exchange rate which touched the ceiling rate by 1898–9. This can be seen in Table 6.14.

TABLE 6.14: SUMS RECEIVED ON COUNCIL BILLS
DRAWN AND STERLING-RUPEE EXCHANGE RATE

Year	Sum Received Against Bill Drawn (£)	Average Rate Obtained per Rupee (s.-d.)
1870–1	8,443,509	1–10.495
1871–2	10,310,339	1–11.126
1872–3	13,989,095	1–10.754
1873–4	13,285,678	1–10.351
1874–5	10,841,615	1–10.156
1875–6	12,389,613	1–9.625
1876–7	12,695,799	1–8.508
1877–8	10,134,455	1–8.791
1878–9	13,948,565	1–7.794
1879–8	15,261,810	1–7.961
1880–1	15,239,677	1–7.956
1881–2	18,412,429	1–7.895
1882–3	15,120,521	1–7.525
1883–4	17,599,805	1–7.536
1884–5	13,758,909	1–7.308
1885–6	10,292,692	1–6.254
1886–7	12,136,279	1–5.441
1887–8	15,358,577	1–4.898
1888–9	14,262,859	1–4.379
1889–90	15,474,496	1–4.566
1890–1	15,969,034	1–6.089
1891–2	16,093,854	1–4.733
1892–3	16,532,215	1–2.984
1893–4	9,530,235	1–2.546
1894–5	16,905,102	1–1.100
1895–6	17,664,000	1–1.638
1896–7	15,526,000	1–2.45
1897–8	9,506,000	1–3.406
1898–9	18,692,000	1–3.978
1899–1900	19,067,000	1–4.067

Sources: DSAL, Digital South Asia Library (nd), *Statistical Abstracts Relating to British India from 1840 to 1865, First Number*, http://dsal.uchicago.edu/ and David Barbour, *The Standard of Value*, Macmillan & Co. Ltd., London, 1912, p. 208.

The years 1893 to 1898 were considered a transition period; the government was able to ascertain whether the rate of 1s.4d. was realistic, what kind of contraction in rupees was required for the rupee to reach this exchange rate, and also to understand the quantum of gold that would have to be borrowed in London to maintain this level. A reversion to bimetallism, especially at the rate of 1 gold = 15½ silver was no longer a relevant option. India moving towards a gold standard, therefore, seemed inevitable. To recommend the road map for the adoption of a gold standard in India the Fowler Committee was appointed in 1898. By the time the report was presented in 1898, the rupee had risen to the ceiling rate of 1s.4d. giving confidence that India was ready to move on to the gold standard with full convertibility of the rupee at this rate; in other words, gold could be converted to rupees and *vice-versa*.

Although we will return to the full implications of the Fowler Committee Report in the next part, two issues faced by the Indian government at this point of time were the availability of reserves and the elasticity of money supply. The change to full gold standard in India in accordance with the Fowler Committee was considered difficult because the government did not have reserves of gold. Under a full gold standard people could demand gold in exchange for rupees at the stipulated rate. There was a danger that the entire reserves could get dissipated in exchange for rupees. The cost of maintaining such large reserves would have been difficult and expensive. At the same time, the failure of the government to honour its commitment to convertibility of rupees to sovereigns would mean a breach of trust. The repercussions of India regressing to silver would be nothing short of cataclysmic.

The other big question raised by the Fowler Committee was whether the rupee rate had increased by forcing an absolute or relative stringency or contraction in the supply of rupees. The argument made against this assertion was that money supply actually increased in the period immediately after closure of mints. This was due to several reasons. First, the government continued to coin rupees against silver received by banks which had been shipped just before or soon after the mints were supposedly closed. Second, dishoarded rupees came into circulation with the higher value of rupee vis-à-vis silver, and finally, rupees from native states and flowing in from outside the country added to the money supply. The quantum of effective money supply also increased because of economies in the use of currency due to expansion of cheque system and improved velocity of circulation of money due to improved communications. Economists in favour of the gold exchange standard argued that rather than a restricted supply it was the increased demand for rupees that was responsible for the appreciation of the rupee to 1s.4d.; this increased demand could have been due to factors like the large borrowings on the Indian account (debt and investment in India), reduction in public remittances from India and from demand for Indian exports.

On the other hand, the argument that there was indeed a relative scarcity, i.e. demand increasing more rapidly than supply, was strong too. Moreover, gradual improvement in world trade and commerce, with a fixed money supply, meant a *relative* contraction of currency. While trying to comprehend the complex monetary standard evolving in India, it is important not to lose track of the simple essentials of money and monetary instruments. At the end of the nineteenth century it seemed as if the fixed exchange rate between the rupee and the sovereign (and in turn gold) at Rs. 1 = 1s.4d. could be maintained. But at what cost? If the relative scarcity of the rupee was indeed a fact, then by the Quantity Theory of Money, India should have faced a deflation. And this may have actually been the case. As evident in Table 6.11, the fall in India's price level was sharper than the fall in Britain's price level; the contraction in money supply was perhaps the reason. One of the biggest challenges countries across the world would face was also clearly emerging in India—maintaining a fixed exchange rate (stability in international exchanges) and, at the same time, stabilizing domestic price level by following an independent monetary policy. As illustrated in Figure 6.16, changes in money supply to control exchange rates also impacts the domestic price level.

Meanwhile, India it seemed had drifted away from any possibility to return to monometallic silverstandard; the moment for India to finally to move on to a pure monometallic gold standard was imminent. Unfortunately that was never to be.

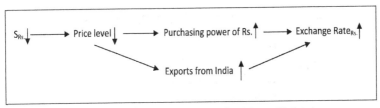

Figure 6.16: Control of Money Supply to Maintain
Exchange Rate of Rupees

NOTES

1. The exchange rates were twofold; for silver it was usually expressed as rupees in shillings and pence and for gold as price of sovereigns in rupees.
2. Unlike the pro-gold lobby (particularly the Chambers of Commerce) there was no anti-gold lobby *per se*. These were more like independent voices of various political and economic commentators.
3. The notation used here for Rupees-anna-pice has been explained in endnote 3 of Chapter 5.
4. Italics my own for emphasis.
5. Ibid.
6. By which year this amount of currency would be required is not mentioned by Lees.
7. Drawing from the work of Bagehot, Mellyn (2009: 75–6) asserts that 'real history' (as opposed to 'conjectural history') views institutions as organic, not mechanical. The evolution of institutions was not always by design; more often than not they are the accidents of 'real history'.
8. This term was commonly used, although it is not found in the literature referenced here.
9. Morys (2012, p. 29) points out that the German states (on a silver standard) 'were swamped with French gold coin' in 1867.
10. 'A banker or bullion-dealer in London desires to send a hundred thousand pounds to India, or China, or Holland, or any country where silver circulates. Silver we will suppose is dear in London, so he sends a hundred thousand pounds worth of gold to his Paris agent, who has it coined and exchanged for five-franc silver pieces, which are then exported to their destination. The French Mint is set to work, and the French coinage is changed to the extent of £100,000, for no purpose whatever but to minister to the gain of a foreign banker' (Ballard, p. 23).

11. To reiterate, these costs include 'seigniorage charge, the cost of melting coins, delays and associated loss of interest, insurance fees, and so on' (Friedman, 1989, p. 8).

12. It is important to mention that this has been especially so in the recent literature; however, if one goes back to contemporary debates, India finds a prominent place in the discussion.

13. To reiterate, value of currency is usually defined to mean weight and fineness of bullion content; we, however, use the term value to refer to purchasing power including its purchasing power over other currencies (exchange rate).

14. The Mapillah community arose primarily from Arab contacts. Mappilahs chiefly reside in the Malabar region of Kerala.

15. For a comprehensive view of the evolution of banking in India, see Goldsmith (1983).

16. But gold sovereigns obviously did not circulate because the market rate of the rupee (as we see) was below 1s.4d. Why give 1s.4d. for Re. 1 at the ceiling rate when at the market rate it was possible to obtain Re. 1 for (say) 1s.2d.?

17. Rs. 300 m/0.38 = Rs. 800 m.

18. As we stated above, this purchase of silver benefitted London silver traders.

CHAPTER 7

The Gold Standard and the Gold Exchange Standard

The fact that the Government of India have drifted into a system and have never set it forth plainly is partly responsible for a widespread misunderstanding of its true character.

JOHN MAYNARD KEYNES

The Indian gold exchange standard that had arisen at the end of the nineteenth century was an interesting and important one. India was consequently on neither; pure silver, pure gold nor bimetallic standard. Under this novel scheme, the exchange rate of the rupee (a token silver coin) was pegged to the British sovereign, which in turn was convertible to gold at a fixed rate. The exchange rate was pegged at a rate which ensured a small positive balance of payments surplus in favour of India (after accounting for all expenditures of the Indian government including remittance of home charges). Through this surplus, new coins were put into circulation. The question, however, arose as to whether this increase in money supply through a surplus in balance of payments was sufficient to accommodate the growing needs of the domestic (Indian) economy. If not, as we have seen above, deflation in the general price level was inevitable or in other words, an increase in the gold price of the rupee. The system of council bills also ensured that gold inflows into India were minimized to just the net surplus in the balance of payments. This was an important corollary to the gold exchange standard because even then the West continued to be weary of India's propensity to hoard precious metals so that gold, once it entered India would be 'consumed', would never leave. The shortages of gold would raise its price, sending the world into deflation and recession.

Over the next decade and a half the Indian government faced many challenges in the smooth functioning of the gold exchange standard and in ensuring stability in its value both in terms of internal purchasing power and external rate of exchange between the rupee and sterling. To an extent, the years before the War were indeed a period of relative stability and it is important to understand why. In any case, the gold exchange standard was never considered to be a permanent solution. The hope was that at some point of time India would have been in a position to move on to a pure gold standard. But before that could happen, something even worse did, that put the entire international monetary system into a state of confusion; the First World War.

7.1: THE ECONOMICS OF INTERNATIONAL MONETARY STANDARDS

If the mechanism works automatically the problem is essentially one of knowledge and intellectual curiosity; if the mechanism demands management, knowledge becomes a prerequisite to action.

HEILPERIN, 1931

The decline of bimetallism had propelled countries of the world towards adopting a monometallic gold standard. India in some sense was kept away from it and was instead put on a gold exchange standard. In either case, countries faced a dilemma in ensuring internal and external stability simultaneously. In fact, it is important to understand the new 'rules of the game' under which the gold standard and its variants had to abide by. Domestic money supply in countries was constrained by the quantum of gold reserves and these reserves could only be enhanced through foreign trade (or through gold discoveries). But it was not domestic money supply *per se* that mattered; rather it was the effect of changes in money supply on the price level and real output to bring out an adjustment in any imbalance in the balance of payments that was sometimes difficult for countries to accept. Although a nation's currency could be revalued upwards or devalued, the essence of the gold standard was that it was a fixed exchange rate regime. In other words, shocks in the external balance were transmitted on to the domestic economy through changes in money supply, which in turn led to changes in domestic price level and output so as to ensure necessary adjustment in the external balance without having recourse to altering exchange rates.

The classical gold standard was a system in which participating countries had to announce the price of their domestic currencies in terms of a fixed amount of gold. National money and other forms of money (bank deposits and notes) had to also be freely converted into gold at the announced rate. Gold coins could be exported or melted into bullion and sent out of the country in payment of goods imported. The US, for instance, fixed the dollar at 1.50463 grams of pure gold where it remained until 1933. The British sovereign was fixed at 7.322381 grams of fine gold. The sterling–dollar rate was therefore $4.86656 = £1. Under the gold (or silver) standard the price of gold (or silver) expressed in terms of the national currency is fixed by law and the precious metal can always be sold for a determined amount of national currencies at the mints or central banks (free coinage). If all countries are on the gold standard, then the ratio of the gold content of their national currencies was called *gold or mint parity*. The gold standard permitted countries to alter the price of their currency in terms of the quantity of gold obtainable in exchange in case they suffered a chronic balance of payments problem but this was neither encouraged nor resorted to by the major players as it would undermine the purpose of the standard itself.

In this section I describe how the gold standard system worked, providing a high degree of stability in exchange rates that fostered free trade and capital flows at the turn of the twentieth century. The years between 1899 and the advent of the First World War were considered the most prosperous years under the classical gold standard system (1880–1913) with the US economy showing definitive signs of coming out of the 1893 depression that had followed a panic triggered off by the bursting of the railroad bubble.

As we have seen, without precious metals, exchanges would simply not take place because of a lack of trust and confidence in the value of the medium of exchange. An over-supply of the medium of exchange could render it worthless and hence its credibility as a means of settlement of claims at a point of time as well as across time would be unacceptable to people. The same issue also pertained to settlements that arise from foreign trade. Like internal exchanges, foreign trade too could be sustained through barter but such a system would have been totally inadequate in a highly interconnected industrializing world. A means of payment that is acceptable to all trading partners was therefore necessary to ensure international goods and capital flows. When payments have to be made across borders, one national currency needs to be converted into another. The question arises as to the rate of exchange. If the two currencies are both based on either a pure gold or silver specie standard then the rate would be in proportion to the gold or silver content of the two currencies. If one is based on gold and the other on silver (like say England and India respectively were) then the exchange rate would in proportion to value (market price) of the gold and silver content of the two currencies respectively. Under international bimetallism since the ratio of gold to silver remained almost constantly at about 1:15½ it was easy to convert one currency to the other, and with a great deal of certainty or with little risk. However, the gold discoveries of the 1840s and massive silver flow to India during the 'cotton famine' changed all that; there was increasing concern that gold prices would fall while silver prices would increase and the gold–silver parity would end. For this and other reasons there was an exodus to a monometallic gold standard across the Western world. This was the beginning of the end of international bimetallism and with it silver went into free fall. There was then no certainty as to the rate at which gold currencies could be converted into other silver currencies and *vice-versa*. This uncertainty in exchange rates, as we have seen, had a negative impact on international trade of goods as well as on capital movements. Many countries, especially in the Western world had by this time moved on to a pure gold standard or what is called a gold specie standard where the monetary unit circulated as gold coins. The US moved on to a *de jure* gold standard system in 1900 when the Congress passed the Gold Standard Act.

In 1893, India moved on to a rudimentary form of the *gold ex-*

change standard. The price of the rupee was fixed in terms of the sterling (Re. 1 = 1s.4d.), which in turn was convertible into gold at a fixed rate. This, however, was a ceiling rate and the rupee was allowed to freely depreciate, the lower bound being the value of silver in the silver token rupee coin. Once the demand for rupees (and supply restricted by closing of the mints) had raised its value to 1s.4d., it was expected that from thereon a more proper form of the gold exchange standard would become operative. Importers of Indian goods could buy an unlimited quantity of rupees at the announced rate and exporters of goods to India could exchange rupees for gold at that rate. A *de facto* gold standard had supposedly been created without gold in domestic circulation. The third variant of the gold standard, the *gold bullion standard* was a system whereby the government guaranteed conversion of currency (paper) to gold at a fixed rate. Under all these standards, although it was possible to issue notes without 100 per cent backing of notes with gold, gold reserves did act as a constraint on note issue given that inadequate reserves could prompt a run on the currency. For sake of completeness we must mention a fourth possible system; a *currency standard* is where the price of the national monetary unit is fixed in terms of the currency of another country by monetary law and is held stable by the monetary authorities of that country. Here national currency would require 100 per cent backing by the foreign currency. When the foreign currency was convertible into gold, the system was nothing but the gold exchange standard.

When all countries adopted the gold standard in any of the variants defined above, the fear of a crash in silver prices was no longer topical. Under the gold exchange standard, for instance, Britain would accept country India's currency (rupees) in settlement of a claim (export of goods from Britain to India) only because it is assured that Indian rupees are convertible into gold (sovereigns) at some fixed rate (i.e. some fixed quantity of gold); in other words, exporters from Britain are assured that they will receive a certain fixed quantum of gold in exchange for their exports to India. As long as countries adhered to convertibility of their currency into gold at the announced rate, the risk and uncertainty of exchange rate fluctuations under the gold standard was minimal.

Before describing India's monetary developments when the world was on the classical gold standard, I will explain the basic tenets of this system. This is important not just from a historical standpoint but also because one can have a more informed opinion when one hears calls on going back to this 'golden era'. While demands for a return to the gold standard usually highlight 'price stability' both of exchange rates and the domestic price level, a fundamental question remains to be addressed—if a country was continuously importing more than it was exporting goods, how could it sustain an outflow of gold over a longer period of time? Exports and imports (after adjusting for autonomous capital flows) had to be brought into a reasonable level of sync. The fundamental problem with the system lay in the mechanism through which this was supposed to happen; the monetary flows pertaining to the external sector had a strong bearing on domestic or internal price level and the real economy.

For a more formal analysis we divide a country's macro-economy into two broad domains—the internal and the external economy. The core variables of concern to the internal macro-economy are price level, employment and growth while the primary concern with respect to the external sector is to ensure balance of payments equilibrium. The balance of payments consists of three main components of interactions between countries:

1. International trade in commodities, goods and services
2. Short-term cash and credit transactions
3. Long-term capital movements including foreign direct investment (FDI)

Of course another important component in international trade is the movement of labour, which apart from its social and cultural implications may be treated as a commodity. Put together these exchanges had to be settled by international payments, which gave rise to a demand for and supply of foreign exchange that was subject to perpetual and continual fluctuations. At the end of a certain period of time, several payments and receipts cancelled themselves out, but a residual remained, a balance to be settled, from which arose the need for international settlements and international indebtedness. If these balances were not settled regularly a chronic balance of payments disequilibrium situation would have to be confronted, requiring a major correction in foreign exchange rates, with severe and disruptive consequences to the movement of goods, capital and labour.

To understand the working of the classical gold standard in bringing about an equilibrium in the balance of payments, I have extensively drawn from the work of Michael Heilperin (1939), a renowned Austrian economist who expressed his overt concern over what he termed as 'monetary nationalism' wherein countries fail to follow 'the rules of the game' for balance of payments adjustments under the gold standard. These rules essentially require that signals from the external sector to domestic economy are transmitted *fully* so that they are allowed to have their necessary and complete impact to bring about an adjustment in balance of payments disequilibrium.

When each currency is convertible to a fixed quantity of gold, a problem arises as to how equilibrium can be simultaneously achieved in the balance of payments. In other words, the question is how an unequal demand and supply can be brought into equilibrium at some given (fixed) price. This problem is illustrated in Figure 7.1. Here D is the domestic economy and F the foreign economy. Suppose the following rates are announced or are determined by the gold content of the currencies: $C_F = 10$ oz. of gold and $C_D = 1$oz. of gold. Then $C_F = 10C_D$ or $C_F/C_D = 10$. Of course, there still remains an element of risk for there could be a revision in the par value of the currency. For example, the rate of currency D (C_D) could be revised from (say) 1 $C_D = 1$oz. gold to 1 $C_D = 0.90$ oz. of gold. Now $C_F/C_D = 11.1$. This is a devaluation of C_D. Imports from F would decline and so would the demand for C_F. D's exports would become more competitive and F would import more goods from D so that supply of C_F increases. Now if at the exchange rate of $C_F/C_D = 10$, the demand for C_F (the foreign currency) exceeds the supply of C_F then *without* recourse to a revision in the par rate (to $C_F/C_D = 9$), the only way in which equilibrium can be restored in the foreign exchange market is through shifts in the demand and/or supply curve for C_F.

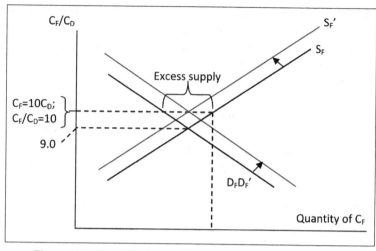

Figure 7.1: Fixed Exchange Rates under the Gold Standard

The exchange rate standards described above are essentially fixed exchange rate regimes. They had the advantage of maintaining stability and minimizing risk from exchange rate fluctuations on trade and capital flows. However, when there was disequilibrium in the balance of payments, since exchange rates could not change in order to restore equilibrium the only alternative was for 'quantity' to change. In other words, *the economy itself had to expand or contract* to increase or reduce the volume of exports or imports; this would be reflected in Figure 7.1 as shifts in the supply of and demand for foreign exchange (C_F) respectively. The 'rules of the game' were to ensure that these shifts happen, endogenously.

An excess supply of C_F implies that country D has a surplus in its balance of payments and F would have a deficit (assuming a two-country world). If so, then gold flows out from F to D. Money supply reduces in F and increases in D. From the quantity theory of money, if velocity remains constant, then the price level must fall in F and increase in D. This would mean that exports of country F increase and of D decrease so that demand for C_F in D increases (shifts outwards). Simultaneously, since imports by F from D will be costlier, F will import less from D so that they will need fewer C_D. This will mean supply of C_F in D decreases (shifts inwards).

Equilibrium in balance of payments is restored at $C_F/C_D = 10$ with D_F' and S_F'. The impact of price level changes on exports and imports requires time and a lot depends on the elasticity of import and export to price level changes.

This process of adjustment whereby D's domestic real economy had to contract could sometimes be painful for countries and often led to internal strife and protests against the gold standard. To neutralize these impacts adjustment was therefore sought by manipulation in interest rates to attract or induce compensating flows. Interest rate hikes (by say F) would no doubt bring in short-term capital from outside and bridge the deficit in balance of payments but would, however, dampen investment in the domestic economy, slow down growth, bring down the price level and reduce imports. In some sense, allowing interest rates to rise would have a similar impact as a decrease in money supply, deflation and a fall in price levels; the efficacy of each of these in bringing about balance of payments equilibrium is an empirical question.

Furthermore, when a country is on the gold standard its scope to issue paper currency is restricted. To ensure settlement of its international dues at the announced rate any issue of additional national (paper) currency is not possible unless it has acquired additional gold through positive net exports. Issue of un-backed paper currency could lead to a run on currency. While this constraint on money supply ensures domestic price stability there is a limitation imposed on the country's ability to deal with unemployment and/or slow growth using expansionary monetary policy. In a situation of adequate gold supplies and positive international growth this issue can go unnoticed; however, when growth slows down and employment rates fall, countries might find it difficult to manage their 'internal affairs' and may consequently be forced to expand money supply while, at the same time, announcing a devaluation of their currency in terms of gold. The latter would entail a revision in international gold parities. Going back to Figure 7.1, it is apparent that equilibrium in balance of payments can also be restored through a revaluation of C_D, say, to $C_F/C_D = 9.0$. However, frequent currency devaluation or revaluation destroys regularity in capital flows and induces erratic movement in short-term funds.

The destruction of confidence would ultimately have caused a break-down in monetary stability and undermined the gold standard. This can only be avoided with a well developed system of induced and automatic stabilizers that restore balance of payments equilibrium within a reasonable period of time.

A similar process of adjustment happens when one country is on a pure gold standard and the other on a silver standard. A deficit in balance of payments necessitates the outflow of (say) silver from F to international markets where it is converted into gold for payments to D. Once again this would mean changes in money supply, price level and volume of exports and imports that would ultimately bring about balance of payments equilibrium. An important aspect of this standard is that when gold is received by an exporter in Britain to settle his obligations the corresponding amount of (say) rupees is removed from circulation in India. A deficit in India's balance of payments must lead to a contraction in supply of domestic money supply (rupees) and consequently a fall in price level so as to bring about the necessary equilibrium in balance of payments through changes in exports and imports. On the other hand, a surplus in India's balance of payment would mean an in-flow of silver so that domestic money supply increases, price level rises and balance of payments restored. At the same time, sover-eigns must be taken out of circulation in Britain, melted, exchanged for silver in the bullion markets and sent to India. The key then in such standards like the gold exchange standard is to ensure that international payments or outflows or inflows of gold or domestic currency have the necessary impact on money supply to set the adjustment process in motion.

Although exchange rates are fixed and announced under the classical gold standard, some fluctuations around these rates are nonetheless possible. The range of fluctuation is determined by the costs of transport, insurance as well as duration for the physical export and import of gold between two countries. In addition, the duration of transportation would involve the opportunity cost of interest lost on account of the metal being transported. For sake of completeness we must also consider the bank's rates of buying and selling gold as these rates would invariably differ. Put together these factors determine the so called gold export and gold import point, illustrated in Figure 7.2 below. Continuing with our earlier example, let the gold parity between C_F and C_D be equal to 10 or $C_F/C_D = 10$. An increase in imports of goods from F would mean an increase in demand for C_F and a shift in D_F to D_F'. C_F will then appreciate (or C_D depreciates) to 10.5; in other words $1C_F = 10C_D$ is now $1C_F = 10.5C_D$. But how is this possible? After all, the gold parity is determined by the gold content of the two coins. Why would anyone give $10.5C_D$ for $1C_F$ when each C_D weighs 1/10th of C_F? The answer lies in the cost of transporting C_F to country D. If the costs of transport, insurance, interest foregone, etc. amount to (say) 10 per cent, then C_D can depreciate till a maximum rate of $C_F/C_D = 11.0$. If there is an increase in demand for C_F to say D_F', then the exchange rate will not go beyond $C_F/C_D = 11.0$ to (say) 11.2 because it would be cheaper to physically ship gold from D to F than pay more C_D for each unit of C_F in the foreign exchange market. Point x then becomes the gold export point (from D). Similarly, point m is the gold import point (into D). An increase in D's exports implies a demand for C_D or supply C_F. However, the C_D cannot appreciate above $C_F/C_D = 9$ because importers of goods in F would simply ship gold to D rather than buy C_D in the foreign

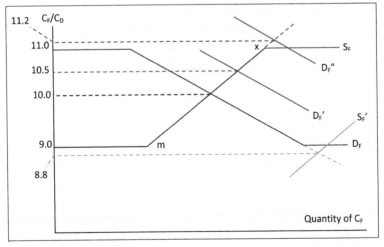

Figure 7.2: Gold Export and Import points under Gold Standard

exchange market at a higher rate of, say, $C_F/C_D = 8.8$ in which case they would get just $8.8C_D$ for each unit of C_F.

Now payments can also be effected through bills of exchange. Obviously the exchange rate for bills too cannot exceed or fall below the gold or silver export and import points as traders would choose to ship the metal itself rather than buy or sell bills at unattractive rates. Under the pure gold standard exchange rates were not fixed but moved between narrow bands.

The gold standard does not mean that countries must operate with gold currencies. Even paper money is acceptable so long as it is administered in such a way that its price in terms of a fixed quantity of gold is fixed. This will only happen when there is an obligation for the central bank or the appropriate monetary institution to buy and sell gold freely in exchange for paper currency at a fixed rate. This actually is a more fundamental requirement, even more than the *fixity of the rate* itself at which gold is bought and sold. This rate can be changed but then the obligation to buy and sell gold at the new rate should not be diluted. Given that the state can usually exercise its authority to change the rate at which gold can be bought and sold implies that the gold standard in a closed economy *by itself* does not serve any real purpose except perhaps a readjustment in the general price level; however, in an open economy caution needs to be exercised as to its impact on international trade and on international relations. For instance, a state could debase a coin with impunity and there is really little one could do about it. However, as already mentioned, this could have a destabilizing influence on international trade and capital flows not only because prior settlements are affected [for instance if D owed F, $1C_F$, then F may now receive (say) 0.9 oz. instead of 1 oz. of gold at the old rate] but also because the element of uncertainty over future rates would creep in. The repercussions on trade and capital flows may be of utmost importance to both F and D.

The most important function of the international gold standard was that it established precise parities between national currencies, fluctuations were then restricted to the import and export points. To make the system functional, the currencies had to be freely converted into gold and allowed to move freely between countries on the standard. The international gold standard minimizes the disturbing effects which the plurality of national currencies can have upon international commercial and financial relations. In other words, it provided the best alternative to an international or world currency.

Reserves served an important purpose under the gold standard. Reserves were required primarily as a backing for currency in circulation and avoidance of a crisis in confidence. To an extent, therefore, reserves prevented an over-issue of currency and inflation; however, it is in the external sector that these reserves become crucial. Reserves were not merely to 'guarantee' the 'value' of bank notes but also to maintain international monetary stability by providing for gold export in case of a deficit in the balance of payments. However, such reserves would have to be replenished so that its effect could be transmitted to the domestic real economy; a monetary contraction would then mean a slowdown in the real economy and correction in the balance of payments. Reserves must not be seen as a way of sustaining perpetual deficits; their role was to ensure that the adjustment mechanism or the rules of the game were transmitted to the real economy in order to correct long-terms imbalances in the balance of payments.

The Bank of England was considered to be an exemplar of central bank behaviour during the classical gold standard. Whenever Great Britain faced a balance of payments deficit, the Bank of England raised the 'bank rate' (rate of interest) so that the economy slowed down and with it imports too. At the same time, the slowdown also brought down the general price level, making English exports more competitive. Such behaviour was more the exception than the norm; France and Belgium, for instance, did not follow the rules of the game. By never allowing interest rates to rise adequately, price levels did not deflate to the extent needed. Another instrument adopted to neutralize the impact of gold flows emanating from balance of payment disequilibrium was 'sterilization' of changes in domestic money supply; for instance, securities could be sold through open market operations when there was an inflow of gold on account of a surplus in the balance of payments. The excess gold is therefore mopped up and does not increase money supply and the price level. In this way the chronic surplus would continue to exist and at the same time the deficit country would have to retaliate so that it does not face a deflationary situation from an outflow of gold. The re-equilibrating mechanism was constricted by open market operations that set about neutralizing the effects of gold flows; deficit countries prevented money circulation from falling and interest rates from rising while surplus countries let money supply increase and interest rates fall. These led to the persistence of chronic balance of payments imbalances simply because the 'rules of the game' were not being adhered to by the players. However, convertibility at gold parity was maintained to a satisfactory extent by most of the major players under the gold standard; this prevented reckless expansion of money supply and control of inflation rates. The average inflation rate between 1880 and 1914 under the gold standard was just about 0.1 per cent.

Throughout the latter half of the nineteenth century and the first decades of the twentieth century there were incessant calls for India to be put on a gold standard. But that never happened. The reason for this was simply because the world feared India's propensity to 'consume' or 'hoard' precious metals; gold and silver once they entered India never left. This would drain the world of gold, raise its price and deflate general price levels, thereby triggering off recessions and depressions. Given that gold standard countries backed their currencies by gold, an outflow of gold to India would render a contraction in paper currency and credit in these countries. At the same time, the propensity to hoard gold would have meant that the rules of the game would not work out. The inflow of gold on account of a surplus in the balance of payments had to raise domestic prices (in India), reduce exports and bring back equilibrium in balance of payments. However, hoarding would have meant neutralizing the inflationary impact of gold inflows. The secondary repercussions of India moving on to gold could make matters worse. Adoption of a gold standard could lead people to perceive the inevitable fall in the status of the rupee. As rupees went off circulation, the Indian demand for gold coins would soar and with it the price of gold. At the same time, the increased supply of silver into the market would mean a crash in its price. China, the only great economy at that time to remain on silver, would have benefited from this depreciation in the price of silver but the fear of a continual fall could have led China too to abandon a silver currency. Some other minor objections to a gold standard were raised like the small value of transactions those meant that gold would not be suitable for day-to-day transactions in India.

Let us now explore the rules of the game under a currency exchange standard where instead of prices of a country's currency being fixed in terms of gold it is now fixed in terms of the currency of another country.

1. The monetary authority (usually central bank) fixes the quantity of the foreign currency (or standard currency) that will be exchanged for a unit of the national currency; in other words the parity between the standard currency chosen and national currency is defined by law.
2. National currency must be convertible into standard currency and vice-versa. The central bank must then maintain this price by buying and selling unlimited quantities of the standard currency at this price.
3. Adequate reserves of the standard currency are required. In case of deficits the reserves diminish, in case of surpluses in balance of payments, reserves accumulate.
4. Monetary reserves are held on deposit in the country whose currency is adopted as standard. If, for instance, India is on the sterling standard, then increases and decreases in reserves of standard currency (sterling) will be held in London on India's account.

How do settlements take place?

1. Between India and England: a surplus (deficit) in India's account will be reflected by an increase (decrease) in £ balances held in London by the Indian monetary authority.
2. Settlement between India and other countries that are also on the sterling standard: Net payments will be made in London by transferring £ from deficit countries to surplus countries and vice-versa. If all reserves are held in London by the Bank of

England, then the latter becomes the clearing house or settlement agency for all the balances.

3. Settlement between India and countries not on sterling standard: Any net payment to be made by sterling standard countries to (say) gold standard countries will be met by a decrease in or the outflow of England's gold reserves. Net payments to be received by sterling standard countries will result in an inflow and increase in England's gold reserves.

How is equilibrium in balance of payments restored under the sterling standard?

1. Between countries on the sterling standard and England: If the balances of (say) India are accumulating while these of England are declining, then to maintain parity India must increase the demand for £ ($D_\pounds$ must shift outward). In other words India buys £ and sells rupees. England, on the other hand, to decrease supply of £ in the foreign exchange market ($S_\pounds$ must shift inwards) must buy £ (to replenish its reserves) and sell rupees from its reserves. This will increase money supply in India (Rs.) and diminish it in England (£). Consequently interest rates decrease (increase), price level increases (decreases), exports fall (rise) in India (England) so as to restore equilibrium in balance of payments. This is illustrated in Figure 7.3.

   India's £ reserves held in England must remain idle and should not be invested by England in earning returns. This would nullify the equilibrating mechanism. Moreover, since the opportunity cost of reserves must be forgone, the sterling standard is not costless.

2. Between countries on the sterling standard; here the impact will have to be borne by the reserves of the two countries. Though the reserves of both countries are held in England, there would be no net impact of money supply on England itself.

Finally, we take a look at the rules of game under the gold exchange standard. Under this system it is gold which remains the monetary standard; however, while the central bank or designated

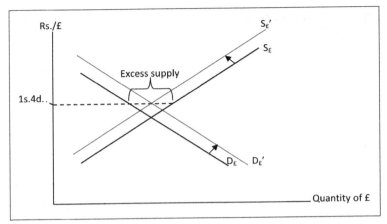

Figure 7.3: Adjustment under Sterling Exchange Standard

institution of (say) India is bound to redeem its notes it can choose to do so in either gold or in foreign exchange of a gold standard country, say, sterling. India maintains the price of gold at the legally prescribed rate by buying or selling it or £ at this rate (in exchange for its rupee). There are few specific rules that are necessary for the smooth functioning of the gold exchange standard.

1. India must consider changes in total reserves of both, gold and sterling (i.e. gold exchange standard) as a basis for policy. An increase in these reserves happens on account of a greater demand for rupees. To maintain the exchange rate, India must sell rupees and buy gold or sterling (increase in $D_£$). This increase in supply of rupees will lead to an increase in Indian money supply and price level, reduce exports and restore balance of payments equilibrium. Figure 7.3 is also applicable to this situation.

2. The reserves held in London for instance must be kept liquid and against any risk of suspension of convertibility by and/or movement of gold from England.

3. The Bank of England must keep 100 per cent reserves to meet the obligations of the monetary authorities of countries like India. Once again these balances must be kept idle and not be used by England.

4. Between countries on the sterling standard. Here the impact will have to be borne by the sterling reserves of the two countries. Though the reserves of both countries are held in England, there would be no net impact of money supply on England itself.

At this point it is important that we take stock of the central issues pertaining to the monetary system of a country. This, as the history of the rupee illustrates, is a question of balance; there are no absolute solutions. While one objective is met, we drift away from the other. In such cases, it is the state that must act in the interests of society as a whole but very often this wasn't the case. The state chose to act in the interest of specific groups so that the burden of their decisions fell on those who simply could not understand what was happening or on to those who had no voice to protest against the system. I came across a recent statement by D. Subba Rao, former Governor of the Reserve Bank of India, that captures this predicament; 'People who want growth are more articulate, they have a platform and they are heard. Not that I do not have sympathy for them, but people who are hit by high inflation do not have such opportunities to be heard (Livemint, 11 February 2013).

First and foremost, any monetary system strives for stability in the value of its currency or its purchasing power. When the price level of goods and services in the economy rises, a currency loses its purchasing power; its value is eroded. This, as we have seen in our discussion of the Quantity Theory of Money, is the result of increases in supply of money that translates into higher prices (under certain assumptions). The repercussions on the real economy on account of instability in the value of money can be critical for a country's economic, social and political stability. I mention a few of the possible adverse impacts of inflation; debtors (gain) and creditors (lose) are affected differently which can throw the credit system of an economy out of gear. There are also distributional concerns that arise when inflation rates are high. Inflation is a general tax on the entire population, making it a regressive one. Capital-labour relations may deteriorate. Sustained inflation alters inflation expectations and pricing policies of firms, developing into a vicious cycle that is difficult to break. Stability in the value of money, or in other words, domestic price stability, is a central concern of any monetary system. At the same time, we must reiterate that it is just not inflation which is a concern; deflation is an even bigger worry as its impact of the real economy could be disastrous. What is therefore required is a stable domestic price level, with perhaps low rates of inflation (which indicates a healthy demand situation in the economy with buoyant prices guiding resource allocation).

Now while domestic price stability is of foremost importance to the sustainability of a monetary system, stability in exchange rates is also critical. Raw material flows, international trade in finished goods as well as capital flows became integral to the development of world capitalism. Instability in exchange rates could easily and quickly endanger working of this fragile but critical interconnected network. Deterioration in international trade and exchange would result in lower standards of living across the world. The decline of international bimetallism broke the stability in gold–silver parity that had existed for several centuries. National monies had expanded beyond their metallic component and included paper currency as well as bank money and credit instruments. In such a world the need for stable exchange rates became more crucial than stable domestic price level. While one might dismiss this by arguing that the external sector might be only a small percentage of total output of a nation, this is not a valid claim. Exports and imports play a very important role *at the margin* for an economy; they may encompass some of the most necessary inputs for all other sectors of an economy (oil for India) and may be also be the trigger of growth and development (India's software exports). We can also easily appreciate the necessity for capital flows, both foreign direct investment and foreign institutional investment for a country like India. Widely oscillating exchange rates could not only throw these sectors into confusion, but could also have major ramifications for a country's growth and development.

Chablani (1939), however, rightly points out that 'instability of foreign exchanges was a symptom of a disease rather than the disease itself' (p. 90). Fluctuations in exchange rates arose from instability in the domestic price level and that usually happens because of excessive supply of money in the domestic economy. Other reasons could be political instability and external shocks. Exchange rate stability requires international coordination and not merely internal management of the monetary system. For instance, if the US pursues prudent domestic monetary policy and maintains inflation at zero per cent while India pursues an expansionary monetary policy that results in 10 per cent rate of inflation, then, all else remaining constant, the rupee would depreciate by 10 per cent vis-à-vis the dollar to maintain balance of payments. In this case, the US cannot be held responsible for the appreciation of the dollar. But what if the rupee–dollar exchange rate was fixed? Then India's inflation may be transmitted (perhaps partially) to the US. The gold standard had in some sense ensured that all currencies on the standard had stable exchange rates but the repercussions of this stability were transmitted onto domestic price levels and the real economy. Nonetheless, in a rapidly integrating world the gold standard provided the necessary impetus to world trade. Transactions costs of hedging against currency fluctuations and conversion of gold to silver and *vice-versa* were also avoided. Uncertainty and risk in the possible disruption of gold–silver parity due to discoveries in different parts of the world was also eliminated.

From 1893 the British Indian Government by and large gave utmost priority to maintaining exchange rate stability. This came at the cost of domestic instability in price level. India was at the mercy of currency changes in Britain. All it could do in such cases was to allow inflation or deflation in the Indian price level, all in the cause of maintaining exchange rates. In the absence of international agreements, the best recourse would have been to stabilize domestic price level and let the exchange rates take the impact. The benefit of a flexible exchange rate policy was observable for a brief period between 1922 and 1926. However, India reverted back to a fixed exchange rate regime after this brief interlude and once again faced several adverse consequences.

Today the world has moved on to a system based on 'abstract' bank money; balance of payments adjustment takes place through 'price' changes in foreign currency. We see later in the book the process is not as painless as it might seem; its impact on exports and imports as well as instability in exchange rates does add to the transactions cost of foreign trade. While India moved on to a flexible exchange rate regime close to a century later, in 1899 it was still engaged in a battle over the adoption of pure gold standard or the gold exchange standard.

7.2: THE FOWLER COMMITTEE AND THE ELUSIVE GOLD STANDARD

The idea that convertibility is necessary to maintain the value a currency is, on the face of it, a preposterous idea. No one wants the conversion of bananas into apples to maintain the value of bananas. Bananas maintain their value by reason of the fact that there is a demand for them and their supply is limited.

B.R. AMBEDKAR

They must adopt my scheme despite themselves.

A.M. LINDSAY

It would be useful to recall something mentioned at the very start of this book—the difficulty of monetary instruments to fulfill all three functions of money simultaneously, effectively and efficiently, both *within a country and internationally*, has been and continues to be the root cause of many national and global financial crises. As the world drifted away from international bimetallism, silver and with it India's silver rupee depreciated steadily over a period of 20 years. Without a possible lower limit, the danger of large inelastic payments (home charges) in gold was expected to cause a budgetary crisis in India. The solution to the problem was to delink the rupee from silver and instead fix its price in terms of sterling, the latter being fully and freely convertible into gold at a fixed rate. In 1892 the Herschell Committee recommended that the Indian mints be closed to the free coinage of both gold and silver, the government retaining the liberty to coin rupees if required by the public in exchange for gold at a fixed rate.

The exchange rate of the rupee was actually fixed in terms of sterling (i.e. how much it would be worth in terms of sterling or a certain quantum of gold). For a while, the rupee depreciated below the ceiling rate of 1s.4d. (= 16d.) but once the demand for rupees stabilized and its supply was controlled (or constrained) by closure of the mints, it reached the stipulated ceiling rate in 1898–9. From here on, any increase in demand for rupees would have to be met by the unlimited issue of rupees in exchange for gold at this rate. In other words, as seen in Figure 6.13 the supply curve of rupees is perfectly elastic at the rate of 1s.4d. Although the rupee could depreciate (which it did) this was not expected to happen since India generally ran a surplus in its balance of payments. A buoyant demand for rupees meant that India would (almost) always be a net receiver of gold sovereigns from which silver could be bought and rupee coins minted for domestic circulation. At the same time, the adjustment mechanism to bring about balance of payments equilibrium was also simple; an increase in India's surpluses would mean an increase in the inflow of gold sovereigns and a corresponding increase in domestic money supply, an increase in prices, a fall in exports and an increase in imports until balance of payments equilibrium was restored.

But was it acceptable to allow domestic fluctuations in price and output for exchange rate stability? The answer lay in the necessity to inspire confidence in national currencies; without an acceptable means of payment, including deferred payment, international exchange would be reduced to barter. With the increasing international division of labour in the early twentieth century, there was a danger for industrialization to come to a grinding halt. For a while the impact of this on domestic instability could be managed artificially but as Heilperin pointed out, without following the rules of the game for long-term balance of payments equilibrium, the system was bound to fail, and it did. Meanwhile, under the gold standard and its variants the world did operate with a system of internationally agreed rules, conventions and supporting institutions to facilitate exchange rate stability as well as international trade and capital flows.

Before we focus on the evolution of the gold exchange standard in India, we must answer a fundamental question. Why did India not adopt a pure gold standard, which would have ensured the same level of stability in exchange rate and also allowed an automatic adjustment mechanism for long-term balance of payments equilibrium? Although many answers have been given, not all are convincing. One of the most common justifications for adoption of the gold exchange standard was that it would economize on the use of gold and make it easier for countries that did not have a sufficient amount of gold to move closer to a gold standard. But more than these condescending answers, the West was concerned about India's hoarding habit. What if large amounts of gold flowed into India (like silver did during the cotton famine) and never returned into circulation? What if India's thirst for gold absorbed significant portions of world production? With net supply available for currency in the world reduced, prices of gold would increase and bring back the spectre of deflation in the general price level. At the same time, India was an important supplier of raw materials to British industry and stability in exchange rates was required. The gold exchange standard was the right alternative for India; a close approximation to the international gold standard but conveniently, without a domestic gold currency.

The Fowler Committee Report presented in 1898 actually recommended a gold standard with a gold currency for India; the gold exchange standard had been suggested by A.M. Lindsay but was considered inappropriate by the Fowler Committee. The authorities neither adopted the gold exchange standard as a consistent whole nor were they fully clear on the expected outcome from its adoption. Nonetheless, by 1900 it had become clear that India was effectively on such a standard managed by the government with the following features (Y.S. Pandit, 1937, p.139):

1. The rupee, a silver token coin, was unlimited legal tender and was not convertible by law.
2. The British sovereign was unlimited legal tender at Rs. 15 = £1 or Re. 1 = 1s.4d. = 16d. The government was bound to give Rs. 15 in exchange for £1. India did not have a mint to coin gold and no Indian gold coin in circulation.
3. Paper currency was also legal tender in India.

4. Although not bound by law, the government was willing to give sovereigns in exchange for rupees. But this was left to the discretion of the government. In 1899, the government was willing to give sovereigns for the rupee but the practice was sometimes suspended when large quantities of gold were not easily obtainable.

5. For international exchange, i.e. Indian imports, the government was willing to convert rupees into sovereigns at the rate of 1s.4d.

6. As a matter of administrative practice the government was willing to sell (reverse council) 'bills on London' in return for rupees at a rate of 1s.$3^{29/}{}_{32}$d. As long as the government did this, the rupee would not depreciate below this level for Indian importers would, at worst get 1s.$3^{29/}{}_{32}$d. in exchange for each rupee.

7. To prevent the flow of gold to India, the Secretary of State for India in London had put on standing notification that he would sell in London Council Bills on India at 1s.$4^{1/}{}_{8}$d; the gold-export point for Britain or the gold import point for India.

Points 4 and 5 have been shown in Figure 7.4. The point 'm' is the gold import point into India (or the gold export point in Eng-

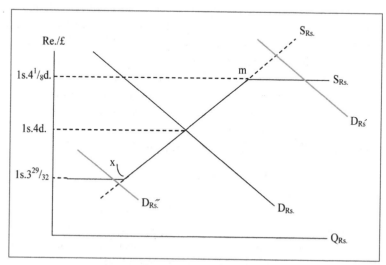

Figure 7.4: Gold Export and Import points in the Market
for Rupees under the Gold Exchange Standard

land). If the demand for rupees were to increase to $D_{Rs.}$' then without the sale of council bills the rate would not exceed 1s.$^1/_8$d. (<1s.4.125d.). Beyond this point it would be better to ship gold out of Britain. Why would anyone pay more sovereigns for a rupee in Britain when they could instead buy a rupee for 1s.4d. in India? The sale of council bills on India was therefore set according to the gold-export (from England) point, m. On the other hand, if the demand for rupees fell to D_{Rs}' then the rupee would have fallen below 1s.3$^{29}/_{32}$d (1s.3.906d.). However, sale of reverse council bills at this rate ensures that Indian importers are able to get at least 1s.3$^{29}/_{32}$d. (> 1s.390625d.) per rupee. If not they could sell rupees to the government in exchange for sovereigns and export the sovereigns directly to England in settlement of their import dues. Point x is therefore the gold export point from India.

If India had a 'perfect' balance of payments (where autonomous inflows were equal to autonomous outflows) vis-à-vis Britain then the rate would be at 1s.4d. If, however, India had a favourable balance of payments (high $D_{Rs.}$) then it would be closer to m, whereas if her balance of payments was unfavourable it would be closer to x. Typically, the exchange rate would fluctuate between the gold export and import points. This can be observed from the actual exchange rates between 1898 and 1914 as presented in Table 7.1.

Given that the balance of payments on the trading account was usually in favour of India, the exchange rate should have been closer to Britain's (India's) gold-export (gold-import) point. However, since India had to remit most of this surplus back as 'home charges' to Britain only a small surplus effectively remained in favour of India and the exchange rate did not usually touch India's gold import point.

Apart from the financing of commodity trade, Council Bills were also used to enable Indian borrowings in Britain. Figure 7.5 shows how lenders could buy council bills in London and send them to borrowers in India who would claim the amount from the Treasury in India. This flow of funds when appended to Figure 6.15 gives a complete picture of monetary transfers between Britain and India under the gold exchange standard.

TABLE 7.1: EXCHANGE RATES FLUCTUATE BETWEEN
GOLD EXPORT AND IMPORT POINTS

Years	Average Rate of Exchange	Years	Average Rate of Exchange
1898–9	1s.3.972d.	1906–7	1s.4.087d.
1899–1900	1s.4.069d.	1907–8	1s.4.031d.
1900–1	1s.3.973d.	1908–9	1s.3.931d.
1901–2	1s.3.988d.	1909–10	1s.4.037d.
1902–3	1s.4.002d.	1910–11	1s.4.060d.
1903–4	1s.4.047d.	1911–12	1s.4.083d.
1904–5	1s.4.045d.	1912–13	1s.4.059d.
1905–6	1s.4.042d.	1913–14	1s.4.069d.

Source: Y.S. Pandit, *India's Balance of Indebtedness, 1898–1913*, George Allen & Unwin, London, 1937, p. 148.

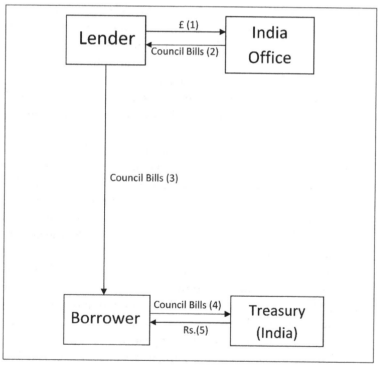

Figure 7.5: Indian Borrowings in London using Council Bills

Indian foreign borrowings were an important component of total sales of council bills. The sale of council bills (in exchange for discharge of the Government of India's liabilities to the Secretary of State on account of home charges) were used to partially offset gold outflows that would have been necessary were it not for this claim on the Indian Government. Table 7.2 shows these actual volumes of each of these components.

The stable exchange rates under the gold exchange standard ensured that Indian commodity exports fed the Western world raw materials for its industrialization; India alone accounted for almost 10 per cent of Britain's trade. However, as mentioned above, the gold exchange standard was not consciously planned solution to the crisis of the rupee; it came to be accepted as a mechanism

TABLE 7.2: COMMODITY BALANCE OF TRADE,
INDIA'S BORROWINGS

Years	Commodity Balance of Trade (Rs.)	Foreign Borrowings (Rs.)	Sale of Council Bills (Rs.)	Sale of Council (£)	Home Charges (£)
1898–9	355.6	40.9	280.8	–	–
1899–1900	270	122.5	284.8	19.07	16.13
1900–1	229.1	130.8	199.8	13.3	16.99
1901–2	348.6	133.7	278.3	18.54	16.88
1902–3	357.5	57.7	277.5	18.5	17.67
1903–4	453.4	17.9	356.8	23.86	17.4
1904–5	385.4	119	365.4	24.42	18.83
1905–6	328.3	249.7	472.2	31.57	17.67
1906–7	276.2	102.9	498.9	33.43	18.33
1907–8	117.6	266.8	229.2	15.31	17.77
1908–9	173.2	142.8	209.6	13.92	18.32
1909–10	422	246.5	410.2	27.42	18.41
1910–11	514.1	72.8	395.5	26.46	18
1911–12	506.7	56.5	403.7	27.06	18.33
1912–13	414.4	53.5	385	25.76	18.99
1913–14	359.6	183.1	466	31.2	19.46

Sources: Y.S. Pandit, *India's Balance of Indebtedness, 1898–1913*, George Allen & Unwin, London, 1937, p. 154; and M.L. Tannan and K.T. Shah, *Indian Currency and Banking Problems*, Ramachandra Govind & Son, Bombay, 1917, p. 93.

In Search of Stability

that effectively replicated international exchanges on the gold standard without India actually using gold as domestic currency. Let me now briefly delve into the circumstances that led to the adoption of this monetary standard.

In April 1898, the Secretary of State for India appointed Sir Henry Fowler to study the question of Indian currency. Overall there seemed to be a consensus that the closing of the mints in 1893 had delinked the rupee from silver and prevented the decline of the former. But there was apprehension over the government's strategy to melt down rupees, which had led to a great shortage of liquidity in the markets. Interest rates had firmed up and loans were difficult to procure even with the best of security. Two proposals were made to the Fowler Committee as suitable variants of a pure gold standard. The first was by Lesley Probyn who proposed a gold bullion standard wherein the authorities would guarantee conversion of rupees into gold bullion; gold currency would neither be minted nor circulated. The other variant suggested by Alexander Martin Lindsay came to be known as the *gold exchange standard*. India became one of the first countries (after Java of the Dutch East Indies) where the gold exchange standard developed, followed by Siam, Philippines and Greece. Both these proposed schemes by conceiving of gold standards without a gold currency were ahead of their time and in fact came to be adopted by many major nations of the world in the second quarter of the twentieth century after the gold specie standard was abandoned. As it was Lindsay's plan that was eventually adopted in India, it is useful to see what he had envisaged for India.

To Lindsay what India needed in foreign trade was for the rupee to have a fixed price in terms of gold. This could be ensured by pegging the rupee to sterling, which in turn was convertible to gold at some fixed rate. Instead of giving sovereigns for rupees and rupees for sovereigns in India, Lindsay proposed that the government should give rupees for sovereigns in London and sovereigns for rupees (only for international trade) in India. The rate of exchange in London would be 16d. + x = Re. 1 where x is the transactions cost (including transport, insurance, etc.) of shipping gold to India and 16d. would be the exchange for Re. 1. On the other hand, the rate of exchange in India would be 16d. − y = Re. 1 where y is the transactions cost of shipping gold out of India. Therefore the market rate would always be between these gold shipping points. In reality no gold would be shipped when the exchange touched these points. Instead the government would buy or sell council bills at the stipulated rate to the full extent of demand. This is precisely what we described in Figure 7.5.

To maintain a fixed rate, Lindsay suggested a fund of £10,000,000 to be kept as gold in London and rupees to a lesser extent in India. The amount would not be available to the government for any of its expenditures. When drafts were sold in London, gold would be received into the fund and rupees paid out from the fund in India. If rupees in India were exhausted, the gold in London would be used to buy silver in the bullion market and sent to India to be minted into rupees. When drafts were sold in India, rupees would be received in India and sovereigns paid out in London. If gold in the fund were exhausted, then either gold would have to be borrowed in the London market or silver shipped from India and used to purchase gold in London. Obviously, there would be a major loss in this case as the market price for silver was below the rupee value of silver coin. Nonetheless, the quantum of funds was considered adequate.

At the same time, given a fixed exchange rate there was then a need for an equilibrating mechanism so that long-term adjustment in the balance of payments was possible. If two countries were on the gold standard then the outflow of/inflow in gold from the deficit/surplus country had to cause a decrease/increase in price level and consequently adjustment in balance of payments. To ensure the operation of an equilibrating mechanism, Lindsay's plan stipulated that the reserve fund be kept entirely distinct from the internal currency system. Any rupees used to buy sovereigns in India (by the public for—say—imports) would add to the rupee fund in India. This would result in a contraction of domestic money supply. Similarly any sovereigns held in the fund in London (say, due to British public buying rupees) must not enter circulation in Britain while any sovereigns paid out should result in a net addition to Britain's money supply. Figure 7.6 schematically describes

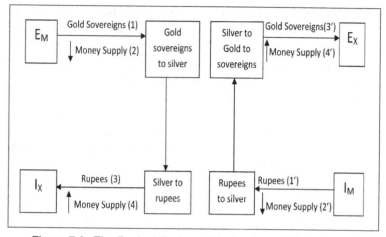

Figure 7.6: The Basic Adjustment Mechanism of Lindsay Plan

the adjustment mechanism under the Lindsay plan. In this way, the effect on price levels would be the same as would have been the case if the two countries were on the gold standard.

But the bankers did not accept the Lindsay plan essentially because it seemed to be highly regulated and managed and was prone to possible manipulation. Instead the Fowler Committee recommended the adoption of a gold standard with gold currency. The sovereign would be made legal tender in India. At the same time, rupee would circulate locally as legal tender. However, the committee did not favour the free convertibility of rupee into gold coins. To maintain the exchange a fund was to be created wherein the seigniorage profits from the minting of silver into rupees (as token coin the rupee's price was greater than the value of silver it contained) would be held in gold. Any depreciation of rupee from its fixed rate of 1s.4d. could then be countered by purchase of rupees (increasing the demand for rupee) using gold held in the fund.

Even as the committee was sitting, the exchange rate touched 1s.4d. in 1898. The recommendations of the Fowler Committee were accepted by the government and implemented. Sovereigns and half sovereigns were made legal tender and government offices were instructed to accept them and facilitate the circulation of gold. Unfortunately, gold did not stay in circulation; it kept coming back to the government treasuries. On the other hand, silver seemed to be the preferred currency in circulation. Between 1893 and 1900 very little coinage of rupees was undertaken. In 1900, however, the Government began minting rupees and the seigniorage profits (value as coin less bullion value) were kept in a special Gold and Silver Reserve Fund (later called Gold Standard Reserve). Between 1900 and 1905 coinage was by and large and steady but never abnormal. In 1905 the government had silver reserves amounting to some £12 million (= Rs. 180 million). From then on the coinage of rupees took place at an accelerated pace. The Government favoured that the fund be kept in India so that when India adopted a gold standard the gold reserves could ensure convertibility of the rupee into gold coin. However, the Secretary of State for India insisted that the reserves be held in London and invested there. If gold was held in India, then at a time when silver (if the rupee was to be coined in silver) was required for the purpose of minting rupees, it would again have to be shipped back to England for purchase of silver in the bullion markets. Furthermore, holding reserves in England strengthened the credit of India to carry out its borrowing operations in Britain. This was the first step in India moving towards a gold-exchange standard.

To avoid the unnecessary movement of gold from Britain to India as well as of rupees from India to Britain for conversion into gold, the Secretary of State for India decided to sell council bills on India in unlimited quantities in London at the gold export point (or gold import point in India) of 1s.4$\frac{1}{8}$d. The surplus of gold collected in London over the payments made on account of 'home charges' then had to be remitted to India. Silver bullion was bought and exported to India where it was minted into rupee coin (Rs. 1.2 billion). The seigniorage profit on the minting (£16 million) was credited into the Gold Standard Reserve. In 1907, the size attained by the fund caused the Secretary of State for India to utilize £1 million from it for capital expenditure in the railways. Moreover, he directed that until the fund reached £20 million, one-half of the increments would be used for capital expenditure. After it reached the stipulated level, the entire increment would be utilized. But, as we will see later, this was putting gold back into circulation in Britain (which should actually have caused monetary contraction in Britain) and against the proper rules of the game.

The gold exchange standard operated smoothly but for a crisis which developed in 1907. That year monsoons in India failed while at the same time the American economy faced a financial crisis. British import demand slumped and the famine which had affected a population of some 13 million meant there wasn't much to export from India. At the same time, Indian imports being highly inelastic continued unabated. The consequences on the rupee-sterling exchange rate were simple; the demand for rupees in London declined, while the demand for sovereigns in India continued at the same levels. The balance of trade had turned in favour of England and with it the value of the rupee began falling from the ceiling rate of 1s.4d. In Figure 7.4 this would mean a movement from D_{Rs}' to D_{Rs}''. But with the Government of India under no obligation to give out sovereigns which could be exported to England let alone giving it at some fixed rate, the rupee was once again heading for free fall. Till now the scheme giving unlimited council bills on India in exchange for sovereigns in London at a fixed rate of 1s.4$^1/_8$d. had worked well; this was when India ran balance of payments surpluses with Britain. However, in 1907, the situation had reversed. The rupee had reached the lower limit beyond which there was a likelihood of it being melted as the silver value of the coin exceeded its rupee value but there was no mechanism to stop its fall.

The exchange banks requested the Government of India to sell them drafts on London at the rate of Rs. 15 = £1 or Re. 1 = 1s.4d. Unlimited supply of bills would render supply of rupees perfectly elastic and prevent decline of the rupee. The government, however, after consultation with the Secretary of State refused. Furthermore, the government decided that gold in excess of £10,000 would not be given to any single individual on any single day. The banks meanwhile pleaded that only up to £1 million were needed to meet India's immediate import obligations and if that amount was forthcoming from the government in the form of bills on London, panic in the market would abate. Finally in November 1907, the

Secretary of State invited tenders in India for £250,000 on him in London at rates not exceeding 1s.3^{27}/$_{32}$d. It was further announced that tenders would be issued from time to time. This eased the situation.

The recession continued through most of 1908 and with it the rupee remained weak. The sale of council bills in London was dismal. The Governor-General in India requested that the Secretary of State in London agree to bills drawn on him in India. These 'reverse councils' drawn at a fixed rate at 1s.3^{29}/$_{32}$d. for the first time in 1908. It ensured that the rupee did not sink below a certain level just as the council bills drawn at 1s.4^1/$_8$d. ensured that the rupee did not appreciate above the par rate of 1s.4d. A total of £8 million reverse council bills were sold until September 1908 but were again discontinued as the sale of council bills picked up. The mechanism of council bills and reverse council bills used during this period is illustrated in Figure 7.7.

By 1909 the crisis had fully abated and the situation was returning to normal with the India's balance of trade turning positive. However, the total drain in gold reserves with just a single year of famine in 1907 had amounted to some £25 million. If the

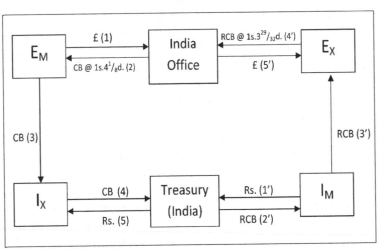

Figure 7.7: The Working Mechanism of Council Bills (CB)
and Reverse Council Bills (RCB)

famine had been severe and had gone into a second year, it would have been impossible to maintain the rupee close to its par rate. The gold exchange standard would have inevitably collapsed. It was, therefore, felt that the reserve fund be increased with a greater part of it to be kept in gold reserves rather than illiquid securities as the price of the latter would in most likelihood crash in times of crisis. With general condition of prosperity returning, the gold reserves continued to accumulate reaching some £22 million at the eve of the war, as more and more rupees were minted.

At the eve of the War, India's currency system was as follows: the rupee was unlimited legal tender and so were sovereigns at 1s.4d. Currency notes to the extent of some Rs. 700 million circulated with reserves of about 15 per cent in silver rupees, 55 per cent in gold in India and England and the balance in securities of up to £140 million. The Secretary of State sold council bills without limit at less than or equal to 1s.4^1/$_8$d. In return the Government of India gave 15 rupees in exchange for a sovereign. This prevented the exchange from rising above 1s.4d. However, there was no statutory obligation to keep the rate from falling below 1s.4d. In normal years this was unnecessary because of the balance of payments were in favour of India and the demand for rupees remained buoyant. However, there was always a possibility for a situation like that of 1907 to turn the table upside down. Although the sale of reverse council bills saved the day, there was neither a real obligation for the government to undertake this nor would it have been possible to sustain this measure had gold reserves diminished further.

The adoption of a full-fledged gold standard for India as had then been recommended by the Fowler Committee Report ended instead with something closer to Lindsay's plan of a gold exchange standard, which in fact had been dismissed off as unsuitable by the same report. It was only in 1913, when the gold exchange standard itself would enter into a phase of crisis, that it was finally approved as such by the Chamberlain Commission. It was also decided that it would not be in India's interest to use gold in internal circulation. Once again a debate which had arisen in the 1860s on the suitability of a gold currency for India was reopened; many considered gold to be superior in terms of its portability and convenience than silver, that a paper currency backed by gold was the ideal currency system while silver was a sign of low price levels and underdevelopment. There were, however, those like Keynes who argued that the demand for gold sovereigns were not for circulation but for hoarding. For the man on the street, given the prevailing price levels and consumption baskets, silver rupees were the most suitable currency. Keynes was supported by the fact that during the period 1898–1913 silver rupees were minted to the tune of £63 million while gold sovereigns in circulation amounted to just about £11 million.

Under a pure gold standard India would have to enforce convertibility of the rupee into gold for which it would have needed a huge store of gold as England. No doubt the people of India did possess gold but the question was whether gold would be forthcoming during times of crisis. At the same time, keeping a large stock of gold to meet a demand that could perhaps arise once in ten years could also be considered an unjustifiable waste. The idea then was to economize on the use of gold for international indebtedness. The economy in the use of gold by countries on the gold exchange standard would mean that the price of gold internationally is below what it would have been if *all* countries were on the gold standard. The latter would have resulted in higher gold prices, bringing in the fear of general deflation. The counter-argument was nonetheless equally valid; under the gold exchange standard, given that a country would require foreign exchange of a gold standard country it was not clear how it is easier to acquire such a currency like sterling as opposed to gold. Moreover, since full convertibility by gold standard countries must be ensured, it was again not clear how the total quantum of gold required under a gold exchange standard is less than a pure gold standard. Another alternative suggested for the late movers on to a pure gold standard (Austrian-Hungary and Russia) was to hold large reserves in foreign bills which could be discounted and exchanged for gold.

Although the rupee was a token coin passing above its intrinsic value, the gold exchange standard did safeguard the rupee from losing value. This was taken care of by the fact that the government could not increase its supply arbitrarily; the supply of rupees could increase only to the extent India's net trade surpluses (including borrowings) exceeded payments against home charges. The gold inflow into India would be exchanged for rupees. In other words, the supply of money expanded (or contracted) in response to the balance on foreign trade. But this brings us back to two critical questions regarding the supply of currency—its elasticity and its adequacy.

Does this mechanism necessarily provide the required *elasticity of supply* in response to seasonal variations in India's *domestic* commerce and trade? Typically the currency in circulation would expand during the season when exports took place. But this need not have corresponded to the necessities of the internal economy. Exchange rates indicate the requirements of foreign trade but it is the rate of discount (interest rates) in money markets that are a better indicator of the requirements of internal trade. For instance, there could be pressure on exchange rates to appreciate while there may not be a similar situation in the money markets and for domestic interest rates to rise. The supply of credit based on pledge of domestic bills of exchange was considered a possible response to shortages in the money market; but India did not have well developed money markets and banking sector for the widespread and reliable use of these instruments.

Apart from elasticity, concerns were also raised on the *adequacy of money supply*—the automatic expansion and contraction of money supply to the requirements of domestic growth. The straightforward measure of adequacy is obviously the domestic price level or (equivalently) the purchasing power of money, an overexpansion or contraction in money supply leading to inflation or deflation respectively. How did India fare when we consider domestic price level as an indicator of the adequacy of currency in circulation? The increase in general price levels between 1898 and 1913 rules out the possibility of an inadequacy in currency and existence of a deflationary situation in India. The price level was fairly steady between 1873 and 1888. Then between 1888 and 1912 the price index shot up from 111 to 182. But there could have been another problem here; consider a situation where internal trade is depressed but on account of large external borrowings, there is net inflow of gold which is converted into rupees. We, therefore, had a situation where exchange was firm while internal trade was depressed and currency in domestic circulation redundant. There was a possibility for internal price levels to rise that could further depress exports in order to bring about an adjustment in the balance of payments. What India faced here was a situation of domestic stagflation on account of high external borrowings; the question of critical importance for the longer term economic prospects of the country would be whether or not the borrowings were used for productive or unproductive purposes.

A key concern raised in the implementation of the gold exchange standard was whether or not 'rules of the game' for balance of payments adjustment were being enforced; instances like that of reserves being re-spent on British capital goods for the Indian railways meant that what should have been taken out from circulation in Britain was in fact coming back into circulation. If so, how could price levels in Britain fall so as to correct its balance of payments disequilibrium? And if they did not how would long-term balance of payments between Britain and India be achieved? The equilibrating mechanism of the gold standard also meant that when council bills were issued in London, there would be a contraction in money supply (in Britain) so that discount rates increased, general price level fell and exports rose. But did this happen? Perhaps not; seasonal spikes in payments made to India meant that a serious disturbance in London money markets was a definite possibility. There was only one solution to protect London money markets; Sir David Barbour assured the Fowler Committee that gold would not leave England. But this was in fact against the spirit of the equilibrating mechanism that was necessary to restore balance of payments equilibrium (see Box 7.1).

Meanwhile, there was also concern over the 'rules of the game' playing out in India. If the money entered circulation on account of a surplus in the balance of payments, it should have raised price levels and reduced Indian exports. But would that be the case? What if Indians simply hoarded the rupees so that there would be no increase in Indian spending and price levels remained unaffected?

Box 7.1: Against the Rules of the Gold Exchange Standard Game

Q.4332. Now you say that under the system proposed by the Government of India, if gold circulated in India, there would be heavy withdrawals, every busy season, of gold from London?—I should have said that there is a risk of heavy withdrawals during any time of active export trade.

Q.4333. Do you think that gold would go back or remain in India?—I think that gold to a great extent would remain in India.

Q.4334. Would not there be the same or similar demand for gold in London under your scheme in a busy export season? People would pay in gold at 1s.$4^1/_{16}$d.in order to get rupees?—The difference would be this, that gold would not be drawn from London for currency purposes in India. The gold would be transferred from certain accounts in the Bank of England to the Gold Standard Account office, and in the autumn here, that is in the slack season in India, a re-transfer would take place; *but the gold would not leave the Bank of England for currency purposes in India.*

Q.4236. You would propose then, that the gold paid into the Gold Standard Reserve should not be set aside specially to meet claims against it, but should be merged in the general balance of the bank which it might use for any purpose—Yes that would be the best way. *There would be then no disturbance of the London money-market.*

Source: *Minutes of Evidence Taken Before the Committee Appointed to Inquire into the Indian Currency*, Indian Currency Committee, Eyre and Spottiswoode, London, 1898, p. 40.

While the objective of maintaining value the rupee may have been acceptable, these arguments against the 'rules of the game' playing out meant that the gold reserve standard may not have worked if a chronic balance of payments disequilibrium situation had developed in either India or England. Herein lay the problem with the pre-War Indian currency system; not only was it managed but more importantly the rules of the game were not allowed to play out. Neither was there any deflationary effect from Britain's deficit balance of payments nor was there a serious inflationary impact from India's surplus in the balance of payments. Even under a pure gold standard adjustment for balance of payments equilibrium was supposed to be automatic; in reality this was a myth. In times of adverse balance of payments, rather than let money supply contract and price levels fall to bring about adjustment, governments resorted to manipulation in discount rates to attract inflow of gold and restore equilibrium. Similarly by using reserves, the deflationary impact from an adverse trade balance may have been avoided but longer-term equilibrium in the balance of payments would not be achieved. Nonetheless adequate reserves of gold were considered to be the only solution in mitigating a crisis under the gold standard and even the gold exchange standard.

The crisis of 1907–8 had exemplified this need. A similar situation on a larger scale could have a catastrophic effect on the Indian currency. Questions were raised on the adequacy of reserves and on where they should to be held. India maintained two reserves— the Gold Standard Reserve and the Paper Currency Reserve. The Gold Standard Reserve began as the Gold Reserve Fund in 1901. The amount accumulated as reserves came from the profit on the coinage of rupees or the difference between the gold price of the rupee (fixed at 1s.4d.) and the gold price of silver. If India's surplus was 1s.4d., a rupee would have to be given in exchange. However, to coin this rupee may have cost the government just (say) 1s.1d. (depending on the price of silver). The profit on this conversion (assuming no other transactions costs) would have been 3d. In 1901, the accumulated profits or Gold Standard Reserve amounted to some £3,000,000. These reserves were shipped from time to time to England and invested in sterling securities (although not in tune with the 'rules of the game'). As the demand for rupees increased, so did its coinage and subsequently reserves in the Gold Reserve Fund. In 1906, the fund had an amount of £12.5 million. The heavy demand for coinage of rupees led the government to create a silver branch of the Gold Reserve Fund. These rupee reserves allowed for quick injection of rupees into the system as and when the need arose. In 1907, the fund had £4 million in Indian rupees (Rs. 60 million) apart from the £12.5 million gold reserves. For a short time it was called Gold and Silver Reserve Fund but was finally labeled the Gold Standard Reserve in 1907.

I will discuss the Paper Currency Reserve in the next section; here it suffices to mention that it was accumulated to provide backing for the paper currency in circulation. Although it could be used to stabilize the exchange, it was the Gold Standard Reserve that was considered to be the first line of defense to maintain the exchange.

The crisis of 1907–8 depleted total reserves from £31 million to just £11 million. In addition to these £20 million used from the reserves, another £4.5 million had to be borrowed in England. A single season of depression had weakened the position of the Secretary of State by a sum of £25 million. Obviously, a chronic crisis would have led to unsustainable levels of borrowing. A crisis like that of 1907 exposed the inadequacies of the gold-exchange standard in India. Although the crisis abated and the reserves once again reached healthy levels, questions remained on the sustainability of the gold exchange standard and the challenges for India to move on to a pure gold standard.

The Royal Commission on Indian Finance and Currency (Chamberlain Commission) was therefore appointed in 1913 to re-evaluate India's currency system. The contention that the gold exchange standard was the most appropriate for India did not seem to be well founded. At the heart of the debate was the purpose and utilization of the Gold Standard Reserve. This reserve had been created from the profits of seigniorage in the minting of rupees from silver. The question was whether its purpose was to steady exchange rates or to ensure convertibility of the rupee into gold on demand. The latter was necessary for India's transition to gold standard under which the management of exchange rates would no longer be required. The convertibility of rupees into gold on demand would ensure stability of the exchange without the need for state intervention. Moreover, in spite of annual home charges that had to remitted by India every year to Britain, India almost always emerged as a net creditor nation given a favourable balance of trade. Usually the concern in adopting a gold standard was that gold could get dispersed in internal markets and would not be available to meet international settlements in gold; but this applied to debtor countries which had to ensure payments. This argument did not hold good for India. Given her balance of trade it was unlikely that the demand for export of gold would not be met by the annual inflows. At times of crisis, if and when this trend was reversed, international payments could be made from the Paper Currency Reserve, i.e. reserves held against issue of a gold-backed paper currency. A chronic deficit (or surplus) in the balance of payments would be taken care of through the rules of the game working out. For instance, if Paper Currency Reserves were to fall due to an exchange of gold for notes, there would be an automatic contraction in paper currency circulating, fall in prices and increased competitiveness of exports.

There were other serious reasons too for questioning the merits of the gold exchange standard. Council bills or drafts were sold in London at 1s.4$^{1}/_{8}$d. in London so as to prevent the rupee from appreciating and reverse councils were sold in India at 1s.3$^{29}/_{32}$d. to prevent the rupee from depreciating. But this mechanism had also effectively transferred India's surpluses on its balance of payments into gold in London and prevented gold from flowing to India. Prior to 1904 the sale of council bills were limited to the quantum of home charges but after the unlimited sale of councils in London began, all natural flow of gold into India was prevented. There was another disadvantage of selling unlimited council bills in London. At a time of crisis as in 1907, the lack of gold in India in fact triggered a panic in the market; the Government of India did not have enough stocks in hand to allow the free export of gold. India's gold reserves were held in Britain and it was only with a great degree of reluctance that the Secretary of State for India ultimately conceded to the drawing of 'reverse councils' on London that allowed gold to be taken from reserves held in Britain, thereby alleviating the crisis in India. If that had not been done it was possible that the rupee could have fallen all the way down right up to the intrinsic value of the coin, i.e. in accordance to its bullion content. Theoretically a fall below this point is not possible since rupees would have been melted into bullion; if this were indeed to happen, then India would have been left without a currency in circulation. Once again the Paper Currency Reserve held in India in gold would have been a more appropriate option. All over the world, international payments were settled through bills of exchange markets and/or the movement of bullion. India too could have resorted to these means rather than holding its gold reserves in England.

It was also contended that under the gold exchange standard, India's gold reserves in Britain were being misused. By 1914–15 more than £30 million were held by the Secretary of State in London. Why then had India continued borrowing in London money markets at 3½ per cent when its cash balances held with the Secretary of State were lent at just about only per cent with little security?In fact, the joint-stock brokers dealing in these securities were reported to have declared dividends of 20 per cent. Was this at India's cost? Meanwhile, the average interest rates in India were 5 per cent going up to 9 per cent during the busy season. Could not have these reserves been put to better use in India? Another criticism of the gold exchange standard was the persistent obstruction by the India Office—influenced by London bankers and bullion brokers —that prevented minting of gold coins in India. In particular it was Lord John Morley, Secretary of State for India who decided, based on inputs received from the London bankers, that India should not be allowed to import and hold any more gold than was absolutely necessary. This later developed into a concerted effort from almost all quarters of the world to see that India did not receive gold against goods exported by her. At that time, the Secretary of State was considered to be one of the biggest money lenders in the London money market, the hub of the financial world. Lending India's gold in London ensured lower market interest rates and cheaper credit—a critical input for economic growth. Of course, the counter-argument was India's propensity to hoard precious metals. But this may have been exaggerated. After all it must not be forgotten that the rest of the world too 'consumed' large amounts of gold for the arts and for reserves. Finally, the Government of India had to face credible charges of corruption in the making of secret and heavy purchases of silver for coinage. Between 1905 and 1907 the Government of India minted coins to the tune of some £42 million, one of the heaviest coinages in world history (until then). Allegations were leveled against government officials and M/s. Samuel Montagu & Co., merchant bankers and bullion dealers,

---

Box 7.2: The Silver Scam

SAMUEL, MONTAGU & CO.
Questions in Parliament
Transactions in Silver
London, July 23

In the House of Commons yesterday the Prime Minister (Mr. Asquith) promised Mr. Bonar Law that he would enquire as to whether or not the banking firm of Samuel, Montagu & Co. silver brokers for the India Office took advantage of the confidential information to make profits for themselves.

Sir Stuart Samuel, M.P. is a partner in this firm. It will be remembered that a few months ago he was forced to vacate his seat for Whitechapel owing to the firm's transactions on behalf of the India Office, but he was subsequently re-elected.

Source: *The Advertiser*, Adelaide, 24 July 1913, p. 10.

---

for manipulating prices at which silver was purchased for coining. But more importantly for the economy, this unnecessary coinage also caused a significant rise in the price level and with it, political and social ferment.

The Indian gold exchange standard was a 'managed system' while most other countries had a system wherein supply was responsive to the demand for money, automatically. It was the 'open mint' without state intervention of any kind where the flow between coin and bullion into and out of the country was 'free' or unrestricted although at some charge. The response of money supply to demand took place on the basis of price signals, namely discount rates in the money market. For instance, a surge in demand for currency would cause interest rates to increase and immediately induce the inflow of gold to the mint (from bullion). The coined gold would then flow into the money market. In India these powers were not in the control of markets but a supreme financial autocrat—the Secretary of State for India who transacted the financial business of the India Office—buying silver for coinage, loaning out cash balances held in reserves, selling council bills, raising sterling loans, as well as managing the Gold Standard and Paper Currency Reserves. And in executing each of these functions it is not surprising to find vested interests for private gain developing and exploited.

Before we end this analysis of the gold exchange standard we make a brief assessment of it from the point of view of whether or not it met the functions of 'good' money. The stability of the gold price of the rupee does not imply that all the other functions of 'good' money were automatically satisfied by a managed rupee under the gold exchange standard. First, the medium of exchange was not merely for the purpose international settlements but also for internal trade and industry. And here it is critical for a good currency system to be responsive to the needs of trade and industry. In this case, the gold exchange standard was a managed system that was driven by the objective of maintaining the gold price of the rupee. Everything else was supposed to follow. The government being in the position of a monopolist was prone to the possibility of an over-issue of coins; after all there was a potential for profits from the difference between the gold price of the rupee and the gold price of silver. As we have seen, this over-issue of coins may have actually happened; rupees were not convertible to gold so that excess rupees (which may have come into circulation on account of large borrowings in Britain) could not be drained off the system. Price inflation, even stagflation, could have been the consequence of this inflexibility. With regard to its function as a store of value, the fall in the rupee's purchasing power (rise in price level) did make it seem like a failure.

There were other criticisms levied on the gold (or sterling) exchange standard; it was not easy to comprehend for the common man. Rupees were converted to sterling at the fixed rate only for the purpose of external remittances and that too only during times of crisis like in 1907. Here too the government was not obliged to do so; it was to prevent a major crisis that it reluctantly agreed to sell reverse council bills drawn on the Secretary of State for India at the fixed rate. The crisis of 1907 also exposed another lacuna in the gold/sterling exchange standard. When the gold price of silver rose or the exchange fell below the gold price of silver, rupee coins would either be melted or exported. This could mean a complete disruption of the monetary system of the country. The automatic expansion and contraction of currency to bring balance of payments into equilibrium (rules of the game) is an important feature of a sound monetary system. In this regard too, the gold exchange standard failed. The government did not always ensure that the issue of council bills and reverse council bills in India affect money supply in England and India respectively. The effects of these bills were sometimes neutralized by the government through sale of securities or otherwise. The utilization of both the Paper Currency Reserves and Gold Standard Reserves were also fuzzy. While the Paper Currency Reserve was to provide backing for currency, it was very often used for the purpose of exchange rate stabilization.

These drawbacks of the gold exchange standard made it a far from ideal system that can be summarized as, at best, 'a fair weather friend'. The positive external environment that ensued in the first decade and a half of the twentieth century allowed the gold exchange standard to survive in India. The crisis of 1907 was only precursor to the dangers of the system.

7.3: PAPER CURRENCY UNDER THE GOLD EXCHANGE STANDARD

This change will pass unnoticed, except by the intelligent few, and it is satisfactory to find that by this almost imperceptible process the Indian currency will be placed on a footing which Ricardo and other great authorities have advocated as the best of all currency systems, viz. one in which the currency media used in the internal circulation are confined to notes and cheap token coins, which are made to act precisely as if they were bits of gold by being made convertible into gold for foreign payment purposes.

A.M. LINDSAY

The most critical issue facing India's monetary system at the beginning of the twentieth century was the inelasticity of supply to meet the fluctuating demands of the domestic economy. The inability of the system to drain excess money not only resulted in inflationary pressures building up at times but the dearth of currency, especially during the most active seasons, inhibited growth of trade and industry. The sluggish circulation of paper currency as well as an underdeveloped banking sector in India transferred the burden on metallic currency to provide necessary liquidity in the economy. Meanwhile, under colonial rule, the supply of currency was targeted at maintaining the value of the rupee to sterling at the stipulated fixed rate of 1s.4d. Moreover, as a fixed exchange rate regime, the gold exchange standard required the support of large reserves in times of crisis to prevent depreciation of the rupee. India therefore ended up maintaining large reserves; unfortunately, Britain took advantage of its colonial status and held a substantial portion of these reserves in London, supporting its own money market rather than utilizing the reserves to provide adequate backing for wider acceptability of paper currency. In this section, I will briefly present the state of paper currency circulation until the advent of the First World War.

Let me begin with a brief recap of India's paper currency system; although some sporadic efforts were made even in the eighteenth century, India's history of paper currency began in 1839 with the Presidency Banks issuing promissory notes payable on demand. These notes were, however, not recognised as legal tender and therefore had a limited circulation, typically being accepted only in the towns where the banks operated. The quantum of reserves held against their note issues being just 25 per cent of demand liabilities, the system did not help the Presidency Banks in instilling confidence amongst people. The trend continued till the end of the East India Company's rule in India; the British Government under the Crown had to start when public confidence was at a low, post-mutiny. It was James Wilson, India's first finance minister (or Member) who took charge of expanding the circulation of paper currency in India. Wilson's proposed that the government issue notes as a public monopoly rather than leave it to private banks which did not have the kind of unquestioned reputation necessary for this purpose. Moreover, the profits accruing from note issue would accrue to the State and could then be used for the general good of society. While Wilson and the Secretary of State agreed on this point, they did not on another key issue—the quantum of reserves that should be held as backing for note issue. The Secretary of State, following the British Bank Act of 1844, was ultra-conservative in his approach stipulating 100 per cent backing of currency by bullion reserves with only a maximum of Rs. 40 million to be issued against Government of India securities. These reserves were held in order to prevent an over-issue of notes and, at the same time, ensured full convertibility of the notes in circulation. Wilson saw no benefit in this approach and felt that issuance of notes was unnecessarily being tied so stringently to bullion reserves but before he could push through his scheme, he died. The stand of the Secretary of State prevailed.

Although the Paper Currency Act was passed in 1861 making notes legal tender, there were several factors which dampened the adoption and extensive use of paper currency in India including the circle system and lack of small denomination notes. While making notes payable outside the circles would have imposed large transportation costs on the government, this scheme prevented the use of notes across circles. Beginning in 1900, the government took many steps that attempted to 'universalize' notes, especially smaller denomination notes. By 1912, notes of Rs. 5, Rs. 10, Rs. 50 and Rs. 100 had been universalized. But there remained another problem and more difficult to surmount; the Indian preference for metallic coin as a store of value. In fact it was this preference that necessitated the use of silver token coins instead of a paper rupee. After all, the rupee as 'a note printed on silver' was an extravagant practice which could have instead been printed on paper, thereby saving the exchequer of major expense. But the government had rightly realized that while this may have worked elsewhere in the world it simply would not have in India. People were willing to accept a rupee only because it had an intrinsic value (its silver content). Even a low denomination one rupee note on paper would not have been accepted by the general public, especially those outside the main urban centres. Their argument was straight and simple: coin could be immediately turned into bangles. What about a note? 'So many notes could only serve to light up his *hukah*' (Tannan and Shah, 1917, p. 137).

The slow growth in the active circulation of paper currency right through the nineteenth century can be seen from Table 7.3 While its quantum showed some improvement towards the end of the century, it is important to see this against the growth of trade in India. Foreign sea-borne trade alone had increased from Rs. 1.23 billion in 1875–6 to more than Rs. 4.8 billion in 1913–14 (ibid., p. 121). When we consider the growth in domestic trade and industry as well, paper currency in circulation was woefully inadequate in meeting the needs of the Indian economy. Although universalization of notes was considered an important step in liberating the usage of notes from the circle system, the fear of 'note runs' (like bank runs) due to the low levels of confidence in convertibility of paper ultimately led to an impasse. In the end it all boiled down to a question of Paper Currency Reserves. No doubt 100 per cent backing of paper by metallic reserves would have alleviated the lack of confidence but this would have only saved some costs (like wear and tear of coin) but not addressed the problem of inelasticity of supply to fluctuating seasonal demand. The decision over reserves thus became a critical one.

Before we look at the issues surrounding Paper Currency Reserves, we briefly illustrate how reserves were impacted by the sale

TABLE 7.3: NOTES IN ACTIVE CIRCULATION
(MILLIONS OF Rs.), 1892–1913

Years	Rs.	Year	Rs.
1865	74.3	1904–5	281.1
1875	112.4	1906–7	339.3
1885	145.8	1908–9	331
1892–3	195.3	1909–10	372.1
1893–4	178.5	1910–11	387.5
1899–1900	212.7	1911–12	418.9
1900–1	220.5	1912–13	453.9
1902–3	234.9	1913–14	466.3

Sources: DSAL, *Digital South Asia Library (nd), Statistical Abstracts Relating to British India from 1840 to 1865, First Number,* http://dsal.uchicago.edu/ and M.L. Tannan and K.T. Shah, *Indian Currency and Banking Problems,* Ramachandra Govind & Son, Bombay, 1917, p. 120.

of council and reverse council bills in London and India respectively. In Figure 7.8(a) the sale of council bills were credited partly into each of the following: the balances held by the Secretary of State, the Paper Currency Reserve and the Gold Standard Reserve. The amount was paid out by the government partly from its balances, the Paper Currency Reserve and/or the Gold Standard Reserve. The opposite took place on the sale of Reverse Councils by the Government of India as seen in Figure 7.8(b).

There were two critical issues that had to be sorted with respect to reserves: first, the location of reserves. It was argued that reserves were held in London as gold and in securities to provide liquidity

Figure 7.8: Impact of Council and Reverse Council Bills on Reserves

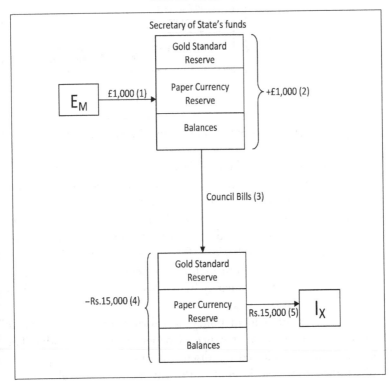

Figure 7.8(a): Impact of Sale of Council Bills on Reserves

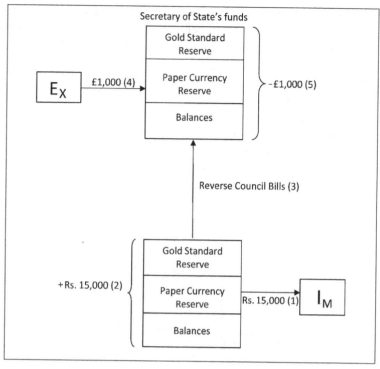

Figure 7.8(b): Impact of Sale of Reverse Council Bills on Reserves

to the money markets there. This was in spite of the tight conditions in the Indian money markets and better yields that could accrue to the government if reserves were held and invested in Indian securities. Second, reserves held against the Paper Currency Reserves were being utilized to stabilize the exchange rate instead of providing necessary backing for a paper currency. The inflow and outflow of funds from each component of reserves was arbitrary and used indiscriminately by the Secretary of State as well as the Government of India.

By 1905, a 'permanent policy' was formulated on the metallic reserves to be held for issuance of paper currency in India. The government was allowed the discretion to decide on the quantum of reserves to be held in gold and/or silver, where it would be held (in England and/or India) and also whether it would be held as bullion and/or coin. Rupee coins, however, had to be held in India only. The cap on notes based on securities too was slowly relaxed from Rs. 40 million in 1861 to Rs. 60 million in 1881, then gradually in small increments over the next few decades. By 1911, the Paper Currency Reserves held in securities stood at Rs. 140 million. Out of this, Rs. 400 could be invested in English securities. The total reserves held against paper currency issued stood at approximately Rs.700 million by 1913. The breakup of these reserves is given in Table 7.4.

The strategy to build up reserves was critical in increasing the issuance of notes; however, there was a vicious circle problem here because the issue of paper currency was necessary for the rapid and substantial accumulation of funds. When paper currency was issued against gold, the entire nominal value of the note was credited to reserves (assuming the gold value of paper and printing to be zero). With silver coin the reserves accumulated only partially, i.e. to the extent of the gold value of the rupee less the gold value of silver.

To accelerate the use of paper currency and at the same time increase its elasticity so as to make it more responsive to the demand for money, it was suggested to correlate the function of note-issue to that of banking. Banks usually discount bills. When they do so they acquire an asset against which they issue notes. Central banks would usually increase their note issue at certain seasons of the year in order to discount more bills thereby injecting the neces-

TABLE 7.4: METALLIC RESERVES HELD AGAINST ISSUE OF
PAPER CURRENCY AS ON 3 MARCH 1913

(*in millions of rupees*)

Form	Amount
Silver in India	164.5
Gold in India	293.7
Gold in London	91.5
Securities	140
Total	689.7

Source: M.L. Tannan. M.L. and K.T. Shah, *Indian Currency and Banking Problems*, Ramachandra Govind & Son, Bombay, 1917, p. 119.

sary liquidity into the economy during the most active seasons of the year. For India the only available alternative was to increase money supply through foreign inward remittances. This, however, was possible only when a sufficient spread in domestic and foreign interest rates existed. But then high domestic interest rates were not conducive to domestic growth of trade and industry. Keynes therefore suggested that India should follow the Europan example rather than that of Britain. India was simply not ready for a cheque system, which was Britain's response to meeting its liquidity requirements. Instead, India could hold a fixed proportion of gold or silver coins as reserves and further amount in government securities including bills of exchange of the highest class. This could have provided the required elasticity in the supply of money.

In 1913 a commission was appointed under the chairmanship of Mr. Joseph Austin Chamberlain to enquire into the methods of maintaining exchange rates and the location where reserves should be maintained. The commission recommended that the Gold Exchange Standard was the most suitable for India and funds held in the Gold Standard Reserve account had to ensure the maintenance of exchange rates. As Keynes had suggested, the commission recommended that the Paper Currency system be made more responsive to demand fluctuations by allowing a greater proportion of the Paper Currency Reserves to be held as Government Securities. However before the suggestions could be considered for implementation, the First World War broke out. While these issues remained to be sorted out, a whole new set of problems surfaced.

7.4: BANKING IN INDIA UNDER THE GOLD EXCHANGE STANDARD

There are famous dates in the history of Indian banking which should serve as 'memento mori'.

JOHN MAYNARD KEYNES

Earlier in the book we traced the genesis of credit money and banking in India. We now update the development of this important economic and monetary institution in India through the final decades of the nineteenth century until 1913. Broadly speaking, the banking sector comprised four important constituents, the first two termed as the European money market and the latter two, the Indian or native money market: (i) Presidency Banks (ii) Exchange Banks (iii) Indian Joint Stock Banks and (iv) indigenous bankers like Shroffs, Marwaris and moneylenders. Although banking had taken firm root in the country, its development was retarded and unlike in the West it was unable to provide the necessary elasticity in supply of liquidity as required by industry and trade. The major challenges facing India's banking sector will be presented in this section.

The Presidency Banks (which included the Bank of Bengal, the Bank of Bombay and the Bank of Madras) had the right of note issue till 1862. In 1876, government representation in the banks also ceased; however, they remained distinct from the native joint stock banks as they came under the Presidency Bank Act of 1876. Even under the East India Company, these banks always came under strict government regulations although it must be remembered that they were private enterprises run by private individuals. As far as domestic lending went the banks were not permitted to give long-term loans of more than six months or upon the security of immovable properties even as the country was in dire need of industrial capital. In spite of these restrictions, the Presidency Banks showed healthy growth in deposits; in 1870 total deposits (public and private) stood at approximately £4.2 million and increased to £24 million by 1912. Although capital and reserves seemed adequate, Keynes expressed some concern over the public deposits held at the branches since these were literally on call. Other banks, which held balances with the Presidency Banks (private deposits), treated these as part of their cash holdings. A sudden spurt in withdrawals could therefore have put some strain on the Presidency Banks. Another important restriction imposed on these banks was their exclusion from all foreign exchange dealings. Foreign exchange transactions during the period of silver depreciation had become highly speculative and concerns over Presidency Banks being involved was justifiable given that they held the government's money. However, under the Gold Exchange Standard with the exchange rate being fixed, the fear of foreign exchange transactions may have been unwarranted.

It must be noted that unlike the Bank of England, the Presidency Banks did not effectively control the money market in India. The Bank of England could not only preserve the central gold stock of Britain simply by adjusting its bank rate but any change in its rate would almost at once force up or down all other rates in the London money market.

The second group of banks serving the European money markets were the Exchange Banks. Although these banks dealt mainly with businesses involved in foreign exchange transactions, they were of critical importance to the Indian economy. This was because they were the effective financiers of Indian trade or, in other words, suppliers of credit to businesses for import-export transactions. We have seen in Figure 6.15 the basic mechanism utilized by the Exchange Banks in transferring money from England to India with the help of council bills. The sequence presented in the illustration was simplified to highlight the use of council bills; we now present in Figure 7.9 the schematic structure of how Exchange Banks organized transactions that made them financiers or suppliers of credit to the Indian market. The Indian exporter (I_X) would receive bills of exchange against shipment of goods to importers in England (E_M). In the normal course, these bills would be payable (say) 30 days after the receipt of goods in England. Effectively, therefore, I_X would receive payment for the goods exported after several months since their production or procurement in India. Without finance or credit, this business may have well have been unviable. Suppose an Exchange Bank stepped in and purchased (discounts) the bills from I_X at a discount, sent it to England where the money was collected from E_M or rediscounted in the market. I_X is now able to turn the goods into money at a faster rate, something critical for a trader. The question arises as to how Exchange Banks would raise money in India to purchase bills from I_X. Exchange Banks typically had their headquarters in London where they received funds through deposits and current accounts. The money may have been available in London but it had to be transferred to India, perhaps at short notice depending on the volume

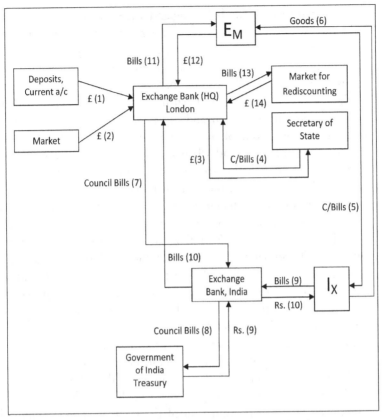

Figure 7.9: The Credit System in India under the
Exchange Banks

of bills obtained for discounting from I_X. Here the council bills
system provided the necessary mechanism. Using their funds, the
Exchange Banks would buy council bills drawn on the Government of India Treasury in London and transmit them to their Indian
branch by telegraphic transfer. They could then be encashed at
the treasury in India, the funds becoming available within a short
period of time for purchase of bills from I_X. Meanwhile, the bills
purchased from I_X are sent to the Exchange Bank in London for
collection or rediscounting making funds available for further purchase of council bills, if required. The terms at which exchange

banks obtained their funds in England were also a crucial component in this credit chain. If the funding came from their own depositors or current account holders, it was relatively cheap. It also
gave them greater flexibility in waiting for the right moment (best
terms) to rediscount bills in London. On the other hand, borrowing
in the London markets could push the Exchange Bank into a tight
corner when rates were stiff and/or pressurized the Bank to rediscount bills at unfavourable rates. This was the most dangerous link
in the credit chain—if and when Exchange Banks were 'called on
to return what they had borrowed in England, and unable at short
notice to bring back what they lent in India' (Keynes, 1913, p. 213).

The deposits of Exchange Banks showed a healthy growth in
India during the period of the Gold Exchange Standard. While
deposits increased from £5 million to more than £16 million between 1890 and 1910, cash balances increased from about £2.3
million to just £2.9 million during the same period. In percentage
terms, therefore, the cash deposit ratio registered a sharp decline
from 46 per cent to 18 per cent. The rapid strides made in raising
deposits by the Exchange Banks was a positive development in
India; nonetheless there were concerns of their low reserves and
whether, at a time of crisis, they would be able to bring in sufficient funds from overseas at a short notice. Although the Exchange
Bank provided services to hedge exchange risks, their business flourished even after the introduction of the Gold Exchange Standard
(that ensured fixed exchange rates), in a risk-free environment. They
were, however, weary of intruders and resisted moves for Presidency Banks (and even a Central Bank) to enter their domain.

Apart from the three Presidency Banks (which were urban based
and their dealings were substantially with the government) and
the Exchange Banks (which focused on foreign transactions) there
were the Indian joint stock banks; banks registered in India with a
paid-up capital of at least £33,000 (Rs. 500,000). Their business
focused on meeting the banking needs of the internal trade of
India since neither the Presidency Banks nor the Exchange Banks
were geared up for this purpose. From the year 1904, the number
of joint stock banks showed a 'great outburst of fresh activity'
(Keynes, 1913, p. 222), the roots of this impetus being the Swa-

deshi Movement. However, the enthusiasm for setting up joint stock banks was followed by a number of bankruptcies and closures, more than 60 in all, within a decade. The rush towards acquiring deposits from public entailed offers of high rates that forced the banks to look for the most lucrative opportunities to lend. This usually meant that lending went into more speculative enterprises. Once again the cash deposit ratio of these banks showed a decline from just 20 per cent to an abysmal 10 per cent between 1890 and 1910. A crisis was staring at the face and it happened in 1913. Nonetheless, there was no denying that the turn of the century was also the turning point in Indian banking history. Table 7.5 below shows the significant growth of deposits in India the thirty years between 1887 and 1917.

The last group of banks in India was the unincorporated banks and indigenous moneylenders. Though they played a key role in the economy, there were several dangers that could have arisen when they started acting as banks, i.e. taking deposits from the public and lending them out. Earlier, the moneylenders and money-changers usually did not accept deposits from the public but this was becoming a lucrative business. The possibility to earn interest on deposits was slowly luring Indians away from hoarding, especially in urban centers, and instead accumulating their savings in a bank. By 1910 there were close to 500 such institutions with large nominal capital and a small paid-up part. But the principles of

TABLE 7.5: GROWTH OF DEPOSITS

(in million of rupees)

Year	Presidency Banks	Exchange Banks	Joint Stock Banks	Total
1887	110	40	10	160
1890	180	70	20	270
1897	120	90	60	270
1907	310	190	140	640
1917	750	530	220	1640

Source: R. Rau, *Present-Day Banking in India,* University of Calcutta, Calcutta, 1922, p. 112.

modern banking were more often than not going unheeded by the unincorporated banks.

Meanwhile, people's deposit in other institutions too showed positive growth. By 1913, the Indian post office deposits had collected almost £15 million from more than £1.5 million people. The credit needs of farmers were also crucial in an economy and Cooperative Credit Societies were seen as the appropriate mechanism to deliver it across India's innumerable villages. The working capital of these institution grew from a paltry Rs. 100,000 in 1905 to more than Rs. 100 million in 1915. As mentioned above, these were healthy trends as it showed a definite move away from hoarding and channeling money into productive activity. A cause of concern however remained; adequacy of reserve to stem a crisis.

What was interesting is that during this period there was a growing recognition of the critical importance of banking and a money market (where borrowers and lenders of money can meet) in the industrial and economic development of India. Here the need to break the hoarding habit was one side of the challenge in order to raise deposits. The other side of the challenge lay in developing sound lending practices by banks whereby the money of depositors is channelized into sound investment. A clear articulation of the circular flow of goods and money (see Figure 7.10) in an

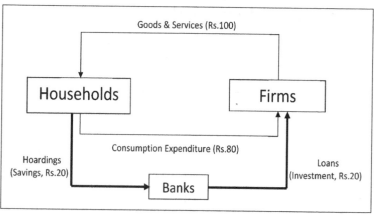

Figure 7.10: The Circular Flow and the Role of Banks
to Channelize Savings into Investments

economy was emerging in India wherein the banking sector was required to put savings (leakages) back into circulation in the form of productive investments (injections).[1] Finally, the need for regulation and disclosure of assets and liabilities of the banks to the fullest extent possible was deemed necessary, without compromise, if Indian banking had to inspire confidence in the masses. There was also a complete skew in the duration of credit available; only short-term loans were possible from banks with a dearth of long-term financing instruments in the market.

Some interesting points that were highlighted close to a century ago included the need for diversification in clientele of the bank, the sectors in which they operate, the nature of collateral securities and their liquidity, the lack of experience in banking business and the close connection or nexus between banks and businesses to whom money was lent, the need for greater specialization in credit instruments, professional lending practices between banks, lending money by lending money against the collateral of their own shares, independent and expert auditors, the danger of excessive competition amongst banks that drives up interest rates on deposits, paying out of dividends from new deposits (Ponzi schemes), capital adequacy norms and the need for greater State supervision and regulation.

India did not have a central bank, an institution to play the role of a 'guide, friend and philosopher' to the banking sector and the government (Rau, p. 4); many felt that the time had arrived for one. Its functions would be to administer note issue, manage the government's cash balances and regulate the foreign exchanges of the country. There was also the need to ensure an elastic supply of money that could respond at short notice to the seasonal demands of trade and industry. The possibility of note discounting to banking and a bank rate policy were two important instruments that could have been utilized by a central bank in managing the elasticity of supply of money and credit in the economy. Unfortunately, the other banks (especially the Presidency Banks and Exchange Banks), and to a degree even the government, were afraid that a Central Bank would intrude into their space so that these proposals were kept at bay.

NOTE

1. Introductory macroeconomic textbooks usually begin with the circular flow model. For sake of completeness we have briefly explained the circular flow model in Appendix 2 of this book.

CHAPTER 8

The First World War

Whatever has overstepped its due bounds is always in a state of instability.

SENECA

Since the 1870s silver had been steadily declining, ultimately forcing the Indian Government to close the mints to the free coinage of silver. Once the rupee touched 1s.4d. it seemed to be safely above the price of silver; however, in 1907 it fell sharply and almost breached the silver value of the coin. There was the danger of coins going to the melting pot. After much hesitation, sale of reverse council bills came to rescue and the danger passed. Thereafter it seemed as if the Gold Exchange Standard had just about settled when a catastrophic disruption descended on the world in 1914: the Great War. The Indian monetary system had again to undergo a major test when silver began to appreciate steeply even as gold prices remained flat. Once again the danger of the rupee being melted down and disappearing from circulation arose. This time the search for stability in the rupee-sterling exchange rate proved even more challenging.

8.1: THE RISING PRICE OF SILVER AND CRISIS IN THE INDIAN CURRENCY SYSTEM

All change is not growth, as all movement is not forward.

ELLEN GLASGOW

In currency as in other matters, we are still in a storm-tossed ocean, and we know not as yet what terra firma we shall eventually reach and when.

SIR W. MEYERS

By the end of the nineteenth century, except for China, most countries had moved away from a silver standard and on to a gold standard or some variant of it. The United States and France did have silver currencies as legal tender but with no new coins being minted, their relative importance in the currency system of these countries was on the wane. Silver, however, did serve as token subsidiary coinage in many countries even as bimetallism had been renounced as a viable option to a monometallic gold standard. India was on a gold exchange standard and although rupees were printed on silver, fluctuations in its (silver's) price did not really matter except when (i) the gold price of the rupee fell below the gold price of silver or, which to an extent can be considered equivalent at least in so far as its implications go (ii) the gold price of silver rising above the stipulated gold price of the rupee. In other words, when the coin as silver was worth more than a coin as rupee, there was a danger of coins going out of circulation and into the melting pot with severe consequences for the Indian economy; an economy that was suddenly left without a medium of exchange. Given that only the maximum limit (of 1s.4d.) was stipulated by the government, this situation could arise when either silver prices rose or when rupee exchange fell.

India had experienced a type (i) situation in 1906–7 when the rupee depreciated below the gold price of silver and faced a threat of being melted into bullion. It came out of the crisis without a major upheaval although at one point of time it did seem that the situation would get out of hand. It was the issuance of reverse council bills (at Re. 1 = 1s.$3^{29}/_{32}$d.) which came to the rescue in meeting the demands of Indian importers. Over the next few years the exchange rate of rupee remained stable until the advent of the First World War. During the war years, the rupee underwent a type (ii) crisis when the gold price of silver began to rise sharply, crossing the upper limit of gold price of the rupee (1s.4d.), the point at which supply of rupee became perfectly elastic. Once this rate was breached, a coin commanded more value as silver than as a rupee. The threat of coins being taken out of circulation and put into the melting pot became immediately imminent. As mentioned at the very beginning of this book the difficulty of monetary instruments to fulfill the three functions of money simultaneously, effectively and efficiently, across space and time has been the root cause of many financial crises. In this chapter we will see the challenge posed in maintaining a stable value of the rupee internally (in terms of the domestic price level) and externally (the exchange rate); this time on account of rising silver prices during the war years.

The war began in August 1914 and the price of silver initially witnessed a fall just like the fall in prices of most other commodities that were not for direct use by the military. International trade was disrupted and a state of depression cast an ominous cloud over the entire world economy. India too suffered from this decline in confidence and the immediate reaction of people was predictable; they rushed to convert their notes into silver or gold. Within just four days of the war being declared in England, some £2 million of notes were cashed for gold in India. The government soon put a stop to this and agreed to cash notes only for rupee coins. The progress of the war initially affected Indian exports adversely. As the demand for Indian goods slumped so did the demand for council bills on India drawn in England. Under a fixed exchange rate regime, the lack of demand for rupees meant a lack of supply of sterling. To add to the problem, with Indian imports being rather inelastic, the usual needs of Indian importers for sterling had to be met. To prevent a crisis developing (like in 1907) from an excess demand for sterling and a sharp fall in the rupee-sterling rate, the government ensured the sale of reverse council bills, amounting to more than £9 million between August 1914 and January 1915. This eased the pressure on any adverse market sentiment building up and soon things were back on track as the depressionary phase abated. But this was just the beginning of an even bigger challenge: the war boom.

As the war intensified, Indian exports of commodities like cotton, wheat, hides and oilseeds to meet the requirements of defense forces grew sharply. With this the demand for council bills too began to show a healthy growth from 1915 onwards. Imports stabilized and India's balance of trade was once again in surplus. The exchange rate of the rupee reached its upper bound and the threat of any major conversion of coin into bullion on account of the fall in the value of the Indian currency abated. But this stability in exchange rates (on account of fixed exchange rate regime) did not mean that there was external sector macroeconomic equilibrium. A chronic balance of payments surplus was building up which required adjustment. The first signs of this were reflected in the quantum of reserves held in the Paper Currency Reserve account. As rupees had to be coined on silver in India against council bills drawn on India in England, the levels of reserves plummeted to just about Rs. 170 million (from double that in the pre-war years). Only 17 per cent of total notes issued and outstanding remained backed by silver rupees. The government had to make record purchases of silver to coin rupees. At the same time, the demand for rupee coins from growing commodity exports and for payment to troops fighting in Persia and other parts of Africa was outpacing the supply of silver.

Between late 1915 and 1920 silver prices began to shoot up consistently in fits and bursts that took it to levels never seen before. All this happened while gold prices remained almost constant so that the gold price of silver increased unequivocally. Table 8.1 shows the fluctuating but overall rise in silver prices and the flat gold prices during this period.

Several other factors contributed to the rise in silver prices; first, as resources were diverted into serving the needs of the military as

TABLE 8.1: SILVER AND GOLD PRICES, 1910–20

Year	Silver (cents/oz.)	gold ($/oz.)
1910	55	18.92
1911	52	18.92
1912	62	18.93
1913	56	18.92
1914	51	18.99
1915	48.7	18.99
1916	65	18.99
1917	80	18.99
1918	100	18.99
1919	130	19.95
1920	70	20.68

Sources: D.H. Leavens, *Silver Money*, Principia Press, Bloomington, 1939, p. 11 and World Gold Council www.gold.org

the war progressed, widespread shortages in supply led to a rise in the general price level, which just like all other commodities, also impacted silver. Second, the significant reduction in production and supply of silver due to a civil war in Mexico and the restrictions imposed on exports of the metal from that country also exerted upward pressure on silver prices. Even as the civil war receded in Mexico, production could not be restored at a quick enough pace so that shortages in supply continued. Third, increased demand for subsidiary coinage all across the world led to a surge in the demand for silver. The war had triggered off massive industrial activity that generated several working class jobs. Since these were people who spent cash rather than used banking services, the need for low denomination (silver) coins increased. Fourth, the inflationary pressures permeating through most of the economies of the world forced people to hold higher average cash balances. This once again increased the demand for subsidiary money and consequently for silver. Fifth, the war had also caused a spurt in the demand for Chinese goods. Given that China was still on a silver standard, this further fueled the demand for silver. It is pertinent to mention that the Chinese demand actually rose sharply only after 1919 but thereafter contributed significantly to the upward trend in silver prices. Finally, the passing of the Pittman Act in the United States (discussed later) that allowed for the sale of silver to Britain and also recoinage of silver dollars strengthened the demand for silver.

Returning to the situation in India, unlike the cotton boom of the 1860s, this time around the increasing gap in the balance of payments could not be bridged through the direct import of precious metals. The only alternative to pay for India's exports was through council bills. But this entailed a payout of silver rupees in India for which bullion had to be purchased in the bullion market. Availability of silver being sparse on account of the various factors stated above, although the rate was maintained for telegraphic transfers to 1s.4¼d., the onus fell on adjustments in the quantity of council bills sold in London. Rationing therefore became inevitable and quotas were fixed from time to time according to availability of silver rupees in stock in India; this quantity varied between Rs. 3

million and Rs. 12 million per week. Further constraints on the quantity of rupees demanded were imposed by restricting foreign exchange dealings to only a few Exchange Banks that were put on an approved list. Restrictions on the goods for which council bills could be used were also imposed; typically priority was accorded to commodities required for the war. In spite of these restrictions imposed on demand, beginning in 1916, the Government of India had to buy large amounts of silver in the bullion market (see Table 8.2) to meet the rupee claims in India.

The escalating gold price of silver in the bullion market ultimately crossed the gold price of the rupee (exchange rate), fixed at 1s.4d. By August 1917, as Coyajee (1930) put it, it was evident that 'the rupee had cut its moorings with the old rate which had been maintained for twenty years'. (p. 189). Let us illustrate the predicament of the rupee graphically. From Figure 8.1 (based on Figure 6.13), the increasing demand for silver (from D_{S1} to D_{S2}) pushed its price up and above the rate of 1s.4d. But at this point the demand for and supply of silver rupees would collapse to zero (or be melted and supplied to the bullion market) since coins would be worth more as bullion than as rupees.[1] With the price of silver exceeding 1s.4d., the Indian monetary system was in a precariously critical condition as more than Rs. 5 billion could have gone out of circulation, the consequences of which can only be imagined.

TABLE 8.2: SILVER PURCHASES FOR RUPEE
COINAGE, 1915–20

(millions of standard oz.)

Years	Silver purchased in open market	Silver purchased from USA
1915–16	8.6	x
1916–17	124.5	x
1917–18	70.9	x
1918–19	106.4	152.5
1919–20	14.1	60.9

Source: B.R. Ambedkar, *History of Indian Currency and Banking*, Thacker & Co., Bombay, 1947, p. 204.

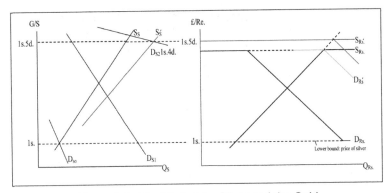

Figure 8.1: The Market for Silver and the Gold
Exchange Standard

The government did all in its capacity to stem the rise in price of silver. Apart from the rationing measures on issue of council bills, strict restrictions on the use of silver for non-currency purposes were also imposed. No ornaments could be made and no silver could be exported or imported without a government license. This was to effectively move the demand for silver (D_S) inwards to lower market price. Increasing the supply of silver (from S_S to S_S') by curbing smuggling of silver was attempted but was not successful in the Indian case like it was elsewhere (like the Philippines). Following Mexico's 1906 example of moving on to a gold currency was also out of question as there was simply no gold available in the world for such a major change. There remained only one option then; raising the rupee-gold exchange rate to the gold price of silver, *pari passu*. In Figure 8.1 this would in effect shift the supply curve up to S_{RS}'. Table 8.3 shows the rates set for telegraphic transfers vide council bills and the corresponding bullion price of silver, 0.925 fine.

Meanwhile, to meet the growing needs of currency, the government issued notes throwing caution to wind insofar as reserves were concerned. Note issue increased multifold between 1910 and 1920 as can be seen in Table 8.4. But the stress on reserves was manifest. When by March 1918 it reached an abysmal 10.8 per cent of notes issued, the fear of a post office deposit run and even a note-run became a real possibility. This would have most dangerous reper-

TABLE 8.3: RATES SET FOR THE TELEGRAPHIC TRANSFER ON INDIA BY THE SECRETARY OF STATE FOR INDIA

Date on which Rate Went into Effect	Rate from T.T. per rupee	Corresponding bullion parity per oz. 0.925 fine
3 January 17	1s.4¼d.	43.8d.
28 August 17	1s.5d.	45.7d.
12 April 18	1s.6d.	48.4d.
13 May 19	1s.8d.	53.8d.
12 August 19	1s.10d.	59.2d.
15 September 19	2s.	64.6d.
22 November 19	2s.2d.	70.0d.
12 December 19	2s.4d.	75.3d.
5 February 20	2s.815/16d.	88.6d.
12 February 20	2s.1027/32d.	93.8d.

Source: D.H. Leavens, Silver Money, Principia Press, Bloomington, 1939, p. 169.

TABLE 8.4: GROSS CIRCULATION OF CURRENCY NOTES, 1911–22

Year	Gross Circulation of Currency Notes, 31 March each Year, Crores of Rupees
1910	54.4
1911	55
1912	61.4
1913	69
1914	66.1
1915	61.6
1916	67.7
1917	86.4
1918	99.8
1919	153.5
1920	174.5
1921	166.2
1922 (Jan. 15)	172.9

Source: Stanley H. Jevons, *The Future of Exchange and the Indian Currency*, Oxford University Press, London, 1922, p. 42.

cussions on not just the economy but also politically in India and, as some contemporary experts argued, even on the war itself. Notes would almost immediately lose value that would be reflected in an increase in all other prices. War supplies from India would be affected by this disruption. It would have also become impossible to float domestic war loans to raise resources for procurement of supplies. There were also fears that bankruptcy of the government would give a great impetus to the nationalist movement in India. Revolts and disorder would then spread amongst Indian troops serving at various fronts and 'would have necessitated bringing out to India, British troops who could be ill spared' (Leavens, p. 171). In fact, had the government been forced to resort to inconvertibility of the rupee, it may have cost Britain the winning of the war. Once again, the colonial government was acting in its own interests, in particular, its war economy, rather than that of India *per se*.

Ultimately the British Government negotiated supplies of silver from the United States that led to the passing of the Pittman Act in 1918. Under the act some 5,670 tons of silver were melted down from dollars and sold to Britain. The arrival of a shipload of silver in the nick of time provided some short-term respite to the government by preventing a note run. Meanwhile the Government of India resorted to several delaying, but which many considered as acceptable tactics to slow down the rate of conversion of notes into silver. These included limiting the availability of staff at its various treasuries and putting caps on the volumes of conversion on any single day. The whole idea was to ensure that there was no panic in India that could lead to a uncontrollable note run.

With the price of silver rising above 1s.4d., the rupee had ceased to be a token coin; India had moved back to being on a quasi-silver standard as the rate between the rupee and silver was made to move in tandem. The problem, however, was that the rupee-sterling rate had to be revalued by mandate to a higher level and not automatically based on supply and demand. But then an even more important question had to be answered and one that became widely debated in India during the last decades of the nineteenth century— should the rise in price of silver be transmitted to the rupee exchange rate? In other words, should not the price of the rupee reflect movements in the domestic price level and trade balances rather than the price of silver? After all, the point of closing the mints in 1893 to the free coinage of silver was essentially to delink silver from the rupee. How then could the government justify raising the exchange rate (forcing the rupee to appreciate) just because silver prices rose in bullion markets? Was this not equivalent (though converse) to the situation which developed in the 1870s when the rupee depreciated just because silver depreciated? To some economists the situation was indeed different; the rise in silver prices *reflected* the surplus of India's balance of trade while in the 1870s silver prices were crashing *in spite of* India's balance of payments surpluses. A rise in silver prices and consequently the exchange rate would enable balance of payments adjustment.

If, on the other hand, revaluation was avoided and the exchange rate was maintained, rupees would have to be coined to meet the increasing demand. The increase in domestic money supply would then cause the domestic price level to rise. This was becoming evident even with the revalued rupee and would only have been much worse had exchange rates been fixed; alongside the increase in coins, notes as well as bank deposits (money supply) between 1914 and 1920, had witnessed inflation in India, food prices having risen by some 93 per cent. Suicides by people facing starvation was reported and food riots erupted in parts of the country (Table 8.5).

TABLE 8.5: INDEX OF TOTAL CIRCULATION OF COINS, NOTES AND DEPOSITS AND PRICE LEVEL (1912–20)

Year	Total Circulation	Price
1912	100	100
1913	102	104
1914	99	107
1915	105	111
1916	119	134
1917	145	143
1918	165	164
1919	195	201
1920	187	205

Source: Stanley H. Jevons, *Money, Banking and Exchange in India*, Government Central Press, Simla, 1922, p. 45.

TABLE 8.6: RUPEES COINED BETWEEN 1912–21

Year	Rupees Coined
1912	124,189,206
1913	163,265,951
1914	48,370,150
1915	15,272,118
1916	212,900,210
1917	264,782,876
1918	413,650,628
1919	427,606,284
1920	108,936,640
1921	11,515,179

Source: Stanley H. Jevons, *Money, Banking and Exchange in India*, Government Central Press, Simla, 1922, p. 37.

Table 8.6 shows the massive amount of silver coinage that took place during the war years. In Figure 8.1 this could be shown by taking D_S to be a function of D_{Rs} so that increase in the latter would push up the price of silver in the bullion market.

Although the exchange rate of the rupee was ultimately increased, the growing demand for rupees continued unabated and consequently raised the price of silver. This in turn necessitated a higher rupee exchange rate to be fixed. A vicious cycle had developed. The post-War boom aggravated the situation to such an extent that one way to control India's balance of payments surpluses was to levy duties on exports. This, it was argued, could have curbed the demand for rupees and its consequent monetization in India.

In 1919, it was under these unfavourable conditions that the Babington Smith Committee made its recommendations for an overhaul of the Indian currency system. The central problem as explained was the growing demand for rupees that was leading to an insistent demand for silver. Three options were considered by the committee before it finally zeroed in on raising the exchange rate of the rupee *pari passu* with the rise in the gold price of silver. First, inconvertibility of notes; eminent experts like Barbour, however, warned that such a step would immediately put coined rupees at a premium, which would then, through the working of Gresham's

Law, drive out coined rupees from circulation. Any possibility of a return to convertibility would become very difficult as new silver may be needed (if it did not return from hoarded stock) so that silver prices could then witness a further rise at that time. The second option was to debase the rupee by lowering the silver content of coins. Once again, Gresham's Law would begin to operate, with only new (overvalued) coins circulating. The old undervalued full-weighted coins would be forced out of circulation. These coins would return to circulation only after being re-minted with the revised silver content. There could also have been a net increase in the demand for silver if the old coins did not return to circulation, implying a possible rise in silver prices in the bullion market. More-over, the process of re-minting all the old coins would take years during which time the country would face a severe monetary crunch resulting in a state of utter commercial confusion. Another danger of debasing coins was inflation. This was already developing into a major issue at that time in India.

The only remaining option for the government was to raise the exchange rate of the rupee. Several benefits would accrue from such a policy. It would effectively curb the demand for rupees with-out its withdrawal from circulation. A further benefit of the up-ward revaluation of the rupee exchange rate was its effect on the domestic price level, which would be lowered on account of cheap-ening imports. Social discontent would therefore be alleviated to some extent. Moreover, given the inelastic demand for Indian ex-ports during the war, the exchange rate hike was not expected to dampen overall export revenues. To the contrary, a higher exchange with an inelastic demand for exports would actually raise export revenues. Indian industry would welcome this measure as it would lower import costs and increase export revenues. At the higher exchange rate, remittance of home charges in terms of gold would entail a smaller amount of rupees. Once a decision was taken to go ahead with this option two questions became pertinent; the choice of the revised ratio and whether the rupee should be pegged to gold or the sterling. Even as this decision was being taken there was a growing concern that once the war boom came to an end, deflation would follow. Prices of silver too would fall. A downward revision of the rate would then become inevitable. The other major challenge was Britain's decision to suspend the convertibility of sterling into gold on account of its burgeoning expenses to fund its war efforts. This led to an inevitable outcome—depreciation in the gold price of sterling. In India, the question therefore arose as to whether the exchange rate of the rupee should be fixed to gold or sterling or in other words, should India choose to be on a gold exchange standard or alternatively on a currency (sterling) exchange standard. The advantage of fixing the rupee to sterling was that since a major share of India's trade was with Britain and other sterling countries, this would make exchange rates more predictable. On the other hand, linking the rupee to sterling would mean that the former would have to share the sterling's fluctuating fortunes. Moreover, at that time, there were conflicting movements in the gold price of the rupee and that of sterling; while the sterling was depreciating the rupee had to appreciate so that India's balance of payments could be brought into equilibrium. It was therefore finally decided to link the rupee to gold and not sterling.

As far as the rate was concerned, the Committee proposed that a rupee exchange rate be fixed at 2s. *gold,* which at that time was equal to 2s.6d. *sterling.* This was equivalent to Rs. 10:1 sovereign or Re.1:11.30016 grains (= 0.732 grams) of fine gold. The other points included in the committee's report were the free and unlimited sale of council and reverse council bills, unconstrained movement of precious metals, minting of sovereigns in India so that gold could be introduced as an auxiliary currency (the option of converting rupees into gold on demand being with the government), encouraging the circulation of gold currency by not converting sovereigns into rupees, discouraging hoarding, and keeping the Gold Standard Reserve in liquid form. The committee also proposed to make the supply of money more responsive (elastic) to demand by allowing note issue up to Rs. 50 million against commercial bills endorsed by the Presidency Banks. As an added precaution it was proposed that these commercial bills be restricted to those issued against goods for export only. Internal bills were not to be considered for note issue as these could have been drawn for purposes of raising money (finance) or speculation. However, the case against inland bills was not accepted and in the Act of 1920, these bills became the basis for providing additional currency when required.

Perhaps the main criticism of the committee's report was the arbitrary manner in which exchange rate was to be raised. Though some experts suggested a step-by-step incremental approach to setting the exchange in order to achieve the objective of domestic price stability and balance of payments equilibrium, this was still like shooting in the dark. After all adjustments do not take place immediately and the lags make it difficult to establish cause and effect. The committee was also criticized for over emphasizing the need for *stable* exchange rates. This, as we know, was seen as playing a critical role in fostering international trade and commerce. In the absence of well-developed foreign exchange markets and hedging instruments this may well have been so; however, economists like L. Abraham were already seeing the advantages of a more flexible exchange rate mechanism. With the post-war boom likely to be followed by a bust and depression, he expected that it was only a matter of time that the price of silver fell and India's position would be reversed, making it necessary to devaluate the rupee. In the meanwhile, if there were increases in the price of silver there was no need to cap the exchange rate and the rupee could still be revalued to a higher rate. The best policy would be through announcements that 'the rupee was likely to be steady at a certain rate and that it was the policy of the Government to keep it steady'. (Coyajee, 211). There, however, remained a problem in the government setting exchange rates in this manner. If they did, expectations would soon develop on the next move by the government, invariably leading to speculation. Suppose the government announced that reverse council were to be sold at 2s., then a few days later at 1s.11d., then 1s.10d. Obviously people would only expect, if the external situation exhibited a similar trend, that it would soon be 1s.9d. Wouldn't it then be wise to buy sterling today and sell it back tomorrow when it appreciates? An artificial demand for sterling would soon arise that would in fact make it appreciate; a self-fulfilling prophecy. While no exchange rate could be considered permanent, setting exchange rates according to a well-defined rule could also have adverse effects.

Other suggestions were made to tackle the balance of payments surplus without recourse to changes in exchange rates. Sir D. Dalal in the Minority Report suggested that instead of adjusting the surplus in balance of payments through receipts of silver that were converted into Indian rupees, the excess should have instead been drained through an outflow of capital, or in other words, invested in securities outside India. Another suggestion made by him was that India should have allowed the free export of silver during the war rather than banning it. This would have prevented the price of silver from rising by increasing supply of silver in the bullion market. Put together, Dalal reiterated that with these measures the exchange rate could have been maintained at 1s.4d. instead of raising it to 2s. (gold).

Let me once again revert to the same issue that I raised in the very beginning of this book—the difficulty of finding stable monetary instruments. Clearly the rupee faced this predicament during the war years. The choice between stability in the exchange rates at the cost of high domestic inflation was clearly apparent. At the same time the war necessitated Indian exports of commodities (and did not want the exchange rates to appreciate too much) but then the colonial state had also to ensure that the Indian economy was not derailed (by inflation), which in turn could lead to social strife and widespread anti-British sentiment, perhaps even endangering the outcome of the war. A problem of maintaining stability in the foreign exchange rate and domestic price level simultaneously was crystallizing in India. This dilemma has been illustrated in Figure 8.2.

Even as this dilemma continued, the recommendations of the Babington-Smith Committee were accepted and in February 1920 the rupee was to be pegged at 2s. gold. But just a few months after this action had been taken, silver prices began moving violently again; this time it was in the opposite direction. By June 1920 the balance of trade began to move against India.

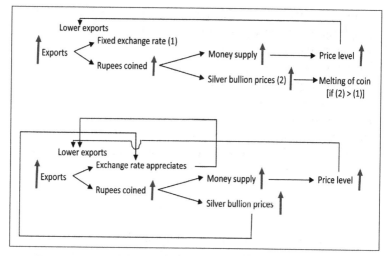

Figure 8.2: Effects on Foreign Exchange Rates and Domestic
Price Level under Fixed Exchange Rates and
Appreciating Exchange Rates

8.2: A FOOTNOTE ON THE INTERNATIONAL
MONETARY SYSTEM DURING THE GREAT WAR

So far as the economic historian is concerned, the First World War is a
thankless episode; for one of the central themes of this period is the destruction of an international economy often nostalgically referred to as 'the
good old days'.

GERD HARDACH

This section, or what may be more aptly called footnote, briefly
describes the situation that was evolving across the world during
the war years (Hardach, 1977). Like in India, the first reaction to
the war in many countries was for its nationals to convert notes
into gold and by foreign investors to repatriate their assets overseas. Obviously, governments reacted by simply imposing a ban
on convertibility of either into gold. While most governments did
this blatantly, others like Britain and the US continued with *de
jure* convertibility but made it *de facto* inconvertible. Governments
also did their very best to lay their hands on all possible available

gold either by according themselves sole purchasing rights of gold or by mobilizing people to surrender their hoards of gold or through confiscations. But all these measures did not mean that gold was actually used to fund their import surpluses; the latter were by and large funded through bilateral credit arrangements. It is no wonder then that Britain had a large imbalance in its trade account while it was still able to show a net accumulation of gold reserves.

Both internally and externally, national currencies were delinked from gold. Conversion of notes to gold was suspended and gold was not remitted to export surplus countries. In fact, the latter resisted the inflow of gold on account of its possible impact on their domestic inflation rates. As we saw, India too was in this predicament. In the neutral money markets of the world, a market for free exchange rates emerged. Even currencies of the belligerent countries were traded, albeit at large discounts, in the foreign exchange markets.

For Britain its biggest problem was maintaining the sterling's exchange rate vis-à-vis the US dollar. With Britain's large deficits with the US, a total of more than $350 million in gold had to be transferred by Britain to the USA in 1915. This was something that both parties were not comfortable with; Britain being keen to maintain its gold reserves while the US was weary of excessively large inflows of gold that could trigger off domestic inflation. Only when the US officially entered the War was the US treasury able to make the necessary dollar credits.

NOTE

1. Also observe that the gold price of the rupee cannot fall below the gold price of silver (as once again coins would be melted); this is shown by the demand curve for rupees becoming perfectly elastic at a rate of (say) 1s.

CHAPTER 9

The Interwar Period

The Indian currency system has been the most unpopular aspect of British rule and administration in India.

N.R. SARKAR

Thus the unthinking assumption, in favour of the restoration of a fixed exchange as the one thing to aim at, requires more examination than it sometimes receives.

JOHN MAYNARD KEYNES

The post-War period saw a slump in the world economy. India turned from a net exporter to a net importer. The price of silver also began to fall precipitously. The rupee exchange rate fixed initially at 2s. gold was reduced to 2s. sterling. But even this could not be sustained with growing current account deficits. It was ultimately allowed to float. This buffered India to an extent at least from the deflationary trend which gripped the world economy in the post war years. But when Britain returned to the gold standard in 1925, it put India back on to a fixed exchange rate regime. The Hilton Young Committee suggested that India adopt a gold exchange standard. But this did not happen; instead India returned to a sterling exchange standard with the rupee pegged at 1s.6d. Many considered that at this rate, the rupee was overvalued. It exports were dwindling even as imports were increasing. The balance of payments deficit could only be covered through export of gold that was actuated on account of the intense depressionary conditions prevailing in the agricultural sector. Meanwhile, in the banking sector there was a realization of India's need for greater channelization of savings to productive investment and also for a central bank. The Presidency Banks were merged into one entity, the Imperial Bank, which was seen as an important step for the expansion of banking in India. However, the Imperial Bank was essentially a commercial enterprise and its objectives could not be reconciled to those of a central bank; it was in 1935 that India's central bank, the Reserve Bank of India, commenced operations.

In spite of these institutional advancements, the message that comes through our study of the monetary system during this period is the priority accorded by the colonial government to exchange rate stability rather than the needs of the domestic economy that was reeling under deflation and depression. The argument advanced by supporters of the government policy was India's dependence on foreign trade, the external obligations of the government and the need for foreign capital for investment in India. Unless exchange rates were stable India would not be able to source these critical inputs for economic development at reasonable terms. The Reserve Bank of India was also mandated to maintain the exchange rate at 1s.6d. and had therefore to subsume the needs of internal currency and credit to their external obligations.

But before we delve into the predicament of the rupee in this period, I begin with a short note to describe the environment in which the Indian economy functioned, which in a word was dismal.

9.1: A NOTE ON THE INTERNATIONAL MONETARY SYSTEM DURING THE INTERWAR YEARS

War can really cause no economic boom, at least not directly, since an increase in wealth never comes from destruction of goods.

LUDWIG VON MISES

Although we will exploite the history of the rupee and the Indian monetary system during the interwar years, it can be fully appreciated only in the context of the upheavals taking place in the world at that time; from the war boom to a slowdown and finally the Great Depression of 1929. These events not only influenced the rupee but also the course of economics. Till the depression monetary economics by and large focused on two objectives—internal as reflected in the purchasing power of money (inflation and the domestic price level) and external stability as reflected in the exchange rates and equilibrium in the balance of payments. The depression raised the need for introducing a third policy objective—unemployment. It is not within the scope of this book to digress into a study of macroeconomics and the debates around it. Here we will limit ourselves to presenting a few facts that had a close bearing on the issues surrounding the rupee in the interwar years. Once again, this brief section is more in the nature of an introductory note than an in-depth study.

With the rise in war expenses, most European countries had to abandon the gold standard. Even the United States had *de facto* abrogated the conversion of currency into gold during the war but was able to return to a gold standard by 1919 as its inflation was relatively low during the war. By 1920 the US had re-instilled a sense of confidence in the revival of the world economy. A boom ensued in the US and the rest of the world was able to ride on it, at least for a while. At the Genoa Conference in 1922 the call for a return to the gold standard was seen as critical in restoring international trade and bringing capital flows back on track. However, some serious concerns had to be addressed: the return to pre-War parities would be difficult given the high rates of inflation in war torn nations, the danger for a rush to accumulate gold and the resulting shortage of the metal that could cause a sudden and massive worldwide deflation. In this regard, a gold-exchange standard (based on the Indian experience) where exchange rates would be set in terms of a fixed amount of gold but with no internal circulation of gold coins was seen as being the most appropriate alternative. Soon after Germany's burden under the Treaty of Versailles had been scaled down by the Dawes Plan of 1924. Capital markets too began functioning normally. The world it seemed was finally out of the effects of war, economically speaking.

Britain too was committed to a return to the gold standard which it did in 1925 but the sterling was no longer the foundation of the regime; it was the US dollar which had emerged as the principal gold-backed currency in the post-War era. Moreover, since the purchasing power of sterling had eroded vide the increases in money supply, it could return to the pre-war parity only through a contraction of money supply. But at the time the decision was made, policy makers perhaps did not foresee the need for significant deflation. After all by the mid-1920s, the price levels in the US and Britain were almost at par (158 in Britain and 160 in the US, in 1925)[1] taking the pre-war levels as the base (1913 = 100). On hindsight, however, it did seem that the pound was rather significantly overvalued; but it was not merely the exchange rates that affected Britain's export competitiveness. There was something more chronic about the disease; there were structural changes that had taken place for which exchange rates were no solution. For instance, coal or thermal power was increasingly being replaced by hydro-power, cotton textiles manufacture in Japan, India and Latin America, and so on. Consequently, exports proved inelastic to the devaluation and export revenues fell. But it is important to mention that Britain continued to have current account surpluses at this time. The major concern was instead large capital outflows from Britain, a significant portion for repayment of its war debts that exceeded the surpluses in the current account so that it was left with deficit disequilibrium. The US had become the ultimate creditor country in the world but instead of encouraging the import of goods and services from the rest of the world (which was resisted by political forces within the US which sought protection of domestic industry) it chose to relend the money back to Europe, in particular, Germany. The latter was being battered with increasing foreign debt at high interest rates (up to 9 per cent) and a dangerously high proportion of short-term borrowings.

There was yet another country's policies which was becoming problematic to the international monetary system: France. In 1928, France returned to a gold standard but with a highly undervalued franc, which resulted in both a current account surplus (high exports from devalued franc) and high gold inflows. Now, if the rules of the (gold standard) game had to play out, higher price levels in France should have restored equilibrium, but France did not monetize the gold inflows so that it continued with a surplus disequilibrium even as Britain remained with deficit disequilibrium. Germany's war repatriations also added to France's burgeoning reserves. This was seen as a way of inspiring confidence in the

franc and in France's economic and political strength. But ultimately, with gold being drained from the rest of the world, its
price rose and deflationary forces were unleashed across the world.

By 1928, the seeds of crisis had begun to germinate. The boom
in the US was proving too attractive for capital so that it remained
back there rather than being lent out in international markets.
France too continued to hoard the yellow metal, not letting its
competitiveness to erode with inflation by instead following deflationary policies and at the same time instituting high tariff barriers. Britain's gold reserves were continually being drained even as
France and the US were busy adding new stocks to their already
bloated gold reserves. By 1933, these two countries held more
than 60 per cent of gold reserves, while Britain's amounted to just
about 8 per cent of their holding. Australia, Brazil and Germany
were left with almost nothing in their kitty. Moreover, Britain was
unable to attract foreign capital inflows since it had to maintain
low interest rates to deal with the internal economy in recession.
The primary producers in the world were also increasingly facing
an impending crisis; food prices had fallen by almost 30 per cent
between 1925 and 1929. This not only hit their own exports but
also led to a downfall in the demand of the industrialized nations.
Agricultural depression spread across the word from Latin America
to the Caribbean, from Africa to India.

The loss of confidence in sterling led to the large-scale conversion
of sterling into gold that ultimately forced Britain to abandon the
gold standard in 1931. Even prior to Britain many other countries
including Hungary, Australia, Brazil and many other Latin American
nations had abrogated their commitment to convert their currencies
into gold. The post-war period until 1931 can be viewed as one in
which countries made arduous efforts to return to a gold standard.
In the end, this was turning out to be a futile exercise. Britain's fall
led to a global contagion; it soon became evident that even the
countries flush with gold had been able to accumulate it only on
account of their inward looking polices. The international gold
standard could never survive without the rules of the game being
played.

Meanwhile, even before Britain abandoned the gold standard,

the US was reeling under the Great Depression, which had commenced, if a moment can at all be identified, with the stock market crash of 1929. It was now the turn of the dollar to face a loss of confidence; as that happened a run on the dollar began that immediately led to a 15 per cent fall in US gold reserves. In 1933 the US was forced to leave the gold standard and returned to it a year later but with a devalued dollar. The parity was reset from $20.67 per oz. to $35 per oz—a devaluation of almost 41 per cent. Once again many countries which had pegged their currencies to the dollar also fell. The only countries which remained convertible in 1934 were those in the Gold Bloc: France, Belgium, Holland, Italy, Poland and Switzerland. They soon began to feel the heat of the devaluations in the rest of the world; a loss of export competitiveness and an outflow of gold that began eroding the confidence in these currencies to maintain convertibility. A vicious cycle had begun and by 1935 the first victim had fallen in the Gold Bloc—Belgium left the fold. As deflation mounted and social tensions grew, devaluation was seen as inevitable. By 1936, all counties had succumbed to devaluation.

The Great Depression had also caused a complete disintegration of international trade. Beggar-thy-neighbour policies based on tariff protection and quantitative restrictions inhibited free trade. This was followed by exchange rate devaluations by one country after another in order to increase exports. However, when country after country resorts to the same measure, the efficacy of the measure is called into question.[2] Gold standard countries, including the USA and France were not only unwilling to inflate (deflate) their currencies with gold inflows (outflows) but were also concerned with their loss of competitiveness with foreign currencies depreciating vis-à-vis gold. They had therefore to protect themselves from an onslaught of foreign goods, when their own industries were succumbing to the depression. They were however left with few options—trade barriers and strict foreign exchange controls. The passage of the Smoot-Hawley Tariff Act in 1930 set off a landslide of protective and retaliatory measures across the world that ultimately worsened the effects of the Great Depression.

The phase of devaluations had also warranted another significant policy measure—controls over the flight of capital. When expectations build up on the possible devaluation of a currency, it is only obvious that people would wish to hold their savings in a currency that isn't going to depreciate. This could then force an even greater devaluation. The only option left was to impose controls on the external outflow of capital. This, however, would plant the seeds for black markets in foreign exchange to develop; this is illustrated in Figure 9.1. Here we consider the home currency to be sterling and foreign currency as the dollar. Initial equilibrium is at £0.5 = $1. When sterling is devalued to £0.6 = $1, an excess supply of $ accumulates as reserves (Bank of England would buy these dollar). However, if on account of this devaluation, expectations of further devaluations are raised, then there will be an increase in the demand for dollars ($D_\$$ shifts). Now the equilibrium rate should be above £0.6 = $1, but supply is restricted to Q_0 (even if the central bank stops buying dollars). With this level of supply, rationing of the excess demand will be necessary. Furthermore, for this level of supply, buyers are willing to pay up to £0.7 = $1, which becomes the black market rate for foreign exchange.

Although there were many who believed that the road to recovery lay in more open economy policies including stable exchange rates as well as free trade of goods and international movement of

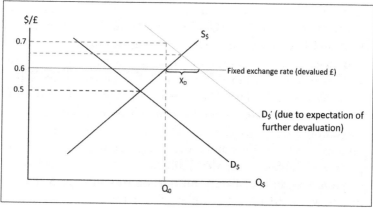

Figure 9.1: Devaluation and Emergence of Black Markets

capital, there were many who believed that addressing issues pertaining to the internal economy, in particular deflation and unemployment required the immediate attention of the state. Franklin Roosevelt was one amongst the latter; he spoke about 'the fetishes of international bankers' and their obstinate pursuit of policies that were targeted at maintaining exchange rates (Singleton, 2011, p. 107). Instead, Roosevelt was keen to pursue policies that would raise domestic demand and real output. These policies prevailed. However, by 1934, the US changed its posture towards adopting protective policies and moved towards greater free trade and even acknowledged the importance of reciprocity in trade negotiations. In 1936, the informal Tripartite Agreement was signed between USA, France and Britain to stabilize exchange rates and abstain from competitive devaluations. In spite of these positive signs, there was no significant change in the world economy as the world drifted into another major event: the Second World War.

It was in this international scenario that the rupee faced a challenge of maintaining stability when countries discarded playing the rules of the game.

9.2: POST-WAR CURRENCY INSTABILITY

At almost every stage in the evolution of the (Indian) currency system, the difficulties of Government have loomed large; and Government all along have looked at the problem more from the point of view of an interested party than a custodian of public interests.

H.L. CHABLANI

The sharp rise in silver prices had compelled the government to revalue the rupee. Finally, the exchange rate of the rupee had been fixed at *2s. in terms of gold.* Since Britain was no longer on the gold standard, the rupee-sterling rate had therefore to be computed on the basis of the London-New York cross rate as the dollar remained on a gold standard. On this basis, the rupee sterling was 2s.10½d. in February 1920. From then onwards forces began to develop that systematically lowered the exchange rate of the rupee. These included (i) the efforts of the British government to deflate their currency so as to make sterling equivalent to gold, in other words, force sterling to appreciate. This monetary stringency led to a rapid fall in the price level in Britain, which in absolute terms exceeded the rate of deflation in India; (ii) an unfavourable balance of trade developing in India's balance of payments on account of a steep fall in post-war exports and the simultaneously high level of imports due to an overvalued rupee; (iii) a sharp fall in the price of silver.

Between June and September 1920 the government tried to maintain the value of the rupee at 2s. gold. This proved impossible as the price of silver crashed by more than 30 per cent between 1919 and 1920 (Table 9.1). In effect the government was collecting (say) 1s.9d. worth of gold in India with Re.1 (i.e. the value of the silver in a rupee coin in terms of gold) but paying out 2s. worth of gold in Britain. What should have effectively cost (say) Rs. 1.30 (worth of gold) to India now cost only Re. 1 worth of gold; this obviously led to a scramble for imports from abroad. The government then tried to peg the rupee to the sterling at 2s. But even this proved impossible as by 1921 silver prices had slipped further to almost 50 per cent of its 1919 price. Even at this rate the (market) sterling value of the rupees (as silver bullion) collected in India was only about £25 million while some £55 million had to be paid out in Britain (to buy gold in the market for sterling). This is illustrated in Figure 9.2. where we map the quantity of foreign exchange against £/Rs. rate. A higher rate means a lower value of the rupee and therefore an increased supply (because of enhanced exports) and lower demand for sterling (because of lower import demand). As can be observed, with an overvalued rupee (of Rs. 10 = £1), there is a massive excess demand for sterling. Given

TABLE 9.1: SILVER PRICES AFTER THE WAR

(New York, cents p. oz, 0.999 fine)

Year	Silver Price	Year	Silver Price
1919	101.125	1921	56.625
1920	68	1922	62.375

Source: D.H. Leavens, *Silver Money*, Principia Press, Bloomington, 1939, p. 212.

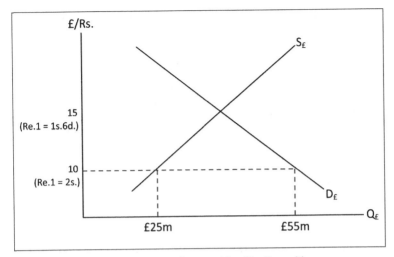

Figure 9.2: Excess Demand for Sterling with an
Overvalued Rupee

that the government wanted to maintain the rupee at this rate, this was ultimately met by drawing from the Paper Currency Reserve held by the Secretary of State in London. Sterling securities were sold at a loss that ultimately cost the Indian exchequer some Rs. 40 million. In spite of this the rate could not be maintained; the rupee had to be devalued. Indian importers who had expected to receive 2s. for every rupee, now had to shell out more rupees for the same number of sterling. At the same time, the adverse balance of trade meant that rupees had to be taken out from circulation to meet net foreign obligations leading to a contraction in domestic money supply, a rise in domestic interest rates and a fall in domestic price levels.

Finally, in 1921, the policy of exchange rate stability was given up. Table 9.2 gives us a picture of India's exchange rates and domestic price levels along with that of other countries during the period 1920–1. By 1921 the rupee had fallen to 1s.2⁷/₈d. (sterling) and lower than 1s. (gold). The shock of severe worldwide deflation thus fell on the exchange rate rather than on the domestic price level in India, with minimal government intervention in the domestic economy.

TABLE 9.2: EXCHANGE RATES AND PRICE LEVEL
IN VARIOUS COUNTRIES

	1920	1921
Sterling rate of rupee	2s.81/2d.	1s.318/32d.
Gold rate of rupee	1s.117/32d.	119/32d.
Index of price level in India	192	191
UK	243	157
USA	179	140
Norway	377	269
France	435	326

Source: H.L. Chablani, *Studies in Indian Currency and Exchange*, Oxford University Press, Bombay, 1931, p. 80.

Till about 1924–5 the Government followed a policy of exchange rate flexibility that allowed for relative stability in the price level. In March 1922, India's balance of trade started turning positive once again and the exchange rose from 1s.4d. in 1923 to 1s.5^{7}⁄₃₂d. in 1924.

The Indian currency system since 1893 had sought exchange rate stability at the risk of its adverse implications on the domestic price level and output. The Chamberlain Commission as well as witnesses in front of the Babington Smith Report reiterated this view. In fact, the report of the latter had even pointed out that exchange rate stability was an important facility rather than an essential condition. In the era before the closing of the mints, even as silver went into free fall, trade did flourish with fluctuating exchange rates (it was the inflexible home charges that became problematic). Moreover, banks and other financial institutions could have developed hedging instruments to take care of the risk and uncertainty introduced into the foreign trade on account of the fluctuations in exchange rates. But India chose otherwise; in April 1925 Britain returned to a gold standard and the Indian government once again chose to adopt a policy of exchange rate stability over domestic price level stability to serve the interest of its colonial ruler.

The rupee exchange rate was now pegged to 1s.6d. gold. However, this time around there was one key difference; instead of guaranteed sale of council bills in London (the rate then was 1s.4d.), the government now introduced the policy of unlimited purchase of sterling in India at the rate of 1s.6d. for Re. 1. By 1924, the system of sterling purchase in India displaced the council bills systems that had been in operation for decades. As shown in Figure 9.3 the supply curve of rupees (S_{Rs}) becomes perfectly elastic at 1s.6d. The rupee cannot appreciate above this rate as the Government would supply rupees at this rate and there was no necessity of a British importer buying rupees for, say, 1s.8d. in the market.

In 1925 the Hilton Young Committee was appointed to report and make recommendations on the Indian currency and exchange system. In 1926 the committee presented its report recommending that India adopt a gold bullion standard wherein silver rupees and paper would be legal tender but these could be exchanged freely with the currency authority for gold bullion, subject to a minimum quantity of 400 oz. (11.34 kg). Currency notes would not be convertible to rupees, although both were convertible to gold bullion. Several advantages were claimed from the adoption of this system; (i) stability of the exchange rate conducive to foreign trade and international capital flows; (ii) simple, clear and a measure that would inspire confidence in the public as currency could be converted to gold at a fixed rate; (iii) automatic expansion and

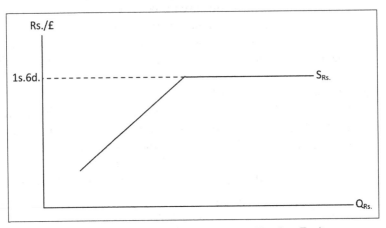

Figure 9.3: The Supply for Rupees in the Foreign Exchange Market with Fixed Exchange Rates

contraction of currency with convertibility into gold—when notes were surrendered for gold there would be a contraction in domestic money supply and when gold was surrendered for notes there would be an expansion of money supply; (iv) gold would remain in the reserves and not get dissipated in circulation; (v) accumulation of gold reserves would pave the way for the adoption of a pure gold standard. In spite of these perceived benefits, only a variant of the gold bullion standard was finally adopted in India.

The next important issue that the committee had to decide upon was the ratio or the standard of value. The rupee exchange was fixed at 1s.6d. (= 8.47512 grains = 0.55 grams of fine gold). The question then arose as to whether the rupee exchange of 1s.6d. was too high (overvalued) as compared to the rate of 1s.4d., which had prevailed prior to 1925. An overvalued rupee would mean that imports become cheaper and exports less competitive, resulting in the balance of trade deteriorating and forcing a correction through lower domestic prices and also lower Indian wage rates. With world prices falling sharply, the fixed rate of 1s.6d. would mean that Indian domestic price levels would be compelled to fall even more to regain its competitiveness internationally. This would hit domestic producers hard. Moreover, the overvalued exchange rate would give a windfall to foreign exporters (to India) as they would now get more sterling for any given rupee sales in India. This would make them competitive in Indian markets. The only recourse once again would be for Indian price levels to fall. Any downward adjustment in nominal wage rates that could follow would then entail a long and bitter struggle between capital and labour and a rise in social discontent across India.

The Hilton Young Commission also recommended the setting up of the Reserve Bank of India; however, strong opposition to the report led to the bill giving effect to the recommendations of the commission being abandoned. The plan to set up the Reserve Bank of India was shelved along with the rest of the report. Instead the Currency Act of 1927 was passed to enforce the new exchange rate of 1s.6d. It was now the statutory duty of the government to purchase gold at Rs. 21-3a-10p per tola (minimum quantity purchased would be 400 oz. = 1065 tolas) and to sell gold (same minimum quantity) in exchange for internal rupees for delivery in Bombay or London in equivalent sterling. India had, therefore, in effect reverted to a sterling (gold) exchange standard.

Between 1927 and 1929, exports and imports grew at a healthy pace. This, it was argued, was *in spite* of an overvalued rupee. A lower rupee may have seen an even healthier trend. The price level saw a drop of about 5 per cent during this period, brought about by a currency contraction to sustain the higher exchange rate. In Figure 9.4 the sluggish demand for rupees had to be countered with a reduction in supply of rupees. This was done by raising the bank rates (rates at which the Government lent money to the Imperial Bank) as well as the sale of treasury bills to prevent an outflow of rupees or to prevent an increase in supply of rupees. Table 9.3 also shows the wholesale price index in Calcutta for the period 1919–20 till 1935–6. As can be seen above although the economy was cushioned against deflation till about 1924–5, a major structural break in deflation is not evident after the introduction of a fixed ratio of 1s.6d.

This opened up a debate as to whether 1s.6d. was really the 'correct' or 'natural' ratio? Here we must return to the central argument

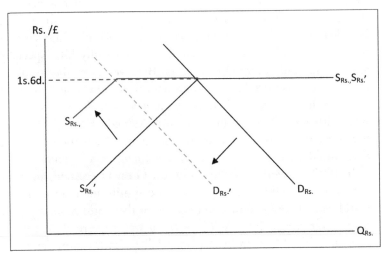

Figure 9.4 Monetary Contraction to Maintain Exchange Rate of the Rupee

TABLE 9.3: WHOLESALE PRICE INDEX IN CALCUTTA
FOR THE PERIOD 1919–20 TO 1935–6

Years	WPI	Year	WPI
1919–20	202	1928–9	145
1920–1	195	1929–30	137
1921–2	180	1930–1	109
1922–3	176	1931–2	95
1923–4	171	1932–3	88
1924–5	171	1933–4	88
1925–6	157	1934–5	90
1926–7	146	1935–6	91
1927–8	147		

Source: H. Sinha and J.C. Sinha, 'The Ratio Question', *Sankhya: The Indian Journal of Statistics*, vol. 3, no. 27, 1937, pp. 125–42, esp. p. 128.

of this book: a question of balance. If the ratio of 1s.6d.gold was correct then, all else constant, prices and wages should have stabilized showing no sharp upward or downward movement. If the rupee was undervalued then it would have resulted in larger surpluses in the balance of trade, increased domestic money supply (inflation of currency), higher price levels and higher wages. On the other hand, if the rupee was overvalued at 1s.6d. then this should have led to a deficit in the trade balance, contraction of money supply, and deflation. Exports would have been badly hit, especially agricultural and commodity exports. But even after the fixed exchange rate was introduced it is difficult to see any major effect on the price level. It could therefore be argued that the rate of 1s.6d. was neither overly overvalued or undervalued. Although the debate over the ratio continued, another major event soon followed that would once more test the fixed exchange rate regime.

In 1929 the world descended into the Great Depression, an event that, economically speaking, was more significant than even the world wars. It resulted in a contraction of the world economy on a scale never seen before. As far as India was concerned, as can be seen in Table 9.4, there was a steep fall in both exports and imports; however, in absolute terms the quantum fall in exports was larger than the fall in imports. This put pressure on the rupee's

TABLE 9.4: VALUE OF INDIA'S TRADE
IN MILLIONS OF RUPEES

Year	Export	Import	Difference in export	Difference in Import
1926–7	3,110	2,410	x	x
1927–8	3,300	2,610	190	200
1928–9	3,390	2,630	90	20
1929–30	3,190	2,500	–200	–130
1930–1	2,260	1,730	–930	–770

Source: D.K. Malhotra, *History and Problems of Indian Currency: 1835–1949,* Minerva Book Shop, Simla, 1949, p. 67.

exchange rate to weaken. The situation was accentuated by the start of the Civil Disobedience Movement in 1930 and the consequent flight of capital. Once again, the only recourse open to the government was contraction in supply of rupees. This was achieved through the issue of reverse councils amounting to some £14 million and meeting these sales by transfers from the Gold Standard Reserve and Paper Currency Reserve and at the same time withdrawing almost Rs. 1,380 million from circulation. These measures to maintain an overvalued currency caused stringency in the money markets and accentuated the fall in the domestic price level as we saw in Table 9.3.

For a brief period it had seemed that the ratio question was settled but the Great Depression and its impact on India's trade and domestic economy once again brought the issue to the fore. In 1931, England went off the gold standard so that sterling was no longer convertible to gold. Now the Indian Government faced a not-so-new predicament—should the rupee be linked to gold or sterling? And at what rate? Two possibilities existed; to either link the rupee to gold at ≤1s.6d. or to link it to sterling at ≤1s.6d. There was also the option to let the rupee float as it had in 1924. The uncertainty over its decision could have caused a note and a bank run so that, as a preemptive measure, the government closed all banks for three working days.

If the rupee was pegged to gold at either 1s.6d. (= 8.47 grains of gold) or 1s.4d. (= 7.53 grains of gold), substantial gold reserves would have been required to overcome any possible depreciation of the rupee. In case of a deficit in the balance of trade there would have been pressure for the rupee to depreciate in which case gold would have to be sold in the market and rupees purchased (so that the increased demand for rupees would have prevented its depreciation). The reserves in the Paper Currency Reserve were very low at that time at just about £32½ million. Rupees would have to be withdrawn from circulation, melted and sold in the market in exchange for gold. This would have entailed severe contraction in money supply and consequently deflation. Once again fixed exchange rates would have transmitted the shock to domestic price levels and even output. Moreover, pegging of the rupee to gold would have meant that the rupee would have fluctuated vis-à-vis sterling (since the sterling was delinked from gold and depreciating). This could have affected trade between India and Britain as well as other countries which were on a sterling standard. The government could have instead chosen a 'free' or 'floating' exchange rate regime; however, they wanted certainty in the rupee-sterling rate since large sterling loans had to be paid off. The risk of a depreciating rupee would have increased the burden of these loans. Adherence to a fixed exchange rate could actually improve India's credit rating internationally and secure debt at much lower costs.[3]

Ultimately, the Government chose to peg the rupee to the sterling at 1s.6d. The linking of the rupee to sterling, however, led to the depreciation of the rupee (as sterling depreciated) vis-à-vis gold (by some 40 per cent) as well as other currencies pegged to gold. This should have made Indian exports more competitive and imports more expensive. While the former did not really happen because of the simultaneous decline in world prices as well as higher import duties imposed by countries, imports became more costly from gold standard countries. Britain and other sterling standard countries benefitted from this improvement in competitiveness. But this benefit did not last long; countries one after the other abandoned gold and moved on to sterling standard.

Soon after the rupee was delinked from gold and pegged to sterling, the price of gold in terms of rupees began increasing as sterling began depreciating vis-à-vis gold. Between September and December 1931, gold prices in India rose by almost 50 per cent from Rs. 21 to 30 per tola. The windfall, along with the abysmal condition of the real economy, induced people to part with their hoards. The distress in the agricultural sector during these years was the hardest hit by the worldwide recession. Agricultural prices fell and the farmers unable to pay their dues to the government resorted to sale of gold. Table 9.5 shows the exports of gold from India between 1931 and 1940. A debate soon broke out to assess the pros and cons of the gold exports from India. From their side the government argued that the sale of gold was undertaken to tide over a period of difficulty and by itself there was no need for the government to intervene in people's decisions. People had the right to sell gold and reap the benefits. This in fact was the very purpose of hoarding gold; in time of contingencies individuals and families could fall back upon their savings. It was also good that gold was coming out of hoards and circulating. Moreover, during this period India's balance of merchandise trade had begun to deteriorate.

TABLE 9.5: GOLD EXPORTS FROM INDIA

Years	Net Gold Exported (million of oz.)	Value (millions of Rs.)	Average Price (Rs. per tola)
1928–9	x	–212	x
1929–30	x	–142.2	x
1930–1	x	–127.5	x
1931–2	7.73	579.8	25-9-0
1932–3	8.35	655.2	30-9-0
1933–4	6.7	570.5	33-4-0
1934–5	5.69	525.4	35-7-0
1935–6	4.02	373.6	35-8-0
1936–7	3.01	278.5	35-10-0
1937–8	1.77	163.3	36-1-0
1938–9	1.35	130.5	37-12-0
1939–40	3.16	346.7	41-14-0

Sources: D.K. Malhotra, *History and Problems of Indian Currency: 1835–1949*, Minerva Book Shop, Simla, 1949, p. 79; H. Sinha and J.C. Sinha, 'The Ratio Question', *Sankhya: The Indian Journal of Statistics*, vol. 3, no. 27, 1937, pp.125–42, esp. p. 134.

This was causing pressure on the rupee to depreciate. Adjustment in the balance of payments would then entail contraction of money supply and deflation. Under prevailing conditions of a worldwide slowdown, this would have proved disastrous. Gold exports staved off possible pressure on the rupee to depreciate and intensity of deflation.

The greatest benefit to India from gold exports, however, came from the fact that the large inflow of sterling (to buy gold) was used to payoff India's debt of £15 million. This improved the credit rating of the government which was able to access further loans at substantially improved terms. For instance, the price of 3½ per cent Government Paper rose from just about Rs. 62 in 1931–2 to almost par in 1934–5 (Sinha, 1938, p. 28). It was therefore felt that the cancellation of sterling loans at a time when gold prices were high was a wise decision. Some £80 million worth of gold was sold and sterling was purchased to the extent of some £70 million that was used to settle debt and strengthen reserves. Over all, it was argued by the government that it was good for India to have sold off a dead asset like gold when its price was high and invested a part of it in interest-bearing securities.

While the government's arguments were strong and could not be dismissed off easily, there was at the same time an audible contingent of Indian commercial and public opinion makers who were opposed to the gold exports, which they saw as emanating from an overvalued rupee. They urged the government to instead impose an embargo on gold exports and resort to domestic open market purchase of the gold. At the same time, the rupee-sterling rate should have been re-set at the pre-War level of 1s.4d. The reasons forwarded for this argument are also noteworthy: (i) The government was disposing an appreciating asset (gold) for a depreciating one (sterling). Them losses incurred in this swap exceeded the amount earned from investing in sterling securities. (ii) Although the future of gold currencies became increasingly uncertain as countries gave up the gold standard, gold had surely not yet been dethroned from the international monetary system. There was no surety that government had to once again buy gold to return to a gold standard, it may have had to pay a much higher price. (iii) The government could have purchased some gold to enhance its banking reserves. (iv) The gold exports were hiding a chronic balance of trade and debt problem that India was slowly falling into. It would not have been sustainable over a longer period of time. (v) Sir Purshottamdas Thakurdas argued that no other dominion or agricultural country in the world maintained their pre-war parity. Australia and New Zealand devalued their currencies by 10 per cent to 25 per cent while some countries even defaulted on their obligations. India maintained the rate with currency deflation plus export of gold. Between 1931 and 1933, the UK price index showed an increase of 3½ points while the Indian index declined by 3. The total difference between the price levels of the two countries was therefore of 6½ points; this clearly showed that the rupee was overvalued. Lowering the ratio could be the first step in raising the domestic price level. (vi) According to G.D. Birla, the high rupee-sterling rate was maintained to motivate capital to return to Britain during the war and not in accordance with the competitiveness of Indian exports.

This period also saw the sale of silver by the Indian government. Following the recommendations of the Hilton Young Commission, India had begun sale of silver in the Paper Currency Reserves since 1927 and until 1934 had already sold some Rs. 570 million worth of silver in the market. However, in 1933 the government still held more than Rs. 1 billion in silver. The danger of a fall in world silver prices from a sale of silver by India was prevented by an agreement which limited India's sales to a maximum of 35 million oz. annually. The USA meanwhile agreed to buy this amount from the market every year. This stabilized the price of silver internationally.

While external stability in the exchange rate of the rupee was maintained through gold exports, the domestic economy was reeling under depression. The effect of the crisis was especially severe on the agricultural sector. While the prices of both exports and imports fell, given that Indian exports were predominantly agricultural and commodity exports, the international terms of trade showed a marked deterioration. Between 1929 and 1932, the price of exports fell some 47 per cent while price of imports fell by just

16 per cent (Malhotra, 1949, p. 95n). In other words, a larger quantity of exports was necessary to buy the same quantity of imports in exchange. In a fixed exchange rate regime, this put pressure on the domestic price level to fall by way of monetary contraction. Tables 9.3 and 9.6 show the severe deflation of the Indian economy between 1930 and 1939 that was even greater than Western economies. Possible reasons for this may have been the increased spending on defense in these countries in contrast to India's over dependence on agriculture which was the worst hit because of the inelasticity of demand.

Table 9.7 shows exchange rate fluctuations between 1930 and 1938. As can be seen, without gold exports the exchange rate would have fallen sharply and probably even forced India to abandon the rate of 1s.6d. Post-1938, the exchange rate again faced pressure to depreciate and went down to 1s.5^{15}/$_{16}$d. Forward rates weakened and the Government also attributed the depreciation to speculators who wished to move funds to Britain and bring them back when the exchange fell.

The movement for a revision (devaluation) of the rupee rate grew stronger with country after country devaluating its exchange rates; England, Scandinavian countries, Egypt, Japan, United States,

TABLE 9.6: PRICE INDEX IN VARIOUS
COUNTRIES, 1929–36

Year	UK	USA	Australia	Japan	Canada	India
1929	100	100	100	100	100	100
1930	87.5	90.7	88.5	82.4	90.6	82.3
1931	76.8	76.6	79.2	69.9	75.4	68.1
1932	74.9	68	78.3	73.3	69.8	64.5
1933	75	69.2	78.2	81.6	70.2	61.7
1934	77.1	78.6	81.6	80.8	74.9	63.1
1935	77.9	83.9	80.8	84.4	75.4	64.5
1936	82.7	84.8	85.6	89.9	78	64.5
1937	95.2	90.6	91.9	108.4	88.4	72.3
1938	88.2	82.5	92.9	114.3	82.2	76.6

Source: D.K. Malhotra, *History and Problems of Indian Currency: 1835-1949*, Minerva Book Shop, Simla, 1949, p. 106.

TABLE 9.7: EXCHANGE RATES RUPEE TO STERLING

(*in pence, d*).

Years	Rate	Year	Rate
1929–30	17.85	1934–5	18.05
1930–1	17.78	1935–6	18.08
1931–2	17.91	1936–7	18.1
1932–3	18.06	1937–8	18.09
1933–4	18.02	1938–9	17.09

Source: D.K. Malhotra, *History and Problems of Indian Currency: 1835–1949*, Minerva Book Shop, Simla, 1949, p. 100.

Belgium, France, Holland, Switzerland, Italy and Czechoslovakia depreciated or devalued their currencies in succession. In 1932, the devaluation of the Japanese yen led to the large import of Japanese cotton piece goods into India. The government countered this with an imposition of import duties on all cotton piece goods except those from Britain. The call for lower rates grew stronger and even the Indian National Congress passed a comprehensive resolution on the subject in December 1938. The government was, however, adamant and Sir James Grigg, Finance Member, declared: 'I will be no party to any monkeying about the present ratio' (quoted in Malhotra, 1949, p. 101).

But the situation was also beginning to impact Government finances; as revenues fell due to deflation, the Government took measures that included austerity, retrenchment and taxation. These measures were, however, unable to restore the finances of the government. Provinces under Congress governments faced an even greater problem as prohibition was introduced, depriving them of much needed finances.

These policies threw up some important generalizations on how exchange rates affected an economy like India at that time. India was by and large a high debt country whose net exports had to raise sufficient quantum of foreign exchange to pay off the principal and interest on this debt. Without exchange rate flexibility the only way for this to happen was to force deflation in the domestic price level to increase exports. Where exported goods faced an inelastic demand this contraction would be even greater and obviously more painful. Exchange rates were a shock absorber that would protect the domestic economy from shocks originating in the international economy. However, currency depreciation could have increased the rupee cost of servicing and repaying debt in foreign currency. Domestic budget deficits would have increased. Without a possibility to increase domestic money supply (to maintain exchange rate), the government would have to resort to higher levels of taxation or borrowing. Such policy measures would have adversely affected the real economy and worsened the prevailing depressionary situation. Nonetheless, the possibility to devaluate currency was seen as an important instrument that India was unable to take recourse to. This was also one of the reasons why the country had to resort to gold exports to dampen the domestic contraction of the economy.

9.3: THE IMPERIAL BANK OF INDIA

The Imperial Bank, for all its pompous title and connection with government can hardly be called a central bank par excellence. It is certainly India's premier bank, but it is not India's Bank of England. The peculiarity of the banking system in India is that there is not much system in it.

BHANOO B. DAS GUPTA

The Imperial Bank of India arose in 192 from the merger of the three Presidency Banks: the Bank of Bengal, Bank of Bombay and Bank of Madras. We will not delve on the administrative details here but only highlight those aspects which had a bearing on the monetary system of the country.

Even after the formation of the Imperial Bank, all foreign exchange business still remained with the Exchange Banks. The Imperial Bank was prohibited by its charter to engage in foreign exchange transactions given that it held government balances and should not undertake any business prone to heavy risks and uncertainty.[4] Note issue was also not handed over to the Imperial Bank. In effect then, the Imperial Bank was restricted to the same business as Presidency Banks. In spite of these restrictions, several benefits were perceived. The amalgamation made the Imperial Bank a larger entity with economies of scale in several activities including training of personnel. Given the greater confidence in a large entity, it would be able to raise larger quantum of resources at lower costs and could extend its activities into the interior regions of the country. There would be also greater confidence in the stability of the institution that would enable the bank to attract deposits from the public. This was deemed critical in India where discouraging the habit of hoarding precious metals was seen as a necessary condition to put the country on the road to modernization. Another major reason for the merger of the Presidency Banks would be its enhanced ability to open branches across India and take banking to the interior. As many branches become profitable only with a time lag, the capacity of a large bank to absorb short-term losses at some branches becomes crucial. With extensive branches, the Imperial Bank would also be able to make fuller utilization of government funds by lending money in the interior regions of the country. Millions of rupees locked up in the Reserves Treasury during the busy season caused stringency in the money markets. With access to a larger market, the Presidency Banks would be able to loan out these underutilized resources. This would also improve the elasticity of supply, especially to the agricultural sector—a most critical requirement of the Indian banking system. The Imperial Bank would therefore become responsible for the spatial movement of funds from one part of the country to another; as mentioned early in this book, an important characteristic of money is its movement across space (and time). There would also be decentralization of the Public Debt Department which hitherto was concentrated in Calcutta. This would enable the Bank to mop up small savings and channelize it into productive investment. By extending the reach of the bank, the withdrawal of funds by the government was also put back into the system. The association of the bank with the government also gave the public a great deal of confidence and trust. Finally, pooling of reserves also lead to efficiency as well as economy of reserves.

It was hoped that the Imperial Bank would revise the old belief that India was the world's sink of precious metals. The role of the

Imperial Bank can best be understood using the circular flow model; it was a channelizing institution of putting savings, hoarding and government balances back into the circular flow (see Figure 7.10 and Appendix 2).

It was also expected that the Imperial Bank would act as a banker's bank. By virtue of its size and capital it could stand behind failing banks and come to their rescue. This would add greater stability to India's fledging banking system and make it more credible. When the Alliance Bank of Simla failed in 1923, the Imperial Bank agreed to pay the former's depositors (savings and current account holders) up to 50 per cent of the amounts due to them. This was later incorporated by an amendment by which the Imperial Bank was empowered to advance or lend money to a banking institution with a rupee capital upon security of its assets with the specific object of averting or facilitating a winding-up. Indian joint-stock banks also hoped that the Imperial Bank would look after banking policy and provide better coordination amongst various banks, which otherwise was a source of conflict especially during times of stress. For instance, when a rumour began to float that the Allahabad Bank had approached the Imperial Bank for assistance it was looked upon as a loss of prestige and the former had to announce that it would never borrow money from any other bank. The adverse effects of a breakdown of inter-bank lending, as we saw during the 2008 recession, can aggravate a financial crisis. The Imperial Bank was also expected to become the central rediscounting agency in the country. This would further assist all the joint-stock banks as well as agricultural and industrial banks in the country. Furthermore, a bank with enormous resources, expanse and clientele and resources would be able to influence the entire banking sector; for instance, the bank's rate would become the norm for the entire sector. However, a question of competition arose vis-à-vis joint stock banks. It was alleged by the Allahabad Bank to the Hilton Young Commission that the Imperial Bank by setting unfair and uneconomic rates was abusing its power and forcing smaller bank's out of business. The Imperial Banks ability to obtain funds at a lower cost than other banks was also seen as detrimental to fair competition in the banking sector. But the question here was whether these attractive rates accrued on account of managerial efficiencies; if so, it would be wrong to penalize it on this count.

The big question on the role of the Imperial Bank was whether it would be able to combine its commercial and central banking functions together. The model followed here was that of the Banque de France which had both, Banque d'Affairs (industrial bank) and the Caisse des De'pot et de Consignations (central banking) functions. This compartmentalization of functions could allow for reconciliation of conflicting objectives; a commercial bank pursues its goal of profit maximization while a central bank was entrusted with responsibilities aimed the general good of society. Consider an economy facing a recessionary situation. As a central bank the Imperial Bank would have to signal a rate cut in the market while as a commercial bank as long as demand for its funds existed there is no incentive to do so. During a boom, when rates are rising and security prices are rising too, the central bank sells off securities at a low price (even incurring losses) as part of its open market operation to stabilize the economy. On the other hand, when the economy sinks into a recession, interest rates fall and security prices rise; in such a situation the central bank has to buy these securities so as to inject much needed liquidity into the system. This, however, may not be a commercially prudent step. How then should the bank act? It is therefore not surprising that central banks have statutory or voluntary limits imposed on their rates of dividend so that they are not driven by the profit motive.

The Imperial Bank's biggest failure was its inability to control the very large seasonal variations in interest rates and the very high rates they reached at certain times of the year. The Imperial Bank which had some of the privileges of a central bank and a few of the responsibilities, preferred to raise the rate to the point of maximum profit rather than allow its cash to fall low in the interest of stable rates. The motive of private profit was hampering a more sound policy for the benefit of society-at-large. The conflict of purpose in the Imperial Bank as a commercial bank and as a central bank made it an inappropriate institution to take charge of the latter role. The Imperial Bank was no banker's bank. As one economist put it, more than an apex bank in a pyramidical structure we had a tall tower standing amongst several other shorter ones.

Even as the Imperial Bank was slowly consolidating its position, there were two great obstacles that the banking sector had to contend with—ignorance of the Indian public on the principles and benefits of banking, both to individuals and the economy at large, and the inability of banks to reach out to the masses. Unfortunately, the struggle to overcome these hurdles and develop a more inclusive banking system in India continues till this day.

9.4: THE RESERVE BANK OF INDIA

Whoever controls the volume of money in any country is absolute master of all industry and commerce.

JAMES A. GARFIELD, PRESIDENT OF THE
UNITED STATES OF AMERICA

In 1934, the Reserve Bank of India Act was passed under which the Reserve Bank of India (RBI) was established in 1935. With this the Imperial Bank ceased to be banker to the government and the government withdrew from management of the bank. However, the Governor-General in Council was permitted to appoint up to two members to the central board. They could take part in discussions but not vote. However, their constraints on business and operations were relaxed.

With respect to the RBI, the government sought to minimize political influence over the bank's actions by making it a private shareholders' bank but with several government-appointed Directors. The RBI was assigned the sole right to issue bank notes which gradually replaced Government of India currency notes. The notes were legal tender and guaranteed by the Governor-General in Council. It would transact business of the government and was also empowered to undertake open market operations to expand, contract and stabilize the quantum of credit flows in the economy.

The RBI was assigned the responsibility to engage in foreign exchange transactions of buying and selling bills of exchange, gold and silver in India and England. It was placed under a legal obligation to maintain the rupee-sterling exchange rate at 1s.6d. by buying sterling at a rate not higher than 1s.6³/₁₆d. for a rupee and selling sterling for immediate delivery in London at a rate not lower than 1s.5⁴⁹/₆₄d. for a rupee. The amount of sterling bought or sold had to be greater than or equal to Rs.10,000. The maximum and minimum rates are illustrated in Figure 9.5.

The bank had an Issue Department and a Banking Department. The liabilities of the Issue Department were those that arose from note issue while the assets were gold coin and bullion (minimum Rs. 40 crores) plus sterling securities (total of which should be ≥40 per cent of liabilities), rupee securities, rupee coin, bills of exchange and promissory notes payable in India. Of the total gold coin and bullion not less than 85 per cent had to be held in India. The typical balance sheet of the RBI (29 March 1946) is shown in Box 9.1.

The RBI was a banker's bank and Scheduled Banks had to maintain 5 per cent of their demand liabilities and 2 per cent of their time liabilities with the RBI. The idea was to give the RBI power to influence the credit policy of member banks. A problem that remained, and remains until this day, was for the RBI to influence the activities of India's indigenous banking sector. It was also stipulated that the RBI pay the government a fixed dividend of 3.5 per cent (till 1942), which was raised to 4 per cent after 1943.

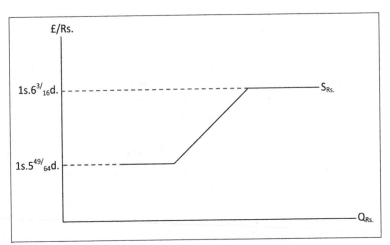

Figure 9.5: Supply of Rupees in Foreign Exchange Market as Maintained by the Reserve Bank of India

Box 9.1: Balance Sheet of the Reserve Bank of India

The liabilities and assets of the Issue Department of the Reserve Bank of India for the week ended 29 March 1946 (in rupees):

Liabilities		Assets	
Notes held in the Banking Department	19,63,56,000	A. Gold coin and bullion	
Notes in Circulation	12,18,77,42,000	(a) Held in India	44,41,45,000
		(b) Held outside India	...
		Sterling securities	11,20,32,89,100
		Total of A	11,64,74,34,000
		B. Rupee coin	15,82,59,000
		Government of India Rupee securities	57,84,05,000
		Internal bills of exchange and other commercial paper	...
Total notes issued	12,38,40,98,000		
Total liabilities	12,38,40,98,000	Total assets	12,38,40,98,000

Source: D.K. Malhotra, *History and Problems of Indian Currency: 1835–1949*, Minerva Book Shop, Simla, 1949, p. 90.

A central bank of issue is necessary for the development of banking resources of the country. In times of need banks will be able to obtain larger resources from it. It provides national control over sound and elastic currency and credit system. By discounting bills of exchange or granting advances to banks it provides necessary elasticity to the currency system of the country. Smaller banks can be relieved of pressure for funds. As early as 1936, the bank recognized the rural credit problem and studied how it could provide finance to cooperative banks. The RBI was also assigned the task of regulating the banking sector and enhancing confidence and trust in the monetary system of the country.

The most crucial feature of the central bank was the necessity to be free from national and international political pressure.[5] It is vested with monopoly power over the output and intake of legal tender currency. The government loses control over it. Moreover, the resources of the government will come under unified and systematic management. Sir Purshottamdas Thakurdas raised concerns over the actual degree of control over the RBI by the government. Moreover, there was in England at that time, given the intensity of the Great Depression, a movement for greater control over the Bank of England by the government. Would it then be proper to relegate an outdated system to India? This question was related to a bigger debate over control of central banks—should these banks be a state bank or a shareholder bank or perhaps a combination of both? Examples of pure shareholder banks were the Bank of England, Banque de France and the Reichbank of Germany. Pure state banks included the Bank of Finland and the Bank of Australia while mixed banks were the Federal Reserve Banks of USA and the Swiss National Bank. The advantage of shareholder banks was greater autonomy from government control and greater efficiency by weeding out unviable banks. On the other hand, driven by the profit motive shareholder banks would not take decision in the larger interest of society. In a country like India, the confidence and trust in the banking sector was abysmal. Even inter-bank trust and relations were poor and there would be little chance of their working together on several issues. Under these conditions, state support of a central bank became imperative to enhance these elements.

NOTES

1. Reid, 1954, p.4
2. Eichengreen and Sachs (1985) have, however, shown that those countries which devalued first benefitted from it with their ability to reach 1929 industrial production levels faster than those who devalued later.
3. D. Rothermund (1992) however argues that in spite of the Government of India favouring a freely floating exchange rate, the Secretary of State countermanded this in the interest of India's creditors (pp. 40f.); depreciation on the rupee would have meant less sterling returned for every rupee that had already been loaned out in India.
4. However, by an amendment to its charter in 1927 it was allowed to engage in the foreign exchange business.
5. Several controversies arose over the autonomy granted to the Reserve Bank of India by the Government of India. For critical views on this aspect see, for instance, Mukherjee (1992); Chandavarkar (2000) and Rothermund (1992).

CHAPTER 10

The Second World War

Make wars unprofitable and you make them impossible.

A. Philip Randolph

The Second World War was perhaps the most significant event of the twentieth century and financially it was the period when Britain and the Allies had to raise enormous sums of money to fight the war. Almost 50 per cent of Britain's national expenditure went towards the war effort. This massive government expenditure resulted in its gross domestic product (GDP) rising by more than 25 per cent between 1939 and 1943. Agricultural output increased significantly in pursuit of policies to provide food security. Production of arms and ammunition increased multifold. Resources were moved away from consumer goods, which had to be rationed in view of the collapse of productive capacity during the war. Taxation and long-term loans (mainly from the US) were the main methods utilized to raise public funds. Money supply increased sharply but inflation was suppressed through price controls. Britain's current account deficit widened with its growing imports for the war. For the entire period, 1939–45, the total current account deficit was £10 billion, out of which more than half was financed through US grants and the rest from sale of investments and an increase in liabilities. An exchange rate of $4 = £1 was maintained only through a system of import controls and foreign exchange restrictions.

India as a colony of Britain had to obviously support Britain's war efforts and it was this priority that defined India's monetary policies during the war years. Throughout the eighteenth century and early nineteenth century the East India Company was riddled with debt to fight its wars in India. This was once again the situation with Britain at the end of the war. Its sterling debt in India had increased manifold during the Second World War. It is also interesting to note that soon after the Company acquired diwani in 1765, Bengal faced a cataclysmic famine that took some 10 million lives. In 1943, just four years before India regained independence, Bengal had to once again face another horrendous famine that claimed some 3 million lives. And like the famine of 1770, one important reason for the famine of 1943 has been attributed to (mis)management of money supply.

10.1: THE RUPEE DURING THE SECOND WORLD WAR

Wars are not paid for in wartime, the bill comes later.

BENJAMIN FRANKLIN

The debate over the currency standard (gold or sterling) and correct rupee-sterling exchange ratio receded with the commencement of the Second World War. A few months before the war, gold exports, which had propped up the rupee since the early 1930s, gradually declined thereby putting pressure on the rupee to depreciate. The war, however, changed all that; India's exports once again increased sharply and within months a favourable balance of payments situation developed as can be seen from Table 10.1. To overcome the

TABLE 10.1: BALANCE OF TRADE AND PURCHASE OF STERLING BETWEEN 1939–40 AND 1944–5

Period	Balance of Trade (X - M) (in million of rupees)	Purchase of Sterling (in millions)
1939–40	780.2	70.5
1940–1	685.4	57.1
1941–2	798.8	73.3
1942–3	842.5	91.7
1943–4	913.2	105.3
1944–5	260.8	91.8

Source: D.K. Malhotra, *History and Problems of Indian Currency: 1835–1949*, Minerva Book Shop, Simla, 1949, p. 118.

increased supply of sterling (increased demand for rupees in the foreign exchange market), the Reserve Bank took the step, for the first time, to intervene in the market by buying sterling for forward delivery, shifting the demand curve from $D_£$ to $D_£'$ in Figure 10.1, in order to prevent the rupee from appreciating. The amount of sterling purchased is also shown in Table 10.1.

A simple system developed to maximize India's contribution to financing the war. This has been schematically illustrated in Figure 10.2. The sterling accumulated with the Reserve Bank of India in London was utilized for the purchase of sterling securities. These securities became the asset backing the issue of notes in India. In effect then, India lent out to Britain a huge amount of credit to finance the war. As can be seen from Table 10.2, sterling securities held by the RBI increased exponentially, from about Rs. 600 million in 1939 to more than Rs. 8 billion in 1945.[1] Another important policy measure that emerged during the war was exchange control, a legacy that continued right up to the end of the twentieth century. To ensure this, restrictions were imposed on Indian nationals and firms, under a new act, on the purchase of foreign exchange, capital movement and travel. The act also gave power to the RBI to acquire all foreign exchange in the possession of individuals and firms. Restrictions were also imposed on imports from 'hard currency' (currencies convertible to gold) areas,

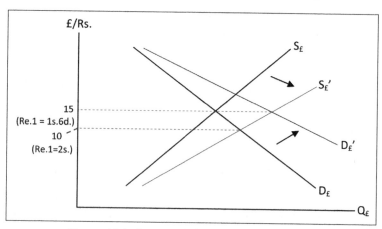

Figure 10.1: Intervention by RBI in maintaining
Exchange Markets

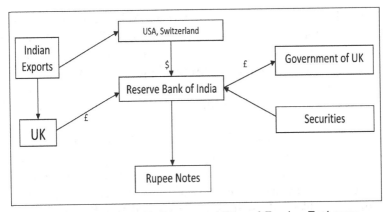

Figure 10.2: Schematic Diagram of Flow of Foreign Exchange
to RBI and Rupee Note Issue in India

TABLE 10.2: NOTES ISSUED AND RESERVES
IN INDIA AND ABROAD

(millions of rupees)

Period	Notes Issued	Gold & Gold Coins in India	Rupee Coins in India	Government of India Securities	Gold & Coins	Sterling Securities	Total Private Deposits
1939	1,585	321	490	251	23	484	2,775.2
1940	1,912	321	244	401	23	907	3,078.1
1941	2,058	324	243	513	–	962	3,565.8
1942	3,210	324	170	728	–	1,272	4,810
1943	5,327	324	81	400	–	4,514	6,787.3
1944	7,241	309	81	342	–	6,493	8,543.5
1945	8,904	308	81	490	–	8,001	1,0261
1946	10,013	324	134	301	–	8,689	12,206.7

Source: D.V. Ramana, 'Determinants of Money Supply India, 1914–50', *Indian Economic Review*, vol. 3, no. 4, 1957, pp. 1–33, esp. p. 16.

in particular, the USA and Switzerland. Balances held in these countries were acquired by the RBI and rupees given in exchange. Export of gold, gold jewelry and/or coins was also banned. The inflow of notes into India was also tightly controlled to prevent counterfeit notes from entering the country. All Japanese accounts in India were frozen. Even remittance of profits by firms was restricted except to free sterling area nations. These controls were aimed at acquiring all possible foreign exchange for the government and at the same time minimizing the utilization of sterling and/or hard currencies outside the 'free sterling area'; the latter included all countries in the British Empire except Canada, Egypt and some others. This ensured that all foreign exchange earned by Indians was available with the government to fund the war and was not held abroad.

While the sterling holdings as well as other foreign exchange by the Reserve Bank of India increased significantly, it led to a simultaneous expansion in the issue of rupee notes. This can be seen in Table 10.2. In the initial years of the war, note absorption was smooth unlike at the start of the First World War. But by May 1940 when silver shortages arose on account of its industrial demand, the situation changed; people went on a spree and began hoarding rupee coins. The coin reserves of the RBI fell steeply. It was ultimately decided to put a stop to this trend by passing a notification that any hoarding of rupee coins would be a criminal offence. The Government of India also, as an emergency measure, issued one rupee notes by an Ordinance. Moreover, all 'old' silver coin were required to be returned to the RBI and 'new' coins with a fineness of just ½ (instead of 11/12) were issued. This took care of the problem that had arisen in the previous war on account of the increase in silver prices; however, it also meant the effective demonetization of silver coins in India. Table 10.2 also shows the decrease in circulation of rupee coins during the war years. Other small coins, including low denomination copper coins, were also taken out of circulation and replaced by coins with lower intrinsic value.

10.2: CURRENCY ABUNDANCE AND FAMINE

The 1943 (Bengal) famine can indeed be described as a 'boom famine' related to powerful inflationary pressures initiated by public expenditure expansion.

AMARTYA SEN

As seen in the previous section and in particular Table 10.2, the increase in sterling assets held by the RBI led to a corresponding spurt in money supply—coins, notes as well as deposit accounts with banks. Convertibility of notes was restricted so that accumulation of metallic reserves did not pose any constraint. Production growth was sluggish and lagged behind the growth of money supply. It was the fall in velocity of circulation of money that, to an extent, dampened the impact on the domestic price level. Nonetheless, Table 10.3 reveals the significant increase in the domestic price level in the late 1930s and first half of the 1940s. Exchange rate stability is also shown for this period in the same table.

Inflation had not only been unleashed in India but had a differential impact on the population. Bigger landlords and landowners benefitted with the increase in agricultural prices. Small cultivators gained from the increase in prices but were partially hurt since they also depended on the market for some of their consumption needs. Their net position may therefore not have changed significantly. The landless labourer was the worst hit; not only were wage rates low but inflation directly and adversely impacted their daily real wage. Small traders suffered too, due to the want of supplies. Artisans like cobblers, blacksmiths, etc., were badly hit as expenditures on these commodities and products plummeted as budgets were unable to even cover basic food needs of the people.

TABLE 10.3: RUPEE-STERLING EXCHANGE RATE (PENCE, D) AND INDIAN PRICE LEVEL

Year	Exchange Rate	Wholesale Price Level
1938	$18^1/_8$	95
1939	$18^7/_{32}$	108
1940	$18^5/_6$	129
1941	$17^{31}/_{32}$	124
1942	$17^{31}/_{32}$	148
1943	$17^{31}/_{32}$	185
1944	$17^{31}/_{32}$	256
1945	$17^{31}/_{32}$	264
1946	$17^{31}/_{32}$	265

Source: D.V. Ramana, 'Determinants of Money Supply India, 1914–50', *Indian Economic Review*, vol. 3, no. 4, 1957, pp. 1–33, esp. p. 11.

Bengal was perhaps the worst affected by these conditions unfolding across the country. More than 3 million perished on account of widespread starvation and deprivation. Although famines were not a rare occurrence under British rule, this famine brought back memories of the Great Bengal Famine of 1770, which gripped the region just five years after the Company had acquired diwani. And just four years before their 182 year colonial rule ended (1765–1947), Bengal once again reeled under a massive famine. Several reasons have been studied as the possible cause of the famine and have in fact become a hotly debated[2] subject amongst economists and historians in recent times. It is beyond the scope of this book to delve into this debate; nonetheless, inflation was one important reason for people simply not being able to afford food. If (at least some of) the roots of the Bengal Famine of 1770 lay in *scarcity of coin*, it is interesting to note that in the Bengal Famine of 1943 (at least some of) the roots lay in the *abundance of notes*. Indian monetary history under colonial rule had come full circle.

The concerns over inflation triggered off concerted efforts by economists to pressurize the Reserve Bank of India to check it by curtailing government expenditure, increasing taxation, stimulating production and encouraging imports. It must be noted here that at this time that the quantity theory of money (QTM) provided the dominant rationale that 'inflationary expansion of currency creates a vicious spiral of rising prices' (Malhotra, 1949, p. 185). Interest rates as a policy measures to curb inflation was viewed with skepticism; while a rise in interest rates would bring in more savings, it would inflate the cost of borrowing and subsequently the price level as well as budget deficits (ibid., p. 167). But even savings did not show any positive shift with public investment in bonds (to mop up excess liquidity in the system) was not forthcoming; Sir Purshottamdas Thakurdas argued that this was more on account of political factors than economic and unless India secured a truly national government this problem would not be resolved. Easy money also meant a spurt in speculative activity, especially in commodities. Indian markets were not physically integrated. Wide divergence in prices encouraged hoarding, speculation, corruption and profiteering. At the same time, government intervention through price controls, rationing and control over supplies increased in order to stem the rapid rise of inflation. Even forward trading in grains, oilseeds, sugar, cotton and bullion was prohibited in 1943 by the Government of India. The roots of India's legacy of the controls and state intervention in the working of markets must be traced to the war years. At the same time, the war years once again revealed the challenge facing the rupee; to simultaneously maintain its purchasing power internally and a fixed exchange ratio vis-à-vis other international currencies.

NOTES

1. India signed a moratorium on the eve of Independence which precluded an immediate recourse to India's reserves held in the Bank of England.
2. The Amartya Sen versus Peter Bowbrick debate (and the many others who joined in) is more than an academic debate; it was charged with and full of personal insinuations. Nonetheless, it is also of fundamental importance in policy formulation on a subject of great importance—famines.

CHAPTER 11

The Bretton Woods Era

It has been our task to find a common measure, a common standard, a common rule acceptable to each and not irksome to any.

JOHN MAYNARD KEYNES

Although the World Wars and the Great Depression had led to disintegration of the gold standard and the fixed exchange rate regime, the world saw a return to the latter as a necessary condition to foster the healthy growth of international trade and commerce. Gold, which had till then provided an anchor for exchange rates, was no longer available in sufficient quantities in many countries at the end of the Second World War. How could these countries return to a gold standard without gold reserves and if they were unable to, how would they rebuild their economies? Imports and capital inflows were after all necessary for them to do so. While the external economy was critical to their future, the Great Depression and the wars had also turned the focus on the need for internal or domestic stability that not only included stable prices but also full employment (or at least low unemployment) and a high rate of GDP growth. The latter elements sometimes warranted inflationary monetary policies that had become a necessity for political survival. Finding a solution that would allow countries to pursue fixed exchange rates and independent monetary policies at the same time was the task-on-hand at the Bretton Woods Conference (United Nations Monetary and Financial Conference) in 1944.

At the end of the war, there were major political changes in the world; the center of world economic and political power had moved from Britain to the USA. Just three years after the war, India too got its independence from Britain; it was in this dynamic context that the rupee continued its tumultuous journey, facing new challenges in meeting the objectives of 'good' money.

11.1: A LAST ATTEMPT AT FIXED
EXCHANGE RATES

Life is not orderly. No matter how we try to make life so, right in the middle of it we die, lose a leg, fall in love, drop a jar of applesauce.

NATALIE GOLDBERG

Between 1870 and 1913 the world was on the international gold standard, which gave precedence to external stability of currencies over the internal stability of their economies. Balance of payments disequilibrium under exchange rates fixed to gold content of currencies meant that adjustments had to happen through inflation or deflation of the domestic economy; the hardship imposed by this process was increasingly becoming painful and politically unsustainable. The gold standard finally broke down during the First World War. Post-War there were attempts to go back to the gold standard but the advent of the Great Depression put those plans to rest. In fact, countries had now to consider a third element of stability in their policy objectives: full employment. The quantum of money in circulation had a bearing, and moreover conflicting, on these three important elements of macroeconomic stability— unemployment, the price level as well as exchange rates. The external sector was also now considered as subsidiary to stability in the domestic economy. As a step in this new-found direction, with no adherence to the convertibility of domestic currencies to gold, countries engaged in a series of competitive devaluations to boost exports and curtail imports. Quantitative restrictions on imports and capital controls were also viewed favourably as an effective policy to boost the domestic economy. And even if it is obvious that they would be no net gain when all countries engage in a similar devaluation, the existence of a first mover advantage could not be denied. Moreover, even if one country did not want to engage in such policies, it would be compelled to if others utilized them. In the end this was a lose-lose game; there were no winners in this game. International trade and capital flows lay in shambles without really having solved the internal problems of these countries. Just when the world was coming to realize the folly of such currency wars, the Second World War cast its dark clouds over the world. At the end of the Second World War the need for a new system was manifest; it had to combine the stability of fixed exchange rates but at the same time allow, to some degree at least, individual countries to pursue independent fiscal and monetary policies that were necessary to address their concerns over domestic stability in output (employment) and price level.

A solution to the problem was proposed at the Bretton Woods Conference. All supporters of the Bretton Woods system were essentially capitalist states that believed in the free market system, although with differing degrees of state involvement. France and India, for instance, preferred a greater degree of planning and of public sector participation in the economy (or what is called *dirigisme*) while the US wanted very limited state intervention (*laissez faire*). But overall it was accepted that the governments had a key role to play in economic stabilization (inflation and unemployment) and growth. Keynesianism had emerged as the dominant economic philosophy in the post-Great Depression era. Since the stability of the Indian rupee was inextricably linked to the international monetary system in existence, we will first outline the essence of the Bretton Woods system, how it worked, the policies that had to be pursued by member countries and finally, the reasons for its failure. The implications for the rupee will be discussed in subsequent sections of this chapter.

The essence of this planned system was to create a new international currency; recollect that ultimately currencies are nothing but a receipt, a token that a person (or a country for that matter) has given goods worth a certain value to another (person or country) and any person in the latter country (or in the member countries) would have to honour that claim at any point of time, now or in the future. Gold (and silver) had proven to be a satisfactory token due to its intrinsic value. Its general acceptability across the world was critical for international settlement of claims. Unfortunately there were three major problems with gold at the end of the Second World War; first, most countries had very little reserves left with them after making their purchases for the war. Second, almost 60 per cent of the world's $40 billion reserves were with the US. A return to an international gold standard was, therefore, not feasible. Finally, the total supply of gold was seen as inadequate to meet the needs of the growing volumes of trade and credit. Inadequate supplies and a possible increase in gold prices once again raised fears over deflation (fall in price of other goods relative to gold), recessions and even depressions. Several suggestions were made to institute such a new international currency; in the end it was decided that the US dollar would be the currency to settle international claims of all member states whose representatives would ratify an official agreement to the effect.

But why would countries 'trust' the dollar? Wouldn't the US behave like the villagers in Chapter 1 who ended up manufacturing too many nails? This was indeed a problem and to overcome it, the US had to agree to the convertibility of dollars to gold at a fixed rate, which at that time was set at $35/oz. There were other reasons too for the acceptance of dollars as reserve currency; the economic and political power of the US economy at the end of the War and its gold reserves were certainly important factors. Moreover, there was no other contender; Britain did not have sufficient gold reserves to commit convertibility of sterling to gold, communist Russia was no longer on the same side as the West. South Africa was the only other country with substantial gold reserves but was not considered a politically-correct option given its policy of apartheid and its limited economic power. The convertibility clause, however, meant that acceptance of the dollar as international currency was not just a 'privilege' to the US but also a responsibility to keep its own inflationary monetary policies under control as it would lead to a run on the dollar. Nonetheless, the US accepted the role of 'big brother', possibly under threat of its Cold War rival, the USSR, if it were to step back.

The US dollar was made convertible to gold at the rate of $35/oz while other currencies were pegged to the US dollar. In other words their par values were fixed in terms of a certain number of dollars. For instance, the British pound was set at $4.86 equal one pound, the German mark was set at $0.25 to the mark and the Japanese yen was set at 360 Japanese yen to the dollar. This, in effect, was a currency (dollar) exchange standard wherein the constraint on money supplies in the world economy was gold; since gold was limited, the issue of dollars would be limited and this in turn would put limits to the issue of national currencies (as they were convertible to dollars). Fiscal deficits would be held in check and wasteful expenses avoided. The result would be an emphasis on enhancing productivity and production with inflation kept in check. The Bretton Woods system would impose monetary discipline on the member countries as well as on the US whose banking sector and currency authority would be compelled to refrain from excessive credit expansion.

However, the world soon realized that if the rules of the game for balance of payments adjustment of a currency exchange standard (see Section 7.1) were to be strictly adhered then in effect it was as harsh as the gold standard. The only possible solution was then to allow more dollars to circulate. This was possible as long as all countries agreed to accept them in settlement of claims and countries with a surplus did not rush to convert their dollars into gold. In fact, Germany did just this; it had agreed to hold dollars and not to compel the US to convert dollars to gold. But for Germany to run surpluses there had to be others running deficits, perpetually. And this was actually possible simply because dollars were forthcoming. The deficit countries could run balance of payments deficits without having to deflate their domestic economies (as in the gold standard); in fact they could even follow an expansionary monetary policy at home. The question obviously arises as to what really were these strange rules of the game under the Bretton Woods system? It is impossible to answer this question by keeping the economics of Bretton Woods separate from the politics of that time.

With its rise as a superpower at the end of the War, the US was keen to dismantle the old trading blocs created by Britain and France during their colonial expansion. There was an urgent need for trade and investment opportunities to be opened up to their expanding companies given the imminent possibility that the US would not have been able to sustain its growth and general prosperity after the war with the sharp decline in European demand. This was accentuated by the growing pressure imposed by unions in the US for a wage increase on account of high domestic inflation rates. Strikes had become widespread and post-war recession loomed large. The Bretton Woods system was seen as a mutually beneficial system; the US would export capital (dollars) to Europe for rebuilding its war-torn economies, while Europe would use this capital to buy goods and services from US companies. In the immediate post-war period, the US had large trade surpluses; dollars were coming back to the US. But a system of giving perpetual state grants and loans in return for imports from US corporations was not an economically sustainable system. While the US continued to inject new dollars into the world economy by running large deficits on account of the arms race with the USSR, the war in Vietnam and 'supporting' friendly (non-communist) countries, its current account surpluses with Europe turned into deficits. By the 1950s with recovery well underway, European nations began protecting domestic industry, discouraging imports and deciding instead to maintain larger dollar reserves.[1] The US complied willingly. It continually ran trade deficits so that Europe could hold greater amount of reserves. This led to a proliferation of dollars in circulation or what was called as 'dollar glut'. In a proper currency exchange standard, Europe should have followed deflationary policies. Instead, as long as the dollars kept coming, the European countries freely pursued inflationary monetary policy at home by imposing strict controls over capital movement (the need for this condition will be explained later).

The Bretton Woods system was conceived from the basic need to provide international money that would be acceptable to all countries in settlement of claims with the condition that first, the exchange rate between this international money and domestic currency remains fixed and second, that there will be an elastic supply of this currency so that a balance of payments surplus or deficit does not strain international or domestic liquidity. These contradictory rules of the game were managed by an institution created by the Bretton Woods system for this specific purpose: the International Monetary Fund (IMF).[2] We will now explore the basic economics of the Bretton Woods system and the role of the IMF in managing it. This, as we will see later, had a direct bearing on the stability of currencies, including the rupee.

Individual nations held their reserves in gold and dollars and they could sell their dollars to the Federal Reserve in exchange for gold at the rate stated above; $35/oz. Exchange rates could move within +/- 1 per cent of the announced exchange rate but if it deviated to anything beyond this, intervention in foreign exchange markets through purchase or sale of dollars was necessary to bring back the rate within the band. Countries were also allowed up to +/-10 per cent in adjusting their parities in case of a 'fundamental disequilibrium'. These devaluations and revaluations were rare under the Bretton Woods system. In the entire Bretton Woods period Britain, for instance, devalued only twice, first in 1949 from $4.86 to $2.80 per pound sterling and then in 1967 to $2.40.

The basic operation of the Bretton Woods system can be understood using a simple demand-supply model. Suppose the foreign exchange market is in equilibrium at a rate of 1£ = $5 or 1$ = £0.2 as in Figure 11.1(a) and 11.1(b), which is from the US and the UK perspectives respectively. Now suppose the US undergoes a bout of inflation but the UK does not. The higher price level in the US would mean that people in the US would prefer British goods (at the going exchange rate of 1£ = $5). This would lead to

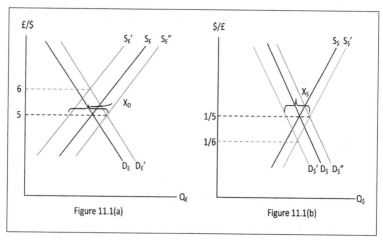

Figure 11.1: Intervention by the Central Bank in Foreign Exchange Markets to Maintain par rate

an increased demand for pounds or a shift in $D_£$ to $D_£'$ in Figure 11.1(a). At the same time, British nationals would not want to buy costlier US goods and so their demand for dollars falls which means that the supply of pounds reduces from $S_£$ to $S_£'$ in Figure 11.1(a). The new equilibrium with $D_£'$ and $S_£'$ would be at a rate of $6 = £1 in Figure 11.1(a), i.e. the dollar should have depreciated. Now this was not permissible under Bretton Woods. The rate had to be maintained at $5 = £1, but how? At this rate, given $D_£'$ and $S_£'$, there exists an excess demand for pounds in the market; the US Fed would therefore have to intervene in the market and sell pounds, effectively shifting $S_£'$ to $S_£''$. How would it get the pounds to sell? Three options were available; (i) from its own sterling reserves (ii) by selling gold and buying the pounds it needed (this would, however, put pressure on the pound to rise further before coming down – the net effect being rather ineffective) and (iii) by approaching the IMF to buy pounds at parity. If it procures the pounds and then sells sufficient quantities in the market, the rate would return to $5 = £1. If the US cannot procure adequate pounds due to a fundamental disequilibrium, then the IMF would permit a devaluation of the dollar to $6 = £1.

How do things look from the UK perspective? In Figure 11.1(b), the market for dollars is at equilibrium at an exchange rate of £0.2 = $1 (= 1/5) where $D_\$ = S_\$$. With inflation in the US, the demand for US imports and consequently the demand for dollars falls from $D_\$$ to $D_\$'$. At the same time, the increased demand for UK goods by US nationals would mean an increased demand for pounds and a corresponding increased supply of dollars from $S_\$$ to $S_\$'$. The pound therefore appreciates from £0.2 to £0.17 (= 1/6) per dollar. To maintain parity, the Bank of England must take action too; to restore the rate of £0.2 = $1, there is excess supply of dollars in the market. The bank must therefore step in to buy these dollars in exchange for pounds. The pounds are its own currency and it must therefore create this and supply it to the market. The dollars will accumulate in its reserves. Consequently the demand for dollars shifts from $D_\$'$ to $D_\$''$ and the rate of exchange returns to its par level.

Furthermore, selling pounds and buying dollars would have the effect of increasing inflation rates in UK and reducing inflation rates in the US; this was the self-correcting mechanism built into the Bretton Woods system. But just as in the case of the gold standard, playing by the rules of the game was not easy; neither would the US be willing to face a recession to maintain the exchange rate nor would Britain like to see higher inflation rates at home. Sterilization policies were then adopted to nullify the consequences of maintaining fixed exchange rates.

Countries with deficits in their trading account (like the US in our above example) would approach the IMF for purchase of dollars to sell in markets at the par rate. This was the key role of the IMF—providing easy dollars to deficit countries in exchange for domestic currency without having to going to the market (which would have propped up the dollar) or contracting their economies to control imports. A few words on the IMF could therefore be in place here. It was set up in 1945 but commenced its operations in 1947. Its objective was to ensure exchange rate stability, prevent currency wars and contribute to stability of international trade and investment thereby facilitating domestic growth and employment. It provided funds for short-term stabilization of exchange rates. Countries contributed a subscription quota from which each country could borrow 25 per cent of its contribution in one go. Countries could request more if it proved insufficient. However, each request was usually followed by the IMF imposing stricter rules and norms for the management of the domestic economy, especially control over budget deficits and domestic government spending. The IMF provided for purchase of foreign currencies by nations in exchange for gold and national currency. The 'purchases' (they were not called loans by the IMF) had typically to be paid back in foreign exchange within a period of 5 years. The currencies usually borrowed from the IMF (at that time) were the US dollar, UK sterling, Japanese yen, Deutsche marks and French francs. The US was of course the largest contributor to the IMF and controlled most votes. Politically speaking, the purpose of setting up the IMF was to ensure that the US Fed did not end up having complete power over the allocation of dollars.[3]

The problem with a fixed exchange rate regime is that a country loses its power over monetary policy unless it imposes control over capital flows. Suppose, for instance, a country has a sudden fall in exports. With fixed exchange rates, this would lead to a contraction of GDP. One way to offset this would be to lower domestic interest rates through an open market operation purchasing securities. However, when sellers obtain domestic currency for the sale of securities, they could convert it into foreign exchange at the fixed rate and buy foreign bonds with a higher yield. Capital flight would render domestic monetary policy impotent as foreign reserves are depleted. This is the famous *trilemma* in monetary economics; it is impossible to have fixed exchange rates, capital account mobility and an independent monetary policy at the same time. The remaining options would be fiscal policies or restrictions on imports to balance the trade account. These may, however, not be efficient solutions; fiscal policies are sluggish and tariff policies may incite others to retaliate. In the post-war period, countries often chose to have an independent monetary policy to maintain full employment and instead enforced controls over capital flows. The emergence of international banking consortia since 1964, however, led to easier capital movement between countries and provided an opportunity for almost zero risk speculative gains that ultimately made it impossible for governments to sustain a fixed exchange rate regime.

Going back to our example in Figure 11.1, suppose the US obtained a sterling loan from the IMF, which could then be sold in the market. The dollar could then be maintained at the par rate of £1 = $5. If for some reason, the IMF thought it was a fundamental disequilibrium situation and the dollar had to be devalued then the dollar would depreciate to £1 = $6. A speculator could see a great opportunity here; if she bought £1 million with $5 million today in the foreign exchange market it could be sold for an additional million tomorrow if the dollar were to depreciate. If not, she gets her $5 million back. In fact, when the speculator bought pounds it would actually put pressure on the pound to appreciate so that the US would have to sell more and more pounds in the market to keep the dollar at its par rate. For this it must take recourse to larger and larger purchases of pounds from the IMF, inevitably resulting in a devaluation of the dollar. If speculators could hammer the dollar sufficiently, it results in a self-fulfilling prophecy for speculators, and moreover one without risk. This was a very dangerous situation indeed for currencies that came under attack of speculators.

The fall of the Bretton Woods system was inevitable given that the gold backing of the dollar slowly dwindled. If countries had approached the Federal Reserve for conversion of dollars to gold they would have to go back empty handed as there was simply no gold available. And as this fear grew, it was only a matter of time before some country would want to rush to the Fed to be the first in line. But for several years countries had held on to the dollar as the reserve currency, simply holding dollars with the hope of future consumption.[4] At the same time, countries really did not want to question their faith in dollars as long as it was available in plenty and kept the wheels of their economies circulating. Moreover, under Bretton Woods system, gold convertibility was optional, not mandatory. Countries could instead hold dollar reserves, which even earned interest. But the possibility to convert still existed.

The decision to switch to gold depended on the market price of gold on the London exchange, called the 'morning gold fix'. If the market price exceeded the rate of $35/oz. then governments would exchange their dollars for gold with the Fed and then sell the gold on the London exchange for even more dollars. A truly paradoxical situation was emerging; while US trade deficits were required to keep the system rolling with liquidity, the greater the deficits the greater was the danger of US's inability to convert dollars to gold and the consequent depreciation of the dollar. It was therefore agreed upon to create a 'London Gold Pool' to offset any spikes in the price of gold. Gold could be sold in the London market from the pool to keep prices at near about the dollar-gold rate. But this was not sufficient to stem the tide. In 1967 there was an attack on the pound that effectively also led to an attack on the dollar and on US gold; with £1 you could get $4.86 or 0.139 oz. of gold.

Once the pound depreciated, the same amount of gold would yield more pounds. The British government was ultimately compelled to devaluing the pound to £1 = $2.80 so that 0.139 oz. of gold which was earlier worth £1 now gave back £1.7375. The incentive to convert pounds into gold reduced with the devaluation.

The fear of a run on the dollar prompted the IMF to create a new international reserve asset, Special Drawing Rights or SDR by which it was hoped that nations would be prevented from buying pegged gold and selling it in the market. While the US was preserving the world capitalist system by spending heavily on defense and military exports, other countries were in fact, purchasing American defense policy by taking a loss of holding dollars instead of converting to gold. Europe also began looking at the dollar with envy; after all the US was able to extract 'world seigniorage' from the dollar which had become the international reserve currency. As Europe regained its lost position, US hegemony was questioned and there was no better way of doing this than undermining the dollar. However, there were costs to doing this. A run on the dollar would have meant reverting gold but then its limited availability may have been too severe; difficulty to obtain dollars may have kept inflation in check (both in the US and internationally) but high gold prices would have meant the return of deflation, currency shortages and slow growth of the domestic economy.

These costs of a run on the dollar were, however, insufficient to ward off the danger of it happening. By 1970 the system was on tenterhooks. The gold backing of dollars had fallen to just 22 per cent (US gold reserves had fallen from $25 billion in 1945 to around $10 billion in 1970) and capital flight began from the dollar to other currencies. Controls were imposed to check capital movements but with little effect. West Germany and Japan could have revalued their currencies to correct the surpluses in their balance of payments but they had no intention to do so even if it meant accumulating dollars. The US was experiencing high inflation and as the government felt that the market price of gold was inching above the $35/oz. level, a rush to convert dollars into gold was becoming increasingly imminent. In 1971, US President

Richard Nixon took the world by surprise; in a single stroke he abolished convertibility of dollars to gold. This was the end of the Bretton Woods era and fixed exchange rate regimes.

The learnings from the Bretton Woods system are many. The rationale for fixed exchange rates may be sound; it reduces risk and uncertainty in international trade and investment flows and pegging exchange to a low inflation country would minimize domestic inflation by encouraging discipline in domestic monetary policy. Nonetheless, a fixed exchange rate regime is by itself not a panacea for all macroeconomic problems; in fact, it is only when each country's budget deficits are under control, and inflation is under check, that a fixed exchange rate regime will work. If this is not so inflation will cause balance of payments disequilibrium that will need adjustment sooner or later. But the Bretton Woods system attempted to circumvent the rules imposed on the Gold Standard; it was a fixed exchange rate system with flexible rules instead of a fixed exchange rate regime with rigid (fixed) rules. By injecting the system with a virtually unlimited quantum of international currency (dollars) it allowed governments to pursue inflationary monetary policies in spite of running balance of payments deficits. Countries with balance of payments surpluses would also pursue policies that encouraged even greater exports while restricting imports (through trade qualitative and quantitative trade barriers) and severe penalties on capital movement. Par values were arbitrarily set by the IMF so that the balance of payments was perpetually in a state of disequilibrium. Dollars were always available from the IMF to fund domestic inflationary policies. The worst case scenario was a devaluation of the currency. While the world enjoyed the benefits of easy international liquidity, the system was slowly but definitely being undermined by its own logic; it depended on just one country for convertibility to gold. In the end, there was very little gold available (whose quantity had remained more or less constant) to back the quantum of dollars in circulation. With a run on the dollar becoming closer to certainty, the US reneged from its promise to exchange dollars for gold. Another attempt at an international fixed exchange rate regime had reached its logical end.

11.2: THE INDIAN RUPEE UNDER
BRETTON WOODS

While it is not true to say that if we take care of our balance of payments we
take care of the economy, it is certainly right to assert that if we take care of the
economy, the balance of payments will take care of itself.

I.G. PATEL

India's first major post-Independence monetary crisis happened
almost two decades after Independence, in the year 1966, when
the rupee had to be devalued by almost 50 per cent against the
dollar. This crisis is a classic case of the issue repeatedly stressed as
to the dangers of a fixed exchange rate regime without simultaneous domestic monetary discipline; it is inevitable that at some
point of time, something must give way. Before we move on to the
1966 crisis, we draw attention to a rather minor but similar event
that happened in 1949: the devaluation of the pound.

In September 1949, with the agreement of the International
Monetary Fund, Britain decided to devalue the pound sterling
from $4.86/£ to $2.80/£, a fall by some 30 per cent. India had a
decision to make; it would either continue with parity to the dollar
(or revalue in terms of the pound), further devalue the rupee to
1s.4d. (instead of 1s.6d.) or maintain parity with the pound and
let the rupee be devalued vis-à-vis other international currencies
including the dollar. Given that many others in the sterling bloc
had already decided to follow the third option, for India to follow
the first option would have been dangerous. The second option of
further devaluation the rupee would have raised the price of imports and given the inelastic demand for imports, this could have
adversely affected inflation rates. The most satisfactory choice was
to allow the rupee to depreciate along with the pound. A negative
fallout of this decision was that sterling balances held in London
(during the war) lost 30 per cent of their value in terms of the
dollar.

Apart from this event, for much of the early post-Independence
period, the rupee was a stable currency with even some calls for a
revaluation of the rupee. While the rupee had been accepted as

legal tender in India, it was obviously not acceptable as a means of international settlements. Foreign exchange was therefore required in order to settle international claims on India. A country's (like India) major sources of obtaining this foreign exchange comes from: (i) surpluses in the balance of trade and current account transactions, (ii) capital inflows either on account foreign direct investment or institutional investment, (iii) loans (also on the capital account of the balance of payments), including short-term and long-term debt (iv) borrowings from the IMF, and (v) drawing down on reserves of gold and/or of foreign exchange.

When demand for foreign exchange is steadily increasing (the demand curve for foreign exchange is shifting out) but supply is dwindling (supply curve for foreign exchange is shifting inwards), it is inevitable that an equilibrium can only be achieved through either (i) letting the domestic currency depreciate, (ii) shifting out the supply curve through the sources mentioned above and/or, (iii) forcing the demand curve to shift inwards by imposing strict control on foreign imports and/or export of goods and, in particular, capital. Here the word 'strict' may be a euphemism; a more accurate description might include words like brutal or oppressive. By definition, since (ii) becomes increasingly difficult at a time of crisis, we are left with only two options; (i) and/or (iii). This was precisely the situation that India confronted in the mid-1960s. However, when additional curbs over imports of goods and export of capital became increasingly difficult, it had to let the rupee depreciate. This process of adjustment is illustrated in Figure 11.2.

The roots of the 1966 crisis can be traced to the inability of the Government of India to curb its burgeoning budget deficits.[5] The deficits may have been unavoidable; first, to fund the war against Pakistan in 1965 and second, to mitigate the effects of the drought of 1965. With rising inflation, India's balance of trade surpluses turned negative that was sustained only through large receipts of foreign aid. The inability to raise resources domestically or from foreign sources to fund the deficits made it increasingly becoming dependent on aid. Meanwhile, the U.S. was pressurizing India to devalue the rupee; aid for devaluation was their clear motto. The World Bank too joined the chorus and obviously supported the

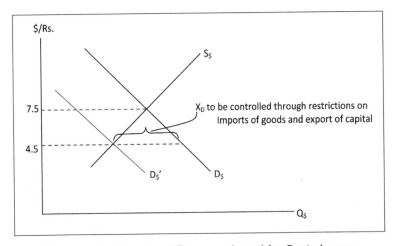

Figure 11.2: Overvalued Rupee and need for Controls over Imports of Goods and Export of Capital

US Government's stand. The crisis began building up in April–May 1965 when reserves dipped to an all time low of just £7 million. When inflows were reduced to a trickle, speculative forces came into play. Illegal capital outflows and withholding of foreign exchange outside India until devaluation contracted supply further. As with many other instances of financial speculation, devaluation became a self-fulfilling prophecy. India was ultimately left with no choice but to devalue the rupee. On 5 June 1966, the rupee was devalued from Rs. 4.76/$ to Rs. 7.50/$, i.e. by 57 per cent. A rupee was equal to 0.118489 grams of gold. The sterling-rupee rate was set at Rs. 18 to the pound. Domestic stability of the rupee was also dismal; between 1955 and 1965, the rupee had lost 80 per cent of its value internally. In 1965–6, inflation rate was 12 per cent and increased to 15 per cent in the following year. Table 11.1 captures the macroeconomic situation as it evolved in the first two decades after Independence. The effect of the devaluation can be seen after 1968 when exports begin to increase while imports fell significantly.

India had adopted a policy of overvaluing the rupee to keep imports, especially of capital goods cheap and meet the targets of the Five Year Plans. Exports from India were limited by its indus-

TABLE 11.1: KEY MACROECONOMICS VARIABLES IN THE POST-INDEPENDENCE PERIOD

(in crores of rupees)

Year	Exports	Imports	Trade Deficit	Foreign Aid	MI growth Rate (%)	M2 Growth Rate (%)	WPI
1950	947	1,025	78	–	–	–	–
1951	1,106	1,379	273	102	–	–	–
1952	873	1,002	129	72	–	–	–
1953	813	855	42	29	–	–	–
1954	918	998	80	27	–	–	–
1955	922	1,024	102	67	–	–	–
1956	977	1,423	446	178	–	–	–
1957	1,001	1,633	632	417	–	–	–
1958	903	1,424	521	537	–	–	–
1959	1,008	1,515	507	465	–	–	–
1960	997	1,768	771	617	–	–	–
1961	1,033	1,718	685	396	3.26	1.85	–
1962	1,069	1,783	714	512	8.81	9.86	–
1963	1,241	1,927	686	643	9.68	8.81	100
1964	1,282	2,126	844	791	8.77	10.21	–
1965	1,264	2,194	930	819	8.2	10.23	119.5
1966	1,153	2,078	925	–	7.32	11.22	133.8
1967	1,193	2,008	815	863	6.46	9.22	153.9
1968	1,354	1,909	555	528	8.36	10.69	–
1969	1,409	1,567	158	444	11.36	13.16	–
1970	1,524	1,624	100	340	11.84	13.25	166

Source: Devika Johri and Mark Miller (nd), *Devaluation of the Rupee: Tale of Two Years*, 1966 and 1991, Centre for Civil Society, ccsindia.org/ ‫... ا ا‬... ‪Eed....w/ medine/wp0028.pdf‬, p. 86; WPI data from Pranab Sen, 'Devaluation in India: A Reappraisal', *Economic and Political*

trial capability and only tea, jute and cotton were competitive in the world market. However, an overvalued rupee meant that all imports were cheap. With limited foreign exchange reserves, it became necessary to ration the available supply. This called for a policy of what T.N. Srinivasan referred to as '*de facto* devaluation'— the imposing of quantitative restrictions and physical controls over imports. Import licenses were issued only for restricted purposes. There were even calls to nationalize the entire import and export trade of India. The overvalued rupee had another adverse effect; it made exports uncompetitive internationally. To overcome this impact on exports, subsidies were meted out liberally. These policies were stretched to their limit; when they could be taken no further the external price of the rupee had to be cropped.

Devaluation, however, was not an unequivocal panacea for India's problems. Demand for Indian exports was inelastic, imports too were inelastic, and devaluation also meant an increase in the monetary cost of external debt. With tighter control needed over government expenditure, the Five Year Plans were suspended for a period of three years following devaluation. The 1966 devaluation was also a turning point in India's political history; the backlash not only led to a split in the Congress Party but also led Prime Minister Indira Gandhi to lose faith in expert advisors and to rely on her own intuition for economic decisions. On her return to power, a number of private banks in India were nationalized which gave the state greater control over savings and thereby to the flow of credit.

The 1966 episode had taught India one critical lesson. While the need for increased amount of currency in circulation, for credit and for state spending was obvious, there were limits on how much money supply could be increased. An excessive amount of money in circulation would not only lead to an accelerating inflation that destabilized the internal value of the currency but also developed into a foreign exchange crisis wherein the rupee was compelled to lose value vis-à-vis other international currencies. The only remaining option of controlling imports and export of capital beyond a point proved destructive to the system, breeding inefficiencies and corruption that had severe long-term consequences on productivity and incentive structure in a market economy.

Some quotes[6] from the Governors of the Reserve Bank of India succinctly point out the need for getting the quantum of money supply right;

A fundamental question in any developing economy is the degree to which stability is maintained during the development process. (Governor H.V.R. Iyengar, August 1959)

It (deficit financing) is certainly an unmitigated, though very necessary, evil during war time, when it is utilised for financing defence expenditure, which, of course, must necessarily be unproductive. Even in peace time, it should be condemned as a means of raising money for unproductive schemes. It can, however, be justified in the case of schemes which are productive within a short period. (Governor B. Rama Rau, April 1960)

Monetary policy has to be used in such a way that it brings about conditions in which funds required for the growth of the economy are available to the various sectors in the right magnitude and composition and at the right time. (Governor P.C. Bhattacharyya, February 1966)

But a remark made by Governor Manmohan Singh (later the Prime Minister of India) clearly articulated the need for stability in the purchasing power of the domestic currency; 'Economic policies must have a strong systematic bias in favour of minimizing inflationary pressure. By now, there is a convincing amount of evidence that inflation distorts Plan priorities, can play havoc with the balance of payments and brings about highly arbitrary shifts in income distributions leading to disruptive social tensions' (November 1982).

This crisis once again illustrates the rupee's journey in search for stability in value, both internally (purchasing power) and externally (exchange rate). That, as we have come to understand, depends on getting one thing right—how much currency and credit should be in circulation, neither too much (so as to cause inflation) nor too little (so as to lead to deflation). But the challenge has become even greater today; it is not the quantum of money in circulation alone that influences the rate of inflation. In a world where the velocity of circulation of money (V) cannot be simply assumed as constant, it becomes all the more difficult in terms of policy to target MV (in equation 1.1) and consequently the price level, P. Furthermore, in a dynamic world, the quantum of currency and credit requirements are in a state of continuous flux. Economists and central bankers are grappling to this day to find an answer to the problem.

NOTES

1. Accumulation of dollar reserves beyond a point must not be seen as a safety net for imports of essential goods. Instead, reserves are accumulated as a policy to maintain domestic currency at an undervalued rate by buying dollars in the market. China's reserves of $2 trillion are a consequence of its policy to undervalue the yuan vis-à-vis the dollar. More on this has been discussed in the Epilogue.
2. It might be of interest to note that the International Bank for Reconstruction and Development (later World Bank) was also created under the aegis of the Bretton Woods system. However, from a monetary standpoint it was the IMF that is of greater relevance to us.
3. For a detailed history of the International Monetary Fund, see James (1996).
4. Countries may not even care too much about future consumption. If the main objective of reserves is to maintain home currencies at a depreciated level to increase exports and sustain high growth rates then in some sense the purpose of these reserves is met there and then. Future consumption and access to world resources are added benefits of holding dollar reserves.
5. This is not dissimilar to the crisis of 2013, which we discuss in the Epilogue.
6. From N. Jadhav (nd).

PART III
EPILOGUE, POST-1971

Epilogue

I am afraid this country of ours, great and blessed as it is, enjoys no such divine dispensation of immunity from monetary laws—which are after all, only reasonable approximations to the laws of supply and demand which at least business men should not belittle or deride.

I.G. Patel

The end of the Bretton Woods era saw the acceleration in global capital flows and dismantling of capital controls. With this, a fixed exchange rate regime was no longer a viable option. With all efforts to find a new system of multilateral monetary management having failed, the world was clearly moving towards a floating exchange rate regime by 1973. Today, in the advanced economies, although governments do intervene in foreign exchange markets, it is an exception rather than rule. Such a freely floating exchange rate regime has, however, brought with it a need for hedging risks against exchange rate fluctuations. In these financial markets where hedging products are offered, currency markets for buying and selling of foreign exchange as well as markets for real goods and services are increasingly interlocked. The proliferation of hedging instruments has also brought with it the privatization of risk, an explosion of financial innovations and the increasing financialization of the economy. Global financial flows have at the same time undermined the close relationship which domestic money supply had on price level and output so that it (money supply) has now been abandoned as an instrument of monetary policy and replaced by interest rates in the direct targeting of inflation as the primary (if not sole) and final objective of monetary policy.

The rupee, however, did not strictly follow the course of the international monetary system. In 1971 it was still pegged to the sterling pound. This was modified in 1975 when the rupee was pegged to a basket of currencies rather than the sterling, which was seen as enhancing the stability of the rupee. The basket and the weights assigned to each currency was left to the discretion of the RBI and not announced publicly. The rupee-dollar exchange rates remained below the Rs. 10 to the dollar mark until 1982–3 and below the Rs. 20 level until 1990–1. It was only in 1993 that India moved on to a market-determined exchange rate system, although with significant interventions by the RBI. Between then and now, the rupee has depreciated from Rs. 20 to Rs. 60 to the dollar. In fact it is the crisis in the external value of the rupee (July 2013) that prompted me to write this epilogue that briefly explores the post-1971 period but particularly the current challenges faced in preventing its depreciation.

During the period 1971 to 1991, India's monetary policy was directed towards realizing its development objectives through the intermediate target of priority sector lending. The RBI supported the government's efforts at mobilizing resources for the public sector. This was achieved through measures aimed at encouraging savings but then ensuring that the funds with banks were directed towards meeting the government's needs. The instruments or operating procedures used included interest rate regulations (bank rate was increased from 6 per cent in 1971 to 12 per cent in 1991) and enhancing the statutory legal requirements (from 25 per cent to 38.5 per cent by 1990), cash reserve ratio (raised from 5 per cent in 1973 to 15 per cent in 1989) and priority sector lending policies. General credit policy controlledthe flow of credit to non-priority sectors. The outcome of these policies were sluggish growth in real GDP along with high inflation rates, especially during the oil shocks in the 1970s when it soared to 25 per cent in 1974–5 and then fell moderately to about 15 per cent in 1980–1.

1991 was truly a landmark year in India's post-Independence economic history; when the country descended into another balance of payments crisis, the move to liberalization and globalization had ultimately to be accepted by the Indian government. India's slow growth and its inability to overcome poverty 40 years after gaining freedom clearly indicated that the policies adopted thus far had not been entirely satisfactory. The phenomenal growth of China and the collapse of socialist and communist economies also pushed India on to this new path. But this transition has in fact made the search for a 'perfect money' even more arduous. In a market system that accepts free (or even limited) capital mobility, exchange rate flexibility and independent monetary policy, the challenges of maintaining the stability of the rupee have become even greater. In this Epilogue, I will present a simple model of open economy macroeconomics that helps us understand (i) the problem of persistent budget deficits and its implications on the stability of the rupee and (ii) implications of volatile capital flows on domestic monetary and economic stability. The latter has recently been accentuated by the policy announcements of Ben Bernanke, Chairman of the U.S. Federal Reserve pertaining to the withdrawal of quantitative easing (QE) and the availability of 'easy money' that had found its way into global markets including India.

This simple model expands on the notion derived from the circular flow of income that we developed in Figure 7.10.[1] For macroeconomic equilibrium we must have:

Leakages = Injections $\qquad$ ... (E.1)

In other words, leakages from the circular flow of income must be matched by injections so that macroeconomic equilibrium in domestic income and output can be achieved.

$$S + T + M = I + G + X \qquad ... (E.2)$$

Where S = savings; T = tax; M = imports, I = investment; G = government expenditure, X = exports.

From equation (2), we get the twin deficit equation,

$$(S - I) + (T - G) = (X - M) \qquad ... (E.3)$$

The twin deficit equation states that net domestic private savings $(S - I)$ plus net government savings $(T - G)$ must be equal to the net balance on current account $(X - M)$.

Consider a situation where, $S = I$ but $G > T$, then

$$[(S - I) + (T - G)] < 0$$

From E. 3 we must have,

$$(X - M) < 0$$

In an economy like India where budgetary deficits have been persistently growing, a current account deficit in the balance of payments becomes inevitable. But what does this deficit in the current account signify? To understand this, we turn to the Balance of Payments (BoP) accounting identity.

The basic BoP has a current account and a capital account, with the sum of balances in the two accounts being equal but with the opposite sign. A current account deficit must therefore be matched by an equal surplus in the capital account. Restricting transactions on the current account to X and M, and on the capital account to F (foreign direct investment), H (portfolio or financial institutional investment – FII – or hot money), L (lending) and R (reserves), we know that:

$$(X - M) = K_O = (+/-) R (+/-) F (+/-) H (+/-) L \qquad \ldots (E.4)$$

where $+ K_O$ is defined as net capital outflow and $- K_O$ is a net capital inflow. $(+/-)$ R denotes *increase/decrease* in foreign currency reserves (equivalent to an outflow/inflow into the capital account), $(+/-)$ F and $(+/-)$ H are foreign direct and portfolio capital outflows/inflows respectively, and $(+/-)$ L is net lending/borrowing. While we cannot specify the sign of each component, we can clearly see from equation E.4 that the sum of R, F, H and L must be negative if there exists a current account deficit, i.e. when $(X - M) < 0$.

A situation where $(X - M) < 0$ implies that this deficit must be matched by a net capital inflow, i.e. $K_O < 0$. In other words, a deficit of savings in the domestic economy (private plus government) when $(X - M)$ is < 0 has to be counterbalanced by a net capital inflow into the country. India, as we know, faces such a situation of $(X - M) < 0$ so that K_O must be negative. To study the impact of current account deficits on the economy suppose in Equation E.3 above let us begin with S = I and T = G so that the current account is in balance. Now if G increases, then $T - G < 0$ so that a current account deficit must emerge, all else remaining constant. This happens because as G increases, the country's output increases and with it M increases. The deficit problem could be solved if domestic savings (S) can be enhanced not merely from higher income levels but also through specific incentives and schemes. Another policy possibility that can bring about current account balance even with higher government spending is to reduce the level of unproductive investment in the economy which would mean a larger surplus in private savings that would help fund the government expenditure; this would keep the current account deficit in check given that the need for foreign capital inflows is no longer required. But with the government spending burgeoning, this is unlikely. Moreover, we must understand that government expenditure leads to multiple credit expansion through the banking system. On the contrary, a lack of adequate liquidity in the system can have adverse impacts on the ability of the country to realize its full economic potential and growth of output.

Now the current account deficit means a net inflow of capital (or $K_O < 0$) that actually funds the budget deficit. As long these inflows from abroad can be sustained the government can continue to run budget deficits. But there are some critical issues that need to be confronted if a country has to depend on such net capital inflows from abroad. Foreign direct investment (FDI) inflows are obviously the most preferred option as their outflows are unlikely and limited. As long as they are buoyant there will be no immediate problem in funding the current account deficit. However, in a situation when FDI inflows suddenly dip either on account of the internal situation (political uncertainty, high inflation, economic policies, etc.) and/or on account of the external conditions (higher interest rates in the US and Europe, political and economic uncertainties internationally, etc.) the country would have to rely either on increased FII inflows, higher borrowings and/or utilizing reserves. Each of these will have economic and political repercussions. If these alternatives too are not preferred then the only option left is to let the country's currency depreciate. When this happens, exports increase and imports fall so that the current account will once again be balanced. This would lead to an increase in income and consequently taxes so that G = T. Also, as income increases, savings (S) should increase so that for a given I, $S - I > 0$ so that equilibrium will be restored;

$$(S - I) + (T - G) = (X - M) \qquad \dots (E.5)$$

A problem, however, arises when demand for exports and for imports are inelastic. In such a situation a massive depreciation of the rupee might be necessary so that current account balance is restored. Moreover if budgetary deficits continue with government expenditure unabated, all else constant, depreciation of the domestic currency will continue. If F and H slow down, reserves could fall to dangerous levels. This is a crisis situation and drastic measures, including emergency borrowing from the IMF or pledging gold becomes necessary. India was able to sustain large budgetary and current account deficits through significant FII inflows. However, in May 2013 when Ben Bernanke announced the possible end to quantitative easing, the possible contraction in available liquidity in the US immediately meant the return of scarce capital back to the US. Foreign institutional investors reacted and began exiting from emerging economies including India. The immediate repercussion of this outflow meant that India would not be able to fund its current account deficit; its reserves would begin depleting and it would have to borrow in international capital markets. But even before this could happen, the rupee began to depreciate sharply. With depreciation going into free fall because of inelastic exports and imports, the only recourse to the central bank was to reduce the availability of rupees in the market or force a scarcity of rupees in the market. Open market operations were resorted to mop up excess liquidity (of rupees). This contraction in domestic liquidity obviously impacted growth rate of the real economy. In effect then, in trying to maintain stable or 'fixed' exchange rates, the RBI has had to make rupees scarce even if it means deflating the domestic economy so that current account balance could be restored. As we have seen throughout Part II of this book, this has been the general course of Indian monetary history.

I recently came across a quote by Stephen Hawking in which he proclaims that 'there are grounds for cautious optimism that we (physicists) may now be near the end of the search for the ultimate laws of nature'. If only economists and central bankers could say the same about money! Our exploration of the history of the rupee has revealed that the search for money which is stable in terms of purchasing power (internally) and exchange rate (externally) has been relentless. The multiplicity of monetary and credit instruments has no doubt made exchange easier and smoother across space and time, allowing a greater division of labour and specialization and improving standards of living; these have, however, made it even more difficult for the government and the central bank to stabilize the purchasing power of money by exerting control over the quantum of money in circulation. The close relationship which was once observed between money supply and inflation and output no longer seemed to hold post-1980s when international capital mobility was unshackled. Central banks have therefore taken to inflation targeting using interest rates as their primary instrument. But this has not solved the problem. India, for instance, continues to grapple with close to double digit inflation even as growth has slowed down and the burgeoning current account deficit has forced depreciation in the rupee. Some would perhaps see the single most important cause of this predicament to be excessive government spending or, in other words, large budget deficits. But in a country which needs massive doses of capital infusion to put it on a higher growth trajectory and meet the aspirations of its teeming millions, there is no alternative but for greater state involvement in directing the country's economic story. The government and the central bank will therefore continue to walk a tightrope using instruments of fiscal and monetary policy to balance their objectives of the rupee's internal and external stability along with high and sustainable growth of the economy.

> *Til forever, on it goes*
> *Through the circle, fast and slow,*
> *I know; It can't stop, I wonder.*
> Have you ever seen the rain?
> Credence Clearwater Revival

NOTE

1. Also see Appendix 2 for a brief introduction to the circular flow model and macroeconomic equilibrium.

APPENDIX 1

Exchange Rate Determination and Fluctuations in Foreign Exchange Markets

FOREIGN CURRENCY SUPPLY AND DEMAND

The economic forces that determine foreign exchange rates are rooted in supply and demand, both of which are determined mainly by foreign trade activity.

Consider India as the home country (Rs.) and USA as the foreign country ($). What gives rise to the supply of foreign exchange or $?

- Export of goods and services from India to USA
- US investment or capital inflows to India
- Foreign borrowings being remitted to India

What gives rise to the demand for $?

- Import of goods and services from USA to India
- Indian investment or capital outflow to USA
- Foreign lending from India

Given that these are the factors that affect demand and supply, we now explain the reason for a downward sloping demand curve for $. We start from a rate of Rs. 65 = $1. If the exchange rate moves to Rs. 60 = $1 or the rupee appreciates, then imports from the US become cheaper and if imports are elastic[1], the demand for $ increase along $D_\$$. However, when the rupee appreciates, the US demand for Indian exports will decline and given that US demand for Indian exports are elastic, the supply of $ will decline; we move long $S\$$.

Let us understand how exchange rates are determined in a floating exchange rate system. What happens when the exchange rate is Rs. 60 = $1. In Figure A.1, there is an excess demand for $ which will push up the price of $ or in other words, the rupee will depreciate till we reach Rs. 65 = $1.

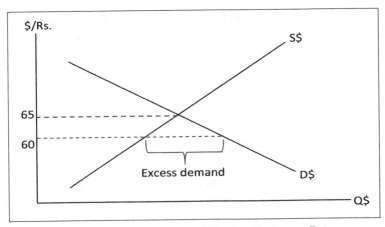

Figure A1.1: Determination of Foreign Exchange Rates

In a foreign exchange market, these rates are in a state of perpetual fluctuation. At the rate of Rs. 65 = $1, you go to the bank to buy dollars because you are visiting the US. Then there is small shift in the demand for $ curve (at a rate of Rs. 65, there is an *increase in the demand for dollars*), which means the equilibrium rate of the rupee will depreciate (say) to Rs. 66. Now at the same time, a person might go to a bank in New York to buy rupees for her visit to India. In that case there will be a shift in the supply curve of $ (she would have to supply

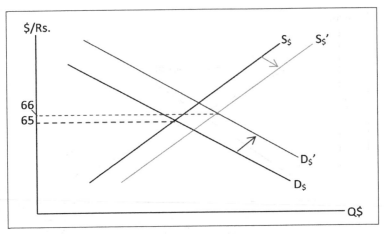

Figure A1.2: Fluctuations in the Foreign Exchange Rates

dollars and exchange them for rupees in order to spend in India). This pulls the rupee back towards Rs. 65 = $1. At every moment of time there will be shifts in demand and supply of dollars vis-à-vis rupees in the forex market. This gives rise to fluctuations in the exchange rate.

In Figure A1.3 we show what happens under a fixed exchange rate system. Suppose the equilibrium exchange rate is Rs. 65 = $1, but the government wants to keep it at Rs. 67 = $1 (to encourage exports). At Rs. 67 = $1, there is an excess supply of $. The RBI would have to buy $2b @ Rs. 65 = $1. If they do not buy dollars, the exchange rate will fall to Rs. 65 = $1.

Business news reporters often employ colorful turns of phrase to describe economic events. When a report states that the 'rupee rallied' in a day's trading, it means that the rupee strengthened against most currencies. When a reporter says there was a 'sell off' of the rupee or that the rupee 'was attacked,' it means that the dollar weakened against most currencies. In this situation, the rupee is said to have depreciated against other currencies. Other ways of stating this is to say that the rupee lost value, lost ground, or weakened against the dollar. This sounds worse than it is. All it means is that India may have demanded more imports from the US. But this kind of language is used for a simple reason: the rupee buys less dollars than it used to in India—after the increase it takes (say) Rs. 67 to buy a dollar while it would have taken only Rs. 65 earlier.

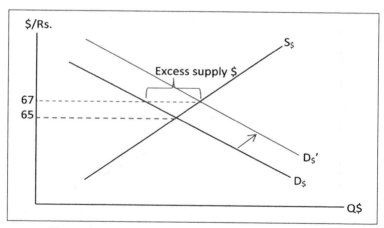

Figure A1.3: Pegging the Exchange Rate; Intervention by Buying Dollars

APPENDIX 2

Circular Flow of Output and Income

The circular flow model is a simplified view of a market economy. It is an approach towards trying to make sense of the market system. The circular flow model divides the market system into a few, highly aggregated sectors which are connected by a few, highly aggregated markets.

Let us begin with a simple economy with only households and firms. The dotted line shows 'physical' flows of factors of production (labour, capital, land and entrepreneurship) from households to firms. In return for (1), funds flow from firms to households through factor markets in the form of wages, interest, rent and profits respectively as returns to factors of production. We now need to define the concept of macroeconomic equilibrium; it is the level of income and value of output that can be maintained over a period of time, without any expansion or contraction. In our simple economy, if factors to production receive Rs. 100 as aggregate income in exchange for providing firms with these factors, then in order for the level of income to remain at Rs. 100 in the next period, households must purchase goods worth Rs. 100 from firms. In other words their consumption expenditure in each period of time C_i must be equal to the level of income (Y_i). Only then can Rs.100 flow back to firms and back to households—in perpetual succession. The concept of circular flow and macroeconomic equilibrium is illustrated in Figure A2.1.

Suppose, however, a leakage from the circular flow in the form of hoardings or savings by households exists. Households do not wish to consume their entire income, they decide to save or hoard 10 per cent of their income. When firms pay out Rs. 100 in period 1, households spend only Rs. 90 on consumption expenditures and save 10 per cent or Rs. 10. In period 2, firms will have only Rs. 90 to pay out to households, who now save 10 per cent or Rs. 9. Firms, in period 3, now have only Rs. 81 to pay out to households. We are now faced with

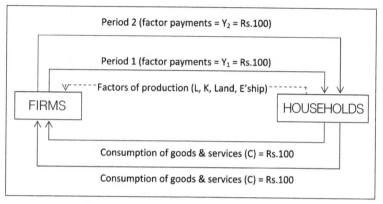

Figure A2.1: Macroeconomic Equilibrium

a situation of macroeconomic disequilibrium with falling aggregate income and output.

For macroeconomic equilibrium to be restored we need an injection into the system that counterbalances the leakage (hoarding or savings). This injection into the system is 'investment' spending by firms. Firms may wish to purchase goods as investment from other firms which then give firms the possibility to put back Rs. 100 into the circular flow in period 2. Macroeconomic equilibrium is therefore restored with this injection (investment) by firms as illustrated in Figure A2.3.

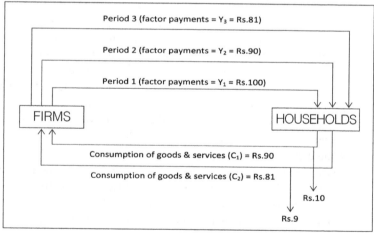

Figure A2.2: Macroeconomic Disequilibrium with Leakages

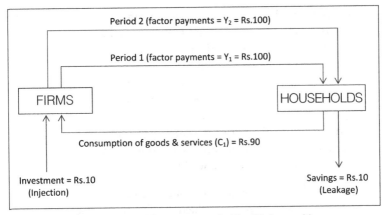

Figure A2.3: Macroeconomic Equilibrium with
Leakages and Injections

We now extend the model to include all the 4 sectors of the economy—households, firms, government and the rest of the world. The 4 'markets' here which bring these sectors together are the market for goods and services (buyers or households and sellers of goods or firms), and financial markets (for savings and investment), government sector (taxes and government expenditure) and exports and imports (through international trade market). Figure A2.4 illustrates the complete circular flow model.

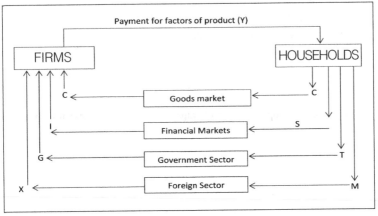

Figure A2.4: Macroeconomic Equilibrium in a 4-Sector
Circular Flow Model

1. Households allocate a part of their income to consumer spending (C) that goes to firms through the goods and services market.
2. Via financial markets, private savings (S) are channelized into investment spending (I) by firms.
3. Households pay taxes to the government (T) which is then spent by the government on government expenditures (G) to pay purchase goods and services from firms.
4. Exports (X) to the rest of the world generate flow of funds to the domestic firms while imports (M) lead to a flow of funds from the economy to the rest of the world.

The circular flow diagram shows how incomes give rise to spending, which in turn gives rise to production of output, which gives rise to incomes. Withdrawals, or leakages, arise from income that is not passed on in the circular flow through spending (C + S + T + M), while injections are spendings that do not arise out of incomes but are exogenous (C + I + G + X).

The concept of macroeconomic equilibrium is illustrated as a tank containing water. If the level of water in the tank (Y) is to remain constant, the total quantum of leakages or withdrawals (W) into the tank (W = S + T + M) must be exactly offset by the total quantum of injections (J) into the tank (J = I + G + X).

To put it algebraically;

$$W = J \text{ implies}$$
$$C + S + T + M = C + I + G + X$$
$$\text{or} \quad S + T + M = I + G + X$$

NOTE

1. A 10 per cent appreciation in the rupee results in a > 10 per cent in quantity of imports.

Bibliography

Accounts and Papers (1860), Thirty-Five Volumes, Session 24 January–28 August 1860, vol. XLIX, London.

Adams, Brooks (1897), *The Law of Civilization and Decay: An Essay on History*, The Macmillan & Company, New York.

Ambedkar, B.R. (1947), *History of Indian Currency and Banking*, Thacker & Co., Bombay.

Ambirajan, S. (1984), *Political Economy and Monetary Management, India: 1766–1914*, Affiliated East-West Press, Chennai.

Anderson, Adam (1787), *An Historical and Chronological Deduction of the History of Commerce*, vol. II, J. Walter, Blackfriars.

Andreades, A. (1909), *History of the Bank of England 1640–1903*, 4th edn., Frank Cass & Co., London, rpt. 1966.

Arrighi, Giovanni (1994), *The Long Twentieth Century: Money, Power, and the Origins of Our Time*, Verso, London.

Bagehot, W. (1877), *On the Depreciation of Silver*, Henry S. King & Co., London.

Ballard, Colonel R.E. (1868), *Remarks on a Gold Currency for India*, Bombay Mint, Bombay.

Bank of International Settlements (2007), *Quarterly Review*, March, http://www.bis.org/ press/ p070314.htm.

Barbour, David (1892), *The Silver Crisis: India's Financial and Commercial Sufferings, Letter by Sir David Barbour, K.C.S.I.* (Finance Minister to the Indian Government), Macmillan & Co., London.

—— (1912), *The Standard of Value*, Macmillan & Co., London.

Barclay, Robert (1894), *The Silver Question and the Gold Question*, Effingham Wilson & Co., London.

Barrett, Ward (1990), 'World Bullion Flows, 1450–1800', in James D. Tracy (ed.), *The Rise of Merchant Empires: Long Distance Trade in the Early Modern World, 1350–1750*, Cambridge University Press, Cambridge, 1990, pp. 224–54.

Bombay Chamber of Commerce (1864), 'Memorandum to the Right Honourable Sir John Lawrence, Viceroy and Governor-General of India in Council dated 8 February 1864', *Accounts and Papers: Twenty-Nine Volumes*, Session, 7 February–6 July 1865, vol. XXXIX, 1865, pp. 5–9.

Bowen, H.V. (1991), *Revenue & Reform: The Indian Problem in British Politics 1757–73*, Cambridge University Press, Cambridge.

Boycott, Dr. (1870), Untitled Report, *Journal of the Society of Arts, 4 February 1870*, pp. 211–13.

Buchan, Bruce P. (1994), 'The East India Company1749–1800: The Evolution of a Territorial Strategy and the Changing Role of the Directors', *Business & Economic History*, vols. 23(1), pp. 52–61.

Buchanan, Francis (1807), *A Journey from Madras Through the Countries of Mysore, Canara and Malabar*, vols. I, II and III, Asian Educational Services, New Delhi, rpt. 1999.

——— (1833), *A Geographical, Statistical, and Historical Description of the District, or Zila of Dinajpur in the Province, or Soubah of Bengal*, Baptist Mission Press, Calcutta.

Burn, Richard (1797), *The Justice of the Peace and Parish Officer*, vol. 1, A. Strahan & W. Woodfall, London.

Cain, P.J. and A.G. Hopkins (1980), 'The Political Economy of British Expansion Overseas, 1750–1914', *The Economic History Review*, New Series, vol. 33, no. 4, November, pp. 463–90.

Campbell, George (1870), Untitled Report, *Journal of the Society of Arts*, 4 February 1870, pp. 213–14.

Cassels, W.R. (1864), 'Letter to His Excellency Sir Bartle Frere, K.C.B., Governor of Bombay', 1 January 1864, *Accounts and Papers: Twenty-nine Volumes*, Session 7 February–6 July 1865, vol. XXXIX, 1865, pp. 11–21.

Cassels, Andrew (1869), 'On a Gold Currency for India', *Journal of the Society for Arts*, 24 December 1869, pp. 101–3.

Chablani, H.L. (1931), *Studies in Indian Currency and Exchange*, Oxford University Press, Bombay.

Chandavarkar, Anand (2000), 'Central Bank and Government: An Untold Story from RBI's Early History', *Economic and Political Weekly*, 35(34): pp. 3048–60.

Charles Earl of Liverpool (1805), 'A Treatise on the Coins of the Realm in a Letter to the King', Oxford University Press.

Chaudhury, Sushil (2006), 'Indian Merchant/Bankers to the Rescue of the European Companies, Eastern India, *c.* 1650–1757', *XIV International Economic History Congress*, Helsinki, 2006, pp. 1–18, www.helsinki.fi/ehc2006/papers3/Chaud.pdf.

Chesney, George T. (1870), *Indian Polity*, Longmans, Green & Co., London.

Cooke, Charles Northcote (1863), *The Rise, Progress and Present Condition of Banking in India*, Bengal Printing Company, Calcutta.

Copy of Financial Letter from India, dated 2 July 1852, no. 36 (1852),

Accounts and Papers: Thirty-Five Volumes East India, Home Accounts; Banks; Finances (India); Public Debt; Revenue; Income Tax, Session 24 January 28 August 1860, vol. XLIX, 1860.

Coyagee, J.C. (1930), *The Indian Currency System: 1835–1926,* Thompson & Co., Bombay.

Daniell, Clarmont (1884), *The Gold Treasure of India,* Kegan, Paul, Trench & Co., London.

Dickens, Charles (1864), *All the Year Round: A* Weekly Journal conducted by Charles Dickens, no. 258, Saturday, 2 April.

Digby, William (1901), *'Prosperous' British India: A Revelation from Official Records,* Unwin, London.

Dodwell, Henry (1920), *Calendar of the Madras Despatches, 1744–1755,* Madras Government Press.

Douglas, James (1893), *Bombay and Western India: A Series of Stray Papers,* vol. II, Sampson, Low, Marston & Co., London.

DSAL, Digital South Asia Library (nd), *Statistical Abstracts Relating to British India from 1840 to 1865, First Number,* http://dsal.uchicago.edu/

Eichengreen, B. and J. Sachs (1985), 'Exchange Rates and Economic Recovery in the 1930s', *Journal of Economic History,* vol. XLV, no. 4, pp. 925–46.

Einaudi, Luca L. (2000), 'From the Franc to the "Europe": The Attempted Transformation of the Latin Monetary Union into a European Monetary Union, 1865–73', *The Economic History Review,* New Series, vol. 53, no. 2 (May 2000), pp. 284–308.

Ellstaetter, K. (1895), *The Indian Silver Currency: An Historical and Economic Study,* translated by J.L. Laughlin, University of Chicago Press, Chicago.

Faucher, Leon (1853), *Remarks on the Production of the Precious Metals and on the Demonetization of Gold in Several Countries in Europe,* 2nd edn., Smith Elder & Co., London.

Fisher, Irving (1912), *The Purchasing Power of Money: Its Determination and Relation to Credit Interest and Crises,* Cosimo Classics, New York, rpt. 2007.

—— (1918), *The Elementary Principles of Economics,* Cosimo Classics, New York, rpt. 2007.

Five Letters from a Free Merchant in Bengal to Warren Hastings, Esq. (1782), London.

Francis, W. (1908), *The Nilgiris: Madras District Gazetteer,* Government Press, Madras.

Friedman, Milton (1989), 'Bimetallism Revisited', *Working Papers in Economics E-89-24,* The Hoover Institute, Stanford University, August.

Gilbart, James (1849), *A Practical Treatise on Banking,* vol. II, Longman, Brown, Green and Longmans, London.

Goldsmith, Raymond (1983), *The Financial Development of India, 1860–1977*, Oxford University Press, New Delhi.

Grant, James and R.A. Fisher (1865), *A Treatise on the Law Relating to Bankers and Banking*, Hodges, Smith & Co., Butterworths, London.

Habib, Irfan (1982), 'Monetary System and Prices', in Tapan Raychaudhuri and Irfan Habib (eds), *The Cambridge Economic History of India, c.1200–c.1750*, vol. 1, Cambridge University Press, rpt. Orient Longman, New Delhi, 2004, pp. 360–81.

Hamilton, C.J. (1919) *The Trade Relations between England and India (1600–1896)*, Thacker, Spink & Co., Calcutta.

Hardach, Gerd (1977), *First World War, 1914–18*, University of California Press, Berkeley & Los Angeles.

Heilperin, Michael A. (1939), *International Monetary Economics*, Longmans, Green and Co., Alabama, rpt. 2007.

Hendriks, Frederick (1869), 'Untitled Remarks', *Journal of Society for Arts*, 24 December 1869.

—— (1870), 'Untitled Remarks', *Society for the Encouragement of Arts, Manufactures and Commerce, A Gold Currency for India: Report of Conferences held by the India Committee of the Society of Arts*, Bell and Daldy: London, pp. 16–23.

Historical and Chronological Deduction of the Origin of Commerce from the Earliest Accounts (1789), vol. IV, London.

Hunter, W.W. (1868), *Annals of Rural Bengal*, 2nd edn., Leypoldt & Holt, New York.

'Index to the Executive Documents no. 14 (1868), Printed by the Order of the Senate for the Second Session of the Fortieth Congress of the United States of America', pp. 1–110, Washington, 1868.

Invararity, J.D. (1864), Minute by the Honourable J.D. Invararity, Bombay, dated 29 February 1864, *Accounts and Papers: Twenty-nine Volumes, East India, Home Accounts; Banks; Finances (India); Public Debt; Revenue; Income Tax*, Session 10, 7 February–6 July 1865, vol. XXXIX, 1865, pp. 10–11.

Jadhav, N. (nd), 'Central Bank Strategies, Credibility and Independence: Global Evolution and Indian Experience', www.drnarendrajadhav.info/drnjadhave_web_files/Published papers/Final Paper on Central Banking Strategies1.pdf

James, H. (1996), *International Monetary Cooperation since Bretton Woods*, IMF Publications, Washington.

Jennings, Samuel (1881), *My Visit to the Goldfields in the South-East Wynaad*, Chapman & Hall Limited, London.

Jevons, Stanley H. (1922), *Money, Banking and Exchange in India*, Government Central Press, Simla.

———— (1922a), *The Future of Exchange and the Indian Currency*, Oxford University Press, London.

Johri, Devika and Mark Miller (nd), 'Devaluation of the Rupee: Tale of Two Years, 1966 and 1991', Centre for Civil Society, ccsindia.org/ccsindia/policy/money/studies/wp0028.pdf

Journals of the House of Commons (1803), 1 August 1714–15 September 1718.

Kanda, Sayako (2010), 'Forged Salt Bills and Calcutta's Financial Crisis in the late 1820s', *KEIO/Kyoto Global COE Discussion Paper Series*, DP2009-010.

Kaye, John William (1854), *The Life and Correspondence of Henry St. George Tucker*, Richard Bentley, London.

Kemmerer, Edwin Walter (1944), *Gold and the Gold Standard: The Story of Gold Money Past, Present and Future*, reprinted by Ludwig von Mises Institute, Auburn, 2009.

Keynes, John Maynard (1913), *Indian Currency and Finance*, Macmillan & Co., Limited, London.

Khan, S.A. (1923), *The East India Trade in the XVIIth Century: In its Political and Economic Aspects*, Oxford University Press, London.

Kling, Blair B. (1976), *Partner in Empire: Dwarkanath Tagore and the Age of Enterprise in Eastern India*, University of California Press, Berkeley.

Knight, Charles (1870), *History of England*, Bradbury, Evans & Co., London.

Leavens, D.H. (1939), *Silver Money*, Principia Press, Bloomington.

Lees, Nassau W. (1864), *The Drain of Silver to the East, and the Currency of India*, Wm. H. Allen & Co, London.

Levi, Leone (1864), 'Resolution 1325 Government of India (Financial Department) on a Gold Currency for India', Simla, *Annals of British Legislation*, New Series, vol. 1, pp. 395–418.

Lord Clive's Speech in the House of Commons (1772), London.

Macaulay, Thomas Babington (1896), *Lord Clive*, Pitt Press Series, rpt. 1921.

Macleod, Henry Dunning (1863), *A Dictionary of Political Economy*, vol. 1, Longman, Brown, Longmans, and Roberts, London, pp. 567–617.

———— (1898), *Indian Currency*, Longmans, Green & Co., London.

Malhotra, D.K. (1949), *History and Problems of Indian Currency: 1835–1949*, Minerva Book Shop, Simla.

Mansfield, W.R. (1864), *On the Introduction of a Gold Currency into India*, London.

————, (1866), 'Report of the Commission to inquire into the Operation of Act XIX, 1861', *Home Accounts of the Government of India, East India (Home Accounts)*, pp. 3–11.

Mechanics' Magazine, The (1837), 8 April–30 September, vol. XXVII, London.

Mehta, Makrand (1991), *Indian Merchants and Entrepreneurs in Historical Perspective*, Academic Foundation, New Delhi.

Mellyn, Kevin (2009), *Financial Market Meltdown: Everything You Need to Know to Understand and Survive the Global Credit Crisis*, ABC-Clio, Santa Barbara.

Milburn, William (1813), *Oriental Commerce*, vol. I, Black, Perry & Co., London.

Mill, James (1826), *The History of British India*, vol. III, Baldwin, Cradock & Joy, London.

Minutes of Evidence Taken Before the Committee Appointed to Inquire into the Indian Currency, Indian Currency Committee, Eyre and Spottiswoode, London, 1998.

Monson, E.G. (1914) *The Silver and Indian Currency Questions: Treated in a Practical Manner*, Effingham Wilson & Co., London.

Morys, Matthias (2012), 'The Emergence of the Classical Gold Standard, Centre for Historical Economics and Related Research at York', *CHERRY Discussion Paper Series, CHERRY DP 12/01*, pp. 1–55.

Mukherjee, Aditya (1992), 'Controversy over Formation of Reserve Bank of India, 1927–35', *Economic and Political Weekly*, 27(5), pp. 229–34.

Muranjan, S.K. (1952), *Modern Banking in India*, Kamala Publishing House, Bombay.

Naoroji, Dadabhai (1870), 'Untitled Remarks', *Society for the Encouragement of Arts, Manufactures and Commerce, A Gold Currency for India: Report of Conferences held by the India Committee of the Society of Arts*, London, pp. 13–16.

Narain, Brij (1926), 'Exchange and Prices in India 1873–1924', *Weltwirtschaftliches Archiv*, 23 Bd., pp. 247–92.

Nolan, E.H. (*c.* 1878), *The Illustrated History of the British Empire in India and the East*, vol. I. Virtue & Co., London.

Pandit, Y.S. (1937), *India's Balance of Indebtedness, 1898–1913*, George Allen & Unwin, London.

Papers Relating to the East India Affairs (1813), Copy of a Financial Letter from the Governor in Council of Fort William, to the Court of Directors of the East India Company; dated 23 August 1809, 22 June.

Ramana, D.V. (1957), 'Determinants of Money Supply India, 1914–50', *Indian Economic Review*, vol. 3, no. 4, pp. 1–33.

Rau, R. (1922), *Present-Day Banking in India*, University of Calcutta, Calcutta.

Reid, William S. (1954), *Economic History of Great Britain*, Ronald Press Company, London.

Rickards, R. (1832), *India; or Facts Submitted to Illustrate the Character and Condition of Native Inhabitants*, Smith Elder & Co., London.

Rollins, Montgomery (1917), *Money and Investments*, George Routledge & Sons Limited, London.http://chestofbooks.com/finance/investments/Money-Investments/Council-Drafts.html#ixzz2443wvzJl

Rothermund, Dietmar (1992), *India in the Great Depression, 1929–39*, Manohar, New Delhi.

Ruding, Rogers (1840), *Annals of the Coinage of Great Britain and Its Dependencies*, vol. II, John Hearre, London.

Russell, Henry B. (1898*), International Monetary Conferences: Their Purposes, Character, and Results*, New York and London.

Safalra.com (nd), http://safalra.com/other/historical-uk-inflation-price-conversion/; data obtained from 2004 paper 'Consumer Price Inflation Since 1750' (ISSN 0013-0400, Economic Trends, no. 604, pp. 38–46) by Jim O'Donoghue, Louise Goulding, and Grahame Allen.

Schmidt, H. (1886), *The Silver Question in its Social Aspect: An Enquiry into the Existing Depression of Trade, and the Present Position of the Bimetallic Controversy*, Effingham Wilson, London.

Scott, Walter (1812), *Tracts, of the Most Interesting and Entertaining Subjects*, vol. VIII, London.

Scutt, G.P. Symes (1904), *The History of the Bank of Bengal: An Epitome of a Hundred Years of Banking in India*, Bank of Bengal Press, Calcutta.

Second Report from the Secret Committee on Commercial Distress with the Minutes of Evidence (1848), House of Commons, London, pp. 1–143.

Sen, Pronab (1986), 'Devaluation in India: A Reappraisal', *Economic and Political Weekly*, vol. 21, no. 30, 26 July, pp. 1322–9.

Shirras, Findlay G. (1920), *Indian Finance and Banking*, Macmillan and Co., London.

Singleton, John (2011), *Central Banking in the Twentieth Century*, Cambridge University Press, Cambridge.

Sinha, H. and J.C. Sinha (1937), 'The Ratio Question', *Sankhya: The Indian Journal of Statistics*, vol. 3, no. 27, pp. 125–42.

Sinha, J.C. (1938), *Indian Currency Problems in the Last Decade (1926–36)*, University of Delhi, Delhi.

Sketch of the Commercial Resources and Monetary and Mercantile Systems of India, 1837.

Smith, Colonel (1870), 'Untitled Remarks', *Society for the Encouragement of Arts, Manufactures and Commerce, A Gold Currency for India: Report of Conferences held by the India Committee of the Society of Arts*, London, pp. 9–10.

Statistical Abstract of the United States (1955), 76 Annual Edition, U.S. Department of Commerce, Washington DC.

Steuart, James (1772), *The Principles of Money Applied to the Present State of the Coin of Bengal.*

Stevenson, Richard (1943), *Bengal Tiger and British Lion: An Account of the Bengal Famine of 1943*', Universe, Lincoln (USA), rpt. 2005.

Sundara Rajan, V. (1955), *An Economic History of India, 1757–1947*, East & West Book House, Baroda.

The Asiatic Journal (1827) and *Monthly Register for British India and its Dependencies*, vol. XXIV, October.

The Bombay Quarterly Review (1856), vol. III, January and April 1856, London, pp. 46–7.

The Calcutta Review (1860), vol. XXXV, September–December.

The National Magazine (1857), vol. X, January to June, New York.

The Spectator (1865), no. 1928, 10 June.

Tannan.M.L. and K.T. Shah (1917), *Indian Currency and Banking Problems*, Ramachandra Govind & Son, Bombay.

Tavernier, Jean Baptiste (1676), *Travels in India*, edited by Valentine Ball and William Crooke, rpt. Asian Educational Services, New Delhi, 2001.

Taylor, John (1836), *A Catechism of the Currency*, Taylor & Walton, London.

Taylor, James (1863), *The Mystery of Money Explained*, Walton and Maberly, London.

Thurston, Edgar (1890), *History of the Coins of the Territories of the East India Company and Catalogue of the Coins in the Madras Museum*, Asian Educational Services, New Delhi, rpt. 1992.

Trevelyan, C.E. (1864), 'Minute of a Gold Currency for India, Chambers of Commerce and Native Associations of Calcutta and Bombay (1864)', *Accounts and Papers: Twenty-nine Volumes*, Session, 7 February–6 July 1865, vol. XXXIX, 1865, pp. 70–90.

Turner, J.R. (1919), *Introduction to Economics*, C. Scribner's Sons, New York.

Urban, Sylvanus Gentlemen's Magazine and Historical Chronicle (1793), Nichols, Son & Bentley, London, p. 342.

Vakil, C.N. and S.K. Muranjan (1927), *Currency and Prices in India*, D.B. Taraporewala & Sons, Bombay.

Verelst, Harry (1772), *A View of the Rise, Progress and Present State of the English Government in Bengal*, J. Nourse, London.

Wacha, Dinshaw E. (1910), *A Financial Chapter in the History of Bombay City*, Cambridge & Co., Bombay.

Walker, Francis (1896), *International Bimetallism*, Henry Holt & Co., New York.

Walras, Leon (1877), *Elements of Pure Economics*, Routledge, London, rpt. 2003.

Webster, Anthony (2007), *The Richest East India Merchant: The Life and Business of John Palmer of Calcutta 1767–1836*, The Boydell Press, Woodbridge.

West, Algernon (1867), 'Sir Charles Wood's Administration of Indian Affairs', in *Blackwood's Edinburgh Magazine*, vol. 65, July–December, pp. 686–701, American Edition, New York.

Wheeler, James Talboys (1862), *Madras in the Olden Time*, vol. III, 1727–48, Madras: J. Higginbotham.

Wood, H.W.J. (1864), 'Letter to E.H. Lushington', Secretary to the Government of India, Financial Department, dated 19 February 1864, *Accounts and Papers: Twenty-Nine Volumes*, Session, 7 February–6 July 1865, vol. XXXIX, 1865, p. 4.

World Gold Council, www.gold.org

Index